RICHARD WAGNER
AND THE JEWS

RICHARD WAGNER AND THE JEWS

Milton E. Brener

McFarland & Company, Inc., Publishers
Jefferson, North Carolina, and London

ALSO BY MILTON E. BRENER
AND FROM MCFARLAND

*Vanishing Points: Three Dimensional
Perspective in Art and History* (2004)

OTHER WORKS BY MILTON E. BRENER

The Garrison Case: A Sudy in the Abuse of Power (1969)
The Other Side of the Airport: The Private Pilot's World (1982)
Opera Offstage: Passion and Politics Behind the Great Operas (1996)
Faces: The Changing Look of Humankind (2000)

**Frontispiece: Richard Wagner, in London, about age 64. From
Weltgeschichte in Karakterbildern by Wilhelm Kienzl.**

LIBRARY OF CONGRESS CATALOGUING-IN-PUBLICATION DATA

Brener, Milton E., 1930–
    Richard Wagner and the Jews / Milton E. Brener.
        p.   cm.
    Includes bibliographical references and index.

    ISBN-13: 978-0-7864-2370-5
    (softcover : 50# alkaline paper) ∞

    1. Wagner, Richard, 1813–1883 — Relations with Jews.
    2. Antisemitism — Germany — History — 19th century.
    I. Title
    ML410.W19B8   2006
    782.1092 — dc22   2005034178

British Library cataloguing data are available

On the cover: portrait of Wagner ©2005 Corbis Images;
background www.8notes.com

Manufactured in the United States of America

McFarland & Company, Inc., Publishers
  Box 611, Jefferson, North Carolina 28640
    www.mcfarlandpub.com

To Eileen
and to my fellow Wagnerians
the wide world over

Table of Contents

Part III. Munich

Part IV. Lucerne

Part V. Bayreuth I: The First Festival

Part VI. Bayreuth II: Levi and Neumann

Part VII. Bayreuth III: The Second Festival

Acknowledgments

I wish to thank Dr. Gabriele Timmerman of New Orleans, who provided very helpful advice on translating some of the German texts.

I also acknowledge with thanks the courtesy and efforts of Frau Annelore Teckelmann of the *Gesellschaft der Freunde von Bayreuth*, the Society of Friends of Bayreuth, and Herr Gunter Fischer of the Richard Wagner Museum in Bayreuth, for making available to me copies of unpublished letters between Wagner and Hermann Levi. Though other authors have quoted parts of them, certain other parts, significant to the content of this book have been largely ignored.

My most heartfelt thanks to my wife, and editor, Eileen, for her continued enthusiastic help, especially with the finer points of English grammar, not at all my own strong point.

Preface

THIS BOOK IS NOT A BIOGRAPHY of Richard Wagner. It focuses principally on his relationship with the Jews—only one aspect of his remarkably complex personality. But that aspect cannot be understood, even partially, except in the context of the whole man and his work, and some of that context is necessarily included here. The essential fact about this nineteenth century colossus is not that he was anti–Semitic, but that he changed dramatically the course of the operatic and symphonic music of the Western world. Less known is the fact that its impact has extended to much of the world's literatures.

Wagner's life has been studied like few others. A Wagner biographer, Guy de Pourtales, writing in 1932, reported about 10,000 books and scholarly articles about him by the time of his death in 1883 and estimated that by 1932 the number may have tripled. Martin van Amerongen, in a volume entitled *Wagner: A Case History*, first made the oft repeated claim that more had been written about this man than about anyone in history except Jesus and Napoleon. One thing is certain: the flow has not slackened. It seems to increase every year.

His tremendous impact on the world of art is but one of the reasons for this huge output of Wagnerian literature. Another is the plethora of available source material: thousands of his letters, thousands of others to or about him; diaries, both his own and his wife's; essays, memoirs, his 800-page autobiography, and the eight-volume collection of his prose works; not to mention the analyses by countless scholars and critics of his opera libretti and of his music. The diaries of his second wife alone extend to 2,000 pages covering the last 14 years of his life. The correspondence between Wagner and King Ludwig is in six volumes, averaging about 220 pages each. These are invaluable sources and I have relied heavily on them among many others.

1

That vast literature reveals a life filled with contradictions. I have been reading and researching this material for approximately thirty years and have found the contradictions inherent in Wagner's relationship with the Jews the most baffling, and intriguing, of all. That relationship divides sharply and inevitably into two. On the one hand is his relationship with *the Jews,* in his mind an impersonal specter, a demonic monolith that haunted his world, its tentacles penetrating his native culture. He perceived that group to be alien and inimical to his goal in life: the acceptance of his grandly conceived artwork, whose roots grew from Germanic soil. On the other hand is his personal relationship with many of the talented individual Jews who abounded in the music world of his time and place.

That he was anti–Semitic is undeniable. One cannot read what he wrote or accounts of what he said and refuse anyone the use of that opprobrious term. But nothing about this man is so simple. Unavoidably his disdain and contempt for that amorphous entity, *the Jews,* often came into head-on conflict with his single-minded, all-encompassing goal. The conflict arose from his contact with individual Jews who stood in awe of his music, who understood his art, and who stood ready to assist him as singers, conductors, pianists, entrepreneurs or financiers.

Unlike the apocryphal anti–Semite some of whose best friends were Jews, Wagner sometimes seemed to be surrounded by them. At one point, with two Jewish friends living as part of his household, he laconically told his wife that their home would soon be a synagogue. At the time of his death, four of his very closest friends were Jews, and two were among his 12 pallbearers. Never did he refuse the help or the friendship of any Jew, or anyone else, for reasons of race or religion, from which fact some questions naturally arise.

In view of his avowed anti–Semitism, what was the nature of his relationship with these individual Jews on a personal level? How much tension did it create? How did he reconcile his calumnious statements about *the Jews* with his close association with so many of them? How were so many Jews able to work so closely with him in view of his slanderous description of their culture and its roots? It is these matters that are the focal point of this book.

Prior to the advent of Hitler and his Nazi horde, the subject was not a burning issue. In those relatively innocent days it was even permissible to write about the man's many faults, failings and peccadilloes without mention of his anti–Semitism. But for at least 40 or 50 years after the war and the discovery of the horrors of the death camps, the subject was not only uppermost in prominence in the continuing Wagner literature, it was no longer one for reasoned analysis.

It was deemed, instead, a most egregious omission to write about Wagner or his work, even, at times, to review certain of his operas, without the obligatory reference to this eternal stain on his reputation. It was part of the social and political climate of the time that one could not be only partially anti–Semitic. The discovery of any such prejudice colored every aspect of the miscreant's character. And the vehemence of Wagner's writings was such that not the slightest chink in that encasement of racial hatred could be acknowledged; any seeming act of genuine friendship between Wagner and a Jew must be seen only as one of cynical manipulation on the part of the composer.

Perhaps for the last fifteen years reason has dared to stick its head, meekly, above that churning morass. But those first faltering steps of rational analysis have been timid indeed. Wagner's anti–Semitism cannot be even remotely understood in the abstract. It must, of necessity, be seen against the background of the whole man. But to this day the vast Wagner literature lacks even a single comprehensive study of his anti–Semitism that places it fairly in perspective with his life and work and the scope of his genius. Those volumes that deal primarily with this subject do indeed often still examine it in the abstract, divorced from any broader study of the man or his work.

Many of them still skew the facts by highly selective inclusion and place the worst possible interpretation on everything said or done by the composer. The most obvious acts of friendship, the most harmless acts or statements, are still too often the subject of contorted interpretations imputing malice. The possibility of warm, genuine friendships, despite all evidence of it, some Wagnerphobes can never admit. Those volumes that treat the subject more fairly are usually general biographies that paint too little of this aspect of his life to be of much value.

The subject is aflame with emotion. The flame is kindled by the grotesque, barbaric events of the Nazi regime on the one hand, and on the other by the devotion of mesmerized Wagnerphiles who dismiss the anti–Semitism as unimportant. To an understanding of his art it truly is unimportant, the arguments of some scholars and pseudoscholars to the contrary. He saved his vitriol for his personal life; he would not and did not sully his art with it. To an understanding of the man, however, it is quite important. It was a significant expression of his emotional makeup.

Everyone who writes about the subject has his or her biases, and I am certainly no exception. I have set out to write an objective examination of the subject, but I know that there is no such thing. Perhaps, however, I can at least objectively state my own bias. I might as well; it will be evident soon enough: I do not believe that, at the deeper levels, the man who created *Tristan und Isolde*, *Parsifal* and *Der Ring des Nibelungen* could possibly have been the monster that so many have painted.

A Note on Translations

FOR A NUMBER OF THE VOLUMES and articles in my source materials there are no published translations from the German, in which cases I have used my own translations. Where published English translations of original German sources exist, I have generally used them, at least as starting points. I have on occasion, when I perceived the published ones as being inadequate or excessively stilted for modern readers, chosen to use my own translations instead. I have also found some translations to have been partial only, having omitted text irrelevant to the translator's context, but, I found, not irrelevant to mine. In cases where I had any uncertainty about the accuracy of my own translations I have had the benefit of the review and advice of Dr. Gabriele Timmerman of New Orleans, a native German speaker and scholar, for whose interest and efforts I am most grateful.

My summary of "Judaism in Music," which appears in Chapter 5, requires a special explanation. It is drawn from the 1894 translation by William Ashton Ellis, which appears to be the only English translation available; I have, unfortunately, no access to the German. The summary makes use of some of Ellis's exact language, but I have included quotation marks only where I deemed particular text crucial to the content of the essay. The quotation marks signify that the exact words are vital to an understanding of the text. For those who are interested, the translation of Ellis is reproduced in full as an appendix to this work.

My life is a sea of contradictions,
from which I can only hope to emerge through death.
— Letter of Richard Wagner to Otto Wesendonck,
September 10, 1856.

The world has my works.
Let the world put up with my follies.
— Letter of Richard Wagner to Dr. Joseph Standhartner,
April 12, 1864.

Part I

Zurich

1

The Asyl

On a rise of ground in Zurich's Enge District is a stately mansion from another age. It is today the Rietberg Museum, home to impressive collections of Oriental and African art. It was once, as a private dwelling, called the Villa Wesendonck; the elevated ground, the Green Hill. From a smaller less auspicious neighbor, now named the Villa Schönberg, there still resound, for those who can hear them, faint echoes of music — and of sometimes angry voices. They linger from a century and a half ago, from a time when the Schönberg was called the "Asyl"; when the Villa Wesendonck was new; and the Enge District, now within the confines of Zurich, was a rural suburb.

The owner of both structures was Otto Wesendonck. He came from Wuppertal, in Germany's lower Rhine Valley, but by October 1850, at the age of 35, had done well enough in his New York–based silk trading firm to relocate in Zurich. He had the means now to offer a lifestyle befitting his attractive, educated, and artistically inclined 21-year-old wife, Mathilde; befitting also perhaps as a partial alleviator for grief. Just a year earlier the couple had suffered the loss of their firstborn, a son, barely four months old. Their second child, a daughter, was born in Zurich 17 months after their son's death. Within a year after their arrival in Zurich Otto had purchased a large plot of ground on the Green Hill and commenced to build a luxurious mansion. It was to be one delightfully suited to Mathilde's musical, literary, and social dreams.

It was almost six years in the making. Not until August 1857 were the Wesendoncks able to take possession. They must have considered it a worthwhile wait. The approach to the home lay through a winter garden, followed by an open walkway bounded by palms and exotic plants. On the walls of the entrance hall paintings of old Italian and Dutch masters peered down on white marble busts of Socrates, Demosthenes, Sappho and Augustus among others. Each of these giants of classical times stood guard next to one of the hall's stately columns. Elsewhere there was a visual feast of glittering crystal chandeliers aglow with candles, black marble frames for mirrors, gold ones for windows, Italian Renaissance–style furniture of massive mahogany or dark oak, carved glass cabinets, brown-gold leather relief tapestry, and red carpeted sandstone steps. The elegant upstairs dining room, adjacent to a projecting terrace, afforded a stunning view of both the town and the Lake of Zurich.[1]

The home became a meeting place for writers, artists and intellectuals. Franz Liszt, composer and pianist; his daughter, Cosima von Bülow; and his pupil and son-in-law, Hans von Bülow, were among the leading actors in a tortured drama that would shortly begin to unfold there. Other visitors included Johannes Brahms and Gottfried Semper, an architect and a political refugee from the Saxon capitol city of Dresden. Among other structures to his credit is the Dresden opera house that still bears his name. One visiting writer said of the Wesendonck home that its wealth, taste and elegance beautified the life within. Perhaps it did. But material wealth has rarely been sufficient to calm volcanic emotions, raw nerves, or clashing temperaments. This was to be no exception.

The entry of the German couple into the artistic and cultural life of Zurich began well before the completion of their new home. The driving force was Mathilde; her husband a willing and financially able participant. It was a ripe field. The city's reservoir of intellectual and creative activity had been swelled by numerous immigrants, who, like Semper, were refugees. They had been involved in the mostly unsuccessful revolutions that ignited in the German states beginning in 1848. In late 1850, the time of the Wesendoncks' arrival, among the most prominent of these was a five-foot-five-inch, 37-year-old fugitive, also from Dresden. His name was Richard Wagner. He was already renowned as a composer of grand opera and fairly radiated supreme confidence in his own genius and in his destiny.

Despite his short stature he must have been easy to spot in a crowd. Almost all of the descriptions that have come down to us speak of the large head, with emphasis usually on the strikingly broad and sloping forehead. Mentioned almost as frequently, and revealed prominently in paintings and photographs, were the thin lips, hooked nose and the jutting chin. One biographer has gone to some length to show statistically that five feet, five inches was not unusually short for a man in those days, at least in that part of Europe.[2] Nonetheless he is described, by almost all of his many contemporaries who have taken it on themselves to do so, as being quite short, with a proportionately long body and short legs.

About his temperament his contemporaries are not nearly so unanimous. He was undoubtedly moody, tempestuous, voluble, and highly opinionated. Otherwise, the closest composite picture we derive is one of contradictions in behavior, dramatic and extreme to a degree that brought comment from friend and enemy alike. There was clearly a nervous excitability about him, with passions sometimes violently expressed. He is credited with being enchanting, filled with witty insights, full of fun, a born mimic, and a fascinating teller of tales about his rich experiences. At other times he has been called sullen, arrogant and offensive.

Very often words tumbled out in a never ending and very rapid stream, always in his thick, distinctly Saxon accent, one that is not considered by fellow Germans to be the most sophisticated. It may perhaps correspond in its distinctness to accents of the country or mountain peoples of America. It happened on occasion that even his rapid fire speech was outrun by his active imagination and he was forced to grope and sputter for words.

From the comments of more than one acquaintance, Wagner must have eaten like he talked, too fast, for which he paid the price in his perpetual problems with digestion, among other nagging, sometimes serious, health problems. Many have attested to his explosive temper, the most violently expressed when contradicted, something worth remembering when reading some of his outrageously extravagant pronouncements.

Wagner had arrived in Zurich, then a town of about 33,000, in May 1849. Three months later he was joined by his wife, Minna, deeply embittered by her husband's revolutionary activity and the consequent upheaval in their lives. But without friends or money he soon made himself the center of a group of admirers. Without any intent to do so, and in spite perhaps of a deep reluctance, he became the moving force in creating a viable musical presence from what had been a society of amateurs. On the day of the Wesendoncks' arrival, October 21, 1850, he conducted in the Zurich City Theater a performance of Bellini's *Norma*. Both the magic of his music and the magnetism of his personality quickly attracted the attention of Mathilde and Otto. The following March Mathilde was present as he conducted the overture to his own *Tannhäuser*, which she, as many others of the time, found thrilling beyond belief.

Wagner was introduced to the Wesendoncks by a writer, a fellow refugee from Dresden, though exactly when is not certain. It appears quite likely, however, that it was at least partially at the urging of Mathilde that Wagner agreed to conduct in the following April four complete performances of his *Der Fliegende Holländer (The Flying Dutchman)*. The opera is his rendition of the tale of the legendary sea captain doomed to sail the seas forever for having called on the devil to help overcome unfavorable winds. Shortly thereafter Wagner gave up the frustrations and aggravations of trying to mount full operatic performances, something he was loath to undertake to begin with, and limited his conducting to concerts.

Apart from conducting, he worked and otherwise moved at a frenetic pace, just as he had always done and would always do. His last three years in Dresden and his first three years in Zurich have often been called his prose years. He had brought with him a prose sketch for a new opera, which at the time he called *Siegfried's Death*, concerning the mythical hero of northern mythology who forges the magic sword, slays the dragon and awakens the sleeping warrior maiden. But it was soon to be extended into a four-opera series, called collectively *Der Ring des Nibelungen (The Ring of the Nibelung)*. The expanded series involved many episodes from the same mythologies, populated, among other creatures, by gods, giants, dwarfs and humans, and centered around the destruction of the race of gods and the inheritance of the world by humans, and the triumph of love over power.

He wrote not a note of music during this six-year period, except for themes scribbled in the margins of his texts, but seemed absorbed with working out in his mind the nature of the new musical forms he felt necessary to convey the force of his drama. Further, convinced of the cosmic importance of this grandly conceived artwork, he felt compelled to expound to the public his thoughts on the world and on life in general, always as seen through the prism of his concept of the ideal work of art.

This he did in many essays, expressing opinions on almost every conceivable subject. Publication was often with his own funds, usually borrowed from others. About some of his boundless topics he knew much: theater, music, opera, literature, drama, acting, and conducting. About other subjects he knew little, or, perhaps better said, he distilled the facts he did know through such a fine mesh of his unalterably fixed opinions that they were scarcely recognizable: history, philosophy, politics and religion, to name a few. Rarely if ever, are his writings salted with such palliatives as "I think...," "I believe...," "possibly...," "I could be in error," or "There is another view." His beliefs are set forth as though sculpted in stone, received from On High, and destined to last through the ages.

There may be an instance or two in which he acknowledged he may have been wrong; if so, they are most difficult to locate. And if he ever blamed any of his many setbacks and adversities to any degree on his own faults or shortcomings, the evidence of that is likewise elusive. He held himself entirely blameless; the fault lay entirely with others such as *the Jews*, by whom he often meant the press, convinced as he was that the press was dominated by Jews; or the theater managements, convinced as he likewise was of Jewish dominance in that quarter; "philistines," a term of even more elastic definition, meaning usually anyone who failed to appreciate his work; Jesuits; or occasionally the French; or, sometimes, the world at large.

He has generally been seen as a supreme egotist. But there is strong basis for dissent. It was not the glory of Richard Wagner the man that he sought to advance. It was, rather, his conception of art, and of what art should be, that consumed his tremendous energy to the exclusion of all else. He pursued relentlessly the creation of works he called music dramas. Their outlines spontaneously, instinctively, took shape within him, however much his endless analyses of them may make it seem to superficial listeners or critics that they were systems, or created by formula. Whatever he wanted, whatever he felt he needed to achieve success, whether material luxuries, or human companionship, he begged, pleaded for, or demanded. But the purpose was not luxury nor companionship for its own sake, or for idle pleasure. It was to enable him to bring to life the artworks, the music dramas, that were the sole purpose of his existence. He was often frustrated and disgusted with the world, and lived in deadly fear that he would die before his work was done.

To all matters not directly bearing on the creation and production of his works he was oblivious, including generally accepted norms of behavior. He was often heedless of the sensitivities, and unconcerned with the needs, of others. Many, nonetheless, under the spell of his overwhelming creative genius, willingly invested in him, financially and emotionally. To any consideration of the development of his own traits of character as a human being, he seemed equally as unconcerned. Whatever did not advance the realization of his art was a matter of no consequence. Good and bad, right and wrong, were judged almost invariably by that one criteria. When they conflicted with his artistic goals, such concepts as gratitude, empathy, tact and diplomacy were foreign to him. When there was no conflict, he could be charming, gracious and considerate.

All of the prose writing in this six-year period was contemporaneous with the creation of the prose drafts and then the poetic texts of his planned four-opera magnum opus, *Der Ring des Nibelungen,* a task he completed in early December 1852. Later that month he read the entire text of the four intended operas to a small group of friends in nearby Mariafeld, over a period of two days according to Wagner, three according to the hostess, a novelist named Eliza Wille. The following February he treated a somewhat larger gathering in the Hotel Bauer au Lac to the same privilege in four three-hour sessions. Never satisfied merely to read, he acted out all of the roles, in a manner, according to many witnesses then and later, uniquely his.

He found time also during his years in Zurich to indulge his love of the outdoors and hiking. There were numerous adventurous expeditions in the Alps, to, upon and through peaks, passes and valleys, many of whose names are familiar to persons of similar bent: the Kleine Scheidegg, Lauterbrunnen, Grindelwald, Mont Blanc, and Monte Rosa.

The Wagners and the Wesendoncks became friends. By May of 1853, Otto was contributing modestly to cover losses sustained by Wagner in connection with a series of concert performances of his own works. A number of loans were in later months to be transformed, sometimes imperceptibly, sometimes overtly, into gifts. This was not at all a rare occurrence in Wagner's life, and Otto was to be merely one of a large number of such donors. They visited with each other at their respective residences, the Wesendoncks in the stately Hotel Bauer au Lac, the Wagners in their more modest ground floor apartment on the Zeltweg. The apartment had been furnished, not luxuriously, but well enough that Wagner soon found himself in financial straits, not by any means a new experience. The problem was alleviated by Wesendonck, who forgave Wagner's 7,000-franc debt to him. In November 1853, he began the composition of the music for *Das Rheingold (The Rhinegold)*, the first of his four operas of *The Ring*.

One Baron Robert von Hornstein, an acquaintance of both Wagner and Wesendonck, described an evening with the Wagners at their home in 1854. Other guests included Otto and Mathilde; another young friend, Karl Ritter, and his wife; and one other musically inclined couple. Normally, says Hornstein, Wagner, on such occasions, could be utterly charming, as he usually was on the many long walks he took with Hornstein and Ritter. But not always.[3]

Hornstein described this particular occasion as an instance when the composer, as host for the evening, was "quite unbearable." Each of the guests was conversing with his or her neighbor, probably the usual lighthearted talk of people at such functions. Suddenly, Wagner uttered a brief, piercing scream that stopped all talk dead in its tracks. The host then announced that he would read a literary piece by Amadeus Hoffmann, which he did. At the conclusion of the lengthy reading, Wesendonck ventured the opinion that this work was a type of romanticism for which he had scant time. Wagner's response was to shout at his generous benefactor in a rage. Hornstein's implication is that Wagner demanded to be the center of attention.

The details of his life considered, it seems more likely that the composer of *Der Ring des Nibelungen* could not abide the painful boredom caused him by the usual talk, among even intelligent people, of things he possibly considered trivial: the weather, children, the peccadilloes of friends, or local gossip, including possible extramarital interests of others— if this was indeed the nature of the various conversations. The diaries of his second wife, beginning about 13 years later, may throw some light on the matter. In them we hear nothing about the neighbors or such things as whether the roof needed repairing. With almost deadly regularity, his uncontradicted pronouncements to her and to their many guests included judgments about philosophers from Plato and Aristotle to Kant and Schopenhauer; statesmen from Solon and Pericles to Disraeli and Bismarck; musicians from all nations and times; and readings from Sophocles and Aristophanes to Shakespeare, Cervantes, Calderon, Goethe and Ibsen.

On this occasion, in the course of his angry fulminations, he let it be known that among other trivialities that plagued his existence, he was being pursued by creditors for his purchases of the furnishings in his home. The

Otto Wesendonck. From *Nun sei bedankt* by Marcel Prawy.

next day, Wesendonck paid his bills. Such was his abiding admiration for this eccentric, mercurial composer.

During the course of construction of Wesendonck's villa, the owner of the neighboring property made it known that he planned to build there an insane asylum. Whether it was an honest statement of intentions or a bluff, Wesendonck decided to take no chance and purchased it at an undoubtedly handsome price. At Mathilde's urging, it was renovated into a home for their new friends, Richard and Minna Wagner, to be rented to them for life at a nominal rent.

If not so spacious or opulent as the home of their benefactors, it was everything that either of them could have desired. A few steps above the garden was a parterre, the domain of Minna. Her husband's workroom was upstairs next to a veranda. His desk, next to a large double window, afforded a magnificent view of the lake and the Alps. The room also harbored a writing desk, used when writing both prose and verse, another pulpit-like desk

The Wesendonck Villa and the Asyl, at far right, Wagner's home from April 1857 through August 1858. From *Richard Wagner: Sein Leben, sein Werk, seine Welt* by Julius Kapp.

where he stood when composing, and for his further convenience, a chaise longue. It was often his practice to pace back and forth as he worked, and from time to time to enter the adjacent room, the music room, to try out a few phrases on his piano. He would then return to the workroom to write the approved musical notations at his "pulpit." It was Wagner who named their new home the Asyl, a term signifying asylum or refuge, and tells us something about his prior life.

So it was, beginning in late April 1857, after moving into the Asyl, still two months before completion of the Wesendonck's villa, that he continued with work on *Siegfried*, the third of his four dramas of the *Ring*. Already written was the music for the first two operas and for the first act of the third, *Siegfried*. About three weeks later, on May 22, his birthday as it happened, he began the composition of the second of the three acts. But two months thereafter, almost concurrently with the completion of the large villa and the arrival on the Green Hill of the Wagners' new neighbors and benefactors, he turned aside from his *Ring des Nibelungen* to another project. A new opera, *Tristan und Isolde (Tristan and Isolde)*, was crowding in on his thoughts and his nerves. It was to embody the many medieval accounts of that Celtic tale of the pair of illicit lovers who, unable to unite in life, do so in death.

To his friend, Franz Liszt, then living in Weimar, he wrote of the emotional toll it took on him to abandon work on the *Ring*: "I have led my young Siegfried to a beautiful forest solitude, and there have left him under a linden tree, and taken leave of him with heartfelt tears.... I have torn [him] from my heart, and placed him under lock and key as one buried alive."[4] He then proceeded to write the full text for *Tristan und Isolde* over a period of three weeks, reading each act as it was completed to a small intimate group. His audience consisted of Minna, the Wesendoncks, and a young couple on their honeymoon, living in the Asyl as house guests, Hans von Bülow and his 20-year-old wife Cosima, the daughter of Liszt. He then composed the music for the first act, and made a musical sketch for the second. Another year had passed.

It was Wagner's forty-fifth birthday, May 22, 1858. Minna was not present in the Asyl. She was at a facility known for treatment of diseases of the heart at nearby Brestenberg and was not due to return permanently until mid–July. The purpose was undoubtedly both treatment and a rest, the one for her congenital heart condition, the other for her frayed nerves, each of which seemed to aggravate the other. A gangly youth with curly hair knocked on Wagner's door. His name was Karl Tausig. At the callow age of 16 he was already an accomplished pianist and a protégé of Franz Liszt, from whom he carried a letter of introduction. Despite some minor strains in the relationship of late, Liszt was at least as good a friend, and as generous a benefactor to Wagner at the time, as was Wesendonck.

The friendship between Liszt and Wagner notwithstanding, a hypothetical stranger happening on the scene, fully aware of Wagner's present situation and life's history, might have predicted that the composer would give the awkward youth short shrift. In deference to Liszt, our fictional observer might have expected for the boy a polite if stiff reception and audition, a courteous response and a quick farewell. Though to the young pianist the scene on the hill may have appeared idyllic, and the position of the famed opera composer one of financial and emotional security, all was not as it seemed. For a number of reasons, had Tausig been more informed, he might have felt little expectation of any but the most formal courtesy.

2

The Fugitive

FOR ONE THING THERE WAS the distraught composer's status for the previous nine years as a political refugee. It weighed heavily on him; too much so, it might have seemed, for him to have much interest in a precocious young pianist. In May 1849 he had been obliged to flee his residence and his position as director of the Royal Opera in Dresden for having participated in a civil uprising. Though successful uprisings are not criminal, this one was singularly unsuccessful. Under threat of arrest, trial, and lengthy imprisonment, he was effectively barred from entering not only his native Saxony, but all of her sister German states. Each of the states in this loose confederation, at this juncture of German history, was independent. However, their various kings, princes and dukes respected the interests of the others, most particularly when there was blood relationship between them, as was frequently the case. The target of this particular revolt was Wagner's employer and benefactor, King Frederick Augustus II of Saxony.

With the aid of troops from Prussia, the uprising was quickly crushed, and shortly thereafter Wagner's picture and description adorned publicly posted arrest warrants. The unlikely revolutionary made good his escape to Switzerland only with the aid of a "borrowed" passport and advice from Franz Liszt as to the safest route. Many of his less fortunate friends and co-revolutionaries were captured and sentenced to death. They were later the recipients of the king's grace in the form of lengthy prison terms in lieu of the gallows.

Though in later years he attempted to minimize his participation, accumulated evidence reflects that the king's music director wrote many a fiery tract fanning the flames of revolt. These were usually written anonymously, but there were few indeed who did not recognize Wagner's authorship. The evidence also reflects that he kept company with the ringleaders of the plot, both foreign and domestic; attended meetings during which the intimate details of the uprising were planned; ordered grenades from a brass foundry; assisted in the publication of a seditious, inflammatory journal; prepared and distributed posters urging the Saxon troops to desert; attempted to raise reinforcements for the revolutionaries after the conflict had begun; and, with several comrades, ascended the tower of the Church of the Holy Cross to direct the fire of the riflemen below against the king's troops. This the tower lookouts accomplished with handwritten notes attached to rocks, which they threw to their confederates on the ground.

The purpose of this uprising, in the minds of most of the participants, was identical with that of revolutionaries across Germany and much of Europe at the time: freedom, democracy, liberty, and other high minded ideals. Despite his fiery speeches and manifestoes, some of them anonymous, and naively urging immediate full democracy, the evidence seems to point to Wagner's motive as one born of professional frustration, most particularly the king's refusal to order a production of his newest opera, *Lohengrin*. He often seemed governed by a congenital inability to understand any viewpoint but his own, and the refusal of the king and the management of the Royal Theater to order a production of *Lohengrin* constituted, for him, the last straw. The government's precarious financial and political circumstances at the time that weighed so heavily on the king meant nothing to Wagner. In the great universal scheme of things such matters, to him, were trifles in comparison to his timeless artwork.

Whatever his disclaimers in later years, he seems to have found the excitement of revolution exhilarating. It was a welcome change from the stifling routine of his position, the superficiality of the theater culture, the "philistines" to whom he was obliged to answer, and for whose permissions he was compelled to beg. There are reports attesting to his nonstop, night-long stream of monologue to his fellow occupants of the church tower, on subjects beyond their understanding and irrelevant to their present predicament. The group was protected from hostile fire by the fortuitous presence of a few straw mattresses, which undoubtedly were of more protective value than Wagner's braggadocio claim that the bullet that could lay him out had not yet been cast. To a friend below he reported that the combined sounds of bells and cannons was "intoxicating." His fortunate escape from the inferno of the collapsing revolution was in a finely appointed coach, courtesy of several fellow revolutionaries who stopped to pick him up. One of them reported that "all the din, the shouting, and the rattling of arms were drowned out by the flaming talk of Wagner."

Once in Switzerland, we see in sharper relief the contradictions in his behavior and expressions of intentions, as well as the wide mood swings that were to be a defining pattern of his existence. The one exception was his dogged, single minded determination to fulfill what he felt to be his destiny. This sole unchanging purpose in life was to bring to fruition the music dramas that absorbed his every thought. In striving for that ultimate goal there would be neither equivocation or compromise. He saw them as the ultimate artworks, and unique in all history. We could perhaps find a touch of humor in such grandiose thoughts, not to mention the corresponding behavior, but history has found nothing humorous in it. The number of those in agreement with him seems to swell with every passing decade.

In September his wife joined him, and he seemed elated in what he saw as his newfound liberty. To a Dresden friend, Theodor Uhlig, he exulted in a sense of freedom and a lighthearted propensity to snap his fingers at external worries. In a letter to the Dresden chorus master he referred to his former struggles in that city as being against ignorance and insolence, and his status there as that of a victim of "spite and calumny."

The euphoria, like most states of euphoria, did not last. By November, he acknowledged to Uhlig that he was not so cheerful anymore. And in 1850, he was obliged to endure the painful frustration of being unable to attend the premier of his *Lohengrin* in Weimar, under the baton of Liszt. However, he still vacillated. By April 1851 he was still adamant that even should he be granted amnesty, he would stay in his "beloved Switzerland" and not deign to set foot in his native land.

But the maintenance of a happy facade was impossible; the futility of life in Switzerland, unbearable. The atmosphere was not at all conducive to either the composition or the production of his work. "If I stay here I shall certainly go under before long," he wrote to Liszt. "What am I to do? Must I sue for pardon from the King of Saxony?" The frustration, he insisted, had little to do with "mere animal instinct of self-preservation," but rather with the lack of stimulation to his artistic life.

He did indeed seek amnesty, as did Minna in his behalf, and as did a number of German princes who admired Wagner's early operas, *Rienzi*, *Der Fliegende Holländer*, *Tannhäuser*, and *Lohengrin*. They were played with increasing frequency throughout the German states. Particularly galling was his inability to hear, unlike thousands of other Germans, his *Lohengrin*, which he had never heard in performance, and was destined not to hear until 1862 in Vienna.

His lengthy and emotional pleas for amnesty, both direct and through intermediaries, were met with consistent and curt denials, based usually on the irrefutable fact that he had never submitted himself to a court of law for determination of guilt or innocence, something that Wagner steadfastly, and wisely, refused to do; and on the equally unanswerable proposition that many other revolutionaries were languishing in prison.

Throughout his life, those most willing to forgive Wagner's indiscretions, rudeness, duplicity and mendacity, and in this case, criminal behavior, were always those most susceptible to the spell of his music. Those who judged him most harshly were those the most deaf to it. The issue of his amnesty was no exception.

In 1856, came a brief but well-considered rejection of Wagner's personal appeal to the Saxon king. But the Grand Duke of Saxe-Weimar, Charles Alexander, indulging his own taste for music, proposed to admit Wagner for a limited time to his domain to oversee production of his works there. To this end, the grand duke sought the approval of King John, brother and successor of Frederick Augustus and for two years now the reigning monarch of Saxony. John was also the cousin of Charles Alexander. John's answer stated the obvious, that Charles was free to do as he pleased, but made clear his own disapproval, something that Charles was not prepared to ignore. Thus the matter ended. A year later, Grand Duke Frederick of Baden made a similar request of King John with similar results.

It was Frederick Augustus, of course, who was the party most directly affected by the uprising of 1849, and he had been bitterly resentful of the ingratitude of his appointed conductor. But even his personal resentment, tempered somewhat by his admiration of the supplicant's extraordinary talents, paled beside the unbending determination of his successor, King John, to uphold the letter of the law in this as in all cases.

The new king's son, the Crown Prince Albert, was, however, of a different temperament. A musician himself, he was an ardent admirer of Wagner's works. In mid–February 1858, two years after his futile direct appeal to King John, Wagner, through an intermediary, sent a letter to the prince begging his intercession with his father. The composer poured out several pages of unrestrained, turbulent emotions, a not unusual occurrence as is evidenced by much of his correspondence. But several passages of this letter summarize forcefully the expressions of his previous attempts at amnesty, and describe most clearly the agonizing frustration of his predicament:

> Is it fair that the overwrought mood of an optimistic dreamer who lives only in his art should be judged withthe same severity as the ambitious plottings of a political fanatic?... No composer was ever so dependent as I upon the support of those who speak his native tongue. I have never been able to compose except to my own text — both words and music are firmly rooted, in a manner unprecedented, in the German language and the German spirit; hence my struggles, ever since my exile, to find a new home for myself on foreign soil have been without success.[1]

Even in German speaking Switzerland, he continued, the theaters were so inadequate as to be of no use to him. Yet so completely did his life depend on exercise of his art that he was engaged on a new composition. Nevertheless, he said, "So broken is my heart with grief and misery, so crippled and hampered is my spirit by the desolating thought that this work also must remain unproduced, that I feel my strength is giving way."

Finally, he told Prince Albert, he hoped that "once you are acquainted with my compositions as a whole, you will acknowledge that I have always endeavored to depict what is noble and sublime, and that if a man of this type can for a moment seem base and ignoble it is merely the result of a passing cloud of error."

The letter was dated February 20, 1858, barely three months before young Karl Tausig knocked on Wagner's door. The composer had still received no answer to it. This was one aspect of the state of mind of the man to whom Tausig handed the letter of recommendation from Franz Liszt.

But there were still other matters crowding in on Wagner's thoughts and emotions that day in May when young Tausig appeared at the Asyl.

3

Minna

THE WAGNER HOUSEHOLD WAS no harbor of idyllic matrimonial bliss. Richard and Minna were temperamentally, intellectually and artistically poles apart. He was 21; she, four years his elder, was an actress of some repute when, in 1834, he met and relentlessly pursued her. It began in the tiny village of Lauschstädt, in southeast Germany, where the small traveling musical company that Wagner directed had quartered for a short stay. The lengthy, highly emotional, overwrought letters of the young conductor to the object of his passion, written during their inevitable separations, tell us much about his volatile temperament and tendency to extravagant expressions of emotion. She, like many another woman later in his life, was unable to resist him. They were married two years later.

Minna must have recognized early on the impossibility of this union. Most threatening of all were his profligate ways that threatened to destroy her financially. A little more than a year into the marriage she twice ran away, first from Königsberg, the city known today as Kaliningrad, where she was employed, and where Wagner was unsuccessfully seeking steady work. She left with the help of an admiring businessman named Dietrich. She first went to her parents' home in Dresden. Wagner sought her out, and for a few days, reconciliation seemed possible. But, in company with her illegitimate daughter Natalie, she fled once more, and stayed with her admirer in Hamburg. Natalie had been fathered by an officer of the Royal Saxon Guards when Minna was but 15, and was passed off throughout Minna's life as her younger sister. Not until shortly after the marriage did Wagner learn of her true relationship to Minna. Not until late in life did Natalie herself become aware.

Minna's infidelity with Dietrich broke Wagner's determination. He accepted employment as music director in the town of Riga, Latvia, imagined his marriage to be at an end and took steps for a divorce. But Minna, possibly motivated at least in part through guilt, decided that she could not permanently abandon her husband, and, after obtaining Richard's assurance by letter that she was forgiven her transgressions, traveled to Riga to join him. He gladly accepted her back. He asked no questions nor burdened her with accusations of guilt.

Her return was a tragic misjudgment. The instincts that led to her flight may have been more sound, whatever the conventional mores of the time dictated. The life Wagner led, and the goals he pursued, did not seem ideally suited to this world, whereas Minna's desires were such as to fit quite comfortably in it. She believed in a stable existence with steady income, living within one's means, prompt payment of one's debts, and respectability among the members of the society in which one lived. These goals required prestigious, or at least honorable employment, all matters of rather small import to Richard.

Her beliefs did not include the necessity of running from the town of Riga across the Russo-Prussian border one summer night in 1839 to escape creditors, nor taking a back road in Prussia to avoid the city of Königsberg, home of many other of his creditors. Throughout Europe at the time the penalty for failure to pay debts was imprisonment. It was while traversing one of these back roads that their wagon overturned, causing injuries to Minna that may have left her unable to bear children; so she later claimed to Natalie.

Neither did Minna's notions of a desirable existence include traveling to Paris by way of a

Minna Wagner. From *Wagner in Exile* by Woldemar Lippert.

stormy and dangerous sea voyage to London in a heaving, bobbing two-masted schooner; nor living a Bohemian life in Paris for two miserable years, while her husband sought vainly to find fame and fortune with his early operas. But she endured those hardships willingly, working and striving in a multitude of ways to keep their joint heads above water. It was a task made doubly difficult by her eternally optimistic husband's proclivity to spend money he anticipated receiving, well before he even expected to receive it, and which usually failed to materialize at all. Her most frantic moments must certainly have come during her efforts to secure Richard's release from a debtor's prison, in which he spent about three weeks.

Her six years in Dresden, during which Richard served as Royal Orchestra director, were certainly the happiest of her married years, which is not really saying a great deal. His appointment came in February 1843, several months after their arrival in the Saxon capital from Paris, and the position was quite prestigious. He had already, shortly after arriving, conducted the premieres of his early operas *Rienzi* and *Der Fliegende Holländer.* He had been frustratingly unsuccessful in having either produced in Paris, but now both became immediately popular throughout Germany. Also produced in Dresden, in 1845, was his *Tannhäuser,* composed during Wagner's employment there. Minna, at long last, was enjoying a measure of financial independence. Her years of sacrifice and menial labor were, so she thought, over.

But Wagner was gnawed by doubts. He seemed to feel that the creative powers growing within him were being traded for a sterile and worthless security; the tranquility of mind necessary to realize his creative potential, stifled. He had suffered misgivings about even accepting such employment, Minna's enthusiasm notwithstanding. In June 1842, en route from Paris to Dresden, he and Minna had stopped in Teplitz, a spa in what is today the Czech Republic. From there he wrote his Jewish friend from Paris, Samuel Lehrs, about whom we will hear more later. He told Lehrs that when he realized that a "banal, tiresome good fortune" might be necessary to survive, "a shudder came over him." For opera houses and theater people he had only contempt: "My future lies in the hands of the theater riff-raff: May God enlighten their lordships and open their hearts to virtue!"[1] As he later wrote in his autobiography, when considering a lasting contract with even one of the finest German opera houses, he felt "degraded again" and a deep contempt. But he wondered what else he could do to hold his ground "between disgust and desire in this strange world."[2]

He had been offered and had accepted the employment, but the profligate Wagner found it impossible to live within his means. Efforts of the king and his ministers to assist him were of no avail. Wagner was not built for steady, routine employment, nor to interpret the works of others. He was born to create, for which he required freedom — of time, and from financial worry. But the world was not then, nor is it now, set up to care for creative artists striking out along new paths, such as those along which Wagner was being inexorably led by his overworked creative instincts. They were paths leading to a revolutionary new art form, one that most of his contemporaries, including his wife, would find incomprehensible, and which would be almost impossible to realize in production in the theaters of the time.

Then came the revolution and Wagner's precipitous immersion in it. He may have seen his flight from Dresden as a door to freedom, but to his angry wife it was a return to penury and humiliation. She was now obliged to endure her husband's grandiose schemes for unintelligible and unproduceable works requiring years without income, living off the generosity of friends and admirers, and dealing with impatient creditors. Her reunion with her husband in Switzerland was not with a high degree of enthusiasm, as was made abundantly clear in a letter to him from Dresden in July 1849: "What sort of future do I face? What have you to offer me?... What proof of love have I had from you?" Yet she seems to have no other choice: "Dresden cannot be my future place of residence; I would play a sad role as your abandoned wife."[3]

He told her he had borrowed money to pay her way to Zurich; she answered that it was depressing that he was not able to provide for her and must live on the charity of friends. "Don't take this amiss," she told him, but "it is very doubtful whether you will ever be able to pay it back since you never adapt yourself to the world as it really is but demand that the whole world adapt and form itself according to your ideas."[4] His behavior she knew well; his potential, not at all.

Once in Zurich, Minna's bitterness only increased, exacerbated by his inability, or unwillingness as she saw it, to earn money. The necessity of living on borrowed funds or on gifts, she found abhorrent.

And she soon had an episode of infidelity to contend with. Its roots were in Dresden, though it blossomed in Paris. In 1848 a young woman, no more than 22 years of age, English by birth but living in Bordeaux with her French husband, attended a performance of *Tannhäuser* in the Saxon capital. The opera is Wagner's rendition of the legend of the nobleman who resided for an untold number of years in the infamous mountain called Venusberg with Frau Venus. His lust having been sated, he finally returns to the outside world, but upon revealing his past whereabouts earns the contempt of his former comrades and the pity of the chaste Elizabeth, his former beloved.

It was conducted by Wagner, and the young woman fell in love with both the music and the composer-conductor. In early 1850, in the forerunner of a scenario destined to play out eight years later on the Green Hill in Zurich, she and Wagner met again in Paris, possibly by chance, possibly not. Her name was Jessie Laussot. She was, like Mathilde Wesendonck, rich by marriage, attractive, talented and cultured. Also like Mathilde, but unlike Minna, Jessie understood Wagner both as man and as artist and appreciated the scope of his genius.

Many of Wagner's biographers and other detractors paint a picture of him as a lustful womanizer, unscrupulous, and forever seeking sexual flings and affairs without limit, regardless of consequences. For such titillation of their readers, they should look elsewhere. Much salacious material is readily available in the lives of certain other composers, as well as many writers and artists. Wagner was certainly no less libidinous than other men, but, as far as the ample record of his life shows, his liaisons were never motivated by a passing hankering for sexual gratification. He needed, more than anything, feminine understanding. In any who did not understand his art and his goals in life, male or female, he had little interest.

His early life may give a clue. He had three older sisters and a younger half sister. It is apparent from his autobiography that they doted on him, perhaps to the exclusion of an older brother, and lavished on Richard their attention, admiration and encouragement. The half sister, Cäcilie, was his almost constant companion in childhood. But it was his oldest sister, Rosalie, ten years his senior, who earned a special place in his affections. He described his relationship with her as one of purity and sincerity that "could vie with the noblest form of friendship between men and women." Sadly, at age 33, she died in childbirth, a shattering blow to the young musician. It is possible that it was this abundance of encouragement and praise that contributed to his unconquerable confidence in himself; possible also, that he spent much of his adult life seeking a substitute for this childhood idolization by four sisters.

Jessie soon influenced her wealthy wine-merchant husband to financially support the penniless composer, but through some rather convoluted circumstances, the plan never came to fruition. Those circumstances are complex and interesting, but it is sufficient for us to know that Minna, alarmed at the possible motivation for her husband's journey to Paris, or at least about his behavior once there, made the difficult journey to the French metropolis by coach. Through Richard's artifice, aided by a bewildered and reluctant friend there, Ernst Kietz, she was unsuccessful in finding him. Frustrated and angry, she returned to Zurich. In fact, Wagner and Jessie had made plans to run off together to Greece. In mid–April he wrote

Minna a long and agonizing review of their failed efforts at a happy marriage. He wept over the separation that was so necessary, but said that a separation there must be.

The plans went awry. Partially through the influence of her mother, in whom Jessie saw fit to confide, the young woman retreated and refused further contact with Wagner. The affair, if such it was, soon become public knowledge, and her husband in Bordeaux threatened to kill Wagner should he ever get sight of him. The thoroughly distraught and dispirited composer, whom no one has ever accused of cowardice, went to Bordeaux, to explain, to Jessie's husband, Eugène. He advised him by letter in advance of his arrival, hoping to make one more attempt to salvage the situation. In a show of his not unusual naiveté, Wagner wanted to ask why he insisted on holding on to a wife who did not wish to remain. "There lies before me either a speedy death or a new life,"[5] he wrote to a friend. But the irate Eugène, through the exercise of sound discretion, was not at home. He and his family had left, placing the matter in the hands of the police. The gendarmes treated the frustrated composer with courtesy and understanding, but, pointing to his expired passport, ordered him out of the country. The relationship ended. Wagner returned to his wife, who was now still more deeply hurt and embittered.

Wagner, of course, was living with his own frustrations. The last opera that he had written that was within her musical understanding was *Rienzi*, an opera in the traditional grand opera style, one that Wagner now found odious. *Rienzi* itself, in later life, he all but disowned. Even the relatively accessible *Der Fliegende Holländer* she then found beyond her grasp, though late in life she claimed that it was the last opera Wagner wrote that she found worthwhile. For his part, Wagner, though expressing in correspondence apparently sincere sympathy, even pity for her, found what he considered to be her petty middle class values both frustrating and stifling. Further, Minna saw his relationship with Jessie only as a typical sexual attraction to a younger woman, one more character flaw, and had not the slightest grasp of her husband's intense craving for feminine understanding and approval.

These same circumstances combined to arouse eight years later almost inevitable romantic feelings, if not a physical romance, outside of his home. The object of his passion this time was the musically knowledgeable, artistically inclined, attractive young wife of his benefactor Wesendonck. As early as 1853 their relations, in her words, "became more friendly and more intimate." Mathilde apparently found the company of this creative romantic infinitely more stimulating than that of her business oriented husband. Forty-three years later, at the age of 68, she wrote of Wagner, "It is to him alone that I owe all that has been best in my life."[6] The deep feelings each harbored for the other could not have remained invisible to their spouses. Circumstances indicate that they did not.

When, in September 1857, the Wesendoncks moved into their new home on the Green Hill, Mathilde and Richard were now adjacent neighbors. Otto was frequently away or attending to business in town, and Richard visited Mathilde in the larger villa almost daily. What transpired between them cannot be stated with any certainty. Many circumstances, including the correspondence of the principals, strongly suggest an absence of any physical intimacy, but a strengthening passion nonetheless. In

Mathilde Wesendonck, from a painting by von Dorner. From *Richard Wagner: Sein Leben, sein Werk, seine Welt* by Julius Kapp.

December 1854, he had written to Liszt about an overly optimistic schedule for finishing his *Nibelung*, after which he would begin work on a new opera based on the love tale of *Tristan und Isolde*. He explained his motive. "Since I have never experienced the true bliss of love, I must build a monument to the most beautiful of my dreams." But he could not wait to finish the *Ring*, or even *Siegfried*. *Tristan* was beginning to breathe with a life of its own. In August of 1957 he completed the orchestral sketch of the second of the three acts of *Siegfried*, then, as we have already seen, put the opera aside and turned to writing both musical themes and the text for *Tristan*.

Much ink has been spilled over the intriguing but unanswerable question of whether *Tristan und Isolde* was inspired by his love for Mathilde, or whether Wagner, who always seemed to feel the need to act out his dramas, found in Mathilde the embodiment of the Irish princess Isolde, about whom he had read so much in the medieval romances.

Whatever the truth of that matter, there can be no doubt of the depth of his feelings and his passion for Mathilde. The inevitable eruption of this simmering volcano came on April 7, only six weeks before the visit of Karl Tausig. It came in the form of a lengthy letter by Richard to Mathilde, wrapped, interestingly enough, in a penciled draft of the *Tristan* prelude, the delivery of which was entrusted to a servant. As the messenger traversed the garden between the two buildings on the Green Hill, the highly jealous and suspicious Minna, tormented by the sight of notes going back and forth, relieved him of his package.

In the calm light of day the letter does not appear to contain evidence of a clandestine relationship, and seems rather to imply the contrary. It is couched in Wagner's usual effusive and extravagant style, but concerns primarily an expiation of jealousy arising out of the hospitality of the Wesendoncks to one Cesare DeSanctis, a visiting Italian musician and friend of Giuseppe Verdi. He had an obvious interest in Mathilde. It did not matter. What was clear to Minna from the letter was the existence of a mutual rapport between her husband and this brilliant and attractive young woman, an understanding, and a depth of feeling that was impossible between him and herself. If she believed that there was more afoot than rapport, however, she might well be forgiven. Nestled among the philosophical discourse about Goethe's *Faust* lay such language as "My whole day was a struggle between melancholy and longing for you.... When I look into your eyes, then I simply cannot speak anymore.... How blind the one who would not recognize your glance and find his soul there!"[7]

Minna wasted no time on calm reflection. She dashed immediately into his room and delivered an unrestrained diatribe, venting all of her grievances, real and imaginary. Ignoring her husband's pleas, she also confronted Mathilde. The explosive anger, probably insultingly expressed, must have shocked and greatly upset her. Whatever the provocation, it resulted in Mathilde's permanently bitter animosity and disdain for the older woman.

Wagner seemed both then and thereafter convinced that the outburst and the almost unbearable tension it precipitated between the Wesendoncks, Minna and Richard resulted from his wife's conviction that the letter evidenced a physical relationship. The pain that might have been caused merely by the obvious spiritual closeness, he never addressed nor, apparently, considered. For him this was not an unusual reaction. For many years, Wagner seemed to believe that because he fired no shots nor planted any bombs in the Dresden revolution, that he was guilty of no crime. For the balance of his life he seemed to claim that because there was no physical relationship with Mathilde, he was entirely blameless in the maelstrom that followed.

Whatever Minna actually believed, she had obviously reached her breaking point. Further ignoring her husband's pleas, she confronted Otto.

But Otto knew of the closeness of his tenant with his wife, was convinced that she had committed no infidelity, and was understanding and tolerant of it. Minna also spread her complaints directly to her Zurich friends and, by correspondence, to relatives and other friends wherever they might be. Life at home for Wagner was all but intolerable and continued work on *Tristan* hardly possible. Finally, about a month before the appearance of Tausig, Wagner convinced his overwrought wife to enter the institution at nearby Brestenberg.

None of these matters could have been known to the youngster who appeared at Wagner's door. But there was one other matter that rendered a warm reception even more unlikely. About this, the young man may have been aware. Almost everyone, especially in the musical world, was.

Eight years previously, in the midst of his "prose years," and almost concurrently with the Jessie Laussot episode, Wagner had written and published an inflammatory and scurrilous essay entitled "Judaism in Music." In it he spoke of the Jews in general, and of a few in particular, in contemptuous terms, describing them as repugnant in appearance and in speech, and essentially denying their capacity to create or to appreciate true art. Considering that Tausig was but eight at the time it was published, it is possible, though not likely, that he remained unaware of it for the next eight years. But he could not have remained oblivious to it forever, for Karl Tausig was a Jew.

4

The Paris Jews

Exactly when this intense hatred of the Jews and Jewishness began to take root in Wagner's psyche is not completely clear. Before September 1850 there was no public awareness, nor indeed, public evidence of it. But during the short separation between himself and Minna in the course of the Laussot episode, in the continuing correspondence filled with mutual recriminations there was one revealing statement about the tome that here concerns us. In one of her letters, in May 1850, Minna complained, "Since two years ago when you wanted me to read that essay in which you slander whole races which have been fundamentally helpful to you, I could not force myself to listen, and ever since that time you have borne a grudge against me ... you never again let me hear anything from your works."[1] The reference could only have been to "Judaism in Music." Hence the essay must have existed, in draft form at least, two and a half years before its publication in early September 1850.

Her reaction resulted from what Wagner habitually referred to as Minna's "bourgeoisie" outlook, namely her mores, manners, gratitude and sense of propriety. This outlook rebelled at the sweeping nature of the scathing indictment of a people, many members of whom had indeed been good to the Wagners during their two-year period of hardship, deprivation and penury in Paris.

Wagner mentioned in his autobiography having sought, successfully, during his Paris sojourn, financial assistance from one of his wealthy friends in Leipzig. The friend was a Leipzig merchant, a Jew named Axelfeld, though his religion is not mentioned in the autobiography. There were also a number of German Jews living in Paris during that time and some, in advantageous positions in the theater, had extended helping hands to one they saw as a compatriot in need. But perhaps the closest of these Jewish expatriates was one unable to directly assist anyone, including himself. He was a sickly, fellow victim of poverty named Samuel Lehrs, the one to whom Wagner later wrote from Teplitz about his apprehensions concerning a director's post. He was a philologist and scholar of philosophy, and what little he earned was through his writings.

He was seven years senior to Wagner, and his family had converted to Christianity about 15 years or more before his friendship with the composer. The family name had been Kaufman. Samuel's name had been changed to Siegmund, but as a young adult he preferred Samuel, and it was as Samuel that Wagner knew him. By Wagner's own fiat, as subsequently expressed inferentially in "Judaism in Music," and more overtly in a much later essay, "Know Thyself," Lehrs was indeed Jewish regardless of the name. The later essay will be examined more closely in subsequent pages. Jewish heritage was enough, in Wagner's mind, to settle the question, and Lehrs probably always thought of himself as Jewish.

Lehrs was one of a triumvirate of close friends sharing a Bohemian life with the Wagners in their Paris days. The other two were Ernst Kietz, the talented but unreliable artist who later assisted Wagner in his deception of Minna, and Gottfried Anders, employed at the National Library. Within weeks after leaving Paris in early 1842, Wagner, in a letter to his half sister Cäcilie, living with her husband in that city, referred to his three friends as a "cherished *trefoil.*"

Lehrs and his two companions, like Richard and Minna, were obliged to struggle daily for bare existence. Wagner described at length how Lehrs, on a wretchedly hot day, was obliged to walk the streets of all sections of Paris to seek forbearance from his numerous creditors. He took an iced drink, says Wagner, and from that day developed a hoarseness, and finally an incurable tuberculosis, then known as "consumption." He grew weaker and weaker for months, filling Wagner and his companions with acute anxiety. One day, Wagner looked for him in his room, which he found to be icy cold. Lehrs was huddled at his writing table, and explained that his employer was pressing him for advances made.[2] The minister of education later tried to help, but little money was available for subsidies. Lehrs received perhaps enough to keep the fire going in the frigid room, but when the Wagners left Paris the following spring, it was with the conviction that they would never see him again.

It was April 1842, and Richard and Minna were leaving for Dresden, where great interest had been shown in a possible production of his *Rienzi.* The emotion at parting from his three friends, Wagner described as "almost overwhelming." He was concerned for all of them, but he felt there could be no doubt of Lehrs's fate.

Wagner credits Lehrs and his infectious absorption with philosophy, in part, with his own lifelong interest in it.[3] He partially credits his Paris friend also with his interest in the classical side of medieval poetry,[4] and it was Lehrs who furnished Wagner with the source materials for his *Tannhäuser* and *Lohengrin*.

In May, just a month after leaving Paris, Wagner wrote to Kietz, responding to news that Lehrs had rented a place in the country: "I am very glad that the good Lehrs likes his country house so much. That his material circumstances seem to improve more and more is priceless luck: may all this help his badly shattered health." In September he complained to Kietz that he did not get a direct answer from him about Lehrs. In late 1842 Kietz wrote that he would not give details as it was all too sad, to which Wagner replied, insisting on full information. In February 1843, he took Kietz to task for waiting two months to reply, concluding his lengthy letter, "I don't want to know anything about you, only about Lehrs."[5]

On April 7 Wagner finally heard directly from Lehrs, and answered at once. He was fearful, said Wagner, but now has hope. After a lengthy narrative bringing his friend up to date on his and Minna's lives, he ended his letter, "Answer me soon, and be of good courage my dear brother. Sooner or later we must be together again. So long and enjoy the beautiful spring air which will bring you strength."[6]

Lehrs died a few days after receiving this letter, one year after the last farewell in Paris. Wagner learned of his death two months later by letter from Cäcilie. He replied that the news left him dumb, speechless for almost eight days, and hardly able to lift his head.[7] In August, writing to Anders, he termed the death of Lehrs "heartbreaking ... this brave, wonderful and so unfortunate man will to me be eternally unforgettable."[8] Twenty years after the first publication of "Judaism in Music," in the course of dictating his autobiography to his second wife, Wagner referred to his relationship with Lehrs as "one of the most beautiful friendships of my life."[9]

Any charge of ingratitude stemming from his infamous essay would center not on Lehrs or Axenfeld but on one who was, probably innocently, a root cause of Wagner's intense anti–Semitism, perhaps the major one. The friend who unwittingly aroused Wagner's antipathy and contempt was Giacomo Meyerbeer. Before immigrating to Paris, Meyerbeer, formerly Jakob Beer, like the parents of Lehrs had changed his religion and his name. This was not an unusual move for German Jews of the day, attempting, most often unsuccessfully, to avoid the prejudice and the stigma that attached to their heritage. His operas, in the grand style, had been produced with the utmost opulence in Paris, then the opera capitol of the world. They had won him international fame and a handsome fortune.

It required no small amount of self assuredness, and perhaps a touch of brashness, for the 23-year-old, unknown, untested conductor of backwater theaters to introduce himself to the foremost opera composer of the day. Wagner did so by letter from Königsberg where, seeking work as an assistant conductor, he lacked permanent or steady employment. In the letter he tells Meyerbeer that it was his, Meyerbeer's, works that pointed out the new direction in music, changing Wagner's own outlook, which had previously been centered around his admiration for Beethoven. It would be futile, the young Wagner continued, "to deny that it was your works which suggested this new direction to me.... I cannot forbear to add that in you I behold the perfect embodiment of the task that confronts the German artist, a task you have solved by dint of your having mastered the merits of the Italian and French schools in order to give *universal* validity to the products of that genius."[10] Wagner left Königsberg shortly thereafter, and if there was an answer to the letter Wagner never received it.

Three years later however, upon crossing the English Channel, en route to Paris by way of Boulogne-sur-Mer, he met two Jewish women, mother and daughter, who knew the famous composer well, and knew also that he was presently in Boulogne. They furnished Wagner with a letter of introduction. In his autobiography, Wagner admits to a favorable impression of Meyerbeer upon that first meeting, particularly "as regards his appearance," one that inspired confidence. He adds, however, that "the years had not yet given his features the flabby look which sooner or later mars most Jewish faces." He had apparently not noticed any such cruel effect of time on other faces. It should be noted however that this mild passage may be the only expression of an anti–Semitic sentiment in his entire 800-page autobiography, save only his brief and restrained, if self-serving, explanation for "Judaism in Music."

By all objective evidence, Meyerbeer seems to have genuinely tried to help the young Wagner to gain a toehold in the economic and artistic jungle that was Paris in the mid–nineteenth century. There are not only the letters of Wagner to Meyerbeer, flattering, fawning, and obsequious in tone, but his even more convincing letters to others. To his brother-in-law, Edward Avenarius, for one example, he wrote a year after arriving in Paris of the very helpful assistance rendered by Meyerbeer, his "great friend and protector." Then there are the letters of Meyerbeer himself, obviously genuinely impressed with his readings of the scores of Wagner's *Rienzi*, and his newly completed *Fliegende Holländer*, written in Paris, borne of his adventures in the North Sea en route to England. On the strength of these works he recommended the young composer to the power brokers of the town.

That he was unsuccessful in advancing the neophyte's career does not, from the vantage point of 160 years, seem to be the fault of Meyerbeer. With

Meyerbeer's help, wrote Wagner in a letter to Avenarius, one Paris theater had accepted his *Rienzi*, but later went bankrupt. Meyerbeer was further instrumental in having *Der Fliegende Holländer* accepted by the director of the Berlin Opera, a fact that Wagner himself acknowledged. But the director was soon replaced by one who had no interest in it. Neither of these disappointing events were matters that could be laid at the door of Meyerbeer.

The celebrated composer also lent his considerable weight to Wagner's successful efforts to have *Rienzi* accepted in Dresden, where it was performed under Wagner's direction in 1842. His letter to the director of the Dresden Court Theater, extolling the virtues of both Wagner and his opera, was perhaps not crucial, but must certainly have been helpful. There is no evidence of bad faith to corroborate the subsequently angrily voiced objections of Wagner that the renowned composer had only pretended to try to assist, and that he was in fact either indifferent, or worse, interested only in sidelining a potential rival.

But if there is little reason to credit Wagner's overheated opinions about Meyerbeer's sincerity, there may nonetheless be good reason to credit his opinions of Meyerbeer's operas, opinions sharply expressed in his essay about the Jews. Those works are the antithesis of everything that Wagner believed about the basic nature of art, and of the essential qualities that any opera should exhibit. The older man had a genius for melody, and memorable tunes abound in his works. They often, however, have little to do with the drama onstage, hanging more like ornaments to hold the attention of the audience. His works can be superficially eye-and ear-catching, opulent and grandiose, but have little depth or artistic unity.

Questions of ingratitude or hypocrisy aside, Wagner, his own concept of the operatic art considered, can perhaps be forgiven for his denigration of that of Meyerbeer. His projection of their faults as something inherently insidious and degrading about the entire Jewish nature, however, transcends the bounds of logic or rational human understanding. Yet there seems little doubt, from the intrinsic evidence, that Wagner's hatred of Meyerbeer did not stem from the fact that he was Jewish; it seems much more likely, rather, that his hatred of the Jews stemmed in significant part from his contempt for Meyerbeer's operas, which ultimately transferred to Meyerbeer himself, thence to the entire culture of his heritage.

It is tempting to conclude that Wagner never mentioned the fact of an individual's Jewish heritage except in regards to those of whom he disapproved, and ignored that uncomfortable fact about those whom he liked or admired. And sometimes so it seemed. But a large number of exceptions undermine the second part of that conclusion.

One glaring exception is the case of Jacques Halévy, a composer 14 years older than Wagner, living in Paris during Wagner's sojourn there. He is best known today for his opera *La Juive*; in English, *The Jewess*. According to Wagner, Halévy openly claimed to have been Jewish, but to have converted only for the sake of his wife. It is doubtful, however, that Halévy ever did convert. It appears rather, that he simultaneously maintained two families, one with his Jewish wife, the other with his Christian mistress, by both of whom he had children. Wagner, nonetheless, in his autobiography, tells us he admired the candor of Halévy's admission, as he did his denigration of the value of the operatic works then in vogue. Wagner's first contact with Halévy resulted from his employment to prepare a piano score for this older composer's operatic success, *Reine de Chypre*. Wagner tells us further that he had taken a great fancy to Halévy, and had a very high opinion of his "masterly" talent. He refers also to his many enlivening talks with that "peculiarly good hearted and unassuming man," though lamenting that his talent deserted him all too soon.

But, says Wagner, it was Halévy's candor that attracted him most, something that he concluded "justifies the participation of all Jews in our artistic concerns."[11] These lines were dictated by Wagner, in or shortly after 1869, for inclusion in his autobiography, destined for public distribution. He was speaking of a time 10 years before his essay on the Jews, but dictating it 19 years after that essay, and almost contemporaneous with its republication. Such a statement as this cannot be reconciled with his almost simultaneous reaffirmation of his peremptory denial of any Jewish creativity, or understanding of true art. It must remain as one of the baffling contradictions of his fractured world outlook.

And that account in the autobiography does not tell the full story. Over a period of four days, from February 27 to May 1, 1842, he published in the *Gazette Musicale* a 25 page essay, "Halévy and *La Reine de Chypre*," filled with laudatory comments about that opera as well as *La Juive*. He found the essential characteristic of Halévy's inspiration the "pathos of high lyric tragedy." His music "issues from the inmost and most puissant depths of human nature. It is terrifying, and makes one dizzy to gaze into the awful caverns of the human heart.... I avow that never have I heard dramatic music which transferred me so completely to a given reach of history." More to the point of our focus, Wagner also let it be known that "whoever can appreciate the solidity, the dignity of German music, to him the influence exerted on one of its most important branches by the author of La Juive will not seem one of his smallest titles to glory."[12]

It is to be wondered if he ever reflected on that essay when, in later years, he wrote of the unbreachable difference between German and Jewish music and art.

5

The Essay

IN LATE AUGUST 1850, Wagner, the expatriate from Germany, forwarded a copy of his manuscript about the Jews to a friend and benefactor, Karl Ritter, whom we met earlier as one of Wagner's dinner guests in Zurich. Ritter, like many other of Wagner's friends, had gone to Weimar for the first production of Wagner's *Lohengrin*. It was conducted by Liszt. The opera is the story of the Swan Knight, who comes to do battle in a trial by combat in behalf of a maiden falsely accused of the murder of her brother. By cover letter he asked that Ritter give the manuscript to Theodor Uhlig, the friend from Dresden, also in Weimar for the performance. Uhlig was in turn asked to give the document to Franz Brendel, the editor of a small musical journal in Leipzig, *The New Journal for Music,* in which it was published the following month.

Wagner had signed the essay under the pseudonym *Freigedank,* or "Free Thought." As he explained disingenuously in his cover letter to Ritter, "Everyone will guess it's me, but it doesn't matter." Through the fictitious name, he continued, he might obviate a "useless scandal." What scandal? Should the Jews try to make this out to be a personal squabble between himself and Meyerbeer, continued Wagner, and to throw back at him the personal favors by Meyerbeer, he would reveal the "true" value of those favors. But, he added, he had no wish to bring about such a scandal. Whatever the motivation for the pseudonym, Wagner's fingerprints, namely his well-known complex, sometimes contorted, prose style, were all over the essay. Further, though his rabid anti–Semitism was not so well known, his penchant for anonymous essays was. During his revolutionary days in Dresden, they flowed from his pen. Neither then, nor now, did they fool anyone. Nor did Wagner ever deny being the author of this incendiary document.

Nonetheless, Brendel took the brunt of the firestorm ignited by the publication of the essay, vitriolic even by the contemporary standards of that hotbed of anti–Semitism that was central Europe in the mid–nineteenth century. Brendel was a professor of music history at the Leipzig Conservatorium, an institution steeped in admiration, almost in reverence of its founder, the recently deceased composer Felix Mendelssohn. Because the essay contained some rather unflattering remarks about Mendelssohn, born of parents who were originally Jewish, all of Brendel's colleagues requested his resignation. He refused either to resign or to divulge the name of the contributor.

In the same journal about 10 months later, despite a passing mention of regret that "a few harsh expressions" of the essay had not been omitted, Brendel expressed, in somewhat milder and more moderate form, thoughts quite similar to those of the essay. More interestingly, he referred to the "perfect tempest" that the essay had stirred up, giving rise to "now friendly, now hostile notices in a crowd of other papers."[1] Making due allowance for the self-congratulatory nature of the observation, it may nonetheless tell us something of the controversy the writing produced. Considering the intense and heated nature of public debate at the time over the proper place of the Jews in German society, it would be difficult in any event to believe that such a missive would pass unnoticed.

Though Brendel continued to refer to Herr Freigedank, Wagner's identity as the author was by this time an open secret. In the spring of 1851, Liszt wrote to his friend asking if he were, as had been bandied about, the author of "the Jewish article." "Why do you ask," was Wagner's reply; "you know very well I was." And he offered his explanation:

> I long had nursed a secret grudge against this Judaism, and that grudge is as necessary to my nature as gall to the blood. An occasion came, when their cursed scribbling vexed me more than usual, and I suddenly let fling.[2]

His use of the word "necessary" cannot pass unnoticed. One does not usually refer to strongly held emotions, whether of hate or of love, as being "necessary to my nature," and Wagner did not choose words carelessly. Such emotions, we generally assume, are irresistible and inevitable because of the nature of the person or object that causes the emotion. The declaration, in short, says something about the object of the emotion, whether a person or a thing. Wagner's statement clearly tells us more about himself than about the Jews. It is perhaps all the more interesting for the fact that many years later, Friedrich Nietzsche, the German philosopher and onetime friend of the composer, said of Wagner that he hated the Jews because he "had to."

Whether the attack on the Jews was or was not a sudden impulse as he suggests in his letter to Liszt, the convictions it expressed remained in the firmament of his unalterable opinions. True, this was one of only two essays— of the many he penned — that were devoted entirely to the subject of the Jews, the other, "Know Thyself," being written and published in 1881, near the end of his life. It is true also that throughout his life he demonstrated an apparent tolerance of, or indifference to the religion, or "race," of individual Jews with musical talent or appreciation of his art. Yet in his subsequent voluminous prose writings, compiled in eight volumes, each of about 400 pages, and in his prolific correspondence, there is a sentence here, a paragraph there, a page somewhere else, echoing the same intense antipathy.

Further, and most notably, we shall subsequently see this propensity in more detail in frequent comments to his second wife, Cosima, as recorded in her diaries during the last 14 years of his life. They are replete with expressions of profound contempt for *the Jews*, often gratuitous and extraneous to the subject under discussion. They are expressed sometimes, though rarely, in mild, offhand remarks, more often in vitriolic ones. Nineteen years after the publication of this essay, to the consternation of almost everyone, he published it again. Even those who shared his sentiments were confounded by this republication, seen as an invitation to animosity at a time when he badly needed friendships.

Though this essay does not, by any means, assure us of an understanding of Wagner's attitude toward the Jews, it was certainly his self-proclaimed creed on that subject for the rest of his life.

Often in this essay,[3] he uses the editorial "we," thus claiming to speak for the whole German nation, or at least the vast majority of it. It is, of course, clear from the context that the thoughts and experiences of which he speaks are his own. The nation itself was, emphatically, far from being of one mind on this subject. It was often the increasing rights and liberties afforded the Jews that precipitated his most opprobrious outbursts.

The following summary or condensed version is drawn from the 1894 translation by William Askton Ellis.* Quotation marks signify that this precise wording (drawn directly from Ellis) is crucial to an understanding of the text.

◆　◆　◆

The purpose of this article is an explanation of "that unconscious feeling which proclaims itself among the people as a rooted dislike of the Jewish nature" in respect to art, and most particularly to music. It has nothing to do with religion or politics. In religion the Jews have long ceased to be our hated foes, the

---

*The full essay is reproduced as an appendix to this work.

Christian religion having itself earned the people's hatred. In politics there has never been a conflict, as we have granted them the erection of their own Jerusalem. The liberal battles we fought for the rights of Jews was motivated more by abstract ideas rather than for a concrete case. We fought for the rights of a people without knowledge of the people itself and despite a dislike for any contact with it. It is now we who are obliged to fight for emancipation. It is the Jew who rules and will rule so long as money remains the all powerful force it is in the world today.

This involuntary repugnance results from, for one thing, the Jew's appearance, in which there is something disagreeably foreign, and renders him unthinkable as a subject of art. But far more weighty is the effect the Jew produces on us through his speech. From generation to generation the Jew speaks the language of the nation in which he dwells, but always as an alien. Since we are not concerned now with the cause of this phenomenon, we will not cast blame on the Christian civilization for this forced separation of the Jews from it, and we can scarcely blame the Jews for it. We are interested here only in the aesthetic character of the result, namely that the Jew speaks modern European languages as learned languages, and not as mother tongues. He is thus barred from expressing himself idiomatically and in conformity with his nature.

A language is the result of an historical community. Only one who has "unconsciously grown up within the bond of this community, takes any share in its creations."

Wagner seems, both here and later in this essay, clearly to imply that art is the unconscious expression of his often used "spirit of the *Volk*," the German word that, though having no exact English counterpart, refers to an identifiable ethnic group. It refers to people who share common history, language, customs, traditions, and mores. The composer thus appears, 50 years before Sigmund Freud or Carl Jung, to refer to the unconscious, even to a collective unconscious, notions advanced respectively by each of these two early psychiatrists. In even the worst of Wagner's prose writings, of which this may be one, are to be found some valid insights.

But just as the Jew has remained outside such community as a rootless stock, so has his language been preserved as a thing defunct. To make poetry in a foreign tongue has been impossible even to geniuses of the highest rank. Yet through almost a thousand years of intercourse with European nations, the remarkable stubbornness of the Jewish pronunciation has remained intact. Hence when a Jew speaks, what we hear is an outlandish and unpleasant "creaking, squeaking, buzzing snuffle," and a use of words foreign to our tongue and a twisting of our phases, all of which creates an "intolerably jumbled blather." As a result our attention is drawn to the repulsive speech itself rather than the content. Though in daily human intercourse, even the Jews may be able to express emotions effectively among themselves, in art they are speaking to us.

If the qualities of their dialect make artistic enunciation of feelings almost impossible through speech, how much less is that aptitude through song, which is speech aroused to its highest passion. Music is the speech of passion.

How then does it happen that the Jew, in music, now rules public taste? In the evolution of our society money has become the virtual patent of nobility. To the Jew, usury had long been left as their only trade. When modern culture became accessible to no one but the wealthy, and had sunk into only venal luxury, culture became less closed to him and we now have the phenomenon of the cultured Jew. This cultured Jew has taken great pains to strip away all similarities with his co-religionists, in many cases even taking Christian baptism to wash away traces of his origin. But it has been a fruitless quest, and has led only to his isolation. "Alien and apathetic stands the educated Jew in the midst of a society he does not understand, with whose tastes and aspirations he does not sympathize, whose history and desires have always been indifferent to him."

The Jews give birth to thinkers, but not to poets. The poet gives voice to the common unconscious spirit of his community, from which the Jew is excluded. The true poet, in every branch of art, gains stimulus from the instinctive life among his people (a further reference to the collective unconscious). *Where is the Jew to find his people? Not in the society in which he plays his role as an artist. Any connection at all with it, for the Jew, will be only as an offshoot of it, not with the healthy stem.*

Why, then, cannot the Jewish artist express the spirit of his own people? When the Jew goes, as he must, to the taproot of his own native stem and "draws water from that well," only a "how" and not a "what" will reward his efforts. The reason? The only musical expression available to the "Jew composer" from his own people is the ceremonial music of the synagogue. But for thousands of years nothing has unfolded in that art through an inner life. There has been only a fixity of form and substance. A form which is never quickened through renewal of its substance must fall to pieces in the end. In the synagogue of the Jewish people one feels the greatest revulsion upon hearing the confounding "gurgle, yodel and cackle," which no caricature can make more repugnant than it is.

Those tones and rhythms of the synagogue usurp the musical fancy of the Jew in the same manner as do the strains and rhythms of our folksong and folkdance shape our vocal and instrumental music. There is not one whit of likeness between his music and ours. Even when the Jew attempts to listen to our music, he listens to the barest surface of our art, but not to our life-bestowing inner organism. The Jew composer hurls together diverse forms and styles of every master. It is ultimately a clatter that results from offering at each new instant a new call for attention by a change of outer expressional means.

With this comment on the works of Jewish composers, Wagner seems to be approaching a discussion of his nemesis, Meyerbeer, whom he does not mention by name. But first he must directly face a problem that could scuttle the efficacy of his entire argument, the musical output and career of Felix Mendelssohn, one whose name he does unhesitatingly mention.

Wagner prevaricated and dissimulated about many things during his life, mostly about matters that concerned the advancement of his artistic goals, but also those that are the downfall of so many others: women and money. But he seems to have had difficulty departing too far from the truth on matters involving the merits of music or musicians. His opinion of Mendelssohn is a case in point. Mendelssohn, four years older than Wagner, died at age 37. We can here pretermit the details of their early friendship and later enmity. Wagner's offense here lies not in prevarication, but in spurious and unfair comparisons.

Nature had endowed Mendelssohn with specific musical gifts as very few before him. He had the most ample store of talents, the finest and most varied culture, the highest and most tender sense of honor.

Wagner proceeds to acknowledge several virtues in Mendelssohn's music, but never without an odious comparison with Beethoven by name, or with "our genuine art heroes," an obvious reference to Beethoven, or perhaps to Beethoven and Mozart jointly. Most of his treatment of Mendelssohn is, in fact, a heavy emphasis on the negative, generally explained through a pointless contrast of his work with that of Beethoven. There must have been hundreds of composers of the day turning out thousands of compositions, none of whom, or whose works, would have shown to advantage in such a comparison. It would not appear that an adverse comparison with Beethoven would amount to a denigration, but Wagner makes it sound so.

Thus, when we hear a piece by Mendelssohn we feel "engrossed," and he does indeed string together the "most elegant, the smoothest and most polished figures," but nothing beyond our most "amusement-craving fantasy is aroused." There is nothing to take the "shape of deep and stalwart feelings of the human heart." The "washiness and whimsicality" of our present musical style has not been brought about by Mendelssohn, but it was he who brought it to its utmost pitch, though in the most interesting and spirited manner possible. Mendelssohn can indeed express a "soft and mournful resignation," but it is one that derives from his "oppressive feeling of incapacity," and confesses its own powerlessness. Further, in the domain of art, "if we are to give our sympathy to the sheer personality, we can scarcely deny a large measure of it to Mendelssohn."

He seems, then, to acknowledge that his former friend was a great composer, but to lament that if only he had not been Jewish he could have been an even greater composer. It should surprise no one that, having set out to find weaknesses in Mendelssohn's music that would stem from his Jewish ancestry, he claimed to have found them. In an essay that is in such large part contrived, the treatment of Mendelssohn's music is perhaps one of the most contrived aspects of all. In later years, his remarks to his second wife, as recorded in her diary, contain numerous, more genuine expressions, including his offhand statement to her that he often found himself humming themes from Mendelssohn's compositions.

Wagner then turns his attention to Meyerbeer, who is referred to by such appellations as "a far-famed Jewish tone-setter of our day," but never by name. However, no one at all conversant with the musical scene could have been left in doubt as to the identity of this "tone-setter." But there is a much more important distinction between Wagner's treatment of these two Jewish, albeit converted, composers. In his description of the music of Meyerbeer, there is nothing that appears contrived or forced. On the contrary, it seems to come from the gut.

Our halls of entertainment today are filled by people whose only motivation for being there is utter boredom. Boredom however cannot be cured by "sips of art." It can only be duped into another form of boredom. To cater to this deception, the "famous opera composer" has made the task of his artistic life. He knows completely how to dupe by taking that jargon already described and palming it off on his bored audiences as a new utterance, though it in truth comprised the same trivialities that had been so often set before them. That this composer uses thrilling situations by weaving emotional catastrophes is not surprising, as that is what is wished by those for whom time hangs heavily on their hands. This composer pushes his deception so far that he ends by deceiving himself. He writes operas for Paris and sends them touring around the world, the surest means of earning art-renown, though not as an artist.

So long as music had a real organic life, down through the time of Mozart and Beethoven, a Jew composer was nowhere to be found. An entirely foreign element could not take part in the formative stages of that life. Only when the inner life is dead, can the outside elements lodge in it and destroy it.

Or, to use Wagner's elegant metaphor: *"the body's flesh dissolves into a swarming colony of insect life."*

There remains one more matter that Wagner felt obliged to address before giving his solution to this entire vexing problem of Judaism. There was the disturbing presence of the poet Heinrich Heine, like Mendelssohn a converted Jew, but nonetheless by Wagner's lights and the lights of many other Europeans, a Jew. Like Mendelssohn, he was renowned as one of the great artists of his genre. Like Mendelssohn he had been a friend of Wagner, until enmity, unrelated to his Jewishness, took its place. And Wagner's solution to the Heine problem was a duplicate of his solution to the problem of Mendelssohn.

As long as there were true poets such as Goethe and Schiller there were no Jew poets. "He was the conscience of Judaism, just as Judaism is the evil conscience of our modern civilization."

What, then, is the answer to this threat to civilization? He points to another Jew, a friend from his revolutionary days in Dresden.

Ludwig Börne "came among us seeking redemption." He learned however that redemption required first, genuine manhood, which, for a Jew, meant first ceasing to be a Jew. And Börne has done it. It did not come through mere conversion with a cold indifference or complacence. It came through sweat, anguish, suffering and sorrow.

Thus Wagner announces to the Jews: *You must take part in your deliverance through regenerative work leading to self-annulment. Then and only then will we be one united people. But, he cautions again, "only one thing can redeem you from the burden of your curse — the redemption of Ahasuerus — going under."*

There would seem to be sufficient material in Wagner's writings to justify the contempt of the present day Wagnerphobes without their spurious creations of more. Some of them point to the phrase "going under" as evidence that Wagner was the first German to advocate the physical annihilation of the Jews. Such a conclusion is nullified, if ever warranted in the first place, by the reference to Ludwig Börne as an example of the "going under," something accomplished by study and hard work, not by death.

But it is clear, of course, that without such "going under," the door to true artistry, or even true understanding of genuine art, Wagner sees as closed to the Jew irrevocably.

◆ ◆ ◆

In later years Wagner often adopted the stance that this was an entirely logical position, taken for a reasonable purpose, and free of rancor. The goal was simply to enlighten the public, including the Jews themselves, as to the source of the problem, namely the existence of a foreign element in German society, and to point the way toward an acceptable solution. He may indeed have been genuinely disappointed that the Jews did not en masse flock to his banner, eager to embrace his happy solution. Many Jews, not too surprisingly, saw it as a declaration of war. In truth, the entire tenor of the article makes clear that there is something very personal to him in this matter, and something very personally threatening about the Jewish presence in Germany. It is no exaggeration to say that the essay almost drips with malice.

It is probably no mere happenstance that it was written, along with many other weighty articles, just as he was preparing to begin his grandly conceived four-opera artwork. His heroes, Beethoven and Mozart, had been gone for decades, and he saw a degeneration in German musical taste. While he did not blame the Jews for the decline, he saw them as profiting from it, and deplored the new music in which second rate composers, especially Meyerbeer, were taking the lead. More likely than not, he feared that after writing his great magnum opus there would be no audience for it.

His expressions of bitterness and contempt for *the Jews* began but did not end with this essay. Evidence of it persists in his correspondence, especially to his close friend Liszt, but also to Minna and to the Wesendoncks. The collected correspondence with Liszt consists of 316 letters, probably over half from Wagner's pen, a matter to be borne in mind when reading some of the relatively few containing derogatory remarks about the Jews. Those few, however, reveal something of his mindset and are part of the entirety of his anti–Jewish animosity.

In February 1853, he wrote Liszt that he must now set the *Nibelung* poem to music "for the Jews of Frankfurt and Leipzig — It is just the thing for them."[4] Almost a year later he wrote his friend again, lamenting that he had had to break his resolve and let the theaters produce his *Lohengrin*, thereby "meekly submitting to the yoke of the Jews and the philistines."[5] In the late summer of 1854 he described to Liszt his desperate financial plight, and ended by saying, "so *Tannhäuser* and *Lohengrin* must go to the Jews,"[6] meaning he must permit their performances even under less than ideal conditions.

The following March, from London where he was conducting the Old Philharmonic Orchestra owing to his dire need of funds, working under conditions he found odious, he wrote that "only a blackguard and a Jew can succeed here."[7] Ten months thereafter came another missive describing the "cold and indifferent way" that others listened to his music of himself and that of Liszt. His description of this ignorance: "something typically Jewish."[8] In June he wrote about Buddhism, which he admired: "Christianity is a contradictory phenomenon because of its mixture with narrow-hearted Judaism."[9] In January 1858 he was once again in dire straits and asked Liszt to send money, even if from "the most Jewish of Jews."[10]

There were a number of separations from Minna during the Zurich days, and consequently, there was correspondence. During the eight-year period between the publication of "Judaism in Music" and the appearance of Tausig, there were 125 letters from Richard to Minna. Eight contain passing references to "the Jews"; never to an individual, but nonetheless all derogatory. In mid–October 1851, he wrote from Alisbrunn that he had received an honorarium from Schwerin, but "with a deduction of 2 louis d'or for the Berlin Jews, of course." Whether the "Jews" were creditors or officials of the Berlin opera, or other individuals is not clear. There was no suggestion that the obligation was unjust, merely that it was resented. Wagner, of course, had his own definition of "Jews."

On March 30, 1855, conducting in London, much to his displeasure, he wrote Minna, "Tomorrow, I dine with Ernst, who has married another Jewess here." After registering his complaints about the sorry condition of his life in the English capital, he notes that "only the Jews and scamps can make money as 'artists' nowadays." On the twentieth of April he complains about a procession for the French emperor and the English queen: "On boxes and boards stood lofty England, to treat the Chief of the French gendarmes, Jews and Jesuits, to its enthusiasm." Wagner's hatred of the Jesuits, it should be noted, was almost as fierce as his hatred of the Jews. The two, as appears from the diaries of his second wife, were often mentioned in the same breath.

On the fourth of May, suspicious always of Meyerbeer's hand in anything gone wrong, he referred to a particularly harsh critic of his conducting: "It is certain," he wrote Minna, "that he has been bought by Meyerbeer's agent (a Jewish music-dealer named Brandus) to pull me down, to prevent me making my way here lest I might have a shot at Paris later." On the twenty-fifth of that month he said he had accepted an invitation for next Sunday of one Benecke, "when, as I hear, he also has invited all the music-Jews of London in my honor. God, how absurd I appear to myself here!"

On the twenty-ninth, he wrote, "Last Sunday I had the good fortune to dine with the family Benecke in the company of a number of music-Jews." On the first of June he was looking forward to his return home: "The beautiful Seelisberg shall narrate us more news than this whole big political and artistic Jew-world, to which I, at least, am dead for good. God rest its soul!"

He had also been writing to the Wesendoncks. On April 5, 1855, he wrote Otto from London about the miserable state of the press there and said he preferred not to "dirty my hands" with the London newspapers. As always, he equated the press with the Jews: "Anyone who understands anything ... does not mix with this Jewish rabble."[11] Later that month he wrote of his bad press in England, which continued despite his great popularity. He blamed it on the remarks in his *Judaism* essay about Mendelssohn. The

Jewish composer, he noted to Mathilde, was a great favorite in London, adding, "In the dear God of the Jews is a very real thirst for vengeance."[12]

Without doubt, Wagner was treated quite shabbily by the London press, and his contempt for the authors of the many sneering, narrow, pedagogic reviews was entirely justified. In attributing them to the Jews, however, he was probably off target. The names of these pompous gentlemen, some rather prominent, include George Hogarth, H.F. Chorley, Henry Smart, J.W. Davison, W.H. Glover, John Ruskin, Samuel Butler, Sir Hubert Parry, and W.J. Turner. None gave any hint of Jewish ancestry.[13]

This, then, is the man on whose door Karl Tausig, the young Jew, knocked in May 1858, seeking encouragement and approbation for his musical artistry.

The letter of introduction from Liszt that he carried was brief, but to the point:

> I send you today a *wonderful fellow,* dearest Richard; receive him kindly. Tausig is to work your Erard thoroughly, and to play all manner of things to you. Introduce him to our mutual friends at Zurich — Herwegh, Wille, Semper, Moleschott, Köchly — and take good care of him.[14]

The Erard Liszt mentioned, an exceptionally fine piano, was, according to Wagner's autobiography, a "gift" received just a few months earlier from the widow of the piano's developer and manufacturer. The subject of Tausig is far more important than the piano, particularly with regard to our subject matter. But a slight diversion to the subject of that instrument can give us a delicious insight into the technique of Wagner as beggar, in which art he also showed some genius.

In July 1856, he had written to Liszt that a divine idea had struck him, namely that he must have an Erard. "Write to the widow," he told his friend, "and tell her that you visit me three times every year.... Tell her a thousand fibs, and make her believe that it is for her a point of honor that an Erard should stand in my house. Do not think, but act with the impudence of genius."[15] Whatever license he thought Liszt had as genius, we may be sure that Wagner apportioned to himself considerably more. A couple of months later he told Liszt to offer the widow 500 francs a month, a proposition that Liszt doubted would be acceptable.

The next we hear of the matter is in Wagner's letter from Paris to Minna on the first of February 1858. He said he would be delayed returning home to Zurich as he could not leave "the kindness of Mad. Erard unrequited." She had counted on his presence on Tuesday and invited many guests including "Rossini himself." Obviously, some progress had been made. The kindness he referred to can certainly not be a purchase for full value, and undoubtedly, was not a purchase at all.

On April 20, almost two weeks after the volcanic eruption on the Green Hill, Minna was in the hospital in Brestenberg. Among the matters he reported to her is that he had received a second message from Erard's that the piano had been shipped the previous day. Two weeks later he exulted, "The Erard, good Minna, has just been unpacked and set up in spite of rain and weather. What a delight it is to play on such an instrument, only the player himself can fully appreciate: the lightest pressure, scarcely touching, at once brings out that gentle bell-like tone.... One joy at least, then, has stolen like a friend into my life." Modestly, he did not mention the very great assist he had given it.

It would be interesting to hear an account from Madame Erard as to how it came about that she made this generous donation. But we have no such account. It is an interesting, but small matter. The subject of Tausig is more important.

6

Tausig

TAUSIG WAS A NATIVE of Warsaw. After early training by his father, Aloys Tausig, a professional pianist and composer, he became, at age 14, a pupil of Liszt in Weimar. His tutelage under the great virtuoso thus began just two years before his journey to Zurich and to Wagner. Shortly before that journey he had made a public appearance in Vienna and was hailed as "another Liszt."

There is at least an implication in the sketchy nature of the letter of introduction that Wagner had known of Tausig, and most probably that the precocious pianist had already been mentioned to him by Liszt. Tausig had not yet attained such fame as would otherwise have brought him to Wagner's attention. No reference to him in any of the prior correspondence is to be found. Either a letter containing such a reference has been lost, a not impossible circumstance, or mention was made of the boy in a personal meeting. However, as far as is known, there had been no personal meeting between Wagner and Liszt since October 1856, almost two years previous.

It is only, perhaps, a minor curiosity. Much more important, Wagner, as requested by Liszt's letter, did listen to Tausig play, and, notwithstanding those other matters that weighed so heavily on him, and notwithstanding the fact that this young pianist was a Jew, his attention soon turned to absolute astonishment. He was obviously thrilled by what he heard. More, he took an instinctive paternal interest in the youth. Wagner had no children at this time. His marriage to Minna was, and remained, childless. Tausig stayed nearby for several days at the Hotel Sternan before Wagner found for him a smaller, no doubt less expensive place. The two artists, the composer and the virtuoso, became fast friends, and the youngster's days as Wagner's almost constant companion included long walks with him in the bordering mountains. Minna was due to remain in Brestenberg for about another three weeks.

Cosima and her first husband, Hans von Bülow, were house guests of Wagner in July, and she was at this time less than enchanted with the man who was to be her second husband. The couple had visited the Wagners in August and September 1857 on their honeymoon, as we have already seen, and had heard the composer read his poem of *Tristan*. Now, about this later visit, she wrote to a friend that Wagner had almost threatened to take the piano transcription of *Tristan* away from her Hans, and give it to "the Jew Tausig."[1]

Liszt himself, not at all inhibited in his expressions of anti–Semitism, counted more than one Jewish youth among his many protégés. Tausig is often considered among the most gifted of all, Jewish and Christian alike. Liszt once said that he had "fingers of steel," and that his technique was infallible. In later years he

Karl Tausig, probably a few years before his sudden death at 29. From *Richard Wagner, the Man, His Mind and His Music* by Richard Gutman.

was praised by critics for his technical dexterity and endurance. His touch was described as "exquisite" his repertoire as extensive and wide. He composed a few pieces for piano, but today is best known for his piano transcriptions of instrumental and vocal works of others, including Wagner.

Once having listened to Tausig, it is not surprising that Richard Wagner would have been captivated by his artistry, the nonsense of his essay notwithstanding. More perplexing perhaps is his deep and long-lasting friendship and affection for the talented youth.

Wagner must have written to Minna about his new companion at once as there is a letter to her dated only three days after his arrival, May 25. It is obviously not the first in which Tausig is mentioned. In it, he told her that "little Tausig played magnificently yesterday, almost a second Bülow," no small compliment. Hans von Bülow was one of the finest conductors and, like Liszt, one of the great pianists of the day. Tausig's formal debut, in

Berlin later in that year of 1858, was at a concert conducted by Bülow. "He gives me great delight," Wagner's letter continued, "affording me distraction, entertainment and incentive. Today, I have again been able to compose well." A few days later he wrote his wife a short note, which he abruptly terminated, saying, "Don't be angry with this accursed scribbling, but Tausig has just arrived for dinner (with a crooked haircut)." A week later, he boasted that another friend "opened his mouth to his ears at Tausig's piano playing."

On June 9, he wrote her, "Tausig is gradually worming his way into my heart; small bad habits apart, he is really very intelligent, sympathetic and good-hearted youngster; he seems much attached to me, and often surprises me with a torrent of thanks for my kindness to him.... Owing to the great heat in his room, he often works in yours beneath me now, where he makes his nest from 12 o'clock without a sound."

By the end of June Wagner was preoccupied with a revival of his *Tannhäuser* in Dresden, where 13 years earlier he had conducted its premiere. Now of course he was barred from Dresden and all of the German states. He wrote Minna that the only report he got was from Tausig's father, who had attended and had written his son that it was "extraordinary, unprecedented, the enthusiasm not to be described." We may assume that the father's attendance was motivated at least in part by his son's new relationship with the increasingly famous composer. His curiosity finally compelled him to visit Zurich.

On July 9, Wagner told his wife, "Tausig's papa surprised us by arriving yesterday; a nervous little manikin, who will probably depart tomorrow." If papa Tausig felt a bit nervous about visiting the infamous arch anti–Semite, it should not be surprising. To Mathilde Wesendonck, to whom he was still writing during her travels despite the recent unpleasantness, he introduced Tausig as "my little musical homegoblin; may he find a kind welcome!"

The extent and depth of his feeling for the homegoblin, however, shows most clearly and directly in a letter to Liszt of July 2. After discussing some matters of mutual interest, he continued with unusual and uncharacteristic enthusiasm:

> You have given me great pleasure with little Tausig.... He is a terrible youth. I am astonished, alternately, by his highly developed intellect and his wild ways. He will become something extraordinary, if he becomes anything at all.

The boy smoked "frightfully strong cigars," Wagner continued, and drank no end of tea, "while as yet there is not the slightest hope of a beard." He assured Liszt that the youth would get no whisky or rum from him. The young guest seemed to be a source of endless fascination:

I should, without hesitation, have taken him into my house, if we had not mutually molested each other by pianoforte playing. So I have found him a room in a little hole close to me, where he is to sleep and work, doing his other daily business at my house. He does, however, no credit to my table, which, in spite of my grasswidowerhood, is fairly well provided.

Wagner shared the universal complaints of parents. Having been child-less those many years, he did not realize that in some respects his guest was just a quite normal 16-year-old. He seemed quite amazed: Tausig sat at the table every day saying he had no appetite, then gorged himself on sweets and cheeses. Biscuits, which were doled out grudgingly by Minna even to Richard, Tausig devoured. He said he hated walking, yet insisted on walk-ing with Wagner, although he could not keep up with the inveterate hiker. "My childless marriage is thus suddenly blessed with an interesting phe-nomenon, and I take in, in rapid doses, the quintessence of paternal cares and troubles. All this has done me a great deal of good." Of course, said Wagner, the boy pleased him in many other ways, ways that must have gratified the composer immensely:

Although he acts like a naughty boy, he talks like an old man of pronounced character. Whatever subject I may broach with him, he is sure to follow me with clearness of mind and with remarkable receptivity. At the same time it touches and moves me, when this boy shows such deep, tender feeling, such large sympathy, that he captivates me irresistibly.

And then, perhaps, the most important matter of all: "As a musician he is enormously gifted, and his furious pianoforte playing makes me trem-ble."

"I must always think of you," he told Liszt, "and the strange influence you exercise over so many, and often considerably gifted young men. I can-not but call you happy, and genuinely admire your harmonious being and existence." After turning to other matters, including a rather pessimistic report on Minna, whose condition alarmed him greatly, he ended the let-ter: "I am with you, especially when Tausig is seated at the piano."

It is interesting to compare his letter to Liszt written six weeks after the appearance of Tausig at his home, with his description of those weeks 11 years later when, recalling them from memory, he summarized them in dictating to Cosima his autobiography. None of the glow, none of the exu-berance was lost. It was, if anything, more pronounced. His immediate affection for Tausig, and his fascination with him, exuded from every line. He recited how the young visitor "astonished everybody by his dainty appearance and his unusual precocity of understanding and demeanor." He mentioned again his horror of the strong cigars. But that he made up his mind to spend some time nearby pleased Wagner greatly:

I could appreciate to the utmost his amusing, half-childish, though very intelligent and knowing personality, and, above all, his exceptionally finished piano-playing and quick musical faculty. He played the most complicated pieces at sight, and knew how to use his astonishing facility in the most extravagant tricks for my entertainment.

He also accompanied Wagner upon some of his visits to his wife at Brestenberg. Wagner followed the results of her treatments there, but neither Minna's conversation nor Brestenberg itself held any interest for the restless Tausig, who did his best to avoid those journeys. But evenings at home with him cheered Wagner unreservedly.

One of Wagner's own favorite performers of the leading tenor roles of his early operas, Joseph Tichatschek, came to visit from Dresden. Wagner held the man in great esteem but, being absorbed with the sketch of Act II of *Tristan*, was somewhat annoyed by the visit nonetheless. To Wagner's relief, Tausig came to his rescue by playing cards with the aging tenor, thereby saving the composer from much embarrassment. It was not the only time the gregarious Tausig used his social skills to perform yeoman's service. On another occasion, as reported by Mathilde following Minna's return to the Asyl from Brestenberg, Tausig played dominoes with the ailing, excitable wife in order to prevent her from disturbing the composer's afternoon nap.

Wagner's letter of July 2 to Liszt probably crossed in the mails with one by Liszt to Wagner dated July 3. Most of that one concerned other matters, but there was a postscript asking that an enclosed letter to Tausig be delivered to him and inquiring as to how the boy was getting along in Zurich.

Wagner's next letter to Liszt, on July 8, revealed that not everything involving the boy was coated with sugar candy. It speaks of a matter involving "T" and "X." T is most certainly Tausig. Who X is no one seems to know. In their correspondence there are at least eight different persons, or in one case a couple, or group, referred to in the same way: "X," or, in the one case, "The Xs." In this instance involving Tausig we know that X is male, but nothing else. Perhaps in any event the identity would add nothing to our knowledge of Tausig.

The letter of Wagner of July 8 makes it clear that Tausig had talked to Wagner about its contents. And it is apparent that Liszt had some harsh things to say to his pupil. The affair of T and X, says Wagner, has become "very significant to me." How seriously Wagner took the contents of Liszt's letter and how much he had invested in Tausig emotionally are at once apparent. He seems appalled at how certain actions can be perverted beyond recognition into their opposite:

I look with horror upon the cares of this world, where everything is ruled by confusion and error to the verge of madness. It was absolutely terrible to me to read your charges against T. What I felt is difficult to describe; it was like a longing for death.

As to what it was that Liszt wrote, we are left in the dark. Referring to his own letter of July 2 to Liszt, pouring out his unreserved enthusiasm about Tausig, he refers to it now as very unconventional, which, for Wagner, it was indeed. Two things, the letter of July 8 continues, made Wagner overlook all Tausig's shortcomings, and become attached to him to the degree that he placed much confidence in the boy. One of these traits was the "boundless love" he showed for Liszt, the cessation of his "impertinence" whenever Liszt was mentioned, and his "most tender and deep reverence" for his mentor. The other, says Wagner, is

the beautiful warmth and genuine friendship which he shows at every moment for X. In the present case also he defended the latter in a really touching manner, and speaks of him always with enthusiastic praise of his heart and intellect. Were it not for these two traits I should not know what to think of this young man who speaks of God and the world in the most ruthless manner.

This comment is one of a very few, and by far the most serious reservation we see, from Wagner's pen about Tausig. Had this spirited youngster already showed a cynicism, or worse, bitterness about life? Whatever lay behind these comments did nothing to dampen Wagner's affection or admiration for him. The letter continues:

Your reproach hit him in this particular point, and when he showed me your letter there was a peculiar desperate question in his glance. With such experiences the boy will become quickly, almost too quickly, mature.

My words will show you how deeply this matter has affected me; it is one of the thousand things which, when they occur to me, estrange me more and more from this world.

Whatever the negative aspects of this letter, it reveals the depth of feeling for the youth who had "wormed his way" into Wagner's heart. Liszt's reply, dated ten days later, seems to have done much to unburden Wagner. He had, said Liszt, felt the "painful rebound of your wounded heart," but the entire matter should, he says, have been private between Liszt and Tausig. X knew nothing of Liszt's admonition to Tausig, and Tausig would have done well, the letter continued, not to discuss it with Wagner. He wrote to Tausig as he did as he felt a duty to act as guardian to him, and the boy's conduct had not been very correct. The "young Titan," said Liszt, sometimes exhibited "an absence of mind and state of overexcitement." But the youngster's talent and genial nature caused Liszt to be overindulgent, and "I do not deny my genuine love and partiality for this remarkable specimen of a 'Liszt of the future.'" His letter ends:

> Be thanked for the kindly friendship and care you bestow upon him. I hope he
> will not only profit by them, but honor them. The rare happiness of living
> near you, and of being distinguished by you, should form and mature him as
> an artist and as a man.

Whether or not the matter under discussion matured Tausig, it is likely that his exposure to the domestic scene in the Asyl after Minna's return may well have done the job. On July 15 Wagner journeyed to Brestenberg to accompany his wife back to the Asyl. Two weeks earlier he had written her that he would come in an "enormously big, wide, and high carriage and will call for you with all the household furniture and bring you to the deserted house which will finally know what it is to have a mistress again." The loving and solicitous tone of the letter was not new. Since the storm had broken in April with the interception of his letter to Mathilde, he had sought to reassure his wife of the innocence of his relationship with their young neighbor. Often his calm and his refusal to reply in kind to her emotional outbursts had only further infuriated her.

In this letter to Minna, he fibbed to her that Tausig, "My little devil of a fellow, however, wants to join me. He has taken a fancy to you." In another note written to her just four days before her release from the hospital, he wrote of the nuisance that his many visitors were unwittingly making, and said that even Liszt need not come, "now only the little and very clever Tausig helps ... (incidentally his father is a very honest Bohemian, thoroughly Christian)."

Why Wagner felt compelled to make this comment about Tausig's father, whom he had previously called a "nervous little manikin," is unclear, but quite interesting. First, it should be noted that Tausig had attracted sufficient attention in the musical world to rate mention in music encyclopedias and biographies of the period. Though reference was often made to the mixed nationality of his parents, Polish and Bohemian, he was consistently referred to, where reference to religion was made at all, as Jewish, without the usual caveat of any differences in the religion of his parents.

Whether or not the father was truly Christian, and whether the parenthetical statement in the letter was true or not, there seems a certain defensiveness evident in it. If, in view of his essay, he felt compelled to defend himself for his affection for this young Jew, it would not be the last time such a perceived obligation lay behind some questionable remarks. On a number of occasions he seemed determined that his anti–Semitism not be seen as compromised in any way, to any degree. It seemed almost at times to be a proudly worn badge. If so, he would have much to defend. His many Jewish friends and companions were often the subjects of such explanations. It is hard to see any other motive for the remark. Neither Tausig's nor his father's race or religion could have been of any moment to Minna. She seemed to be totally without prejudice of that nature. She had already taken her husband to task over his "horrible" essay on the Jews.

By Wagner's own standards, Tausig, with only one Jewish parent, would have been a Jew nonetheless. Such a result is a clear implication in "Judaism in Music," and is made overtly clear in the later essay, "Know Thyself," published in 1881, just two years before his death. The Jew, he wrote,

> is the most astounding instance of racial congruence ever offered by world history. Without a fatherland, a mother tongue, midst every people's land and tongue he finds himself again, in virtue of the unfailing instinct of his absolute and indelible idiosyncrasy: even commixture of blood does not hurt him; let Jew or Jewess intermarry with the most distant of races, a Jew will always come to birth.[2]

In all events, a Jew is what Tausig considered himself. It should be noted that Wagner did not always consider such "racial congruence" a negative trait. In 1872, he wrote to the philosopher Friedrich Nietzsche, with whom he was at the time on good terms. He had been thinking, said Wagner, about the essence of "Germanness": "It is of immense interest to me, and certainly something that is unique in the history of the world, its only counterpart being Judaism, since Hellenism, for example, does not really fit in here."[3] It may be worth pondering whether such offhand and unpremeditated comments may not tell us more of the real Wagner than all of his posturing and polemics.

Part II

Paris and Vienna

7

The Break with Minna

MINNA RETURNED TO THE ASYL on July 15. It seems certain that Wagner was continually, and genuinely, concerned for her health and the strain on her heart. But his solicitations and efforts to heal the breach were in vain. They inhabited different worlds, and their inability to find a common understanding resulted in a miserable month, before Wagner finally departed the Asyl on August 17. Not only Tausig, but the Bülows, again present as house guests, were witnesses to scenes of endless recriminations between the Wagners and between Minna and Mathilde. Minna's view of her perceived rival is neatly summed up in her letter to a Dresden friend: "That cold woman spoiled by happiness." It became all the more intense upon Wagner's declaration to Minna that they could no longer reside in the Asyl. The Wesendoncks insisted that they remain, even if communication between the two couples must cease. But Wagner considered the situation, and further progress with *Tristan*, under the circumstances, impossible.

To Eliza Wille, his friend from Mariafeld, he wrote that his continuing presence in the Asyl was "a form of damnation from which I long every day to be released." All of the "shame and torment" that he suffered during the previous three months he blamed on his failure to leave when the storm first broke. To his sister Klara he wrote of "unheard of scenes and tortures," and that he could no longer endure "these everlasting quarrels and suspicious moods." One of the few episodes to break through the gloomy atmosphere of the impending breakup of home and marriage, temporary though he assumed the rift to be, were the antics of Tausig. The young visitor sang a familiar "Old German Battle Song" with a type of falsetto reachable only by adolescent boys. Wagner says that he and his guests were delighted, but that even Tausig's "pranks" could finally no longer bring cheer.

He left by train on the morning of August 17 for Geneva with the intention of further travel to settle somewhere in Italy and there, in comparative peace and quiet, to complete the composition of *Tristan*. The letter to Crown Prince Albert of the previous February, requesting his intercession with his royal father for amnesty, was apparently treated as a private matter, which the prince probably merely discussed with his father. In any event no answer was ever received. His efforts and those of others in his behalf continued without success for another two years; then he was granted amnesty from all German states except Saxony. Amnesty from Saxony followed a year thereafter.

Bülow and his young wife, Cosima, with tears in her eyes, had left the previous day. Minna, before returning to Dresden, remained for a few weeks in order to dispose of household effects. Unable to avoid trumpeting her misery, she advertised in the local papers that her things would be sold cheaply "owing to a sudden departure," thereby causing further gossip and embarrassment to the Wesendoncks. Tausig made his debut in Berlin later that year and continued his career, often giving concerts with Liszt. He and Wagner remained in contact in a relationship that grew stronger over the years, the physical separation notwithstanding. Creditors descended on the Asyl, but friends, probably including Wesendonck, came to the rescue, and the bulk of the furniture, including the precious Erard, was saved.

The next six years may well be counted among the more difficult and depressing in a life filled with an abundance of difficult and depressing episodes. With only infrequent exceptions, frustrations and hopelessness reigned. Such is the tone of so many of his letters, and such is the external evidence. For the first two of those years, there is little of the matters that are germane to our focus; little evidence of his continuing animosity toward *the Jews*, nor any significant contact with individual Jews, practicing or converted. Sporadic contact and mention of Tausig is one of the few exceptions. Tausig, during this time, was pursuing his own career. In 1860 he toured Scandinavia. It would be another two years before he and Wagner again made personal contact.

Nonetheless, much of significance occurred in this period, and there is much to learn from it about Wagner the man, the forces acting on him, and about his inward state. The events that follow thereafter can be far better understood with at least a cursory summary of that gloomy time.

Wagner arrived in Geneva the evening of the same day as his departure from Zurich, intending to stay for a month for a needed rest. He wrote to Karl Ritter, whom we last saw as courier in Weimar for Wagner's manuscript on the Jews, and who was now living in Lausanne. Wagner was surprised and pleased to hear that Ritter also planned on moving to Italy during his wife's extended absence on family business. With Ritter's offer to be a traveling companion, and upon his assurances of a pleasant climate in Venice, he abandoned thoughts of staying in Geneva and made arrangements to travel to the famed city of canals. That city, however, at the time, was part of the Austrian Empire, an ominous situation causing some hesitation. But Venice, unlike Austria itself, was not part of the German confederation, and the reception there to his inquiries was favorable. After assuring himself of his relative safety from arrest and forcible return to Saxony, he obtained the necessary passport and traveled with his friend to Venice.

He spent one night on the Piazzetta, then searched for a permanent abode. He rejected what is today the posh Hotel Danieli as too gloomy, opting instead for one of the dilapidated Giustiniani palaces, located, like the Danieli, on the Grand Canal. He found the milieu quite suitable for completion of his *Tristan,* and promptly sent for his Erard and his bed.

Wagner and Mathilde had agreed before his departure that there would, at least temporarily, be no communication between them, an agreement she kept to the letter. Some communications he did forward to her were returned unopened. Both, however, kept diaries, his entries there being in the form of letters to her. At the same time he wrote frequently to Minna. It seems clear that when he wrote to Mathilde, he was writing to his Isolde, a conclusion that can be reached even without his specific mention of the opera. His enchantment with his second act music, the high-blown passages, the flights of fancy, the expressions of passion, the references to philosophy and philosophers, and the language of longing and of renunciation, as in the text of *Tristan,* all abound in those letters. He did receive one letter, a sad one, from Otto Wesendonck informing him of the death of three-year-old Guido, born in 1855 during somewhat happier days in Zurich.

The letters to Minna are more mundane, but keenly and genuinely solicitous of her welfare. It seems clear that he anticipated a return to her after completion of the opera. Drowning as he was in a financial quagmire, desperately begging and borrowing while the mountain of debts grew ever larger, he somehow always found the means to support Minna.

He remained in Venice through the winter, seven months in all, and, under the most difficult circumstances, he completed the composition of the second act on March 9. Throughout the entire Venetian episode, in addition to the financial morass there was still the impossible problem of his status. He was closely watched by the Venetian police, who also opened and read his mail. His every move was reported to the city authorities, and sometimes to the Saxon government.

The Palazzo Giustiniani, Wagner's home in Venice from August 1858 until March 1859. It was here he completed Act II of *Tristan und Isolde*. From *Wagner in Exile* by Woldemar Lippert.

Nowhere did the dichotomy in the attitude of others toward his questionable, often erratic, behavior show itself more starkly than in this period of his residence in Venice. As so often was the case, the attitude toward the man depended on the individual's receptiveness to his music. The rather officious chief of police in the Austrian capital of Vienna was one Baron Kempen von Fichtenstamm. We can assume that Wagner's genius meant little to him.

A taste of his steely eyed view of the world, one that brooked no nonsense from revolutionaries, can be found in his first reaction to this refugee's appearance in his domain. To the authorities in Venice, he demanded by coded telegram to know how Wagner got permission to travel and his motive for doing so. But he found no receptive audience among officialdom in Venice. The strongest rebuff must have been that delivered by one Angelo Crespi, the Venetian police councilor. Crespi seems to have been either a devotee of Wagner's music or greatly impressed by his reputation. He went to considerable lengths to investigate the new arrival and, like many another investigator, he found what he wanted. His report must have markedly deepened the scowl on von Fichtenstamm's face.

Crespi acknowledged that the subject was involved "to a certain extent in the disturbances" in Dresden, but that in Zurich he abstained from all political activities and "devoted himself exclusively to his profession, in which as composer ... he has shown genius of a high and original order" and "stands at the head of the musical and aesthetic movements of the day." His physicians, Crespi continued, had recommended a change to some southern climate, but Wagner had been too occupied with composition to follow their advice. He followed with other information detailing the overwrought state of his subject's nerves and other circumstances negating the likelihood of clandestine activity.[1]

The reactionary von Fichtenstamm, obviously outraged, sent a sharp note to Venetian headquarters objecting that far too little importance had been attached to the political aspects of the case. Wagner probably never knew what kind of friend he had in Crespi and others in the bureaucracy, only that he was allowed to continue his work. As he did, the storm continued around him, including the continuing surveillance, about which he must have known.

Successive attempts at amnesty from the Saxon king, buttressed by a personal plea from Minna, who was now in Dresden, met only with failure. Lengthy, piteous pleas and abject admissions, all but confessing guilt, were met with abrupt denials, always suggesting surrender and submission to trial, invitations that he wisely ignored.

The political situation became more and more threatening with the Saxon government making serious demands that the fugitive be expelled from Venice. And there was the further matter of the unbearable heat of the approaching Venetian summer. Wagner was about to begin composition of the third act, and did not want to be interrupted by another burdensome move when he did. So in late March 1859 he moved to the Hotel Schweizerhof in Lucerne, arranging for his Erard to be shipped over the Alps.

Through April and May and part of June he contended, as he phrased it, "with a mood of the deepest melancholy." But progress was made on the composition of the magnificent final act. In April, in his exuberance, he wrote to Mathilde in one of his many unposted letters, kept by him as a diary, "Child! This *Tristan* is becoming something *terrible*. This last act!!!...

Nothing but indifferent performances can save me! Completely *good* ones are bound to drive folks crazy."[2]

Toward the end of May, he wrote to Liszt asking that he "send Tausig" to him. He had heard that he was not busy and Minna, he told Liszt, had said that the boy wished to visit him. To Mathilde he exulted, "Tausig will come to me presently," and that the boy would like it. Otherwise most of his writing was almost morose. But changed circumstances in the environment threw him into a "sincere spiritual ecstasy," evidence of which exudes from every bar of that third act. It enabled him to complete the entire work by the beginning of August. He was visited in Lucerne, much to Minna's distress, by (among many others) Otto and Mathilde, including one trip to celebrate over champagne the completion of *Tristan und Isolde*.

8

Tristan und Isolde

TRISTAN UND ISOLDE WAS something new in music, and its intensity has never been matched. The imagination and the inventiveness that invest its few musical themes and the remarkable unity of its structure are but part of the singular quality of the work. Entirely new were its ceaseless changing of keys to express the perpetually changing tone of the drama, and its ever heightening tension resulting from its succession of unresolved musical phrases. One is always waiting for the closing of the phrase, a satisfying ending. It comes only at the end of the opera, and thus keeps the listener continually waiting, as it is meant to do.

Wagner tells us in his autobiography that he considered it the most daring and most exotic conception in all his work. While composing the tremendous scenes of the final act, a series of monologues that search the psyche of the dying Tristan as words alone never could, he wondered if he was not indeed mad to want to print such a work for the theater. "And yet," he admitted, "I could not have parted with a single accent in that tale of pain, although the whole thing tortured me to the last degree." While composing the second-act music in Venice, a searingly intense expression of physical desire, he had written to Liszt that the opera evoked in him "a kind of convulsive excitement." A year after its completion he wrote from Paris to Mathilde,

> The *Tristan* is as great a wonder to myself as ever. It is becoming more and more inscrutable to me, how I was able to create a thing like that ... supremely talented performers, the only ones equal to the task, are very rare arrivals in the world. Yet I cannot withstand the temptation, were it merely to hear the orchestra.

Lest this all appear as an instance of unwarranted egoism, we should be aware that in later decades many great composers and musically sophisticated listeners found it equally as marvelous and expressed equal astonishment at its intensity and sheer depth and scope. It is not too surprising that to Wagner's heir to the Germanic tradition, Richard Strauss, *Tristan* was his "most treasured opera"; nor that Strauss referred to its great third act as "the supreme emanation of unrestrained melodic wealth." He was reported to have carried the score around in his coat on occasion, like a precious jewel.

Less expected may have been the spontaneous outpouring from the great Italian composer, Wagner's contemporary, Giuseppe Verdi, just three years before his death. Verdi, by nature so much more restrained, so much less complicated than his German counterpart, speaking to a friend, allowed himself some uncharacteristically unrestrained remarks:

> This gigantic structure fills me time and time again with astonishment and awe, and I still cannot quite comprehend that it was conceived and written by a human being. I consider the second act, in its wealth of musical invention, its tenderness and sensuality of musical expression and its inspired orchestration, to be one of the finest creations that has ever issued from a human mind.

"This second act is wonderful," he continued, and, according to the friend, immersed in his thoughts, he kept repeating "wonderful ... quite wonderful."

And there was Verdi's heir to the Italian tradition, Giacomo Puccini. Late in life, composing his last opera, *Turandot*, he interrupted his work to explain something to a friend from the score of *Tristan*. Then he threw it down, exclaiming "Enough of this music! We're mandolinists, amateurs: woe to him who gets caught by it! This tremendous music destroys you and renders you incapable of composing any more!" Fortunately for him, and for us, he did get on with composing *Turandot*, though sadly he did not live to complete it.

His biographer, Mosco Carner, would have understood. Speaking of Puccini's favorite operatic topic, the combination of the life-enhancing and life-destroying qualities of romantic love, he commented that nowhere had it been shown "with such grandeur and elaborated to such psychological and metaphysical depths as in Wagner's *Tristan*."

It knew no national boundaries. In 1879, the French composer Emmanuel Chabrier, then age 38, attended a performance in Munich after having studied the score for years. Upon the first chord, he burst into tears, then, to his startled companions, explained, "I've waited 10 years to hear that A on the cellos."[1]

In 1872, Friedrich Nietzsche attended a special performance of the opera and later termed it "the most stupendous, the most chaste, and the most astounding work that I know. One fairly floats in bliss and exaltation." In 1888, a year before his mental breakdown and a decade after the rupture of his friendship with Wagner, he wrote, "I look about me among all the arts, in vain, for a work of the same dangerous fascination, the same infinite thrill and loveliness as *Tristan*; all of Leonardo da Vinci's unique qualities lose their charm in listening to the first note of *Tristan*."[2]

The fascination with *Tristan* has continued through generations. A mid–twentieth century musicologist expressed well what had been said in various ways by scores of others of his profession: "*Tristan* is the music of passion, almost as beautiful as passion itself ... the music glows, flames, burns with an intolerable heat ... unique in music: nowhere else is passion's fulfillment the very stuff of music itself."[3]

The impact of the opera on the world of music has been immense. There is general agreement among musicologists that there is hardly a serious piece of music written since that does not show, to some degree, the influence of *Tristan und Isolde*. But in 1860 all of such accolades still lay in the future.

For six years following its completion, Wagner's major project in life was the production of this work. It was written in a new musical vocabulary, and to the theaters of the day it was intimidating. One after another of the opera companies in various cities, Carlsruhe, Weimar, Munich, Hanover, Prague and Vienna, considered, in fact vied, for the honor of producing the premiere. They little knew the complexity of the opera and the degree to which it would tax their resources.

Most of those who made the attempt sooner or later abandoned it. Carlsruhe was the leading contender well before the work was finished. The grand duke of Baden was most anxious that Wagner's newest effort be premiered at his theater there. But the projected performance came to nothing for reasons that undoubtedly could have been overcome had Wagner been allowed to be personally present to oversee the preparations. The grand duke, however, was unable to surmount the personal animosities that precluded the composer's presence.

In this late summer of 1859 Wagner made two decisions. One was to try Paris once more. The other was to try to reconcile with Minna. They had now been apart for a year, and he found reason in her letters to believe that it might work. It was agreed that she would join him in Paris in the late fall of the year. He left Lucerne in early September and after visiting with friends along the way, arrived in Paris on the fifteenth of that month. He was 12,000 francs richer than when he left Lucerne, as the redoubtable Otto Wesendonck had purchased from him, for 6,000 francs each, the rights to each of his four *Ring* operas, and thereupon paid for the already completed *Rheingold* and

Walküre. It was not exactly an arms'-length transaction. Wesendonck undoubtedly knew he would get little or nothing as a return, and nothing is what he got, the rights later being sold or pledged to the king of Bavaria, who, financially, also netted nothing.

Wagner first rented a villa with a small garden on the Rue Newton, a side street off the Champs Élysées. In mid–November he was joined by Minna. It was to be a three-year lease with the final two years paid in advance. The wily proprietor knew that the building was scheduled for demolition as part of a general renovation of the city, but neglected to mention this to his new tenant. The Paris we know only from old maps, prints and paintings was about to give way to the Paris of traffic circles and radiating boulevards we see today, all under the guiding hand of architect Baron Georges-Eugène Haussmann.

Wagner's landlord thus refused, even in the face of an offer of increased rent, to perform the slightest repairs, which Wagner finally undertook at his own expense. By February 1860 the rumors of drastic change reached even Wagner's ears. Subsequent litigation went against him, thereby costing legal fees in addition to the improvements and advance rent payments. He and Minna were forced to move, which they did to a more modest home on the Rue d'Aumale.

9

Tannhäuser in Paris

WAGNER'S PLANS FOR PARIS had originally involved the completion of *Siegfried,* and acquainting Parisians with his work, all hopefully leading to productions of *Tristan* and the *Ring.* One of the most encouraging portents was the interest shown by one Léon Carvalho, director of the Théâtre-Lyrique, in producing *Tannhäuser.* In his frenzied desire to impress the director, Wagner treated both Carvalho, and the friend who had recommended Wagner to him, to a solo concert by himself. He sang portions of that opera, accompanying himself on the piano. The account of this rendition tells us too much about Herr Wagner to be passed over lightly.

According to the rather restrained account of the mutual friend, "He shouted, he threw himself about, he played the piano with his hands, his wrists, his elbows, he smashed the pedals, he ground the keys." According to this friend, Carvalho remained totally impassive, uttered a few polite words upon completion of the ordeal, then quickly made his exit.

And we have the account of Carvalho himself. He tells us that when he first laid eyes on the composer, "he was wearing a blue jacket with red braid, and a yellow Greek cap adorned with green fringe." After treating his guests to a rendition of one part of the opera, "dripping with perspiration, he disappeared, to return this time in a red cap decorated with yellow braid; his blue coat replaced by a yellow one embellished with blue braid." Then came the second and last part of the performance:

He howled, he threw himself about, he hit all kinds of wrong notes, and to crown it all he sang in German! And his eyes! The eyes of a madman! I did not dare to cross him; he frightened me."[1]

The mountain of letters and memoirs from the nineteenth century make interesting reading indeed. The modern reader, however, may be forgiven a fleeting wish to be able to swap a goodly number of them for one well chosen videotape.

Returning to matters more directly to the point of our narrative, Wagner made it his business to see, among many other composers and artists he had known, his Jewish friend Halévy, now 61. By Wagner, both the man and his music, bitter controversy had almost always been fomented wherever he went. The attacks by critics and other musicians were usually focused on the music, though often motivated by personal animosity. Halévy had remained an outspoken and steadfast admirer of the music of Wagner, who responded with the kindliest disposition toward the older man, even while lamenting the early lapse of his creativity.

There is also the less pleasant matter of another Jewish composer from Wagner's earlier Paris sojourn, Giacomo Meyerbeer, Wagner's former benefactor. Through one means or another, Meyerbeer had cultivated the most-friendly relationship with the gentlemen of the press. Paris in the nineteenth century was a time and place of bitter rivalries and animosities, and close, if temporary, friendships. It seems in retrospect to have been a veritable minefield. It would be difficult to fault Meyerbeer for his own animosity toward Wagner. But to be a friend of Meyerbeer was also to be an enemy of Wagner, or so the temper of the times dictated. The proposition that Meyerbeer had bribed members of the press to attack his ungrateful fellow German, as Wagner says and as others have implied, has little or no evidence to support it. But perhaps it was not necessary. Whatever the cause, the press in Paris, as in so many other cities throughout Europe, was bitterly hostile to him.

The assault on "the music of the future" began almost at once. That senseless phrase, attached to Wagner's music by some writer, but not by Wagner, had often been used as a term of derision by his detractors. It was sometimes unjustifiably attributed to the composer himself because of his essay *The Art-work of the Future*. Wagner, unlike Meyerbeer, made no attempt to curry favor with the press, nor did he pay its members the usual extra courtesies nor afford them the privileges, such as free tickets, that they considered their due.

He arranged to conduct a series of three concerts beginning in late January, consisting of excerpts from his operas for the twin purposes of acquainting the public with his music and raising money. At the first of those goals he succeeded brilliantly. Despite the empty claim by many critics that his music lacked melody, the audience broke into frequent storms of applause. They heard the melody from these early operas, even if the critics did not.

An intelligent and articulate spectator at the final concert summed up the matter to a friend: "There is something in him — power, an absolute horror of the conventional.... This will perhaps be disputed, for there is no limit to the venality, the ignorance, the spirit of the routine, in a word the infamy of our journalism."

The second mentioned goal was another matter. Wagner was many things, but a businessman he was not. The costs he had obligated himself to pay exceeded his net receipts by 11,000 francs. Months later, a friend, Marie Kalergis, having heard of the financial disaster, donated 10,000 francs to the cause. She also persuaded her own friend Julie Salis Schwabe, a Jewish widow from England, to contribute another 5,000.[2] Wagner insisted on calling it a loan, even furnishing a note for the amount, an act of fairness he would later have cause to regret. And the generous Wesendonck gave him a third payment of 6,000 francs for the third of his *Ring* dramas, *Siegfried*, though it remained still in its uncompleted state.

Wagner tried again in Brussels with equally calamitous results. There were large, enthusiastic audiences for the first two of the three scheduled concerts there, but Wagner wisely cancelled the third. He had been informed by his agent that after traveling and hotel expenses he was due for another huge loss. Years later, in a letter to one of his conductors, Hans Richter, he wrote: "We can't count on any country in which French is spoken: take my word for that ... it seems to go incredibly against the grain with them — to be quite insane indeed — to fork out money."

Writing from Paris on March 3 about the Paris concerts, he told Mathilde that the solitary goal to which he was steering, and on which he had staked everything, was a performance of *Tristan und Isolde* in Paris in May. Already it appears that that goal was falling apart.

But in March, the French monarch, Emperor Napoleon III, thrilled Wagner to his marrow by ordering a production of *Tannhäuser*. The reasons were political: pressures from the ambassador from Saxony, Baron Albin Leo von Seebach, whose efforts came despite the outstanding warrant for the composer's arrest; an assist from one Count Hatzfeld, the attaché to the Prussian Embassy; and another from Princess Pauline Metternich, granddaughter of the former Austrian chief minister, Clemens Metternich. She was the wife of her grandfather's son, that is, to say, her uncle, Richard Metternich. It was a great coup, a tribute both to Wagner's artistry and to his political connections. But the glow was soon to turn to ashes. It seems that for every friend in politics there was at least one corresponding enemy.

The primary enemy in this instance was a politically powerful group of gentlemen known as the Jockey Club. For starters, they did not like the thought of this German composer's work being performed in their leading opera house, the Académie de Musique, known more often as the Opéra, even though it was to be produced in French translation. They were Legitimists, and therefore by political persuasion opponents of both the emperor and of Pauline Metternich. But perhaps most of all they were opposed to an opera that did not have a ballet in the second act.

This requirement of the Jockeys was motivated by their relationships with so many young ladies of the Ballet. These aristocratic gentlemen dined in a leisurely fashion every evening, usually arriving for the second act, at which time they expected to see their mistresses perform. Hence there had to be a ballet, and it had to be in the second act. Wagner's attempts to compromise as to the type of choreography or its place in the opera came to naught. Their stubborn position on this matter ran head-on into Wagner's stubborn position against episodes in opera that made no dramatic sense.

To the Jockeys it mattered not at all that Wagner was going to include in the performance an opening scene that did make sense. It was to be a bacchanal, an orgiastic dance in the grotto of Venus. It was not a ballet in the usual sense, and was not in the second act, but it did involve a dance, of sorts. An account of the rehearsals of that scene by the choreographer, Lucien Petipa, tells us not only something of our composer, but removes any lingering doubt about the credibility of Carvalho:

> The moment we arrived the composer sat down at the piano. He played with an enthusiasm and a fury that no words can begin to describe. His hands ground the keys. At the same time he flung himself around, shouting the names of the groups as they entered and attempting to conjure up the scenes of this terrible bacchanal. "Arrival of the fauns and satyrs, — they — turn everything upside down, — the disorder reaches its climax," the composer screamed at me, hands still pummeling the ivory keyboard, as the musical ravings continued to mount. He banged out a series of chords that caused the whole room to shudder, then suddenly exclaimed: "A clap of thunder rings out, we're all dead."

"What a devil of a man!" continued Petipa. "At the rehearsals he would go and stand at the back of the auditorium." Then Petipa said,

> when he wanted to come down to the orchestra pit to make some remark to the artists, instead of taking the corridor, he would step over the seats, walking as much on his hands as his feet, and risking breaking both arms and legs. One day he leaned too far over the orchestra and burned himself on one of the footlights. You can understand how so demanding a man was bound to annoy many people.[3]

There were, to be sure, other serious problems besides the Jockeys: an incompetent conductor: quarrelsome, uncooperative translators who caused Wagner "the most harassing torments"; and a high strung, pompous lead tenor, one Albert Niemann; not to mention Wagner's rather serious bout of illness, termed typhoid fever by the physicians. It may well have been brought on, at least in part, by the pressure of the mounting problems. But always there was the thought that it all might lead to a performance of *Tristan*. The ever supportive Bülow had come to Paris to observe his friend's conquest of that city. In the midst of these troubles, he sensed, and stated, that Wagner would gladly have given himself up to the executioner, had he been able the night before to conduct a good performance of *Tristan*.

Niemann had been recommended by the theater management, as had, for the role of Venus, a Jewish soprano named Fortunata Tedesco. According to Wagner, she was the only singer in the company who had any claim to brilliance. He described her as "a tragedienne," who, on account of her beauty, would be a very valuable addition to the repertoire of the theater. He also wrote that she was "a rather grotesque but voluptuous type of Jewess" and had achieved many successes. Not completely won over by her talent, Wagner praised her dedication to the role. The admiration, guarded though it was, was in marked contrast to the bitterness he felt toward his tenor. For Niemann he had unrestrained praise for his talents, but contempt for his lack of cooperation and his egotistical fear for his reputation and voice.

After nine months of planning, preparation and 160 rehearsals came the first performance on March 19, 1861. There comes a moment at the end of the first scene of Act I, a transition from the Grotto of Venus to a quiet meadow, when the only sounds from the stage or orchestra are the high pitched but softly murmured melody of a young shepherd boy, and the accompanying English horn. It is an ideal moment, for those who wish to do so, to interrupt the opera with shrill and raucous sounds, offering as it does little competition from the stage or the pit.

During that first performance at the Opéra, the pride of France's operatic life, it was at that point that the stillness was pierced by the first of many shrill whistles. This was soon followed by loud shouting, laughter, hissing and more whistling. It came, of course, from the Jockeys, who were scattered throughout the audience. Most of the balance of the audience rose to the defense, and the performance proceeded with many lengthy interruptions while the main drama was played out in the audience. Somehow the opera proceeded, haltingly, to the end.

The second performance was a repeat of the first, the only addition being the street hawkers outside, who did a lively business peddling what they were pleased to term "Wagner whistles." Wagner requested that the third performance be on a Sunday, hoping that these aristocrats would not attend. They did attend, however, as did the police; not to quiet the Jockeys, but to save them from physical harm by the balance of the enraged audience. Wagner, Minna, the emperor, and most of Wagner's friends avoided that performance. As Wagner received firsthand reports of the melee, it was noted that his hands trembled. He asked for and was granted permission to withdraw the opera. His compensation for the nine months of agonizing trials, tribulations and humiliations was 750 francs.

10

Vienna

WAGNER'S ONE THOUGHT AFTER the Paris fiasco was to bring about a production of *Tristan*. His reasons had as much to do with money as his agonizing desire to see his creation brought to life on the stage. In July 1860 he
had received notice that a request for amnesty in his behalf by von Seebach
had been granted to the extent that His Majesty, King John, would not object
to Wagner entering states other the king's own Saxony to conduct performances of his works, with the further proviso that the state request that Saxony not demand his extradition.

Wagner then set his sights on Carlsruhe as a potential forum for *Tristan*, but first stopped in Weimar to see Liszt. Liszt had arranged rooms for
him as he had for a number of other musicians, owing to a rural festival by
the Society of Musical Artists, in full swing at the time. Among the guests
was Bülow. Tausig appeared briefly but, to Wagner's chagrin, left quickly
to pursue his love affair with a young lady, presumably the one who shortly
thereafter became his wife. Among the new acquaintances he met there was
Leopold Damrosch, a violinist and conductor. He was also one more Jew
whom Wagner was to count among his friends.

He found in Weimar, as he was to find elsewhere in Germany, a warmer
reception and a more enthusiastic response than he might otherwise have
expected, due to the sympathy aroused by his heavy-handed treatment in
Paris.

Just three weeks after the last Paris *Tannhäuser* performance, he presented himself to the grand duke of Baden. Unfortunately, problems with
casting ultimately scuttled his prospects for a Carlsruhe *Tristan*. But while
the project still showed signs of life, he went to Vienna to seek suitable
singers for the intended performance.

He arrived on May 9, and was even more enthusiastically received than in Carlsruhe. For the first time, 11 years after its 1850 premiere, he heard *Lohengrin*, first in dress rehearsal, then in full performance. His entry into the theater was marked by a spontaneous outburst of applause and cheers. With tears in his eyes he accepted the congratulations and expressions of support from the host of well-wishers who crowded around him. The notion of producing *Tristan* in Vienna rather than in Carlsruhe soon surfaced in the minds of both Wagner and the management of the Vienna Opera, and plans were made.

The problems in producing *Tristan* in Vienna were no less difficult or complex than those in producing *Tannhäuser* in Paris, and the Vienna experience was stretched out over two agonizing years, as opposed to the relatively short nine months in Paris. The cruel demands of this opera on the title role frightened the selected tenor, Aloys Ander, as it was later to frighten others. Dark rumors circulated that the opera was unsingable. The tension between Wagner and a powerful music critic, Eduard Hanslick, gave the management its own case of jitters. Wagner's sources of income, always in the form of gifts or advances, were drying up, and his financial situation became more desperate than ever. But it was a slow, if inexorable, process.

In the meantime, beginning shortly after arriving in Vienna, he again had personal contact with Tausig. At 19, Tausig was no longer the boyish companion Wagner knew in Zurich. Three years had made a difference, and the relationship was becoming increasingly one between equals. Tausig's purpose in the Austrian capital was to win, by his concerts, audiences for the music of Liszt. To Minna, still in Paris, Wagner wrote that "the confounded boy" was just as amusing as ever but not so insolent. Aside from amusing Wagner, Tausig introduced him to a friend, Peter Cornelius, about Tausig's age, but with his own aspirations to write opera. Cornelius also became, at least for a number of years, a close companion to Wagner.

Shortly thereafter, he returned to Paris to arrange with Minna for the transfer or disposition of the household furniture of their former residence. En route he stopped in Carlsruhe to explain to the grand duke that he had decided upon Vienna as the preferred site for *Tristan's* premiere. The grand duke, no doubt breathing a sigh of relief, wished Wagner well and predicted great things for him. Tausig overtook Wagner in Carlsruhe as he too was en route to Paris, to see Liszt, and the two friends traveled there together. Wagner wrote to Mathilde of this meeting: "Little Tausig who started from Vienna after me, and punctually caught me up at Carlsruhe — helps me now and then to a playful smile!"[1]

Back in Vienna Wagner wrote to Minna in Dresden that his host, who was also his physician in Vienna, Dr. Joseph Standhartner, had gone to join his family at Salzburg: "I'm quite alone in his abode now. Tausig and Cornelius haven't come back to Vienna yet, so I'm happily protected for the present from the injurious influence of too youthful company on my views of life and general morals; though I hope to expose my weak little mind as little as possible to such contamination even later."[2]

In Vienna, he turned his thoughts again to *Tristan*. He traveled to nearby Mödling to visit his prospective tenor, Ander, inviting Tausig and Cornelius to join him. His intention was to run through various parts of the opera with him. It was a disappointing session. Wagner found that despite his own demonstration of the proper interpretation of the role, the man was unequal to the task. Worse, his fear of the part was now obvious.

A glum Wagner returned to Vienna with his two young companions, who tried to cheer him up, in which task Tausig was apparently more reserved than Wagner felt he should have been. He attributed the reserve to the fact that Tausig had "aspirations in high quarters at that time." We are left to guess, as we are in so many places in his writings, as to precisely what was meant. He was pleased nonetheless when Tausig did accept another invitation for a few days at Hietzing, where Wagner and both young friends heard the prospective Isolde, Louisa Dustmann. He was pleased also that the soprano showed some of the requisite "spiritual susceptibility" for the role.

In late 1861, with prospects for *Tristan* dimming, he turned his attention to a plan for an opera he had long considered. It was for an operatic comedy on a subject that had first seized hold of him many years before, stimulated by a youthful experience. The story of *Die Meistersinger von Nürnberg* (in English, *The Mastersingers of Nuremberg*) was to center around the fifteenth century guild of the German mastersingers. He had sketched the opera in 1845 at the age of 33. Now he obtained an advance of 10,000 marks from his publisher Franz Schott in Mainz, promising to deliver the comedy that was, he claimed, to be in a popular style and easy to produce. It was to be a means of supporting himself and Minna.

11

Penury

IN TRAGIC FACT, HE HAD NO means to support himself or his wife. His propensity for squandering money, most often sums that had been charitably given or advanced for uncompleted works, had once again caught up with him. The small sums that he earned with his concerts were grossly inadequate. His greatest potential for raising money was, as it had always been, his talent for attracting donations from wealthy patrons of the arts, whether businessmen or royalty of both sexes. However, by late 1861 it was becoming widely understood that no matter how great his compositional prowess, one could easily be sucked dry by his extravagant requirements.

It is now, and has been from his own lifetime, customary to draw a clear boundary between Wagner the man, and Wagner the artist; or between the man and his music, with little recognition of the inescapable fact that it was the man who wrote the music. Conventional wisdom is there were two Wagners; the artist who composed some of the most sublime music to resound from either operatic stage or concert hall, and the man who personally lacked elementary decency or respectability. Bursting with creative genius, he was, so the standard biography goes, almost totally lacking in character. One part of him was, despite all hardships and crises, true and faithful to his genius. The other part of him, purposely and intentionally, decided to become an amoral human being, devoid of consideration of his fellow man. In the pages of most of his biographies, in essays and in popular journals, there is too seldom any attempt to search for a possible relationship between the two; any consideration of the one as perhaps the result of the other, the two contradictory aspects of the one man as being two inevitable sides of the same coin.

Wagner himself cried out under the pain of being so drawn and quartered.

In 1851, his early Zurich days, in a biographical sketch titled *A Communication to My Friends*, he wrote,

> I can only hope to be understood by those who feel a need and inclination to understand me.... As such I cannot consider those who pretend to love me as *artist*, yet deem themselves bound to deny me their sympathy as *man*.... The severance of the artist from the man is as brainless an attempt as the divorce of soul from body, and ... never was an artist loved nor his art comprehended, unless he was also loved — at least unwittingly — as man.[1]

Shortly thereafter, in a letter to his co-revolutionary August Roeckel, confined in Waldheim prison and then under sentence of death, he wrote, "I care for no sympathy from those who distinguish between the 'man' and the 'artist.'"[2]

Minna, as has been amply evidenced, poorly understood the phenomenon to whom she was married. It is pointless to blame her. She was constitutionally as unable to change her nature as was Wagner to change his. And she was not alone. Wagner's older brother Albert, for only one example, wrote him during his Zurich days when, penniless and exiled from Germany, he was working on the first of his *Ring* operas with little hope of any kind of performance, let alone a profitable one. The letter was scathing in tone: "You consider people only when and in so far as they can be of service to you: when that is over they no longer exist for you.... Much as I esteem and love your talent, it is anything but so as regards your character."

In truth, at this stage of his brother's creativity, Albert could never have guessed the overwhelming power of what would flow from that "talent" in later years, and may well not have understood it if he had. The letter was admittedly not without provocation. It was prompted by Wagner's attempt to borrow money from Albert's daughter Johanna, about whom he had previously said some rather unkind things.

The title of a recent volume, *Wagner: The Terrible Man and His Truthful Art*, says much about the popular conception of the book's subject, but does little justice to the valid insights within its covers.

We have seen something of the dichotomy between Wagner's anti–Semitic writings, both public and private, of which we will see much more, and his relationship with living, breathing Jews, whom he liked or disliked according to their musical talents, their understanding of his works, or their willingness to assist him, financially or artistically. His polemics notwithstanding, the religion of most of them appears to have been irrelevant.

There is no less puzzling a boundary between his need for money, which he so freely squandered, and the passion of his life, which is ordinarily the means by which one earns his livelihood. A pupil of Liszt once noted that whether Wagner was cheerful or somber depended not on the outward circumstances of his life, but according to the progress of his work.[3] His passion, the creation of music drama of unprecedented power and beauty, was not one calculated to earn him so much as a meager living, yet live he must, sometimes artistic creation seeming to be his only motive for it.

He has been accused of hypocrisy in deriding the universal striving for money, particularly in his calumny against the Jews, while scrounging every franc or mark he could borrow. Yet without prostituting his genius, there has been little suggestion forthcoming over these many decades from his army of critics as to how else he might have survived to complete his life's work. True it is that he was profligate to an extreme degree. It is sometimes difficult to fathom how so much could have slipped through his fingers so quickly. True it is also that, when the opportunity was available, through one means or another, he surrounded himself with luxury.

One of the luxuries, it must be mentioned, was clothing of satin and silk, often lined with fur. He suffered from a rare and painful skin condition known as erysipelas, an acute inflammation of the skin stemming from a blood infection. It most often affects the face and head, but frequently also, as was the case with Wagner, other parts of the body. Healing in one part of the body can be accompanied by the unrecognized onset of the condition in another. Possible complications include rheumatic fever and abscess formation.[4]

Wagner suffered his first attack at age 21, when he was courting Minna, and he tells us that then, and in various periods of his life, his swollen and disfigured face made him loathe to leave the privacy of his room. He referred to the condition as the "roses." In a letter of December 1855 to Liszt, for one example, he wrote, "the thorns of my existence have now been supplemented by blooming 'roses.'"

One of his most frequent companions in London in the spring of 1855, while conducting the Old Philharmonic Orchestra, was Ferdinand Praeger. Praeger also stayed with Wagner in Zurich in July 1857 and saw him in Paris during the winter of 1860–61, as well as on later occasions. He blamed Wagner's nervous excitability and volcanic outbursts, in large part, on his attacks of erysipelas, at which time his "nervous system was delicate and sensitive," causing irritability. The touch of cotton, noted Praeger, caused a shuddering sensation throughout his body.[5]

Wagner's preference for silks and furs next to his skin, rather than cotton, was, hence, based upon reasons more important than appearance. But throughout his life and beyond, he was the target of criticism and ridicule for what has been deemed a predilection for effeminate clothing. Most egregious was the theft of a series of his letters to a milliner in Vienna, detailing his seemingly outrageous requirements of these materials. The letters were purloined and read aloud to a number of friends of the thief including Johannes Brahms, who thereupon read them to a circle of his own friends at their favorite restaurant to the merriment of all.

It was not one of the great symphonist's finest moments. The letters were then offered for a price to Wagner, who refused the blackmail, whereupon they were printed in a journal whose staff generally reveled in such matters. In the attempted extortion, Brahms was not involved; in the sequence of events leading to their publication, he had a hand. The letters were published first in 1877, and again 23 years after Wagner's death.

However, it was not only in clothes that his tastes ran to the luxurious. He claimed always to require rather opulent, sometimes garish, surroundings as a suitable atmosphere in which to compose. Improbable as that may seem to some, no one is qualified to dispute him. Though a more modest lifestyle might have enabled him to avoid much grief, no one can convincingly tell us what impact such a "normal" and routine life might have had on the creativity of his unique genius.

He could also, of course, have followed the advice of his wife and many well meaning friends, and written popular works with conventional tunes that would have left his audiences humming, or filled his stages with marching bands, clashing armies, or perhaps even animal acts, all of which were in vogue at various times in operatic history. And, of course, he could have bribed or otherwise curried favor with critics. Unfortunately for him, but fortunately for many of the rest of us, he obtained the funds necessary for what he deemed a suitable lifestyle in ways that, though offensive to the morals and mores of polite society, were the only ones he had found to be successful. They were the only ones he could endure, and the only ones that permitted him to ultimately realize his vision.

He felt the world owed him a living and said so on a number of occasions. It did indeed. Sadly, he never understood why it was that not everyone agreed. Some of those who did, and so generously financed him, knew full well the probable consequences. The world is all the richer for their generosity. In October 1855 he wrote to Liszt a letter, one of a few, that includes a few telling sentences spelling out what is otherwise clear only from a perusal of his lifetime correspondence and the memoirs of others.

Referring to his popularity in America, where "Wagner nights" in Boston, for instance, were frequent, he mentioned how difficult it would be to reject an offer to conduct there, the compensation being undoubtedly much greater in America. But he would, nonetheless, have to do just that, he told Liszt, as he could never finish his *Nibelung* under such circumstances.

"It is not," he said, "my business to 'earn money,' but it is the business of my admirers to give me as much money as I want, to do my work in a cheerful mood."[6]

All of the mitigating circumstances taken into account, however, acquaintance with the degree to which he too often withdrew from the world around him, disdained the norms of universally acceptable conduct, and ignored the sensitivities of others, can be a humbling experience. An exchange of correspondence in late 1861 with Baron Robert von Hornstein (whose acquaintance he had made, it will be recalled, in 1855 in Zurich) is not a truly typical example. It may be one of the most extreme. But it is worth an extended look for what it may reveal about our subject.

The aggressive crudity of the demand is not completely irrelevant to the vehement and extravagant nature of his expressions of anti–Semitism, opinions similar to those expressed by so many others of that time with somewhat more restraint and balance.

At the time Wagner first met Hornstein he was composing the music for *Die Walküre,* second of the *Ring* dramas. Despite his pleasure in Hornstein's approval of his music, he decided quite early on that the baron lacked both strength of character and intellect. But in 1861 Hornstein had acquired one new quality that interested Wagner greatly. He had come into a small inheritance. In early December of that year Wagner decided to renew the acquaintance. His letter was direct and to the point:

"I hear you have become rich," he told the young man. After laying before him all of his own recent troubles and vicissitudes, he got to the meat of the matter:

> In order to rid myself of the most pressing obligations, worries and wants which rob me of my peace of mind, I require an immediate loan of 10 thousand francs. With this I can put my life in order and start working again. You may find it hard to provide me with this amount, but if you really *wish* it and do not shrink from sacrifices, then I am sure you will find it possible.

He then threw down the gauntlet: "Now let us see what sort of man you are!" The assistance, Wagner assured him, will "bring you in close contact with me, and you will allow me to stay next summer for approximately three months on one of your estates, preferably on the Rhine."

Standing alone, and without context, the letter could be seen as a joke or a deliberate attempt to needle its recipient. It is undoubtedly neither. Nor does Hornstein's answer appear to support Wagner's assessment of the baron as intellectually challenged:

> You should turn your attention to *really* wealthy persons whom you will surely find among your numerous patrons and patronesses all over Europe. I regret

that I am unable to be of service to you. As to your extended visit to "one of my estates," I am not at present prepared for a lengthy visit, but if this should become possible at some future time I will let you know. I have read in the newspapers, with great regret, that the production of *Tristan und Isolde* will not take place this winter.

Wagner, as so often, had the last word:

It would be wrong not to rebuke you for your answer to my letter. It will probably not happen again that a man like me will have contact with you, but it should be a wholesome lesson to you to be made aware of the impropriety of your lines.

It is not your place to advise me in any way whatever, not even as to the relative wealth of individuals. You should have left it to me to decide why I have not approached any of the patrons or patronesses you mentioned.

If you are not prepared to receive me at one of your estates, you should have grasped the singular opportunity I offered you, by making appropriate arrangements at a place of my own choice. Your promise, therefore, to let me know when it will be convenient to you to receive me is an insult.

You would also have been wise to suppress your sentiments concerning my *Tristan*. Your answer could come only from one who is totally indifferent to my works.

Let this end the matter. I reckon on your discretion, as you can on mine.[7]

The Baron seems to have acceded to Wagner's request to end the matter there, even if to no other.

12

Biebrich on the Rhine

So HE BEGAN WORK ON *Die Meistersinger,* the opera that he intended to be light and easy to produce. He had early on thought and said the same about *Tristan.* It was understandable that even he, at times, should want to use his genius as a means of earning the money he so desperately needed. Like his deep and complex opera about love, however, his comedy was destined to be quite taxing and difficult to stage. It was not in him to write light or readily accessible works. His inner daemons propelled him on to deeper, newer and more novel things. These were all traits in which *Die Meistersinger* was to rival *Tristan,* remarkable indeed considering the pervasiveness of the comedy's understated humor.

Yet the two works could hardly be more different. Except in their tremendous power of expression they have little in common. The story of *Die Meistersinger,* entirely original with Wagner, is a conventional romance set against a background of the medieval guild of mastersingers. A young knight must gain entrance to the guild to succeed in winning the hand of his beloved. Though he fails, due to the pedantic boorishness of the mastersinger selected to judge the audition, he succeeds when the townspeople acclaim his Prize Song.

In 1861 Wagner began the sketches for the opera, and in December wrote the entire poetic text. In mid–February 1862, he rented a small set of rooms in a stately, recently completed home in the little town of Biebrich, near Wiesbaden on the right bank of the River Rhine. It was ideally situated on the river's edge, just before its gentle turn northward. Conveniently, it is almost directly across from Mainz, the residence of his publisher, Schott. About a week later Minna, unannounced, joined him from Dresden, where she had taken up residence after leaving Paris.

It was a futile attempt at reconciliation. She seemed obsessed with her role as innocent victim of his deliberately chosen unorthodox life, but seemed also determined that he would not have a free moment to compose. She preferred to torture both him and herself with irrational jealousies. They separated ten grueling days after her arrival.

At a party at Schott's he met a 28-year-old, intelligent, straightforward woman of striking good looks, named Mathilde Maier. In addition, she had what for Wagner was always a much admired quality: she was a good listener. One factor in this quality may have been her partial deafness. She was destined to play, for a while, an important and perhaps stabilizing role in Wagner's life. Living with her widowed mother, she was determined not to cause the lady any grief or embarrassment with her conduct. Wagner seemed content, if not completely happy with the platonic relationship that ensued.

On March 18 he finally obtained a full pardon from the Saxon king, owing in part to proof of dire medical conditions, and was thus permitted to enter Saxony. Together Richard and Minna set up a residence in Dresden for Minna, but Richard returned to Biebrich to work, hopefully in peace and quiet. At the end of April he completed the music of the overture, a stirring, powerful piece, often played in concert today. In November, Richard, at her urging, and against his better judgment, joined her in Dresden. By the end of 1862 they had parted for good. It was to be the last time they lived with or even saw each other. Till the end of her days, four years later, he continued, with the greatest difficulty, to support her as promised.

After completing the overture of *Die Meistersinger* he began composition of the first act, but completed very little of it that year. Apart from the continual shrill accusations of his wife, delivered first by letter, then in person in Dresden, the need to support both her and himself rendered sustained constructive work impossible for over two years.

For the balance of 1862, and four months beyond, excluding only the few weeks he spent with Minna in Dresden in late November, his home was the few rooms he rented in the mansion in Biebrich. Perhaps one of the most fortuitous events to occur in the Biebrich residence was his audition of Ludwig Schnorr von Carolsfeld for the role of Tristan in the opera's premiere, whenever and wherever that might turn out to be. Carolsfeld was a huge bear of a man, of ungainly physiognomy and forbidding aspect. Wagner was at first loathe to hear him, as he was afraid that the tenor's "gross appearance" might color his perception of the man's talents as an artist. Nonetheless, in late May, Wagner heard him perform as Lohengrin in Carlsruhe. He kept his presence concealed from Schnorr, still concerned that he might want to remain unacquainted with him.

This reticence changed quickly and dramatically. It was one of the more memorable happy events of his life. Overwhelmed by what he heard, Wagner invited Schnorr to spend time with him at Biebrich. There, an immediate bond was formed between the two men. As described by Wagner, they ran through much of the *Ring,* and especially *Tristan,* "to their hearts' content,"[1] and Schnorr was destined to become, three years later, the first Tristan.

The audition in Biebrich included Malvina Schnorr, his wife, who sang the part of Isolde, and would become the first Isolde at the opera's premiere. At the piano was Hans von Bülow (who, with Cosima, was visiting at Biebrich), while Wagner instructed the singers as the audition progressed.

Apart from his dire financial straits, other matters slowed his composition of *Die Meistersinger.* His landlord at Biebrich owned a bulldog, Leo, which he kept chained up and, so Wagner believed, sadly neglected. Wagner harbored a fierce hatred for many people, but owned a succession of dogs throughout his life, and had only the friendliest feelings for every one he ever met. Leo was no exception. One hot August day, the inveterate dog lover attempted to have the creature unchained by a servant and obligingly held the animal's head to lessen the man's fright. Wagner was bitten on the upper joint of the right thumb by the ungrateful canine and rendered unable to write for two entire months. He excused the bite as being "involuntary," a more charitable view of the offense than he generally afforded the bites and stings of humans.

Toward the end of 1862, when Wagner returned to Biebrich after parting from Minna in Dresden, he was informed that his landlord desired to occupy the quarters he had been using. Wagner, facing a forced move before the next April, was obliged to begin looking for a new residence at once. He settled on Vienna. He had received in November an invitation to conduct a series of concerts in St. Petersburg, Russia; and Vienna was suitably located with a view toward east and west. Further, there was still the possibility of a *Tristan* in Vienna, or so he was led to believe. In Vienna, he again had personal contact with Karl Tausig.

13

The Vienna Jews

In his first days in Paris, over 20 years earlier, Wagner's trio of friends included Lehrs, the Jewish philologist. Now, in Vienna, Wagner again found himself with a triumvirate of friends, two this time being Jewish. One was Tausig; the other was a 26-year-old native of Prague, Heinrich Porges.

Porges had studied philosophy and law at the University of Prague, but took a greater interest in his private lessons in music. In 1858, at the age of 21, he decided that he wanted to become a piano virtuoso, especially interested as he was in the new directions of German music. During the next three years, in the home of his parents, he came into contact with Liszt, Bülow, and Cornelius. He arranged during this period for Liszt to be invited to Prague to conduct his "Dante" Symphony.

Porges's talents as a musician were apparently not great, his bent being more toward the area of editing and writing on matters of music. From 1859 until 1862 he was active as the Prague correspondent for the *New Journal for Music,* the same journal that had published "Judaism in Music" a decade earlier. In his first article, in January 1859, he reviewed, among other pieces, Wagner's "Faust" Overture. His younger brother Friedrich, known as Fritz, was a physician living in Vienna, and there had met Wagner and, through him, Tausig and Cornelius. To Heinrich he described Wagner as "a damned difficult man."

Tausig and Cornelius hit upon the idea of a Wagner concert in Prague. Porges was happy to join the effort and wrote to Wagner offering him the opportunity to direct a concert for the benefit of "poor physicians," a phrase that probably lacked the humorous overtones it exudes today. Since Wagner wanted a guarantee, Porges organized a subscription for which he set a good example by buying a number of subscriptions himself. Three concerts were conducted in February 1863.[1]

The day after the Prague concert Porges paid Wagner about 2,000 marks. "I laughingly assured him," wrote Wagner, "that this was the first money I had ever earned by my own exertions." This Prague concert was a favor that Wagner never forgot. Porges also introduced him to a number of "intelligent admirers," which in Wagner's view would be a redundancy.

That venture earned for him enough money to travel to St. Petersburg for five concerts in March and April. From those and others in Moscow, he netted 12,000 marks, which, like all other sums that he garnered, quickly disappeared. In his autobiography he referred to Porges as "an out-and-out partisan" of Liszt and himself, and says he was impressed , not only by his personal qualities, but by his enthusiasm.

Throughout most of 1863, Wagner assumed the role of traveling conductor, even as he maintained his hopes about *Tristan* in Vienna. He completed concerts there in January, for which his copyists were Cornelius, Tausig, and one Wendelin Weissheimer. He then conducted in Prague and in St. Petersburg in March and April. He continued his concerts, often including many of his own compositions, in Moscow, Pest, Carlsruhe, Löwenberg and Breslau before returning to Vienna in December. The concert in Löwenberg had been arranged by Porges. The Breslau concert was arranged by Leopold Damrosch, the concert director whom Wagner had met over two years earlier in Weimar. Despite the dismal concert room and lack of guarantee of receipts, Wagner tells us he agreed to conduct so as not to compromise his friend too severely.

Wagner was surprised to find the front section of the theater filled with Jews, and even more surprised to find that his success in that city was due to the enthusiasm of the Jewish population there. The day after the concert, Damrosch arranged a dinner in Wagner's honor, which, again to his surprise, was attended entirely by Jews. As to exactly what he made of these Semitic audiences, Wagner leaves us in the dark, though it undoubtedly did not escape him that Damrosch himself was a Jew. It all tends to lend substance to the observation of Friedrich Nietzsche that "the Semitic races show greater understanding of Wagner's art than the Aryan ones."[2] Nietzsche's comment was also later supported by a list in the *Bayreuther Blätter* (a newspaper founded by Wagner in 1878) of patrons contributing to Wagner's work. It is replete with Jewish names.[3]

In Prague he ran across an old friend, whom he referred to as Marie Löwe, whom he had known from his earliest youth. She was now a harpist with the orchestra, and Wagner recalled that upon the first performance of *Tannhäuser* in Prague she had sent him an enthusiastic report of it. Her admiration had grown over the years, and according to Wagner, she remained "tenderly attached" to him. That he refers to her by her maiden name, or at least a variation of it, is interesting, though puzzling. Her name was Lehmann by marriage. Her oldest daughter, Lilli, traced her maternal lineage back a number of generations in her autobiography, and it appears that there was no Jewish ancestry on her mother's side. Marie's husband, however, Lilli's father, may well have been Jewish. Lilli, who became a much sought after soprano, says flatly, "We were Protestants,"[4] but explains that as a child the family worshipped, and that she was educated, at Catholic institutions due to a paucity of Protestant ones in Prague.

The use of the maiden name by Wagner may or may not be of significance. Lehmann was the family name of many Jews, and was generally considered a Jewish name. Not only is the daughter, Lilli, termed Jewish by most modern Wagner biographers and other

Heinrich Porges, from a photograph by Joseph Albert, Munich, about 1865. From *Geschichte und Kultur der Juden in Bayern*, ed. by Manfred Treml and Wolf Weigand.

writers, but the family was obviously so considered by their neighbors in Prague. Lilli has, tellingly, described how "the Jew-baiting, which we experienced repeatedly in Prague, was confined to window breaking only, and, as far as I know, it never reached anything worse."[5] Her treatment of the entire subject is sketchy at best, and we are left to guess why these Protestants should have been the targets of anti–Semitic attacks.

By Wagner's own standards, as we have already seen, if either parent was Jewish Lilli would be, to him, Jewish also. It is likewise not certain if significance might attach to his spelling of his friend's name as "Löwe." Marie herself, and her parents and children spelled it "Löw," or "Loew." There comes, later in Wagner's life, evidence that he considered Löwe to be a name frequently used by converted Jews.[6]

Lilli was never very fond of her father, and he did not come to Prague for a long time after his family moved there. She explained that her mother feared that "he might endanger us in the modest positions we occupied and which we had obtained with difficulty."[7] The reasons for the difficulty, or the danger, she likewise never explained, and his religious heritage hence remains a clear possibility. In her autobiography she seems unusually preoccupied and sympathetic with Jews and Judaism, and inordinately drawn to both. It is perhaps significant also that although she traces the lineage of her mother quite far back, she makes no reference to that of her father.

Wagner did not mention in his life's story that during this time in Prague he also met Lilli, then 15. In her own autobiography, Lilli tells us that Wagner embraced her "stormily" and kissed her so much it frightened her. Marie, writing to a friend about this visit, said, "Although he is fêted everywhere, the poor man has not enough to live on.... I am much envied because I have his friendship." She also soothed her daughter's fears about him.

Ultimately Lilli was captivated by his music, first by *Tristan,* and later by the *Ring,* in which both she and her younger sister (named Marie like their mother, but known as Riezl) sang supporting roles. Wagner was close throughout his life first to Marie, then to her two daughters, both personally and as singers, and we will have occasion later to look more closely at these relationships. In 1886, three years after Wagner's death, *Tristan* was first performed in America, by the New York Metropolitan Opera. Lilli Lehmann was the Isolde to Albert Niemann's Tristan.

The friendship with Tausig, the acknowledged Jew, continued in Vienna as it had in Zurich. It appears, if Wagner's highly questionable statement to Minna is to be believed, that Tausig's mother, but not his father, was Jewish. As we have seen, it is possible that with Lilli the situation may have been the reverse. Neither situation apparently made any difference to Wagner. Both Tausig and Lilli Lehmann admired his music and befriended him, and were both high in his esteem and enjoyed his friendship.

It is interesting to compare these two cases with that of Eduard Hanslick, a music critic with sufficient literary skills that his poison pen became a force to be feared in the musical community. He was born in Prague in 1825. He studied law, despite his keen interest in music and literature, and was later employed as a government clerk. But in 1848 he changed course and became music critic for the *Wiener Zeitung,* an influential Viennese newspaper.

It appears likely that Hanslick's mother was Jewish, his father Christian. Hanslick had admired Wagner's *Tannhäuser,* but turned quite hostile to the composer's music beginning with his next opera, *Lohengrin.* Wagner's "Judaism in Music" may have been a factor. It is also possible that it played only a minor role or none at all. Hanslick's opinions of these later operas seem at once both insufferably pedantic and superficial, yet there appears no more evidence of malice or personal animosity in them than there does in his reviews of almost every other contemporary composer, Brahms being the most famed exception. He seemed, despite a veneer of erudition and scholarship, incapable of comprehending any but the simplest, most accessible of compositions. Among his favorite composers were Rossini and Johann Strauss, the "waltz king." He liked music that was "light, tuneful, unchallenging," and the genuineness of even his stated admiration of Brahms has been questioned by a Brahms biographer.[8]

His own philosophy of music, expressed in his slim volume *The Beautiful in Music,* first published in 1854, may be explanation enough for his antipathy to Wagner's works. The argument of the book is the antithesis of everything that Wagner believed about the nature of music drama, and everything that gives his music its tremendous emotional impact. Unlike Wagner, Hanslick believed that music was by nature abstract, unrelated to objects or ideas, and that a natural wall separated words from music. In his own words he tells us that his objection to Wagner lay in the composer's

> violation of the music by words, the unnaturalness and exaggeration of the expression, the annihilation of the singer and the art of singing by unvocal writing and the orchestral din, the displacement of the melody of song by declamatory recitation, enervating monotony and measureless expansion, and finally, the unnatural, stilted progression of his diction, a diction which offends every feeling for fine speech.[9]

For opera, he emphasized Mozart's dictum that the words must be "the obedient handmaiden of the music." He never revealed the slightest suspicion that music could reach its greatest heights in conveying the emotional content of words, objects, ideas or dramatic situations.

It seems possible that Hanslick's good will toward Wagner, who had disdained the critic for some years, was deemed by the Vienna Opera personnel to be necessary to a successful production of *Tristan.* Their erratic attitude toward such a production went back and forth, seemingly in tune with the critic's relationship with its composer. Such, in any event, seemed to be Wagner's own assessment. The best Wagner could or would do, by his own account, was to ignore him. He, and some of his biographers, claimed that the tension reached a climax with a reading of the text of *Die Meistersinger* to a small group, including Hanslick, in the home of Wagner's friend and physician, Dr. Standhartner, in November 1862.

According to this telling, the critic immediately recognized the boorish, narrow, pedagogic villain of the piece, the town clerk, as a caricature of himself. That was not difficult, the story goes, as in the original draft of the piece, the villain had been named Viet Hanslich. It is not contended that the draft read by Wagner contained that name. Wagner was persuaded by friends to change the name to Beckmesser. What is contended is that Hanslick fled the group at the first opportunity, the lampoon being obvious, whatever the name.

The story, in one form or another, has been widely accepted. Wagner's own account, however, makes no mention of naming his villain Hanslich or anything else. He states only that the "dangerous critic" seemed more pale and depressed with the reading; that it was impossible to persuade him to stay at the close; that Hanslick took the whole text as an affront to himself; and thereupon the critic's attitude toward Wagner underwent a very dramatic change for the worse. The composer, it should be noted, nowhere denies the justification of the critic's impressions.[10]

Hanslicks's own account of the evening casts doubt on the story. In a volume published in 1894 he quotes his own previously expressed opinion (published, presumably, shortly after the event) of the reading in Dr. Standhartner's home:

> After the sulphurous glow of the *Ring* comes an appealing genre scene of German municipal life, now comic, now touching, based on a simple premise, and motivated by the joy and suffering of simple folk. With *Die Meistersinger,* Wagner will do more for the German theater than with the *Ring*.... Wagner has simultaneously opened up two opposing routes. It cannot be a matter of indifference ... whether he will prefer to appear *before* his nation as a mastersinger or as a Nibelung.[11]

Neither the *Ring*, nor *Meistersinger*, of course, had yet been performed. Hanslick is speaking only about the poetic texts, the verses of which had not been completely set to music. If he did in fact see the poem as a personal lampoon, it either did not disturb him, or else he went to some lengths to appear oblivious to it.

Die Meistersinger was ultimately heard first in Munich in 1868, and then in Vienna in 1870. Hanslick's review of the Munich performance gives evidence of the narrowness of his musical comprehension, as well as the reason he was so feared. Standing alone it may seem to be evidence of malice toward Wagner, but reviews in similar tone of the music of other contemporary composers blunt that argument.

He referred to the overture as "the world's most unpleasant" except for the "even more horrible" Prelude to *Tristan*, which he had heard in its 1865 premiere. He referred to the *Meistersinger* overture as a chromatic flood, tossed about in "a kind of tonal typhoon," contrived, "brutal in effect and painfully artificial." This is a remarkable reaction from a trained musician, especially considering the thunderous applause greeting that overture in concert beginning in November 1862. In a volume published 100 years later by two prominent American music critics and historians, that same "tonal typhoon" was described as "one of the glories, not only of Wagnerian music, but of all symphonic literature."[12] Hanslick's review of the balance of the opera is, with some exceptions, as disparaging as that of the overture: "dry and boring," "restless accompaniment and excessive modulation," "monotonous and clumsy," "brutal shouting and screaming."[13]

Wagner practically ignored Tausig's Jewishness, as he did Lilli's. He never mentioned Tausig's, as far as is known, until after the young man's untimely death. Nor did he ever mention, apparently, the subject of religion with regard either to Lilli's mother or her sister Riezl. But upon republication of his "Judaism in Music" in 1869, he commented as part of a lengthy postscript that Hanslick, despite his "gracefully hidden Jewish origin," produced art criticism that was Semitic and anti–German. Fifteen years later Hanslick answered with an article in the *Deutsche Rundschau* in which he denied being Jewish, and pointed to the fact that his father was Christian; implying, at least, that his mother was not. But to his credit he said that if he were Jewish he would not be ashamed to admit it. He would, he said, be proud to be "burned at the same stake" as Mendelssohn and Meyerbeer,[14] thus proving both his strength of character and, with regard to the second named victim, his lack of musical judgment.

Unfortunately he also added two other comments that do little for his reputation: "Wagner couldn't stand a Jew and consequently he developed the habit of regarding as a Jew anyone he didn't like." That statement had some validity when applied to groups, such as journalists; none when applied to individuals. Had it been true, Wagner would have found himself in a world consisting largely of "Jews," his enemies far outnumbering his friends. Admittedly his understanding of what made a person a Jew was broad, conversion being irrelevant and the Jewishness of one parent sufficing, but no more so than that of the German public in general at the time. Hanslick's error of fact was then matched by an equally palpable error of judgment: "I do not doubt that in 50 years the writings of the Wagnerites will be looked upon in amazement as the relics of an intellectual epidemic."

14

Flight from Creditors

IN APRIL 1863, WAGNER WROTE a preface for a new printing of his text of the *Ring*, which had already been through several. In it the composer lamented the improbability of his work ever seeing the light of day, due, as he saw it, to the degenerate state of the German theater. He described at length the conditions required for the production of a work of such monumental proportions, including a specially built theater, and saw but one solution that had even the smallest likelihood of realization: a German prince who might someday recognize his obligation to German art and undertake the construction of the requisite theater, and production of the *Ring*. His final words: "Will this Prince be found? 'In the beginning was the deed.'"[1] He could not have guessed, even wildly, the impact this preface was to ultimately have on his life and his work.

In May, Wagner, having been obliged to move from his lodgings in Biebrich, set up new quarters in a large, mansion-like home in Penzing. Penzing was then a suburb of Vienna; today, very much a part of it. Though unequal to the scenic setting he had given up, the building itself matched the stateliness of his former home. Despite being in more dire financial straits than in Biebrich, instead of renting a few rooms, he, typically, took its entire upper portion.

With sources of loans or gifts becoming ever more scarce, he conducted more concerts, including, in November, one in Prague. He again saw the Lehmanns, and Marie again wrote her friend about the visit, this time reporting that Wagner was very charming to herself and her daughters, and would "like to adopt Lilli as his daughter. Lilli has declined, and indeed he is not old enough to play father to such a big daughter." There were no doubt very valid reasons for the refusal, but Wagner was 50, Lilli was 15.

Toward the end of the year, Cornelius and Tausig again came to see Wagner in Vienna, but their older friend was nursing a grudge for a perceived slight of the previous summer. This "insult" occurred while the Schnorrs and the Bülows had been visiting Wagner at Biebrich on the Rhine, the occasion of the *Tristan* audition. The two young friends had also been invited. Although Cornelius had at first accepted, he was soon diverted by what to him seemed a better offer from Tausig, and both of the young men went cavorting off to Geneva. Wagner learned of this by means of a rather jolly letter from the pair advising that they had smoked a cigar to his health, with no mention of any regret at being unable to appear in Biebrich.

Now, in Vienna, Wagner let them know in no uncertain terms that he considered their conduct of the previous summer insulting. He seemed irremediably perplexed that they could not understand his lack of sympathy with their preference for the beautiful Swiss countryside to a visit with him in Biebrich. He blamed Tausig as the culpable party and thought the event undoubtedly was connected to his apparent sudden possession of disposable funds.

There was in addition some current behavior on the part of Tausig, while visiting Wagner at his hotel, that irritated the Master. It involved the young friend's refusal to introduce a certain lady to him. But this was forgotten as quickly as the slight of the previous summer, particularly when he found Tausig quite helpful in taking care of practical details of concerts in Vienna. This included transcribing for piano certain of Wagner's compositions, for which Tausig enlisted also the help of Johannes Brahms, then 25. He described the budding composer to Wagner as "a very good fellow." The Brahms-Wagner relationship had started off well enough even earlier, but soured in later years.

Wagner moved into his home in Penzing the twelfth of May, 1863, a period that came between concert tours. Tausig and Cornelius were often invited there to dine with him. On the 22 of June he wrote his good friend Malwida von Meysenbug a lengthy and detailed letter describing his recent activities. He concluded with: "Little Tausig is my only contact with the outside world: an intelligent and quite exceptional young man! In all seriousness he enquires most eagerly after his bride, and asks you to convey to Olga his most tender greetings!" That reference is one of a very few we have about Tausig's marriage.

It happened that during one period there were simultaneous afflictions to both guests, Tausig having a severe illness, and Cornelius an injured foot. But there were visits by Friedrich Porges (the physician called Fritz), and there was a new dog named Pohl, the gift of his landlord. During the heat of the summer, as was his lifelong custom, Wagner took long walks with his dog, and was joined at times by both Porges brothers as well as other acquaintances. But his closest friends were still Cornelius and Tausig. Tausig, however, even when restored to health, sometimes made himself scarce, keeping company with "wealthy Austrian officers," or so Wagner tells us.

His wanderings that year brought him in late November to the home of the Bülows in Berlin. Enroute from Mainz to Löwenberg, he stayed with them overnight on the 28. After dining with them, and while Hans was preparing for an evening concert, Wagner and Cosima went for a drive along a promenade. Both later acknowledged that a silent expression between them was of the utmost significance. Of the details we can not be certain, but in his autobiography Wagner states, "We gazed speechless into each other's eyes; an avowal of the truth mastered us and led to a confession — which needed no words— of the boundless unhappiness which oppressed us."[2] An entry in Cosima's diary for November 28 1877, 14 years after their evening drive, refers to that date as the anniversary date on which "we found each other and became united."[3]

Though he was in fact a pauper, and heavily in debt, for Christmas 1863 Wagner decided to celebrate like royalty. He invited to his Penzing home Cornelius and his two Jewish companions, Porges and Tausig. Wagner wrote to a lady friend in Mainz that he had given Christmas gifts to "my servants, and to Peter, Tausig, and H. Porges: I wish you could have been there." The biggest mystery of course is where he acquired the wherewithal. It was probably another loan that he never repaid. As described by Cornelius, Wagner showered them all with gifts. He wrote his sister that he had received so many expensive gifts that the next day he gave half of them away.

Two days later Wagner took part in a concert by Tausig in Vienna. Throughout the end of the year, he undoubtedly, as was not unusual, had extravagant visions of money to be earned in new concerts in Russia, and possibly marriage to a rich widow. The Russian concerts came to nothing, owing to his lack of travel expenses and the military conflict in the Polish provinces, either of which alone would have scuttled the plans. The marriage also failed to materialize, and thoughts of divorce from Minna he had been entertaining were likewise put on hold. His creditors, even Wagner knew, could not be held off much longer. His friends had reached their limits. His world was caving in. During his last days in Penzing, Tausig vanished for a while, reappearing with his wife, a Hungarian pianist.

Flight was unavoidable, and, encouraged by his realistic friends, he fled. His first stop was Munich, where he learned from Cornelius that Tausig, who had co-signed three notes in Wagner's behalf, and who was then in Hungary, feared on that account to return to Vienna. To a friend Wagner referred to the creditor in question as one least deserving of consideration, but lamented that the three notes to him were endorsed by Tausig, implying that they therefore could not be ignored.

While in Munich, Wagner noted that the population was in mourning, and learned that it was for the recently deceased king of Bavaria, Maximilian II. While walking through the town, he stopped for a few moments to peer at a picture in a shop window of the new king, Ludwig II, then only 18 years of age.

He intended to return to Vienna to try to salvage his wretched financial situation. On the vehement advice of his friends however, and their warnings of dire consequences, he went instead to Mariafeld in Switzerland, where ten years earlier he had first read the entire poem of his *Ring des Nibelungen*. Now he sought shelter with his old friends, François and Eliza Wille, who were his hosts on that occasion. When he arrived he was greeted only by Eliza, François being in Constantinople on business at the time. Until he returned, Wagner had a sympathetic ear in Eliza.

His overwrought nerves permitting but little work, he went for long walks on his own. Eliza wrote later of the terrible experiences he had endured, and concluded that his "nervous irritability and the powerful workings of his imagination made the difficulties of that period a sheer torment for him." Once, suddenly flaring up, he shouted, "Everything might have been fine between me and my wife! It was just that I spoiled her utterly and gave in to her in everything.... She did not seem to understand that a man like me can't live with his wings clipped."

Eliza tried to cheer him. She spoke of the glorious future that lay before him, but succeeded only in increasing his anger. Why speak of the future, he demanded, when my manuscripts are locked away in the cupboard? In his agitation he was pacing up and down the room. Suddenly he stopped directly in front of Eliza. Standing face to face with her, he fairly exploded:

> Mine is a different kind of organism. I have sensitive nerves, I must have beauty, radiance and light. The world owes me a living! I can't live the miserable life of an organist like your master Bach! Is it such an outrageous demand to say that I deserve the little bit of luxury that I can bear? I, who can give pleasure to thousands.

In a moment of defiance he raised his head, then sat down in the chair by a window and stared into space.[4]

When François returned, there was much less sympathy to be had. Though preserving the personally pleasant relationship, he would not offer further help, seeing no end to his guest's financial requirements. The

Wesendoncks would not shelter him either, but offered 100 francs a month, which he refused.

From Mariafeld he wrote to Cornelius on the eighth of April. He mentioned his recurring problems with his bladder, one of only a number of his perpetually nagging and debilitating health problems. He also mentioned Tausig: "If all turns out well, he may succeed in being nailed to the cross for my sake," a probable expression of frustration concerning the notes that Tausig had endorsed for him. He left Mariafeld on the thirtieth of April and journeyed to Stuttgart, where he sought out a friend from his revolutionary days in Dresden, Wendelin Weissheimer, who, as we have seen, served as a copyist for his works.

Wagner was now a fugitive from his creditors as certainly as he had been from Saxon justice. He was without funds and without sources of credit. He had numerous problems with health. Plans to produce his completed *Tristan* in Vienna had come to nothing, and its failure at that prestigious house boded ill for prospects elsewhere. He had completed only two of the four operas of the *Ring* and two acts of the third. He had not completed even the first act of *Die Meistersinger*. Neither the means nor the requisite peace of mind to complete these works seemed within reach. And, not least, he was without the female companionship that was so vital to him.

In Stuttgart, Wagner, in complete despair, stayed with Weissheimer in the Marquart Hotel. "I've reached the end," he muttered, "I can't go on. I'll have to disappear from the face of the earth unless you can stop me." In horror Weissheimer realized that his friend's journey was in fact a flight from creditors, arrest and imprisonment. Not for another four years would the laws permitting imprisonment of debtors be repealed. What he needed, said Wagner, was a quiet and secluded refuge where he could hide away until some solution to his predicament could be found. But he was not meant to be a hermit; he could not live in solitude. He craved, and required to survive, intelligent and responsive companionship. With tears in his eyes he asked whether Weissheimer would accompany him. Weissheimer realized that in such a situation the distraught composer could not be left on his own. Apart from his emotional state he was completely without means.

Without hesitation Weissheimer agreed. In a mixture of joy and relief, Wagner flung his arms around his friend's neck. It was a Saturday. They made plans to leave on Tuesday, as Wagner wanted to see a performance of *Don Giovanni*, to be conducted by a good and devoted friend, Karl Eckert, on Sunday afternoon, and to see various acquaintances on Monday. He told Weissheimer that he considered the last scene of the Mozart opera to be the greatest in the entire operatic repertory. In that performance, the lead role of Don Giovanni was sung by Angelo Neumann, a Jewish singer soon to turn impresario and serve an important function in Wagner's artistic life. As it happened, Neumann was also staying at the Marquart.

Many years later, Neumann was to write that upon returning to his hotel after the final rehearsal, the day before that first performance seen by Wagner, he was annoyed and irritated by an incessant pacing up and down by the man next door, like a "caged lion." Upon complaining he was surprised to learn that his tormentor was Richard Wagner, whom he had known and greatly admired in Vienna in 1862. At that time Wagner was overseeing the opera's rehearsals for the *Tristan* performances that never materialized. Neumann further described meeting Wagner by chance on the street in Vienna during that earlier period, where the great composer was often seen flourishing a red bandanna and talking to himself.

He also relates something Wagner never knew. The owner of the hotel, Herr Marquart, had asked Neumann to tell Wagner that the best two rooms in the hotel and the meals were on the house. Neumann, not feeling well enough acquainted with the composer to do so, asked Eckert to be the messenger. Eckert, believing that Wagner would not take kindly to such an offer from a stranger, decided to foot the bill himself, and sent his wife for the money.[5]

On Tuesday the depressed and discouraged composer and his companion, Weissheimer, were to depart for a nearby mountainous area known as the Rauhe Alb.[6] There could not have been a lower ebb in his life, less basis for hope, or more reason for despair.

He could not have known that the young king whose picture he saw in the Munich shop window had read and taken to heart the preface Wagner had written for the most recent printing of the *Ring* text. Nor could he have known that the new king would soon be the salvation of himself and his work; nor that upon Wagner's own death, 19 years later, this Bavarian monarch would be able, with pride and with full justification, to exclaim in grief, "It was I who saved him for the world."

Part III

Munich

15

King Ludwig

IT IS DOUBTFUL THAT THERE have been many royal heads of state as ill suited or, ultimately, less desirous of serving in that capacity as Ludwig II of Bavaria. On March 10, the new king was 18 years old, and eager to assume the role to which he was called. But it was not long before he became disillusioned and annoyed by affairs of state, politics and war. His interests lay in the beauties of nature, which abounded in the mountains and forests of Bavaria, and in art, most especially as it depicted the world of fantasy. He had a keen interest in the theater and the concert hall; an aversion to pomp and ceremony. In preference to large cities, Munich particularly, with its mass of people, noise, court intrigues and political machinations, he preferred the quiet and solitude of the wilderness.

As Ernest Newman, the great biographer of Wagner and student of the life of Ludwig, so deftly puts it, "He exhibited so many signs of exceptional sanity it was a foregone conclusion that the world would someday declare him to be mad."[1] He has in fact, with no justification, become known as the mad King Ludwig. He was indeed, through political chicanery, ultimately declared insane by four psychiatrists, not one of whom had ever interviewed him or even spoken a word with him before doing so. Why did he come to Wagner's rescue?

In 1858, Wagner's *Lohengrin* had been performed in Munich. The governess of the 13-year-old prince described the performance to him, and her ward was thrilled by what he heard. In February 1861, Ludwig attended a performance of the opera in Munich and upon his continued pleading, his father, Maximilian II, commanded another performance in June. The title role on that occasion was sung by Ludwig Schnorr von Carolsfeld, whom we last saw being auditioned by Wagner in Biebrich on the Rhine, for a possible role as

Tristan. In December 1862 Ludwig heard *Tannhäuser*, and in February 1864, upon his insistence, *Lohengrin* was once again performed in Munich. By this time he was thoroughly entranced by the romantic composer and his works. He immersed himself not only in the poetic texts of the operas, which he learned by heart, but in the prose essays, whose turgid style continues to discourage all but scholars or the most ardent admirers.

At some time during the year before his accession to the throne, he came into possession of a copy of the poem of the *Ring* containing Wagner's preface, with its final words: "Will this Prince be found?" The royal youth resolved that if ever possible, he would be that Prince.

On March 10, 1864, the opportunity came with his sudden accession to the throne of Bavaria following the death of his father. On April 14 he gave the instruction to cabinet secretary Franz von Pfistermeister: Find Richard Wagner. As far as was known in Munich, Wagner resided in Penzing. Upon discovering that his quarry had left the Penzing home three weeks earlier, Pfistermeister so notified his king by telegram. The dismayed king answered by letter, instructing the secretary to find Wagner as quickly as possible, but not to attract attention. "It is of the utmost importance to me that this long cherished wish of mine shall soon be gratified." On May 1, Pfistermeister arrived in Mariafeld and talked to the Willes, with whom he was already acquainted. From them he learned that Wagner had left the previous day for Stuttgart, and that Karl Eckert, the director of the opera there, was his friend.

King Ludwig II of Bavaria. From *Weltgeschichte in Karakterbildern* by Wilhelm Kienzl.

Wagner had remained in Stuttgart over the weekend to hear the performance of *Don Giovanni* on Sunday afternoon. On Monday evening, the second of May, he was at Eckert's home. A servant brought to him the card of a caller describing its owner as "Von Pfistermeister, *Secretaire aulique de S.M. le roi de Bavière* (Secretary to His Majesty, the King of Bavaria)."

No one could have said that Wagner was "born yesterday." He knew a trick when he saw one. He answered as impecunious debtors from time immemorial have often answered calls from their creditors: The servant followed instructions and advised that Herr Wagner was not in. But there was no escape. Upon returning to his hotel, filled with dread and apprehension, fearing arrest and detention, he halfheartedly began to pack his trunk, preparing to travel to the Rauhe Alb with Weissheimer who had ordered a carriage for the following morning.

Presently a waiter brought in a visitor's card with the same inscription. Wagner initially refused to see him, but upon the visitor's persistent demands, he yielded. Weissheimer excused himself and stepped outside. He waited for what seemed an interminable length of time until finally the visitor left. He then returned to the room and found his friend completely overcome. He showed Weissheimer a valuable diamond ring, which Pfistermeister had said was the king's own ring. On the table was a photograph of the new ruler of Bavaria, ring and photograph both having been left for Wagner by the visitor. The overwhelmed Wagner could only mutter, "That this has happened to me — and that it happened now!" Then he broke down completely, threw his arms around Weissheimer's neck, and wept uncontrollably.

16

Cosima

APART FROM THE RING and the photograph, Pfistermeister brought to Wagner a message of much greater value. The king, he said, was Wagner's most ardent admirer, being fully familiar with his writings; everything he required would be available to him and his *Ring des Nibelungen* would be produced in Munich. The import of the entire conversation had been that Wagner's monetary cares were over; that he would be able to complete his life's work in the peace and comfort he so desperately needed. The king would remain good to his word, but in truth, Wagner's struggles were not over. Only one chapter of them had ended; another was soon to begin.

Ludwig had not reckoned with the enormity of Wagner's unpaid obligations. Wagner must have been aware that there were, lurking throughout the land, benefactors who had written off the debts, not desiring to pursue them against the great composer, or who had never, or only half expected, repayment to begin with. It would have been characteristic of him to give little thought to the possibility that many would now say, with justification, that if debts were being repaid they would happily accept their due. In time, the line of creditors seemed endless, and endlessly vexatious. And, as would soon become obvious, there was other baggage Wagner carried that could not be left behind.

The morning following his meeting with Pfistermeister, Wagner wrote an effusive letter of thanks to the king, assuring him that his life, "to its last poetry, its last tones" belonged now to his exalted king and benefactor. Late that afternoon he left with Pfistermeister by train for Munich. The following day he had his first conference with the king.

Ludwig assured Wagner that he was the "sole source of delight from my tenderest youth onwards," and that in repayment, he would now do everything necessary to make up to the composer for what he had suffered in the past: "The mean cares of everyday life I will banish from you forever." The following day Wagner wrote to Mathilde that the king was "the ideal fulfillment of my desires," offering everything needed for a life of creativity and production of his works. The king wanted Wagner to have a place in which they could converse freely, rather than under the watchful eye of scheming courtiers and other enemies of his monarchy, of whom there were many. Hence he made available for Wagner's use during the coming summer months the Villa Pellet on nearby Lake Starnberg. It was but a short distance from Berg, one of the king's own residences.

The promised funds came quickly. On May 7 Wagner wrote Heinrich Porges that he would be in Vienna in a few days to try to settle the most pressing of his obligations. The means for doing this was the first gift from the king in the amount of 4,000 florins,* plus a yearly stipend in that amount. More, much more, was to come. But Wagner's natural bent and habits of a lifetime would not yield to changed circumstances. First, his correspondence, like communications of most harried debtors to both friends and creditors, was often contradictory and at odds with facts, boasting of new wealth, or pleading severe limitations of it, as it suited his purpose. Even more seriously, with tremendous outstanding debts, he was still congenitally unable to renounce the luxuries to which he had become accustomed as a pauper. Much of the king's largess with money from the Bavarian treasury went for more of them.

There was, for one thing, the composer's need for a fine piano. Returning to Vienna, on May 10th to retrieve certain belongings and to settle some affairs, he was distressed to find that his Erard had been sold to pay creditors. The king promptly obtained from Karl Bechstein, manufacturer of an equally fine piano, a made to order specimen which he gave to Wagner on May 22, for his 51st birthday.

But the Erard was not the last instrument to be given Wagner directly from the maker. Benefits apparently accrued to the donors as well as to the recipient. Gracing the main salon in the "Haus Wahnfried," his former home in Bayreuth, now a Wagner museum, is a Steinway grand piano. It was a gift from that American firm in 1876 on the occasion of the first *Ring* performance. Its maker's name fully emblazoned thereon, it is visible to, and often inspected by, several thousands of visitors every summer.

Steward Spencer, in Wagner Remembered (2000), offers the following as helpful in understanding some relative values of monetary units: 1 Austrian florin = 2 marks; 1 thaler = 3 marks. Further, currencies were, in the year 2000, said to be worth approximately 15 times less than in the 1850s. Hence, the 4,000 florins mentioned above would have amounted then to 8,000 marks; in the year 2000, to about 120,000 marks. This, at the exchange rates of 2000, might vary between $70,000 and $90,000 U.S.

Upon returning to Munich, he took possession of the Villa Pellet, where he remained through the summer. He met with the king daily at the nearby royal residence of Berg, where plans were made for the future completion of Wagner's works and schedules adopted for their production. Otherwise the conversations turned mainly on Wagner's other favorite subjects: himself, his struggles and his writings.

That Ludwig was a highly intelligent young man, there can be little doubt. Prince Chlodwig Hohenlohe-Schillingsfürst, who served as president of the Council of Bavaria for four years beginning in 1866, and as German chancellor for six years beginning in 1894, described the new king in a diary entry on April 15, 1865: "His is a noble and poetic nature and his manner is so particularly attractive because one feels that his courtesy is the natural expression of a truly kind heart. He has plenty of brains, as well as character." And Bismarck, who knew him from 1863 to the end of the king's life in 1886, said of him, "He always gave me the impression of a clear headed ruler," and praised his consciousness of kingship and many-sided knowledge.[1]

But the king had been sheltered from many of the basic aspects of life, a circumstance doubly dangerous for this young man. He was homosexual, and did not quite know how to cope with the feelings stirring within him. His diaries, commencing in 1869, tell of his torments and hopeless attempts to restrain his propensities. It was at one time suggested, or hinted, by some of Wagner's many enemies that his friendship with the king included acquiescence in the king's sexual drives. Such a possibility may be safely and totally disregarded. Wagner's life is an open book. The extensive correspondence between Wagner and the king has been long published. There is no hint in it of such a relationship. The extravagance and effusiveness of the language is not unusual, either for Wagner in his prolific letter writing in general, nor for the style of address to the king by any minister or supplicant.

Further there is the almost daily account of Wagner's longing for and courting of women during the few days before being joined by Cosima von Bülow, which, as we shall see, occurred in late June. He kept almost continual company with Cosima thereafter. There is moreover an entry of Wagner in his "Brown Book," a diary he kept beginning in 1865, which, unlike many of his writings, was intended only for himself and Cosima. The entry dated April 1873 is to all appearances a quickly dashed off reflection: "What we cannot ever or in any language understand about the Greek way, is what wholly separates us from it, e.g. their love — in — pederasty."[2]

By the end of the month he was beginning to feel the need of past companionships. Despite his proclivity to alienate so many acquaintances, friendship, male almost as much as female, was vital to him. He had, however, as by now may have become clear, a curious yardstick by which to measure friendships, namely the willingness of the friend to work for his cause, and if need be, to sacrifice his own interest for Wagner's. This willingness was his definition of loyalty. His three best friends in Vienna had been Tausig, Cornelius and Heinrich Porges, the latter's brother Friedrich being of the second rank at best. It was now time to renew old acquaintances. By letter from Starnberg on May 28 he called on one of his two close Jewish friends, Heinrich Porges. Before looking more closely at that summons, it is worth a passing glance at the then-current state of his anti–Semitic mindset. It had showed itself frequently in correspondence in the months prior to his enthusiastic reception of Heinrich Porges into his small circle of favorites, and his happy reunion with Tausig.

During the period of his greatest vicissitudes, his wanderings after leaving the Asyl in Zurich in August 1858, there were matters more pressing to him than his anger toward *the Jews*. From the appearance of Tausig in April 1858 until his last letter to Minna dated November 8, 1864, there are 149 letters to her. They are filled alternately with accounts of his activities, personal health problems, and solicitude for Minna's health and financial well being. From the letters alone, he is obviously making every effort to smooth matters between them. Only two mention his favorite whipping boys, *the Jews,* but they suffice to show that the antipathy is still there.

Six months after leaving Minna, on the 6 of February, he wrote her about attacks of an unspecified nature on concerts by Liszt. The attacks apparently provoked the ire of Liszt's son-in-law Bülow. They had also obviously irked Minna. Don't worry about it, said Wagner; "the consequences seem to be turning out quite well: the young Jews were furious, but he impressed everybody." Liszt, continued Wagner, was in a state of ill humor, but it probably was not due as much to the "scurrilities of the newspaper Jews (to which you might pay less attention)" as it was to other matters.[3] Liszt's own anti–Semitism should not escape notice. In a publication of 1881, *The Gypsy in Music,* he termed the Jews "sullen, servile, cruel and avaricious."[4]

On February 9, 1862, just days before Minna, unannounced, joined her husband in Biebrich, he wrote her about some acquaintances whom he did not think were still in the neighborhood; Alvine Frommmann, for one, "with her terror of the king; the Jews no doubt, too, and reporters, and God knows what besides."[5]

We turn from Wagner's pronouncements on *the Jews* to his appeal to a particular Jew, Heinrich Porges. Porges, at this time, was engaged primarily in teaching music. On the twenty-eighth of May Wagner wrote him from Starnberg: "Now let us be serious. My young king wants me to have everything I need. I need a secretary, but of the kind I need." Wagner then explained what that meant, and it involved business correspondence, manuscripts, literary and musical fair copies, arrangements of scores, etc. "Do you wish to take this on?" It might serve him better, he told Porges, than the "dreary business" of giving lessons. The work would occupy Porges only occasionally, he was told. Though it would keep him busy at times, he would have plenty of opportunity to give lessons if he so chose.

Wagner offered his friend 400 thalers a year when he boarded in Wagner's own home; 600 when he must provide his own board. Porges, he said, was welcome to stay with him both in his temporary residence and his permanent one when completed, and he would have the use of a piano. By way of stressing the generosity of the proffered salary, the composer offered comparisons of it with that of Bülow. Moreover, Wagner could help his friend exploit his literary activity, and had no compunctions about extolling the advantages of association with Richard Wagner. "What does Vienna have to offer you?" he asks rhetorically.

Porges was indeed a writer more than a musician. Wagner's reason for extending the offer to Porges he made abundantly clear, and there is little reason to doubt him:

> If you accept you will make me very, very happy! You know of course that the secretary is merely an excuse for having my friend here with me. If you wish to bind your life to mine (and how long will this life of mine last?), you will, I hope, never have cause to regret it. And how important, how splendid, and how reassuring it will be for me always to have my witty and friendly companion here beside me!
>
> And so—shake hands upon it, and have no scruples about accepting. I know what I am doing, for the friendly will which now provides for me wills it so. I would beg you therefore to take up your appointment punctually of the 1st of June. Your room is ready, and I know you will like it here from the moment you arrive. It is utterly delightful!... Do not make me wait beyond the 1st of June. Here in my splendid isolation I yearn desperately for someone of your stamp, and—given the kind of man I am—I suffer from this deprivation.[6]

He told Porges to ask Tausig to hand over the orchestral parts to his concerts, gave advice as to how they are to be shipped, and told him also to bring with him various books of Wagner's scattered around the residences of Tausig and Cornelius.

He expressed some concerns about Cornelius: "There is something about him that mystifies me." Wagner apparently had previously tried without success to also induce him to share his new life. Nor was this apparently the first attempt to lure Porges. He said it offended him strangely that both Porges and Cornelius were "doubtful and hesitant, ignoring my offer in favor of the pitiful lives that you both are leading!" He had advice for Porges's brother Friedrich, who was currently administering the receipts from productions of Wagner's operas, as Wagner was still in need of whatever funds he could get. He offered Porges "a thousand good wishes to your dear, loyal family," and concluded the letter by advising his prospective secretary as to the best means of travel to Starnberg where a boat would be dispatched to bring him to the Villa Pellet. "Adieu! Come soon! Won't you?"

Porges did not accept the offer, though from his close association with Wagner during the remaining 19 years of the composer's life one might infer that he might as well have. And apparently, as Wagner predicted, he never regretted it.

The letter is interesting primarily in that it is addressed to a Jew, neither a converted nor a "half" Jew, but one who is unequivocally Jewish. But it should not be supposed that Porges was his favorite among the three Vienna friends. There is at least an equal if not greater desire for the company of Cornelius. On May 31 Wagner, from Starnberg, wrote Cornelius in similar vein, begging and cajoling as in the case of Porges, but also threatening: Wagner considered Cornelius's behavior

> insulting.... Either you accept my invitation without delay, and settle down with me for the rest of your life's days ... or — you scorn me.... In the latter case I in turn repudiate you completely and utterly, and shall certainly not include you in whatever arrangements I may make for my life in the future.... My present relationship with you torments me dreadfully. It must either become complete or else break altogether![7]

Cornelius, unlike Porges or Tausig, fancied himself also as a composer and was writing an opera, *Der Cid*. Wagner told Cornelius that his own work on *Die Meistersinger* would no more impinge on his work on *Cid* than the other way around, and even offered the benefit of his advice to the would-be composer.

But Cornelius knew his older friend all too well. He declined the offer. On the fifteenth of June he wrote his brother Karl that Wagner "has treated his best friends in Vienna like bootblacks." Tausig was married, well into his career as a concert pianist, and not a likely candidate to relocate at that point in his life, or to stay and serve the Master anywhere. In not too many years however, as we will see, Tausig would perform important service for him, as would Cornelius.

He was getting nowhere with his male friends, but even more he needed female companionship, if only a housekeeper. He was in the Villa Pellet near Starnberg only through the summer and would be moving to permanent quarters in Munich in September. He complained to Eliza Wille that he soon have to "transplant myself once again to Munich, to set up house, to bother about knives, forks, dishes, pots and pans, bed linen and so on!" A grim prospect indeed. So he turned to Mathilde Maier, whom we last saw in Mainz, where she was introduced to Wagner at the home of his publisher. He asked her to be his housemate and housekeeper. The request apparently caused her some embarrassment, and further, her mother did not want her to leave.

On June 22 he wrote her again and, as usual, was desperate for help. He must, he said, have someone run the house for him. He had invited the Bülows, who were expected shortly, and would stay for two months. But he still needed someone to take over the domestic duties. He could not bear to have no "womanly being" at his side, no educated person to talk to. It would be under the most respectable of circumstances. He was living downstairs, she was to live upstairs. As for her mother, if Mathilde were to marry, Wagner asked rhetorically, she would have to leave her, would she not? He pleaded for a favorable answer. "I beg you," he concluded.

A few days later he sent a letter to Mathilde, but addressed to her mother, Josephine, with the request that Mathilde deliver it. Wouldn't she, Josephine, have the courage to face the world and entrust her daughter to him? he enquires. He promises that Mathilde would be truly cared for and protected against all suspicion or taint. Nonetheless, he added, would it not be possible "without nurturing an impious wish," in the eventuality of his wife's death, to sue for the daughter's hand in marriage?[8]

However on June 29 he wrote Mathilde again, but in an entirely different vein. There had been a sudden change of heart. There had been enough turmoil and roiling of emotions, he said. All he wanted was peace and quiet. He asked her not to give the letter to Josephine. He had not fully considered how it would upset her when he sent it, and for that he apologized. She need have no concern for him either, he said, as he would soon have visitors staying; he hoped that in the fall he could persuade his former maid from Geneva to work for him. The earlier letter had not been delivered to Josephine, and never was.

What had happened between the twenty-fifth and the twenty-ninth of June to cause this sudden change in tone? It was an event that would be of momentous significance in Wagner's life and work, even in the area of our more narrow interest, his anti–Semitism. The entire Bülow family, as we have seen, had been invited to the Villa Pellet. Hans was quite ill, but Cosima came alone with her two daughters. Hans did not arrive until July 7. It is beyond doubt that during those few days Richard and Cosima consummated their long, silent love. The following year, in April 1866, a daughter, Isolde, was born to Cosima.

Whatever uncertainty may have existed then in the public mind about the child's paternity, today the evidence appears convincing that Isolde was the daughter of Richard Wagner. But Hans von Bülow, until his dying day, believed, or claimed to believe, that Isolde was his. In letters, in conversations, and in his will, he affirmed it. Cosima insisted on it herself, at least to the king and presumably to her father, Franz Liszt, whose disapproval she had already earned. But the day came, in 1914, when Isolde demanded to be recognized as the daughter of the great composer, then deceased for 31 years, and thus entitled to her share of his estate upon the death of Cosima.

Cosima refused to make the acknowledgment, and Isolde, already estranged from her mother, brought suit. Cosima, despite her antipathy to Isolde, affirmed under oath at that time, that "from June 12th to October 12th 1864, I had lived in intimate relations with no one but Wagner." Inasmuch as this was detrimental to the result she wanted, we must assume it was true in fact. Evidence from the housekeeper at Starnberg, however, to the effect that she shared Bülow's room with him during his visits, compelled a decision in favor of the even stronger legal presumption that the mother's lawful husband was the father.[9]

The intimacy would continue in the Villa Pellet and thereafter in Munich, and would finally be legitimized in marriage in Lucerne. Wagner had finally found the soul mates he wanted, both in a willing and even devoted prince, and now in a "womanly being." Just how much Bülow knew shortly thereafter, how much he learned only later, exactly when he learned it, and just how much he endured in silence, are matters that cannot now be resolved. Liszt knew quite a bit and was incensed. He counseled Wagner that his daughter would not leave Bülow, and in Starnberg and later in Munich tried to discourage the affair, first with one, then with the other of the couple. It strained the Liszt-Wagner relationship to the breaking point.

On the first of September, 1865, Wagner, as though speaking to Cosima, spilled out in his diary, the Brown Book, his pent-up rage and long smoldering resentment against Cosima's father. Bitterly, he mimics her explanations to him of her absences, as well as all the contrivances of Liszt to convince his daughter that he, Wagner did not love her at all. "He told me a year ago of course 'it would turn out like this, — He would treat me with contempt.'" Wagner's imagination continued to torture him. He visualized the future, more letters from Rome, where Liszt now lived, and where, four weeks previously, he had acquired clerical status as an abbé. Always, Wagner said, there were more excuses as to why she could not join him at the moment. "I shall finally come to hate my friend completely!" wrote Wagner in his private diary, as though writing to Cosima. "I do not believe

Left: Hans von Bülow. From *Cosima Wagner: Extraordinary Daughter of Franz Liszt* by Alice Hunt Sokoloff. *Right:* Cosima von Bülow, about age 30, after George R. Marek: *Cosima Wagner*. Nationalarchiv der Richard-Wagner-Stifiung, Bayreuth.

in his love. He has never loved. He who loves can complain and does not enter into relationships with the Good God.... To me all this Catholic rubbish is repugnant to the very depths of my soul. Anyone who takes refuge in that must have a great deal to atone for.... Your father is repugnant to me. And when I was able to bear him there was more Christianity in my blind indulgence than in all his piety."[10]

Even after the marriage between Cosima and Wagner in 1870, it would be six more years before a reconciliation between Wagner and Liszt could be fully effected. It had started with a graciously worded invitation by Wagner to Liszt to attend the ceremony for the laying of the cornerstone of his new theater in Bayreuth in 1872, one, that for a number of reasons, Liszt did not accept.

17

The First *Tristan*

THE NEXT SIX YEARS in Wagner's life, the period from May 1864 until the beginning of the 1870s, were eventful, even by the standards of his event filled life, though not necessarily so from our narrow perspective. Wagner's close contacts with Jewish friends and acquaintances, concurrently with his continued railings against *the Jews*, gain little further illumination during these years. The most instructive period of that aspect of his life will not begin until the very early 1870s, and will thereafter continue until the time of his death. We will see in those years Wagner's most complex and interesting relationships with Jews, for which his prior ones seem to have been but an important prelude.

During the remainder of the 1860s, his friendships with Tausig and Porges continued, and some issues between him and each of them bear mention. Other events in Wagner's life assumed a much greater importance and cannot be ignored if there is to be a proper evaluation of his later Jewish relationships. There was very soon, however, one contact with a Jew which, despite its brevity, is worth a passing mention.

During the summer of 1864, Wagner's friendship with the king brought him a number of requests for intercession with the monarch on various issues. One of these supplicants was the Jewish socialist Ferdinand Lassalle. Influenced in part by Karl Marx, Lassalle had developed a theory of state socialism. He was influential in introducing the German workers as a significant element in the ongoing struggle between Bismarck and the Prussian liberals, and was instrumental in establishing the first workers' party in Germany. But the help he sought from Wagner was not political.

It was, rather, regarding an affair of the heart. Lassalle was deeply in love with a young woman named Helene von Dönniges, who happened to be the daughter of an official with the Bavarian consulate in Geneva. The dictatorial Dönniges, for reasons not now clear, strongly disapproved of Lassalle. He scotched the affair by keeping his daughter, despite her being of the full age of majority, confined at home and added the further indignity of reading her mail. The incensed Lassalle had a number of influential friends and used many of them in attempts to intercede with the king. One of the friends was Bülow, who was asked by Lassalle to have his "powerful friend" Wagner also make an overture in his behalf. Bülow, despite his own anti–Semitism, had unbounded respect and admiration for Lassalle. In mid–August Lassalle met personally with Wagner in Starnberg. The king was away from Munich at the time, and Wagner agreed to bring the subject up to the king upon his return.

Wagner's true reaction to Lassalle may be more accurately reflected in his letter three weeks later to Eliza Wille. By then much had happened. The distraught and distracted Lassalle had sent a telegram to Wagner withdrawing his request for intercession, implying that Helene had broken off the relationship. Nonetheless he engaged in a duel with a rival and was fatally wounded. Wagner, in his letter to Eliza, mentioned the death of the "unfortunate man," and his appeal for Wagner to intervene. "I am regarded, you see, simply as an all-powerful favorite.... I had never met Lassalle until then; and on that occasion I disliked him immensely; it was a typical love story inspired by sheer vanity and false pathos. I saw in him a typical example of the great men of the future, a type that I can only call Germanic-Judaic."[1] The comment can best be understood, perhaps, by reference to many of Wagner's letters and some prose essays bemoaning the imminent, if not already accomplished, complete victory of Judaism over the Germans, if not all of Europe.

Nonetheless, nothing about Wagner is so simple. In his letter to Eliza Wille he introduced this subject in a sudden switch from a previous comment: "You see, with me nothing goes smoothly! Not even a case like that of Lassalle's death." Then follows his remark about the "unfortunate man." Of what it was that was supposed to go smoothly, and as to whether he was actually sympathetic to Lassalle's request, we are given no clue. As with much else about his writings, essays and correspondence alike, we left to guess.

It is not possible to imagine a Richard Wagner without struggles and painful frustrations. His inherent nature, on the one hand, and that of the rest of humanity, on the other, guaranteed conflict. But after May 1864, his difficulties took on another nature. There were oppressive requirements for money, but the days of poverty were over. The prince that he longed for had come to his rescue, and he was truly Wagner's soul mate. Wagner had what must have seemed to him to be unlimited funds at his disposal. But the prince, now king, had to cope with his own adversaries: political enemies who, whether for good or selfish motives, sought his restraint or removal; newspapers that thrived on reports of malevolent deeds of the composer and his followers; sinister activities and malicious gossip; and the very real circumstance that the funds of the Bavarian treasury were not unlimited.

All of it began to come to a head upon Wagner's removal to Munich, where the king first rented for him, then purchased, property at number 21 Briennerstrasse. Under the terms of the agreement entered into in early October with the king, Wagner was to occupy, rent free for three years, this stately home on one of Munich's most prestigious streets. The elegant structure was half hidden by trees and surrounded by a lush and exotic garden in which he seemed to take the greatest pleasure. According to the French writer Édouard Schuré, "the salon was decorated with dark wall hangings, luxurious rugs, paintings and statuettes barely visible in the mysterious half light."[2]

The rent paid by Ludwig to the owner, courtesy of the Bavarian treasury, was 3,000 florins a year. In return for that plus 15,000 gulden with which to furnish the home, he was to complete the *Ring* in three years, during which he was to receive an additional yearly amount of 2,000 florins. The originally agreed-upon yearly stipend of 4,000 florins considered, he was receiving 27,000 florins for completion of the *Ring* within three years. The work was to be the property of the king — never mind that it had already, unknown to the king, been sold to Wesendonck. At Wagner's request, Wesendonck, ever ready to accommodate his former tenant, renounced his rights.

Until the end of 1864 events unfolded smoothly enough. But anger and jealousy that would later raise their threatening heads, were building. Not all of it was unjustified, nor was it unforeseeable. By November the king had resolved to build the new theater Wagner required for production of the *Ring*. The following month Wagner wrote to his co-revolutionary friend of long standing, Gottfried Semper, the renowned architect, asking that he undertake the project. It was also necessary to train the singers in a new style of singing, an essentially Germanic one, as opposed to the traditional Italian and French. It was, in short, to be "Wagnerian." With the help of the still faithful Bülow, detailed specifications for a new music school were prepared and published in the spring of 1865. Interesting as it was as an abstract document, in many contemporaries it fostered resentment and alarm: in music teachers, musicians, singers, and conductors, among others.

Among the others were the politicians, courtiers and would-be courtiers who may always be found encircling a seat of power. These would

Wagner's home in Munich at number 21 Briennerstrasse, from October 1864 until December 10, 1865. From *Richard Wagner: Sein Leben, sein Werk, seine Welt* by Julius Kapp.

undoubtedly have sought to exercise control over the presumably pliable young king in any event, but the presence of this usurper from outside ignited special fervor in them. Even more incendiary was the influx of friends and cohorts of Wagner. Not always were the Wagnerians the most diplomatic or tactful in their handling of this delicate situation. More and more the vested interests in Munich, musical, literary, theatrical and political, merged into a common front.

There was perhaps justification for Wagner to exercise his influence with the king in the political sphere, as a matter mainly of self defense and protection of the interests so important to him. Whether there was wisdom in it is another matter. The press was almost entirely hostile to him. Not only indiscretions in fact, but words or deeds so perceived by others were heralded by the press as matters of world shaking import. A particular misunderstanding between the king and Wagner in late 1864, causing a minor rift, was magnified manyfold. No one could openly attack, or even criticize, the king. Wagner, however, was not only fair game, but a tempting target. It was he who was thought to be poisoning the mind of their beloved majesty; he who was undermining His Highness's kingship, and working his sinister and insidious ways on the innocence and the ideals of their noble king.

Wagner fought back the only way he knew how: with his pen. He did so gamely, but was no match for the combined might of the press and the enemies at court. His past as a revolutionary, as a socialist, as a squanderer of other people's money, and now the luxury in which he was ensconced on the Briennerstrasse, were all thrown back at him. In the meantime, the line of long-forgotten creditors was lengthening.

In their efforts to alienate the king from him, his enemies failed. Pushed to decide whether Wagner should stay or go, the king begged him to stay. It was apparent, then and later, that the king needed Wagner at least as much as Wagner needed the king, and probably more. In their efforts to drive him from Munich, however, Wagner's enemies were to be successful before the year of 1865 ended.

But before that denouement, there was to be a production of Wagner's long neglected *Tristan und Isolde.* After preliminary preparations, including arrangements for their appearances in the lead roles by Ludwig and Malvina Schnorr, the first of three performances was set for May 15. Bülow was to conduct. But even this event was not to be without the usual Wagnerian complications. At a rehearsal on May 2, the overworked, overwrought, fatigued Bülow asked the theater personnel to enlarge the orchestral area, this opera requiring of necessity a larger orchestra. He was advised that such a change would require the sacrifice of many stalls, front row seats of prime customers. The angered Prussian was at his wit's end. "What does it matter," he bellowed, "if we have thirty *Schweinehunde* [hound dogs] more or less in the place?"

The remark was fodder made to order for the newspapers. It took five days, but on the seventh of the month it exploded and was exploited prominently by the first of the journals. One featured a cartoon of Bülow conducting to an audience consisting, in the front two rows, of hound dogs of every variety. An attempt at apology was of no avail. The Bavarian papers gleefully made capital of the misstep by the "arrogant Prussian," and used the remark as an excuse for a relentless attempt to drive him out of the city and thus cancel or delay the *Tristan* performance. Fortunately for him and for Wagner, the king was determined to hear *Tristan*, and held steady in his support for both men and for the performance.

A ghost from the past also came home to haunt Wagner. It will be recalled that following the 1860 concerts in Paris, Wagner's heavy losses were made up in part by a generous donation of 5,000 francs by Marie Schwabe, an English lady, and Jewish, not acquainted with him. She had responded to a request from one who did know him, Malwida von Meysenbug. It will be recalled also that, although Mme. Schwabe intended the funds as a gift, Wagner insisted on giving a note payable in a year. Not surprisingly, at the end of the year, Wagner asked for an extension, not from Mme. Schwabe (who was not in Paris at the time), but from Malwida, who assured him that her friend considered the funds to be a donation. And so it may have been. But upon hearing that bottomless funds from the king were being disbursed by Wagner to many creditors, Marie Schwabe, now living in Rome, forwarded her note to a Munich lawyer, asking that he place it in line for payment.

In March, almost two months before the scheduled *Tristan* performance, the attorney wrote to Wagner asking that he pay serious attention to his demand for the 5,000 francs, counseling that failure to do so could create embarrassment for him during the preparations for his great opera. Whether purposely, due to inability to pay, or negligently, in the frenzy of the preparations for the opera, the letter was ignored.

On the eleventh of May there was a dress rehearsal before 600 invited guests. On the thirteenth there followed a second, closed rehearsal. For the first public performance on the fifteenth, friends from all parts of Europe converged. These included Leopold Damrosch and Heinrich Porges, now living in Prague, but not Peter Cornelius. Porges had come with his bride, Wilhelmine, as part of their honeymoon trip. Cornelius had come to join Wagner in Munich on December 30, but left shortly thereafter to attend to the production of his own opera, *Der Cid*, in Weimar. Relations between him and Wagner were becoming increasingly strained. Tausig, temporarily, was not on Wagner's horizon.

On the morning of the first scheduled *Tristan* performance, to Wagner's great shock and consternation, he was informed that his lavish furnishings in the Briennerstrasse home were under seizure. Twenty-four hundred florins were needed to release them. He frantically asked that the sum be paid from the treasury and the same morning received word that it would be paid. Cosima was present and, at Wagner's request, accompanied by her oldest daughter, Daniela, aged five, and by the governess of her children, she went to the royal treasury.

She expected to collect paper money. The surly officials were apparently determined to make things as unpleasant for her as possible. Paper money was not available, she was advised, the money would be paid in coin, in several very heavy sacks. Cosima sent the governess for two cabs into which she helped raise the sacks. One of the officials seemed apologetic, expressing admiration for her courage and sorrow that her friendship with Wagner had caused her so much trouble. But the funds had been paid,[3] resulting, in the days that followed, in more shrill outrage, chortling, and cartoons by the press.

The same day as that crisis hit, a second blow fell, one that could not be so quickly resolved. Ludwig Schnorr arrived at the theater to announce, through his tears, that his wife, Malvina, the Isolde of the opera, was hoarse and could not sing. The performance had to be postponed; for how long, no one could say.

This was a shattering blow to Wagner. Later that day, in abject misery, he penned a letter to the king, unusually brief, but pouring out his heart to one of a very few persons who may have been as desolated as he by the forced postponement. As to the delay itself, he claims, he is indifferent. What causes his grief is the disappointment of others, the tears of Schnorr, and especially the dreary hours he is now causing his dear king. As for himself, "I am of no more value in this world. My life has for too long been sacrificed to baseness. My look into the hearts of men shows me an abyss that I cannot fill with any hope." The king answered the same day, with the optimism of youth, "There are many noble and good people for whom it is a true joy to live and to create. And yet you say you are worth nothing in this world?... Love helps everyone to bear and endure. You will in the end be victorious."[4]

Many of the visitors were forced to leave at once, but a number of stalwart friends stayed on for about a week, hoping for a short delay only. The group, including Porges and his wife, were royally entertained at Wagner's home and treated to a number of excerpts from as yet unperformed operas.

It was June 10 before the first *Tristan* performance took place. Despite some hissing, it was a tremendous success and met with resounding applause. For Wagner, a magnificent performance by Ludwig Schnorr of that extremely difficult role was success enough. He could not find words enough to praise him. Those familiar with the opera know very well the difficulties of the role, and the dearth of tenors over the decades that have been fully equal to the challenge. Considering the further difficulty of satisfying Wagner's insatiable demands for excellence in vocal control, in nuance of expression, and in diction, such praise is remarkable. It renders frustrating indeed the absence, at that time, of recording mechanisms.

Wagner could not, at that time, express in words his joy in the artistry of his tenor. But suddenly and tragically, the singer died on July 21, a month after his last Tristan performance. Not until three years later could Wagner find the words to convey his love and admiration for the man and his performance as Tristan, particularly in the severely demanding third act. In an essay devoted largely to Schnorr's interpretation and rendition of that act, written in 1868, he wrote of "the incomparable greatness" of the artistic achievement, of the "miracle of the art of musical and dramatic performance," of the "inexhaustibility of the gift" of this genius, and of the voice that was "full, mellow and lustrous." A new spring of hope, said Wagner, had arrived in his life.[5]

18

Exile from Munich

THE OPERA WAS PERFORMED three times, the last on June 19. A little less than six months later, Wagner was forced to leave Munich. The tearful king had been forced to compel it. It was supposed to be a temporary absence, but as one gleeful newspaper predicted, Wagner never returned to Munich to live.

The events leading up to his December 10 exile are a miasma of bureaucratic infighting, petty jealousies, base journalism and malice. Wagner's biographer Ernest Newman, no wide eyed, uncritical admirer, has little difficulty in drawing a sharp division between the man and the music. For the music his admiration was unbounded. For the man it was quite severely restrained. He has, nonetheless, succinctly summarized the events of the first eight months of 1865, finding Wagner "more sinned against than sinning."

The many courtiers, including Pfistermeister, and numerous others whose names are for the most part of no relevance to our scope of interest, sometimes vied with each other to gain Wagner's favor and the use of his influence with the king for their projects. This they did by offering support for his interests, the theater and music school in particular. Many sought to undercut Wagner's influence with the king out of fear that their rivals had already gained the advantage with him. Others were still seeking to restore the royal prerogatives for the monarchy that had been lost in the Bavarian revolution of 1848. To that end they sought in vain to use Wagner as a pawn. It seems apparent that they projected on both the king and on Wagner the political mentality, the craving for power and glory, the scheming and plotting, that infected almost everyone around them. They understood neither Wagner nor the king, nor the purely artistic interests of both. Wagner turned a cold shoulder to all such overtures.

One project that Wagner did undertake with the king was the improvement of the salary of musicians. He felt that the high fees of singers were unfairly subsidized by the low salaries of ordinary members of the orchestra. Realizing also that the officials surrounding the king were wholly inadequate to the task, not only of restructuring the musicians' salaries, but of building the theater and music school, he suggested to his royal friend that other help was needed. Predictably, there was rising anger by these officials at the suggestion of their inadequacy and at any further expenditure for Wagner's purposes, no matter that it was for the musicians and not for himself. The king, most reluctantly, was compelled to refuse Wagner's request. It grieved him, he answered the composer, that he was bound by irksome restraints that "the world" put on him, but he assured him that he would do everything "possible and advisable" to comply.

The more determined the king became to carry through with the projected theater, for which Semper was in the process of drawing plans, the more opposition he met from his surrounding coterie. Expressions of short temper between them and Wagner were inevitable. The voice of reason on Wagner's side was the diplomatic Cosima. Still married to Bülow, she seemed now to be spending more time in the Briennerstrasse home than with her husband. She managed to divide her time, albeit unequally, between the two households. With regard to her half life with Wagner, she was obliged on occasion to interject honeyed correspondence, into the vinegar that flowed between him and his antagonists.

In the midst of the growing tension, Wagner had once more to endure a shattering blow, the death, on July 21, of Ludwig Schnorr. Circumstances compel the conclusion that he died from complications brought on by the strains of his Tristan portrayal. The last act is severely demanding. Toward the end of the act, the demands on the singer's voice end, but he is then required to lie on the floor of the stage for an extended period. In this theater there was a chilling draft. It was, not unexpectedly, seen by some as one more aspect of the evil of the opera and its composer. Wagner and Bülow traveled to Dresden for the funeral, but due to various delays, including crowds arriving in that city for a performance of the German Festival Chorus, their cab arrived too late at the burial site. According to Wagner, the driver, responding to Wagner's frantic entreaties, explained that 20,000 singers were in town. To that, said Wagner, he silently responded to himself: "*The* singer has just gone."

At least one other important event in Wagner's life occurred during this month. On July 17, just four days before Schnorr's death, Wagner began to dictate his autobiography to Cosima. It eventually covered the period from his earliest childhood until his call to Munich by King Ludwig. Thereafter, beginning on August 10 he kept a diary, the Brown Book, in which he continued to make entries and notations for the balance of his life. Cosima's own diary recording their daily life together commenced on January 1, 1869, shortly after she went to join him in Lucerne following his "exile" from Munich.

By the end of July 1865, Wagner's frustration was such that he could no longer refrain from injecting himself, against his own instincts, into political matters. Plans for the theater were running into every possible snag. On the part of the king, there was procrastination in choosing which of two plans for it that Semper had laid before him. On the part of the coterie there was a surplus of deceit and chicanery. Wagner and the king were not the only victims. Another was Semper, who had been working tirelessly without written contract or any terms of employment.

Many factors contributed to the final denouement in Munich, not all of which can be laid at the door of the cabal, through malice or otherwise. Wagner's home on the Briennerstrasse was a showcase of the finest satins and silks. Pear gray ruffles bordered the ceiling. Cornices of window curtains, mirror frames, and pictures were decorated with pink satin and tied with white satin bows. From the ceiling, a rosette of white satin was trimmed with an off-white lace. It was all ordered from the same milliner whose letters from Wagner were surreptitiously taken from her and made the objects of mirth, extortion and publication. He had attempted to keep the dealings with her secret, but there were no secrets. There were, of necessity, visits to the Briennerstrasse home by officials of court through whom Wagner was often obliged to communicate with the king. They can be forgiven if they did not completely grasp that Wagner considered these surroundings a necessity.

It was only a matter of time before an eruption of the well-known volcanic fury of the volatile composer. The steps leading up to it were initiated by Wagner himself. Unsatisfied with the funds committed for his use thus far, he made new requests for sums sufficient to raise the hackles of the most moderate of his enemies. Their opposition was not always measured, and it soon escalated to a reflexive attempt to undermine the man and everything he desired.

Wagner's response, heated enough at its inception, was to evolve into a rigorous campaign to persuade the king to reorganize his cabinet; to advise him as to who should stay, who should go, who should replace whom, and which department was to have jurisdiction over what functions. His only concern, of course, was to ease the way for the completion of his work, the construction of the music school and of the theater. Any other affairs of state, or of the normal functions of government, were apparently not considered at all. One of these normal functions involved a threatened war between Austria and Prussia and the decision as to whether Bavaria should align itself with Austria or remain neutral.

The ultimate decision, it must be noted, was a poor one. War came a year later, in June 1866, and Bavaria cast its lot with Austria. It ended quickly. On July 3 the Prussians crushed their Austrian enemies at König-grätz, and one week later finished off the Bavarians at Kissingin. The Austrians, with their Bavarian allies, sued for peace. Bavaria got off with a stiff payment in reparations and the loss of some territory.

By all objective evidence, the king was not the simple minded, naive young man that he was sometimes assumed to be by his ministers, nor as he is often still portrayed. Wagner's influence over him stopped at the boundary that separated their joint desire for the fruition of Wagner's work from the affairs of government. On November 27 he wrote Wagner that after calm reflection, he had decided that this was not the time to fire the officials as Wagner wished. Acknowledging that Pfistermeister, one of the major targets of Wagner's efforts, was "insignificant and stupid," and that he would not be allowed to remain much longer, the king determined that it was not advisable to remove him at that time. Nonetheless, emphasized the king, Wagner still had his love and backing and his assurance that all would work out well in the end.

In effecting the changes he advocated, Wagner was singularly unsuccessful. No good came of it, but much harm did, as it was inevitable that such advice would find its way to the ears of the intended victims. Worse, the king's assurances were not enough for Wagner. He wanted total victory. But he was navigating treacherous currents with which he was totally unfamiliar, fighting in a swamp where one misstep could be fatal. Ultimately the misstep occurred. It came in a published letter of the type he had found so useful in the past: anonymous. This one was published on November 29 in a Munich newspaper. It was written in haste and in anger, and without consulting anyone. As with the case of some of his revolutionary tracts in Dresden, and his "Judaism in Music" in Zurich, the anonymity fooled no one. It purported to be from one outside of Wagner's circle, as a disinterested party. It lauded both Wagner and the king and the purity of their ideals, while vigorously attacking both the deed and the motives of certain officials, who were not named but were nonetheless easily identifiable.

At the time of the letter's publication the king was in the royal castle of Hohenschwangau near Füssen, in the foothills of the Alps he so deeply loved. Wagner had already written him on November 26 and 27 urging drastic changes in the cabinet. But before the letter of the 27, he had already mailed to the newspaper his letter for publication, though failing to mention it to the king. Four days after its publication Ludwig wrote Wagner that he was leaving to return to Munich, blaming the furor over the published letter as the precipitant cause and advising that it had embittered the final days of his stay there. He felt, he said, that it was written by one of Wagner's friends, whose intent to help had only hurt their cause. He probably full well knew that the letter had emanated from Wagner himself, who, even more egregiously, had concealed that fact from him. Undoubtedly, though the king had not quite made a final decision, the die was already cast.

The *coup de grâce* to Wagner's position in Munich, a letter dated December 1, had been sent to the king at Hohenschwangau by one of Wagner's most bitter enemies, the minister for foreign affairs, Baron Ludwig von der Pfordten. It was filled with malice toward Wagner, but perhaps no more so than were Wagner's letters filled with hate for the ministers. Von der Pfordten could not shake the king's attachment to Wagner the artist, but he could, and did, undermine his belief that Wagner should remain in Munich. He couched his letter in terms of a choice facing the king, between the love and respect for the people, and the friendship with Wagner.

Upon his return to Munich on December 6, Ludwig was bombarded, as he no doubt feared he would be, by warnings of the danger of this close association with Wagner, and of unrest both at court and in the city at large, due to the huge outlay for the composer and his schemes. The reference to the city beyond the members of the Royal Ministry was probably imaginary. Wagner's music was immensely popular, and the populace there, as is often the case, was largely uninterested in the infighting in court, or in political intrigue generally. The king, fully aware of Wagner's own underhandedness and recklessness in the controversy, still tried to calm the waters, feeling that the situation could still be resolved, but ultimately he succumbed to the inevitable. On the afternoon of the sixth, just hours after his return, his decision was delivered to Wagner: he must leave Munich for six months. The following day Ludwig informed von der Pfordten that the decision was final and would show his people that their love and confidence were of prime importance to him.

Wagner was crushed by this turn of events, but not enough to inhibit a withering verbal blast about Pfistermeister to the king's official messenger. Nor was his pain any greater than that of Ludwig himself. The king no doubt believed that in six months Wagner would return. But Wagner quickly vowed to never again return to Munich, a determination he delayed several months in conveying to Ludwig. Wagner asked that there be no publicity surrounding his departure, and that it be announced instead that he had left for reasons of health. The king promised to do everything in his power to that end, but to that end he had no power at all. The circumstances of his departure were soon known and widely disseminated.

In the early morning of December 10, Wagner left Munich by train. Broken hearted and broken in spirit, he was accompanied on his journey by his servant and his aged dog Pohl. They were seen off at the station only by Cosima, Cornelius, and by Porges and his wife.

Porges had cast his lot with Wagner to a large degree, even if not to the degree Wagner had begged of him. The opening of the projected music school had been tentatively intended for early October 1865. Porges wanted to participate by instructing in piano and lecturing in aesthetics. He also wanted to become editor of a planned newspaper in Munich, the purpose of which would have been to propagate Wagner's aesthetic ideas and interest in his work. Politics, no doubt, would not be a prohibited subject to the extent necessary to support those purposes. When it all seemed to be falling through, after seeing Wagner off to the next phase of his life, Porges and his wife settled again in Vienna. Two years later he was destined to fill both of those desired posts, and many more, in the service of Wagner.

For the next few weeks Wagner traveled about Lake Geneva and the south of France, always on the search for a suitable residence in which to spend the balance of his life. Money was never an object, as he knew the king would stand, with the Bavarian treasury, for any amount required.

Part IV

Lucerne

19

Triebschen

ON THE TWENTY-FOURTH OF JANUARY, Minna, living with her daughter Natalie in Dresden, consulted Dr. Anton Pusinelli, the physician and friend of long standing of both herself and Wagner. The next morning she was found dead in her bedroom by servants. She had suffered throughout her life from a diseased heart and succumbed at age 57 to a heart attack. She and Richard had not seen each other since November 1862, and correspondence between them had been sparse. The agreed payments of support to Minna were among the few obligations on which he had never defaulted.

Despite the bitterness and the invective she heaped upon him in her final years, she refused to bear false witness. When Wagner's enemies in the press, earlier that month, claimed that Wagner had left her penniless, she furnished, at the request of the ever willing Bülow, a written statement of the sufficiency of the allowance she had been receiving. Its publication, however, did little to abate the hatred or the disregard for truth of Wagner's enemies. Wagner received the news of her death by telegram in Marseilles, where it had been forwarded to him through two other temporary abodes. It arrived too late for him to attend the funeral. Whether he would have done so or not, had he known earlier, is a matter only for conjecture.

Between Wagner's departure from Munich on December 10 by the king's order, and February 22, 1866, at least 29 letters and telegrams passed back and forth between the two men. One of the most pressing subjects was the possibility, and desirability, of Wagner's return to Munich. The king yearned for it, but had also to reckon with his duties to the state and to his people. Wagner likewise harbored an obviously sincere and intense attachment for the king. The composer was grateful not only for tremendous assistance rendered thus far, but, more importantly, despite all obstacles, this monarch stood ready and able to bring about performances of the balance of his life's works, some only partially written, and others not even begun.

Nonetheless, on February 22, Wagner wrote to "My beloved and wonderful friend." It was a lengthy and emotional letter, reviewing past events as seen from his rather overwrought perspective, and containing his final and definitive decision not to return to Munich. The king was not ready to have him return at that time in any event, but did harbor a determination that one day it would be possible. Wagner's letter was shattering news for him. The kernel of Wagner's reasoning can perhaps be best seen in one of his final paragraphs:

> My King, I am poisoned by Munich. I still feel a gnawing and searing pain, a creeping ache, as I have never before known, and which was produced by the Munich experience. That is bad ground, my King! And never, never will our work take root there. That is not a seat of "German" art, where the Jews, baptized, and won over by Jesuits, unchastised, teach the "people" and where even the friends of the King, — because they are so loved by Him — can follow, unrestrained, the most shameful slanders.[1]

This is certainly not the only time that Jews and Jesuits were made joint targets of his wrath. Just who these Jews or Jesuits were is something of a mystery. His enemies in chief were Pfistermeister and von der Pfordten. If either was Jewish, it has escaped the notice of historians and biographers, both friendly and unfriendly. Nor, for that matter, is any connection with the Jesuit order to be readily found. It might be well at this juncture, with this unkind cut fresh in mind, to look ahead a bit, at least into the immediate future, at his relationship with the one Jew who was still active in his closest circle at the time, Heinrich Porges.

In Vienna Porges was occupied primarily with preparation of copies of the original score of *Die Walküre (The Valkyrie),* the second of the *Ring* operas. By July 1866 he was again in Munich where he gave private lessons, and with great enthusiasm undertook to write for the benefit of King Ludwig an introduction to *Tristan und Isolde,* the first comprehensive attempt to grasp the psychological development and the ethical foundation of the work. In turn, Wagner put forth great effort to secure steady employment for him. On the first of October 1867, the South German Press, a newspaper formed with public subsidies to propagate Wagner's ideas, published its first issue. Porges was editor of its arts pages. The previous month Wagner had offered Porges a position as one of the administrative officers or "artistic business leader" for the planned premiere of *Die Meistersinger,* then intended for Nuremberg, the city in which the opera is set. This, however, was one more planned performance that came to naught.[2]

The new music school had been opened by decree of Ludwig in July, but Porges, contrary to Wagner's wishes, did not join its faculty. On October 14 of the following year, 1868, Wagner concluded a lengthy letter to Ludwig by laying before him "the destiny of Porges." Wagner had twice had no luck in persuading him to enter the circle of his friends in Munich. "He understands, and, almost alone fully understands me and my truest intentions. Yet he stays aloof and none of the ordinary folks know how to handle him. Still it is my deep conviction that the school is not completely finished if Porges will not take a meaningful part in it."[3] At a later time, we will see more of Porges and his work with Wagner.

In the meantime, Wagner's exile was causing him much agony, resulting not only from his separation from his king, his savior and greatest benefactor, but also from Cosima. This was the woman whose love for him exceeded anything he had thus far experienced in his lifelong quest for feminine understanding, and who stood ready to sacrifice everything for him. Ludwig and Cosima were the two human beings who could truly be termed his soul mates. Their understanding of him both as man and artist, as well as their readiness to forgive his faults, exceeded that of all others. They had come into his life almost simultaneously, and by the end of 1865, and the early months of 1866, he feared he might be losing them both.

Meanwhile, Cosima was enduring her own agonies. Separation from her cold and seemingly unfeeling husband was not made less difficult by the fact that in her marriage to him she had been miserably unhappy. But her determination was irrevocable. On the seventh of March, she, in company of her daughter Daniela, left Munich for Lausanne where she joined her lover. The effect on the dejected composer must have been electric. Just two days later in a country home near Lucerne, "Les Artichaux," he again took up work on *Die Meistersinger,* even as he resumed dictating his autobiography to Cosima. Two weeks later he had completed the first act orchestral score. A week thereafter, returning from an outing to Berne, they chanced to see on the shore of Lake Lucerne the house that would become their home.

The dwelling was near the city of Lucerne, situated on a promontory protruding into the lake. It is a narrow multistoried boxlike structure, whose interesting character derives solely from its gently sloping concave roof. Today it houses a Wagner museum, one of a number of such museums to be found these days in various German and Swiss cities and towns. It is located on the south shore of the lake, a considerable distance from the city center on its northwest shore. In more recent times, the trappings of city life have conspired to surround it. But some things have not changed. The structure itself and its odd configuration are the same, and it still affords a

Triebschen, near Lucerne, Wagner's home from March 1866 through September 1872. From *Weltgeschichte in Karakterbildern* by Wilhelm Kienzl.

splendid view of two of the area's highest peaks. Well to the north of the lake, quite visible on a clear day in all their grandeur, are Mt. Pilatus and Mt. Rigi. This last named peak has, for generations, beckoned the adventurous to climb it in darkness in order to witness the sunrise.

The home sits on the elevated portion of its broad grounds, which slope gently to the water's edge. Properly situated so as to cut oneself off from the sight of modern life, it is still possible to gain some sense of the calm and serenity that must have been the delight of its occupants in quieter times. Two years later, Cornelius, also a composer, and completely enthralled, was to describe the site in glowing terms: "To look out over water, mountains and country like this and not hear a sound of man and his activities! This is the place to dream in, to compose in."[4]

Within the building itself now are some original scores of compositions Wagner completed there, some original essays, and some musical instruments. Encased in glass are a few items of outrageous clothing, somewhat faded now, that once provoked ridicule during the Master's lifetime, and still today sometimes bring smiles to visitors.

Richard and Cosima first spotted the house as they were returning from Berne to their temporary residence in Les Artichaux. Lucerne and its surroundings are in German-speaking Switzerland. As a further advantage, it offered easy access to Munich and the king. The house was named Tribschen, which in German has no particular meaning; it is merely a proper noun. Wagner, exercising once more his wry sense of humor, and the constant references to his search for a haven from the world, added an "e" and the place became Triebschen. The first syllable now implies to German speakers that he has been "driven" there, presumably by the unfeeling world's cruelties, just as he had been "driven" to the Asyl.

The place was in need of repairs. The following day Richard rented it from the current owner for a year. He was obliged to pay at once the full year's rent, which he intended to secure by asking for an immediate payment of his stipend for 1866. In response the king made him a gift of 5,000 francs. He soon found, and so wired Cosima, that the house was entirely satisfactory for everyone. "Everyone" included her two daughters and the expected child of theirs. The king made one more attempt to persuade Wagner to settle again in "his own country," but to no avail. Richard took possession on April 15, and for the next six years Triebschen was to be the home of himself and Cosima and their family. Title to the house on the Briennerstrasse was later returned to the Kingdom of Bavaria.

The removal of Wagner's home from Munich to Lucerne made considerably more difficult the double life Cosima was leading, and more difficult their deception of the king, whom they feared would never understand. It would also inevitably stir up even further the buzzing of Wagner's legions of enemies at court and in the press. Much ink has been spilled over the question of how much Bülow knew, and how soon he knew it. The subject has been investigated, and the highly contradictory evidence analyzed at inordinate lengths, without any clear or definitive verdict.

It appears from correspondence that he must have known of the intimate relationship between his wife and his friend at least by May 1866. But it appears also that his chief concern was that the scandal not become public. Apparently he could better endure the sly innuendoes and insinuations of the Munich press, its sarcasms and cleverly worded but crude hints at immoral happenings afoot, and of salacious news to come, than he could the open declaration of his wife's desertion in favor of his friend and idol. Wagner was indeed his idol. Music was Bülow's life and he considered Wagner's genius to be awesome and unsurpassed. From the music that flowed from his pen, Bülow was mesmerized. Despite the deep hurt, he seemed genuinely concerned that no circumstances should interfere with the work of this creative force. Further, his frequently expressed concern for Cosima seemed still to be a factor in his sometimes perplexing conduct during these tension filled years.

One particularly insulting article in the *Volksbote* at the end of May could no longer be ignored. Bülow, employed now as orchestra director at the Royal Theater, demanded "satisfaction" from the editor, challenging him to a duel. His humiliation could not have been lessened by the fact that the demand was ignored. Bülow then responded in a rival newspaper, the *Neueste Nachrichten*, with a letter that, according to Cornelius, exhibited a mind "that had lost its footing."[5]

In the meantime Wagner and Cosima were making their own desperate moves. They could not permit the steady drumbeat of the Munich press to force a rift between the king and Wagner. In their clumsy attempts to head off that dreaded result, they could well have brought about precisely that. On the sixth of June Wagner wrote the king imploring that he come to the rescue of Bülow, whose honor he claimed was disgracefully slandered. The dishonor to him of course was derivative. The incessant accusations were referring to his wife's adultery. It was one of the quaint cultural idiosyncrasies of the time that the wife's adultery was the disgrace of the husband. Of this adultery, it seemed, everyone including Bülow was now aware, except for the king. The means of this rescue was to be the king's issuance of a document in the form of a letter to Bülow, already prepared by Wagner, which the king was invited to sign and deliver with the understanding that Bülow was entitled to make public use of it.

The letter, after paying homage to his music director's artistry and honorable character, stated that the king himself had "the most precise knowledge of the noble and profoundly honorable character of your honored wife." The king was further to declare that he had no choice but to investigate the "criminal public slandering" against her in order to "get to the bottom of the shameful conduct, and to spare no effort in bringing the evildoers to justice."[6] As is well established by communications among the principals, Cosima and Bülow were privy to every move between Wagner and the unsuspecting king, and were co-actors in the deceitful enterprise. Lengthy letters to the king by Wagner assured him that the love he and Cosima shared was innocent. The king, innocence personified, believed him.

The next day, Wagner, through an intermediary, gambling on the king's emotional dependence on him and their "joint undertaking," sent the hapless monarch a telegram. It said that if his dear friend Bülow were not to get the asked for satisfaction that he, Wagner, would "share his fate" and henceforth be "dead" even to the king. It was an audacious attempt at extortion. But nothing was to be left to chance. The next day, Cosima became an active party in the venture by forwarding her own letter to the king. She begged for the king's understanding that she had three children to whom it was her duty to transmit without blemish the honorable name of their father. The youngest child, Isolde, was of course Wagner's, and she was then pregnant with a fourth child, also Wagner's.

On the ninth, the king, as requested, sent his handwritten letter to Bülow with a friendly cover letter of his own composition. It was published by Bülow on the nineteenth and twentieth of that month, coincidentally with the outbreak of the war between Austria and Prussia. Temporarily this tangled affair was put on the back burner. Wagner, Cosima and Bülow, but especially the two lovers, now had two things to agonize about: concealment not only of the true relationship between them, but also of the artifice they had practiced on their royal friend. On the tenth Bülow joined Cosima and Richard at Triebschen. Apparently the strain and nervous tension involving their respective "honors" bound the threesome together sufficiently to overcome the strain and nervous tension that was working to drive Bülow from them.

Separation from Wagner sometimes seemed at least as difficult for Bülow as the breakup of his marriage. While in Triebschen, he found even more that made a breach with the composer so difficult. He read through the score of *Die Meistersinger*. Though only the composition sketch and part of the orchestration of the second act had been completed, it left Bülow almost breathless. On July 31 he wrote to Alexander Ritter, the husband of Wagner's niece, "My God! All that is ideal and worth preserving in the German spirit lives in this one head, your uncle's." On August 12 he wrote to Joachim Raff, a composer and friend of himself and Liszt, "This work represents the culmination of his genius ... incredibly vigorous, plastic, richer than *Tristan* in musical detail."

But the malignancy, kept secret, could only grow. The existence of two dark secrets, not unsurprisingly, invited a third. It came in the person of Malvina von Schnorr, the first Isolde.

The death of her husband, she felt, had been in the cause of Wagner. Wagner himself believed the same. Malvina was further convinced that it was her mission to see that Wagner lived his life according to the highest ideals as would be befitting the recipient of her husband's sacrifice. She was possibly unhinged by the loss of her husband, and through the good offices of some kind of "medium" felt she was in direct contact with the late tenor. No responsible party that observed or treated her, however, felt that she was at all insane. After Schnorr's death she had been given an annuity by King Ludwig, and was to become a member of the staff of the new music school. Through the spring and early fall her relations with Wagner and Cosima went smoothly enough.

All of that soon changed. In the company of a young woman Isadore von Reutter by name, she visited Triebschen on November 10. Reutter was thoroughly convinced of her own power as a medium, and, further, that she was in communication with the recently deceased Ludwig Schnorr. Whether or not there was any surreptitious motive is only for pointless speculation. Beyond doubt, Malvina believed her. The two ladies remained for two days in Triebschen.

Though Wagner was moved by her description of her husband's last days, the visit completely unnerved both him and Cosima. Wagner had apparently decided, with justification, that the woman, through grief, had taken leave of her senses, and refused to continue any relationship with her. For this, Malvina soon blamed Cosima. Her blandishments to Cosima, urging that she join Malvina in the task of "redeeming" Wagner, were ignored. Malvina, however, did not give up easily. To gain Cosima's help in her divinely appointed mission she threatened to tell Bülow that Cosima and Wagner were having an illicit affair. This frightened no one, as Bülow, fully aware of the truth of the accusation, was certain to deny it.

What did frighten them was the possibility that her next approach would be to the king. On the twenty-second of the month, Wagner, nervously pondering the best defense against such a blow, opted for the move that many other threatened and frightened persons before and after him have found most effective. He struck first. He sent a letter to the king to the effect that his old friend Malvina had lost her reason. "Here I sit," he wrote, "in my lonely fortress by the lake, looking out upon the world in order to write and to compose, but 'madness' knew I was here.... My enemies can no longer disturb me, so it must happen now through a friend."

The noble Cosima, he explained, had tried to protect him from the poor woman's demented and disturbing intrusions, but had succeeded only in bringing down on herself threatening and frightening tantrums. He recommended prevention of possible aggravation of the situation from the machinations of their well-known enemies, whose hands Wagner claimed to see behind all of this. He suggested medical intervention for the poor woman and also police security measures. The king, naturally unable to understand the urgency of the matter, brushed it off in a few lines, hoping only that peace had returned to Triebschen.

To a large degree the preventative stroke succeeded. In early December the king received a letter from Malvina containing allegations of a nature presently unknown, as the letter itself no longer exists. We may be sure, however, they were not complimentary to either Cosima or to Wagner. The king forwarded it directly to Cosima. Whatever it said, it panicked the already jittery pair. Wagner responded with the suggestion that the king should warn Malvina to leave Wagner and Cosima undisturbed or face loss of her pension. On December 20 came another letter from Malvina to the king, which he again forwarded to Cosima. This one contained direct allegations of adultery. Wagner's response was to avoid any overt denial, but to paint the letter as one aimed ultimately at the king himself, and destined to hurt both him and Bülow. On January 9 the king ordered Malvina to leave Bavaria, promising that the pension would continue if she went away. On January 12 she advised the king that she was not leaving.

A compromise was reached. Although the king reportedly said that he could not believe there was anything to the Wagner-Cosima relationship beyond friendship, events show that he was seriously considering that some fire might underlie all the smoke. He offered to restore the pension on condition that Malvina agree to retire, at least temporarily, to some place outside Munich, even if within the Bavarian kingdom. Things quieted for a while, but there was another flurry of activity toward the end of 1867. The matter slowly died a natural death, but not before sorely trying the king's patience. December 9 of that year he wrote one of his ministers that the whole thing had become repugnant to him: "I have shown these people," he wrote, referring to Wagner, Porges, Fröbel (editor of the *South German Press*) and others, so much indulgence and patience ... they ought to have every reason to be satisfied and grateful; the thread of my patience is at last beginning to break." On the 12 he wrote the same minister that he was much disappointed in the "terrible" articles Cosima was writing for the press about the Malvina affair. "If it should turn out that the miserable rumor is true ... Should it after all be really a case of adultery—then alas!"[7]

Alas what? Even when later events left no alternative to acceptance of the fact of the adulterous affair, and of the deceit perpetrated on him, he could not turn away from Wagner the man without turning away from the artist. And that he could not do. That dichotomy can be effected by critics and biographers. For Ludwig it was impossible.

20

Die Meistersinger

THERE WERE OTHER EVENTS occurring in 1867. February 17, Cosima's fourth daughter, Eva, namesake of the heroine of *Die Meistersinger*, was born. Even Bülow knew this child was Wagner's.

Aside from the birth of Eva, there was another happy event that year. On October 24 *Die Meistersinger von Nürnberg* was completed, the last note written. Unlike *Tristan,* this opera waited not six years, but only eight months to see the light of day. At the Munich National Theater, the same that saw the first performance of *Tristan*, the premiere of *Die Meistersinger* took place on June 21, 1868. It was greeted with thunderous applause. The conductor was the still perennial Hans von Bülow. It must have been an extremely painful experience, but, remarkably, the ignominious circumstances did not appear to detract from his artistry in the slightest. Wagner, to the shock and dismay of many spectators, shared the royal box with the king.

The outpouring of awe and admiration heaped upon this opera over the years has almost equaled that lavished upon *Tristan.* Not everyone of course, loved it. General Helmuth Moltke, destined soon to be the German hero of the Franco-Prussian War, said that it reminded him of a meeting of the *Bundestag*, the German federal parliament, except that one could always walk out of a meeting of the *Bundestag*. Others expressed the same sentiments less eloquently, and less humorously.

As with *Tristan*, as with all Wagnerian operas, the voices of the naysayers have been largely reduced to faint whispers. The voices of the admirers have resounded through the years. Liszt termed it "a masterpiece of humor, wit and vivacious grace — lively and beautiful, like Shakespeare." As early as 1882, a critic for the London journal *The Era* wrote that it was "enriched with some of the most masterly touches that ever came from the brain and pen of a man of genius."¹ To Ignacy Paderewski, the great Polish twentieth century pianist and composer, it was the "longest continuous song" ever written.

Wagner's central character is Hans Sachs, an historical figure, a sixteenth century poet and guild master from Nuremberg. The portrayal of this character, according to one modern music historian, results in "one of the few truly full-bodied characters in opera." Through him, this author continues, a "warm and homely wisdom pervades the work.... It soars on a rush of musical wings that carry us to the final curtain all too quickly,"² a rather nice compliment for this four-hour opera. Another recent writer finds Wagner's "Nuremberg vitality" endowing every character "with life, pride of movement, contagious humanity.... It is an art that absolutely absorbs its subject or theme, soul and body." He describes a penetratingly beautiful third-act monologue by Sachs, as "one of the most profoundly moving and human that ever came from the soul of an artist."³

But from the make-believe world of *Die Meistersinger,* the characters offstage had necessarily to return to real life, with all of its pains and sorrows. Bülow kept up the brave front for many months. As we have seen, it was on November 16, less than five months after the first *Meistersinger* performance, that Cosima openly abandoned all pretense and went to Switzerland to remain permanently by the side of Wagner. She had taken the two younger daughters, Isolde and Eva, with her. She was then three months pregnant with her third child by Wagner. Her two older daughters, Daniela, born in 1860, and Blandine, born in 1863, were still with Hans. Though she hoped and assumed that they also would reside with her, she had no such assurance when she left.

Hans von Bülow likewise was now obliged to abandon the charade. He relinquished his posts as conductor at the National Theater and director of the music school. To Cosima's request that he agree to set her free, he answered with an outwardly gracious but self-effacing letter. He took on himself the entire blame, and expressed his understanding that she sought "the necessary substitute" when life became intolerable. She had, he continued, chosen to devote her life "to a being decidedly superior." He compiled at length her admirable traits, which he said, "made up the rock, the very basis of my life. The loss of all these precious things— whose worth I learned not till I was bereft of them — is the undoing of me both as man and artist, and shows me I am bankrupt." There was no irony in this, he assured her, nor was he trying to hurt her, but said, "I am suffering so greatly that I may be forgiven for uttering this cry, though I neither blame, nor seek to blame any other than myself." He agreed that the two older daughters should live with her.

However much it may have appeared that Bülow was accepting of the situation and lacking in anger, concerned only about Cosima and the work of the "superior being," there is abundant evidence of pent-up rage. In a letter of September 15, 1869, to the Countess de Charnace, half sister of Cosima, it came pouring forth. The occasion was triggered, at least in part, by an event of some three months earlier that brought overwhelming joy to Wagner: the birth of a boy to Cosima. Wagner's long yearned for son, born on June 6, 1869, was named Siegfried. Said Bülow:

> For more than three years I took it upon me to live a life of ceaseless torture. You cannot form an idea of the corroding cares to which I was incessantly a prey. When, at long last, it came to the point, I sacrificed my artistic and my material position. There was only one other thing I could sacrifice, and that was my life, and I confess that that would have been the simplest way to settle the difficulty, to settle the inextricable knot.

Why did he not? We see in his reasons the first, and probably only time he allowed himself the luxury of acknowledging a cleft he saw between Wagner and his music:

> Perhaps I should not have shrunk even from that if only I had seen in him, in the man who is as sublime in his works as he is incomparably abject in his conduct, the least indication of a loyal impulse, the most transient sign of desire to act in an honorable and upright manner.[4]

Nor could he any longer resist an expression of resentment against his wife. Perhaps, he said, when she was free, which under Bavarian law would be in another year, and had legalized her association with her lover, "she will be herself again, nor any longer be compelled to prevaricate from morning till night." Is there anything illogical, he asks his sister-in-law, in his desire to seek a legal separation, which he was first not inclined to do? It appears that Cosima's final lie to him was more than he could bear. It harks back to the preceding November, when Cosima left Munich to openly join Wagner in Triebschen:

> Last November I asked her something that might almost have seemed indelicate, as to why she wanted to get away so quickly ... but Cosima had no compunction in swearing a lie. That it was a lie I learned a few months ago, through the newspapers, who ... made public the good fortune of the maestro, whose mistress (so they openly referred to her) had at last presented him with a son, baptized in the name of Siegfried, a happy omen for the approaching completion of his opera.[5]

Bülow's contact with Wagner, the man, ceased. With Wagner's music it did not. He conducted and promoted Wagner's music for the balance of his life, including frequent performances of *Tristan*. After one of them, he was heard to exclaim upon leaving, "Must not everything be forgiven the man who wrote a work like that?"

His reaction was not much different from that of a Jewish acquaintance of Wagner, a great-grand-uncle of the writer Rudolph Sabor. According to Sabor, his forebear loaned Wagner money, but was never repaid. The reaction of this Jewish creditor: "The world is full of people who borrow and don't repay; who steal other men's wives, daughters and sweethearts. But only one of them wrote *Tristan und Isolde.*"[6]

21

Cosima's Diaries

ON THE FIRST DAY OF January, 1869, Cosima began a diary of her life with Wagner. From the first entries it was evident that she was wracked with guilt, some of it for the turmoil caused her two older daughters, but most particularly for her treatment of Hans. She says at the outset that the diaries were "written for you, my children, ... so that one day you will see me as I am." There follows an intense, though not unduly lengthy, expression of the agony of her past life and the wrenching decision to leave her husband and her two daughters with whom she expected to be reunited, a reunion that in fact took place a few months thereafter. She had, she said, a duty to be at Wagner's side.

The diaries cover about 5150 days from January 1, 1869, until the day before his death, February 12, 1883. Whatever their original purpose, they are a remarkable compendium of Wagner's everyday activities and utterances, a chronology of what parts or lines he was setting to music on what days, and his moods while doing so. It records also the comings and goings of the many visitors to the Wagner homes, first in Triebschen and later in Bayreuth, what was said by Wagner during the visits, and what was said afterwards in private. Essentially it is about him, but she frequently interjects remarks and observations of her own. To a larger degree than she may have intended it tells much about her. It is sometimes difficult to tell, without a close reading, what passages are summaries of her husband's thoughts and which are her own. Sometimes it is not possible at all. Her use of quotation marks identifies some remarks as his, but she uses them sparingly.

She has left a gold mine of information for scholars, biographers and researchers of all stripes. But she did her husband no favors. The picture that emerges is not always a pretty one. He said many things in the privacy of his home about many people, friends, acquaintances, and even about enemies, that even he might not have said in other settings. Publication of the diaries did not occur until 1976, 93 years after Wagner's death, and then only by order of a German court. Wagner's heirs contested the publication at every step, in part perhaps because the immediate heirs of some of the targets of his pungent remarks were still alive.

The diaries reveal also the depth of his rancor and malice toward *the Jews.* What had been limited, in essence, to one 23 page essay, parts of a number of others, and sporadic comments in correspondence and other writings, now is shown as a vital, if corrosive, part of his being that surfaced all too often. The bitterness that, on one level at least, showed itself as a contempt for all mankind, showed itself to be centered on *the Jews.* He felt that Jews controlled the press that had treated him so brutally, excepting, of course, the Jewish arts editor of the *South German Press.* He also saw the Jews as the moneyed interest, the bankers, and the dominant officers of the theaters.

It is, nonetheless, impossible for many to accept that the man who wrote the music of *Tristan, Die Meistersinger,* and the *Ring,* and who would, in another decade, write the music of *Parsifal,* truly hated humanity. The contradiction raises a question that, according to one author, can be addressed only by those versed in abnormal psychology. The comment is clever and humorous, but does nothing to explain the man who, early in life, set out his goal of creating what is essentially a new art form, one conveying a depth of emotion never before probed, realizing it in full, then forcing it on a skeptical world on his own terms.

Fifteen years after Wagner's death, in 1898, one of his Jewish friends and devoted followers, Heinrich Porges, answered succinctly, but incisively, just such a question as is raised by these stark contradictions. The letter was to Richard Batka, a musician researching Wagner's life: "Such demoniac personalities cannot be judged by ordinary standards. They are egoists of the first water, and must be so, or they could never fulfill their mission."[1]

As contradictory as any part of the life of this enigmatic, creative giant is his expressed hatred of *the Jews* versus his relationship with individual Jews. Neither the contradictions, nor any possible understanding of the subject is possible without some grasp of the anti–Semitism that abounds in Cosima's diaries. But some factors, preparatory to such a look, should be understood beforehand.

First is the fact that despite his knowledge of the existence of his wife's diary, he never suspected that any of his utterances would be made public, even 93 years later. Such comments, it may be worth noting, and however irrelevant it may seem, are usually not admissible in court against the person making them. For good reason private conversations between husband and wife are considered privileged. The tenor of the remarks, the frequency of them, and the malice with which expressed, exceed that of his essays and letters alike.

Secondly, there does emerge with an extensive reading a sense that the anti–Semitism of these two anti–Semites fed on that of each other. Wagner seemed at times determined to convince his anti–Semitic audience of one that he had not by any means softened his hatred of *the Jews*, even to the point of finding weaknesses and faults with those of that alien race closest to him, and even while maintaining the friendliest relations with them that he seemed ever capable of maintaining with anyone. He seemed with her and others to almost wear his anti–Semitism as a badge of his persona.

It should be emphasized at this point that anti–Semitism exists in many forms, and Richard's hatred of the Jews seems different in its roots and in its form than Cosima's. However wrong his perceptions about the predominant and rising power of Jews in Germany, however paranoiac his fear, however exaggerated and sometimes contrived were the perceived differences between Jews and other Germans, he apparently felt genuinely threatened. He saw the world through the lens of his gigantic artistic concepts, and saw the Jewish presence as menacing, excepting, of course, the individual Jews who were so helpful to him. His contempt for Judaism did not reveal itself until his late thirties.

Cosima's prejudice seemed to stem from childhood, perhaps from her Jew-baiting mother, Marie d'Agoult, who may have been trying to distance herself from a real or imputed part–Jewish ancestry. In Cosima we see a smug innate sense of superiority in religion, a matter of little consequence to Richard, and in culture, not necessarily centered on the artistic. She speaks of "our kind" versus "their kind" and of the impossibility of any real understanding between the two.

She possessed in large measure the certitude of the ill-informed and saw the world through her narrow childhood upbringing. Unlike that of Richard, her hatred of the Jews was unexamined; Jewish inferiority was an unchanging, eternal fact of life. His comments are often laced with at least a touch of humor. Her comments have none. Nor can mitigation be claimed in her behalf due to any spark of genius or creativity.

Nonetheless, unlike her husband, who could be direct and crudely blunt when irritated by a Jew, whether a friend or a real or imagined foe, Cosima seemed unwilling and incapable of purposely causing pain to anyone. Her thoughts were expressed only to like-minded people, and her relationships with her husband's Jewish friends rarely suffered from any act or speech of hers.

And finally it should be understood that when we concentrate solely on the anti–Semitic aspect of the diaries, it may seem that the entire 2,000 pages may be one huge diatribe. That impression is strengthened by the fact that so often the comments, often malicious in tone, are interjected gratuitously, completely irrelevantly, into the subject at hand, and seem alien to the matter under discussion. One modern writer has claimed that the diaries reflect an "obsession with Jews and Judaism that saturates every aspect, almost every moment" of their life together.[2] It is a bit of an exaggeration. The document's anti–Semitism is not its essential thrust, nor its reason for being.

There are between approximately 400 and 450 days on which comments are made about either *the Jews,* or about individual Jews, when the individual's Jewishness is mentioned. The uncertainty in the numbers stems from the composer's propensity to sometimes speak in ways that must have been clear to his wife, but not to us, whom he did not expect to be listening in. There is also the matter of Cosima's understandably unclear shorthand type of notation. Many of the comments were never voiced at all. They are Cosima's private thoughts confided only to the diary.

Often it is difficult to distinguish what is a summary of a comment from Wagner, and what is her own private opinion. All such comments from either of this couple, laced as they are among the 5,150 days spanned by the diaries, average approximately one every 11 or 12 days. The number is large or small, the comments frequent or seldom, depending on the viewpoint. There is obviously much more to the diaries, and to the man, than anti–Semitism.

As a rule an individual's Jewishness is mentioned by Wagner only when he has for some reason been displeased or irritated by that person. Rarely is it mentioned as part of some positive observations, though that too occasionally happens. There may be a half dozen or so such positive comments. There are a few other remarks about *the Jews* that may also be seen as positive. Others are neutral in tone. But at least 95 percent of them range from the mildly anti–Semitic or disparaging, sometimes with an overlay of humor, to the malicious.

Nothing about Wagner is anything less than complex, and these diaries are no exception. But they cover a period involving some of his most complicated and interesting relationships with Jews, two of whom we have already met; one of whom, Angelo Neumann, we have seen only fleetingly; and two more of whom, perhaps the most interesting and complex of all, had not yet entered Wagner's life.

22

"Judaism in Music":
The Second Publication

THE FIRST MENTION OF THE Jews in the diaries is on the subject of the planned republication of "Judaism in Music." Wagner's avowed reason for doing so was to explain the consistently adverse press he was getting, in contrast to the wide and enthusiastic reception his operas receive from the theatergoing public. The new publication, with some minor revisions, was accompanied by a short dedication and a lengthy appendix, about as long as the essay itself. The dedication is to Madame Marie Muchanoff, who, Wagner claims, has asked him in astonishment why he has met with such hostility in the press throughout Europe. We last saw Madame Muchanoff under her maiden name, Marie Kalergis, loaning a significant sum to Wagner in Paris and persuading her Jewish friend Julie Schwabe to do likewise.

Prior to the re-publication of the essay with its dedication, Wagner had written a letter to her on the same subject, dealing mainly with the purity of his motives in publishing the essay the first time. Perhaps, he said, he expected a hopeful acceptance. He thought of

> the great talents of heart and mind from the circle of Jewish society whom I have learned to know and truly to enjoy. Certainly I am of the opinion that everything which oppresses the genuine German character from that side burdens in an even more terrible measure the witty and sensitive Jews themselves.... If the Jewish element is to become assimilated with us ... it is clear that not concealment of the difficulties, but only the open exposure of them can further it.[1]

The thrust of the answer to her question that, he claimed, prompted the second publication is set forth in the appendix. In essence, his argument is that the press is controlled by the Jews, and that, despite the "noble inten-tion" of the essay, he has been maliciously attacked by them in consequence of its publication 18 years previous.

His account of the history of this vengeful endeavor, the recitation at length of episode after episode, reveals his transparently paranoiac tenden-cies. He complained that he was not attacked openly for the essay on Judaism, but rather was ridiculed as the author of the phrase "music of the future" as a description of his work. The press and Wagner's many enemies did delight in heaping ridicule upon him, and did indeed use that expres-sion as a favorite tool.

It has been said that even paranoids have enemies. There undoubtedly was a significant presence of Jews in the press at the time, a consequence of the prohibition against their entry into so many other professions for so many centuries. It was the same prohibition that resulted in the presence of a proportionately high number of Jews in the fields of music and the the-ater, also among the few open to them. Writers friendly to the Jewish cause, for instance, pointed to the large numbers of Jews holding high office in the publishing field as evidence of their worth to German culture. It would have been surprising if many Jews, so situated, did not strike back, even turning to other aspects of Wagner's behavior as more tempting targets than a direct attack on the merits of the notorious essay. Attacks on his many abrasive traits and peccadilloes would have met with a more favor-able public response than an open defense of the Jews.

However, Jews have never accounted for more than about one percent of the German population, and it appears inconceivable that they could have composed any truly significant part of Wagner's tormentors. Certainly the large number of those arrayed against him included many non–Jews, and their motives had little or nothing to do with "Judaism in Music." But Wagner could never concede, even to himself, that the prevalent animos-ity in the press could have been a natural consequence of his uncommon self-centeredness and propensity for ingratitude to friends and benefac-tors.

Whatever the flaws in his reasoning, there can be little doubt that he believed his thesis to the depths of his innermost psyche. His conclusion begins with a statement that may be seen as paranoia or as a final calumny against the Jews. But it is a cry of pain: "As you see, respected lady, I herewith certify the total victory of Judaism on every side." He acknowledges that from his narrative it may appear that his essay was in fact the cause of this victory, but he discounts that idea, claiming, first, that it was his insight into the inevitabil-ity of the downfall of German music that compelled him to trace the causes of it. But he also adverts to the possible and more hopeful prediction made in the essay's conclusion, addressed to the Jews themselves. This, it will be recalled, was the advice to them of the necessity of a "going under," a complete assimilation into the German culture. And he takes up the cudgel again.

He has taken note, this appendix continues, of "the great gifts of heart, as well as mind, which, to my genuine refreshment, has greeted me from out the sphere of Jew society itself." He is certain that whatever burden the Jewish presence places on native German life "weighs far more terribly on intelligent and high-souled Jews themselves." He points out that the best and most entertaining Jewish anecdotes are, in fact, told to Germans by the Jews. There are also heard other frank remarks by Jews about themselves. But to hear it from another, to the Jews is a "mortal crime." He describes how a "very gifted, truly talented and intellectual writer of Jewish origin" had expressed himself with warm appreciation and clear understanding of the *Ring* and *Tristan*, but when asked by Wagner's friends to publish his views, Wagner tells us, "This was impossible for him!"

Nonetheless, he continues, one incentive for this appendix to his essay is "a hope which lies within my deepest heart," that this "openness," as opposed to the use of the pseudonym when first published, though it will gain him no friends among the Jews, may strengthen them to battle for their own emancipation. But as a necessary first step, it must be acknowledged by the Jews that they have displayed a falsification of the highest cultural tendencies of the Germans.

He then touches on a subject that comes closest to a serious escalation of his hostility, one he neatly sidesteps. Whether the downfall of the German culture can be "arrested by a violent ejection of the destructive foreign element" he is unable to decide, as that would require "forces with whose existence I am unacquainted." If on the contrary, he concludes, there is to be an assimilation with German culture so that "in common with us, it shall ripen toward a higher evolution of our nobler human qualities," then is it obvious that no hiding of the difficulties of such assimilation, but only open exposure can be of help.

On January 11, over 18 years after its initial publication, Wagner sent off for republication, together with the dedication and appendix, his "Judaism in Music." Two days earlier, Cosima, asked by him for her opinion of the prospects of immediate publication, replied that she was incapable of saying anything at all about it. What impression it might make, she added, she was completely unable to say. It was just as well. Undoubtedly she could not have prevented his new effort and, had she tried, it would undoubtedly have soured the relationship even before the marriage. Cosima noted in her diary on the eleventh that it made her apprehensive, "yet I did not try to prevent it." When on January 21 she recorded Wagner's announcement that the article was going to be printed, her resigned comment to her diary, but presumably not to him, was "So be it!"

The impression, for the most part, was not good. Even his closest friends were in disbelief. On March 6 Bülow wrote to a friend, exclaiming about the uproar it was bound to cause. Some evidence of the general reaction to it may be gleaned from a letter he also wrote to the composer Raff. He said that a recent composition of Raff's went well in performance in Munich, but that a piece by a Jewish composer, Anton Rubenstein, did not "in spite of the sympathy for Jewish music aroused by Wagner's pamphlet."[2]

It did harm not only to his standing with many of his Jewish devotees, but with significant parts of the non–Jewish public. The article appeared, in pamphlet form, in early March. Until it did, *Die Meistersinger* was being well received, Carlsruhe and Dresden being notable examples. But on March 13 Cosima noted that a Carlsruhe paper had said that by treating a whole race of people, including its eminent composer (Mendelssohn), ruthlessly, and also by treating all his opponents contemptuously, Richard was harming himself and his cause. Two days later came an anonymous letter from Carlsruhe "in the name of 7000 Jews." It was filled with abuse and threats, wrote Cosima, but she resolved that "they may revile me to the end of time, so long as I have helped him, have been permitted to give my hand to him and say 'I will follow you to the death.'"

An old acquaintance of Wagner, Pauline Viardot-Garcia, wrote from Paris. In a letter received on the March 16 she vigorously protested the essay. Cosima's reaction was that "She is a Jewess, that is now quite clear." "Clear" though it may have been to Cosima, she was not. Further, eight years earlier, in Paris, she had invited Wagner to give a chamber concert of the second act of *Tristan* in her home, taking both female roles herself while Wagner sang all the male parts. Cosima wrote out a few lines for Richard to address to her. What they contained we are not told. The following day they received newspaper clippings about the "Jewish Pamphlet. Everyone foaming, raging, jeering." On September 15 1869, Cosima received a letter from Marie Muchanoff: "She tells me that people blame the Jewish pamphlet on me etc. Nice people!"

Not all reactions were negative. Later in March came a favorable anonymous letter, and an article from a Catholic paper, also favorable. A doctor told them that he was glad to know the reasons for the unceasing acts of enmity. But another doctor wrote that the Jewish population in Berlin was "seething." They also received a pamphlet by a "sentimental Jew," an admirer of Wagner, but "indignant" about the essay. Bülow wrote that the Jews in Munich were no longer so eager to see Richard's operas.

The editor of a Viennese paper was enthusiastic about the pamphlet, extolling its "contemplative calm," but an article in another paper called Richard the "Hamann of the 19th Century." In early April a letter from Paris informed them that the pamphlet had stirred great indignation and would probably do harm there to the current performances of *Rienzi*. Another Catholic paper praised both Richard and King Ludwig, who protected him as the "composer of heroic song," a phrase bound to cause exasperation to them both. Cosima noted the accolade, but one can hear the sigh of resignation as she added, "Such is the world."

And what of Wagner's Jewish friends? A performance of *Lohengrin* in Berlin was postponed because of the furor over the pamphlet. On April 7 came a telegram from Tausig: "Huge success of *Lohengrin,* all Jews reconciled." Tausig probably knew the composer too well to have expected a simple thank you. Nothing about this man was so simple. Every possible meaning and nuance had to be dissected.

After telling Tausig that he would have liked to receive some details of the performance, he discussed what Tausig did say, as opposed to what he did not. It would be no bad thing, he said, if the brochure were "properly read by all intelligent Jews, but it seems that people have forgotten how to read." He had hoped that the entire matter would have faded away after this long time, but the insolence of the Viennese press and the lie-mongering about him had persuaded him to take this step, whatever the consequences.

As he saw it, he had now given "some really intelligent Jew" the material he needed to give this entire question a beneficial twist. There must be such a person, but if Tausig did not have the courage to do it, then he, Wagner, was right to describe German Judaism as he did. His conclusion:

> You tell me that *Lohengrin* has reconciled the Jews with me. What I understand by this is really only that my brochure is regarded as over-hasty and, as such, is *forgiven* me. I do not find this very comforting. I have already encountered a very great deal of good-naturedness, especially on the part of Jews. Let one of them show real courage, only then will I rejoice![3]

Prior to this exchange in April 1869, there had been little correspondence between the two men for about five years that is still extant. In all probability there was continuing contact. However, Tausig was admired and loved as much by Bülow as by Wagner, and the young pianist's activities and triumphs are best reflected in the correspondence of Bülow with Karl Bechstein. Bechstein was the manufacturer of the fine pianos, one of which was given by Ludwig to Wagner after loss of his Erard. At least ten times between 1866 and 1871 Bülow mentions Tausig to Bechstein.[4] It is obvious from the correspondence that the young pianist is traveling extensively throughout Europe to widespread acclaim, and to Bülow's immense pleasure.

One letter from another Jewish virtuoso, a renowned violinist and an acquaintance of all of the principals in this tale, tells us much about Tausig. Joseph Joachim, writing to his brother in London in April 1866, described a concert he had given with Tausig, and waxed eloquent about him: "He is the greatest pianist playing in public at present. He has a richness and charm of attack, a varied repertoire , an absence of all charlatanism — in short, an almost uncanny perfection for a man only twenty-four years of age.... You must hear Tausig!"[5]

Bülow, well aware that not only Tausig but a number of other of Liszt's protégés were Jews, could nonetheless write to Wagner his agreement with "Judaism in Music." His letters have as many derogatory remarks about Jews as they do complimentary ones about Tausig. On rare occasion there is an overlap. As early as March 1865, Bülow wanted to know how Bechstein was arranging "the Berlin affair. We can hardly leave out the earthworm (as you call Tausig).... But to keep the Jew pack within bounds we must have a contrast, a damper." He suggests the addition of another performer, free, presumably, from taint of Jewishness.[6]

The jovial Tausig's telegram about the Berlin *Lohengrin* performance was not the last of the tempest. Karl Eckert, who had directed the performance, gave a lecture in that city in which he called the pamphlet regrettable. But on April 18 came a letter from a friend referring to it as a true word spoken at the right time. The matter was gradually cooling down, but was still alive. On May 24 Cosima noted a nice letter received from Wagner's sister Luise, but she was "sad about the Jewish pamphlet." On June 4, two days before the birth of Siegfried, Cosima was upset by having received from a friend a copy of the pamphlet in which a letter from Richard to Tausig is also printed. The contents of the letter are not revealed, but it seems possible that the correspondent may have found the obvious contradictions between the two documents puzzling, and that he may have been trying to say so.

23

Das Rheingold Brouhaha

By summer, Wagner had other trials that must have trumped the fallout from the pamphlet. The entire tetralogy, as the four Ring operas are sometimes called, now belonged to the king as a result of the contract of 1864. Only the first two had been completed, but by the summer of 1869 the impatient Ludwig demanded a performance of *Das Rheingold*, the first of the four.

The opera itself is grand opera in the best sense of the term. The story of its first production is more akin to musical slapstick.

It was to be performed of course in Munich. Wagner wanted complete control over the production, as he did over all performances of his operas, at least for the premieres. His determination was about to be put to a severe test. It led to bitter controversy that resulted in a breach between the king and Wagner, perhaps the most serious in their stormy relationship. It was the first of what would be a number of tests of will. In this one, and in the one immediately following, involving *Die Walküre*, Wagner was the clear loser. But they would be his last such defeats.

Wagner considered his personal appearance for any extended time in Munich to be repugnant. There was the specter of his unsanctified cohabitation with Cosima, so recently the wife of his friend and devoted disciple. On June 6 she had given birth to Siegfried, the third of her children by Wagner. Then there was the malice of the Munich press and of various personnel of the opera and of the court. His solution was to insist on his own conductor for the performance, one pliable enough to do his bidding in all matters. He choose one who was completely devoted to him, but who was untested and unknown. He was Hans Richter, a 26-year-old Hungarian, most recently employed as a horn player in the Kärntnerthor Theater in Vienna.

Underlying the intensity of the gathering storm was the rightful assumption of the king that the center for Wagnerian operas, including the theater that was to be specially built for them, would be Munich. Now, however, finding return to Munich so odious to himself and to Cosima, Wagner was, unknown to the king, considering other sites, including Prussia, as the new Wagnerian capital. It appears that what was occurring was a power struggle for control of the productions. The administrative director of the Munich Opera, Baron Karl von Perfall, was looked upon by Wagner as a hopeless antagonist and as an opponent to be subdued, a view he held for the rest of his days. Bülow, who had resigned as director of both the opera and the music school, was, remarkably, still a devoted Wagnerian in matters involving his art. Unfortunately, he was in no condition emotionally or physically to conduct *Rheingold*. Wagner's choice for the task, the novice Richter, was sadly lacking not only in artistic experience but in the tact or diplomatic skills necessary.

Upon Wagner's insistence, he was installed as opera conductor. Problems and disagreements arose almost at once, centering around the scenic aspects of the production. In this, as in all operas of the tetralogy, scenery is a matter of considerably more complexity and importance than the usual. Wagner, basking in his presumed favoritism with the king, felt certain that His Majesty would yield to any threat of Richter's resignation, and comply with his demands in preference to those of Perfall.

On August 13, Wagner gave his subordinate more detailed instructions as to how the purpose was to be achieved. Richter's demand, counseled Wagner, was to be coupled with a threat to resign were he to be required to obey instructions from the administrative director, the hated Perfall. Thus was a disagreement as to scenery and the like elevated into a test of whether Wagner or Perfall would exercise control. Wagner's confidence that, as the king's favorite, he would certainly prevail was a sad miscalculation.

A dress rehearsal was scheduled for August 27, the performance for the twenty-ninth. They had each been originally scheduled two days earlier, but Richter, citing problems with the scenery, had postponed them. Present at that rehearsal was the king, as were 500 invited guests, including musical celebrities from across Europe. Among them were Liszt, Joachim, Hanslick and Viardot-Garcia. There was also one whose name we have not yet seen, but who was destined to play a leading role in the last four or five years of Wagner's life. He was Hermann Levi, a Jew, son of a rabbi, and conductor of the Carlsruhe opera. At that rehearsal, Richter proved his mettle as a conductor, even if not to everyone's satisfaction.

On the twenty-eighth the king received a telegram from Wagner asking him to postpone the performance scheduled for the next day. The king, ominously, did not reply. The next day Wagner wrote describing numerous problems that must be cleared up before a performance, for which he blamed the laxity of Perfall. The already angry king also received a letter from Richter advising that the performance had been again postponed, till September 2. He had previously, on August 28, in a letter to the king bearing all of the hallmarks of Wagner's obtuse prose, advised of his resignation, to be effective after the *Rheingold* performance. The reason: the difficulties in attaining his "highest life-task," set for himself, with regard to the works of "the great Master Richard Wagner." To perform the opera in the true spirit of the poet-composer will be impossible, said the letter, due to the lack of comprehension by the present director, Perfall. Hence the performance could not take place "so long as this sole authority is not countered by someone with equal sovereignty in certain musical matters." Despite Richter's signature, the Wagnerian prose style gushed from the letter, clear to anyone familiar with it, including the king. The king had now been pushed too far.[1]

Sensing the king's anger, Perfall did not change the scenery to Wagner's liking, so Richter said he would have nothing to do with the planned production of the twenty-ninth. The angry king ordered a meeting of the warring parties. Richter went further than Wagner probably intended. Reminded by Perfall of his contractual obligations, the young director responded that he recognized no authority but Wagner's. Richter was suspended on the spot.

In the meantime Wagner tried to salvage the situation with the king. He would cooperate in the production, he would meet with the theater personnel, with one condition: Richter must conduct. The king was in no mood to consider rehiring the impertinent young outsider who claimed to recognize no authority but Wagner. The monarch's language grew intemperate, but not, perhaps, unwarranted. It came pouring forth in letters to his court secretary, Lorenz von Düfflipp: "Wagner and the theater rabble," he said, were behaving like criminals. He would not tolerate open revolt. Ludwig was obviously enraged at Richter's insolence, and ordered that the suspended conductor be dismissed at once. These "abominable intrigues" of Wagner will not be permitted. He learned that Wagner was coming to Munich to try to salvage the situation and expressed the thought that it would be justified, the Bülow-Cosima situation considered, if there were to be a demonstration against him.[2] Wagner stayed in Munich but two days, then returned to Triebschen empty-handed. Using unusual good judgment, he had not even attempted to see the king.

Neither Wagner nor Richter seemed to understand the depth of the resentment they had provoked. But they did begin to realize that, having overplayed their hand, there was a need to compromise. On the subject of who was to conduct, neither side could give in without a total loss of credibility. The king held all the cards. He was determined that the opera would be performed with a new conductor, but almost every one tapped for the job felt constrained to get Wagner's approval. Wagner, of course, gave approval to no one. Among those refusing to conduct without Wagner's approval was Hermann Levi, the Jewish conductor from Carlsruhe. But he was shooting his last arrow; it was inevitable that the king would, sooner or later, find someone.

That someone was Franz Wüllner, a conductor and pianist, serving as a court conductor at Munich since 1864. Wagner had been angry enough at the mere attempt to have the opera conducted with someone other than of his choosing. By Wüllner's acceptance he was infuriated. On the eleventh of September he fired off a letter to the king's chosen conductor. Wüllner was not a Jew; he was simply a conductor for whom Wagner had little or no respect. When it is appropriate to do so it will be interesting to compare this letter to one the composer was to write to Levi, 13 years thence. To Wüllner, the king's choice, he wrote:

> Take your hands off my score! That is my advice to you, sir; otherwise may the devil take you! Beat times in glee clubs or singing groups, or if you must handle operatic scores, look to your friend Perfall for them! [Perfall dabbled in operatic compositions himself.] Also tell that fine gentleman that if he doesn't make known to the king his incompetence to give my works, I will light a fire that cannot be extinguished by all the scribblers of local rags paid by leftovers from *Das Rheingold* expenses. You two gentlemen will need a lot of instruction from a man like me, before you learn that you understand nothing.[3]

The opera was finally performed on September 22, and was repeated two more times before the end of the month. According to all reports, the performances were quite creditable. The opera was reviewed for one Munich paper by Peter Cornelius, who, for one thing, found the scenic changes that were ostensibly the cause for the imbroglio to have been completely unwarranted, and the entire matter much ado about very little. Whether the premiere of any grand opera has ever been preceded by such low comedy is very doubtful. On September 24 Cosima's diary noted, "Fine letter from Heinrich Porges about *Das Rheingold*."

Despite the tension between them and the sharp language by King Ludwig, it was only a matter of time before a reconciliation occurred. Each was too much in need of the other. Wagner's need for the king was obvious and easy to understand. The king's equally desperate need for the composer was much less so, but vital nonetheless. He had not by any means neglected the duties and obligations that had descended upon him. But his deeper yearnings and dreams, undoubtedly the very stuff that gave his life meaning, were expressed in his partnership in the creation of great art with Richard Wagner. Without him, the bedrock of Ludwig's life, his spiritual underpinnings, would be shattered. As jealously as he guarded the prerogatives of his office, the loss of his collaboration with Wagner would undoubtedly have left him devastated.

It was different for Wagner. However difficult life may have been, and might be, without the support of the king, his creative life would nonetheless be possible. That would now be particularly true after the performances of *Tristan*, *Die Meistersinger*, and *Das Rheingold*. To whatever degree his reputation for honest dealings, tact or other personal qualities may have been reduced to shambles, he was renowned and feted for these creations.

Hence, it should be no surprise that the first move toward reconciliation came from Ludwig. The long silence between them ended in late October. On the twenty-second, the king wrote Wagner that he believed his friend to imagine the royal mantle to be easier than it was:

> To be completely absolutely alone in this bleak, cheerless world, alone with my own thoughts, misunderstood, mistrusted, this is no small thing;... Believe me, I have come to know men. I went towards them with genuine love, and felt myself repulsed; and wounds like these heal slowly.[4]

These morose broodings soon gave way to more earthly matters. He wanted to know if Wagner was working on the final of the four operas, *Götterdämmerung* ("The Twilight of the Gods"), and on the text of what is to be his final work, *Parsifal*.

Friendly correspondence followed, and there is much *mea culpa* on the part of the king. But in the meantime, before communications had resumed, he had given orders for the production of the only other completed opera, *Die Walküre*. Wagner learned this from the newspapers, but he had no intention of returning to Munich. In late September, about the time of *Das Rheingold* performance, he had written to Porges that the baseness connected with that production had alienated him from Munich forever. When he learned of the planned performance of *Die Walküre* he felt strengthened enough in his relationship with the king to lay down conditions. He, Wagner, was to be empowered to handle the entire matter. Further, communications would not be with Perfall, but with the court secretary, who was the more friendly Düfflipp. For his representative he wanted Porges, who would be his secretary with full powers to act for him.

Looming over all of these matters was the subject of Cosima. Both she and Wagner felt she should not be subjected to the calumnies of the Munich press. Exacerbating the situation was the fact that they were still not married, nor could they be until the formality of the divorce from Bülow. This seems to be the reason for Wagner's attempt to postpone the work until 1871. But the king would not postpone the performance that long, nor would he agree to reinstate Richter. Nor could he agree to Wagner's complete control, from afar, of the entire production. Once again, Wagner had overestimated his power over the young king.

24

The Turn of *Die Walküre*

PORGES, WHO HAD REFUSED Wagner's invitation to join forces with him in Starnberg, was now spending a great deal of time in Triebschen. The diary for February 27, 1870, includes Cosima's notation that Porges read to her and Richard an essay he had written about *Lohengrin*. The next night he read more from his essay, and Cosima noted that "his Jewishness becomes apparent only in his inability to listen in silence." That she should have found this to be a Jewish trait is a touch ironic. From all evidence Richard was unable to listen to anyone in silence for more than a few minutes, feeling always the compulsion to dominate the conversation.

On March 3 Porges earned Cosima's deep gratitude, and her tears, by telling her that Richard had never been so tranquil or lively as he had since she came into his life, and that without her, he would never have taken up his *Nibelung* again.

Some of Cosima's notations are cryptic, and others subject to varied interpretations. The following week she observed, "Many curious embarrassments on account of Porges's Jewish origin, every moment brings the Lord Jesus to our lips." Are the embarrassments to Porges, to Cosima, to Richard, or to all three? Is it, as is most likely, their references to Jesus in the presence of a Jew, a nonbeliever, that caused their discomfort? Or is the unlikely but possible cause of their mention of Jesus the presence of the Jew? Any embarrassment to Cosima, however, was most probably hers alone. Whatever her faults, she seems to have been sensitive, and averse, to the possible embarrassment or humiliation to anyone. Her anti–Semitic remarks, justifiably offensive to many today, were almost always spoken to receptive ears or written for receptive eyes. Richard, on the contrary, was often oblivious or uncaring of the sensibilities of others.

The problems with the *Meistersinger* performances, arising out of re-publication of "Judaism in Music," were still ongoing. Quoting a newspaper report, Cosima, in her diary, wrote that Jews were spreading a story that the song of Beckmesser, the villain in that opera, was an old Jewish song that Richard was trying to ridicule. As a result, she continued, there was some hissing, and calls of "we don't want to hear any more," but "complete victory for the Germans." Richard, she says, was upset that Jews should say what they did not want in the imperial theater. Even some determined anti–Wagnerians in recent times acknowledge that this believed misuse of a Jewish song was unfounded.[1] Later that month, there was "violent opposition" to the opera in Vienna from the Jews.

The search for a conductor for *Die Walküre* was the cause of some tension between Porges and Wagner. On the twenty-first of March, Porges, now in Munich, reported that the personnel there did not seem to know what to do. On the fourth of April Porges said that he wanted to start discussions between Perfall and Wagner about this, but the suggestion did not meet with a good reception in Triebschen. Cosima replied, rebuking him, and four days later they received a letter of apology for the intervention. On the eleventh Porges was back in Triebschen, apparently alarmed that the king "assumed" that he, Porges, would conduct *Die Walküre*. He asked Wagner's forgiveness for his lack of caution. What he may have done to cause the assumption, Porges did not say. The following day he returned to Munich. Wagner later voiced the suspicion that Porges would have liked very much to conduct the performance, a suspicion that was probably well founded.

In Munich, knowing that Wüllner was unacceptable to Wagner, attempts were being made to find another conductor. Cosima's diary for April 28 noted the reception of a letter from the conductor Levi, who was employed by the Carlsruhe opera. She noted parenthetically Wagner's comment, "I respect him because he really calls himself *Levi* as in the Bible, and not *Löwe* or *Lewy* etc." A year and a half later, in December 1871, following Richard's and Cosima's first personal meeting with Levi, in Carlsruhe, the comment was repeated. According to Cosima, "Richard says he respects him for the very reason that he calls himself Levi straight out, not Löwe or Lewin, etc." We have already seen Wagner's use of "Löwe," probably inadvertent, for his friends the Lehmanns in Prague. Continuing her entry of April 28, 1870, she said that Levi reported that he was asked to conduct *Die Walküre,* and wanted to know what Wagner thought about it. "Wagner replies calmly and honestly."

His calm and honest answer, for whatever else it may say, is interesting for what it says of the inception of this long-lasting friendship, and

Wagner's respect and admiration for Levi. That relationship was to be the most important but the most problematic of those with any of his Jewish friends. He addressed Levi as "My very dear Orchestra Conductor," and continued:

> Your enquiry does you great honor and deserves an equally honest response. The appeal ... was based upon the assumption that they might eventually find a conductor sufficiently unscrupulous as to perform my work without my personal cooperation. They have not yet succeeded in doing so, since all the most capable conductors who are friendly towards me have refused their help. If they are now similarly mistaken in their assumption with regard to yourself, their search will no doubt have to continue.

There continued an exposition of Wagner's view of the matter, namely, complete incompetence on the part of the theater management, headed of course by Perfall, the impossibility of any decent representation of his work without his own cooperation, and the impossibility of that help. He gave, however, no explanation of the reason for his inability to help. But if the king, to whom he owed so much, persist in requiring an immediate performance, "I have nothing against your conducting my work," but it must be by agreement between Levi and the management, with no demands made upon Wagner. He concluded the letter in a most friendly fashion:

> I am happy to have this opportunity to tell you of my delight at having heard only praise of your performances of my *Meistersinger* in Carlsruhe, and, more especially, that comparisons between the Dresden performance and yours were very much in your favor. How salutary it is for me to be able to welcome a real man of talent as conductor of a German opera-house is something which I probably do not need to affirm.
> Assuring you of my very great respect, I remain,

> Your very devoted servant
> Richard Wagner

Of course Levi did not accept the employment. And of course Franz Wüllner was once again engaged. The premiere was held on June 26, attended by dignitaries from the musical world of Europe, but not including Levi. After a second performance came six performances of each of the first two of the *Ring* operas on alternate days. Among the visitors was the French composer Camille Saint-Saëns, who thanked his good fortune for being alive to hear both of such tremendous works.

Thus, we see once more that when his works were the matter at hand, the religion of the parties to the controversy were of no moment, particularly when they fought alongside Wagner in his cause. Before this relationship has run its course, we will see Wagner's "principled" anti–Semitism put to its severest test. Notice should be taken nonetheless of a diary entry by Cosima on April 22, less than a week before the exchange of letters between Wagner and Levi. It refers to the postponement of the Berlin *Meistersinger* performance until the fall so that passions will have time to cool. "It means," says Cosima, "that a few Jewboys have achieved their aim."

25

Wagner and the French

SOME HAVE CLAIMED THAT Cosima's anti–Semitism may have stemmed, at least in part, from the fear that she had Jewish ancestry. There are disputed claims that one of her maternal great-grandfathers, Simon Moritz Bethmann, member of a family of Frankfurt bankers who died a Lutheran, was a converted Jew. In any event Cosima undoubtedly developed her anti–Semitism long before meeting Wagner, though it was certainly not moderated by that relationship.

But Jews were not the only ones to fall into Cosima's disfavor. Whatever the truth about her Jewish ancestry, there is no doubt about her French lineage. Her mother was French, and Cosima spent much of her young life in France. Yet her diaries reflect a hatred of the French, almost as fiercely expressed on occasion as her contempt for Judaism and Jews, if not nearly so frequently. Her animosity in that direction was most probably almost entirely derivative from Wagner's, but wholehearted nonetheless.

Whether motivated by his two years of hardship and frustration in Paris as a young man, or by the *Tannhäuser* fiasco 20 years later, or by something else, Wagner harbored a hatred of France and the French. The all but idolatrous admiration of Wagner expressed by numerous prominent French writers, artists and musicians, including the poet and art critic Charles Baudelaire, the composer Camille Saint-Saëns and the writer Édouard Schuré, did nothing to temper the animosity. In 1867, he published in the *South German Press* a number of articles about the "degenerate" French and their "superficial culture."

It reached its peak with the outbreak of the Franco-Prussian conflict on July 17, 1870. That struggle began with a French declaration of war based on a perceived insult from the Prussian king. Bismarck, the German Chancellor, had in fact deliberately contrived the supposed insult, counting on the hot-headed yellow journalism of the French press to goad its government into war. On the nineteenth, Bavaria, at Ludwig's direction, cast its lot with Prussia.

That evening Cosima and Richard were visited in their sanctuary in neutral Switzerland by a small contingent of French friends returning to their homeland from Germany. They had been to a Beethoven festival, several Wagnerian performances in Weimar, and a performance of *Die Walküre* in Munich. The group of French admirers included Édouard Schuré, then 29; a strikingly beautiful 19-year-old woman, Judith Mendès-Gautier; her husband Catulle Mendès, a budding novelist of 28; her father, Théophile Gautier, a writer of considerable fame; a 31-year-old friend and poet, Philippe-Auguste Villiers de l'Isle Adam; the composer Camille Saint-Saëns, then 35; and Henry Duparc, also a composer, about the same age as Judith. Wagner was not only far more famous than any of his visitors, but at 57, old enough to be a father figure for all but Gautier, who was near 60. All of these factors may, or may not, explain the passivity of the French group under the insulting blandishments of their German friend and idol.

About a year earlier, at Wagner's invitation, Mendès, in company with his wife Judith, and Villiers, had stopped at Triebschen on their way to an art exhibition in Munich. Judith's beauty seems to have been matched by her intelligence. At 17, among other accomplishments, she had translated a book of poems from the Chinese. On this earlier visit Wagner was instantly smitten by the young woman, and exhibited all the earmarks of a teenager showing off to his first love. This did not escape the notice of Cosima, but the tactful, cultured Judith managed to charm her admirer's wife and to earn her respect and friendship. On July 25, after nine days in Triebschen, the group left for Munich expressing the hope to see there a performance of *Das Rheingold*.

These three friends, together with their four additional companions, now arrived in Triebschen on the first day that pitted Bavaria on the side of Prussia against France. They apparently arrived in hopes of witnessing a wedding, Cosima's divorce having become final the previous day. All circumstances considered, we may assume that they assured the hosts that war would not affect their friendship and that they shared an interest in matters higher than war or politics. If they were expecting a reply in kind, they must have been quickly disillusioned. Cosima's diary and subsequent correspondence tell the tale.

Her diary entry on the nineteenth mentions "feelings of great embarrassment, though the dear people are friendly." The next day, to one of the visitors, she explained to them "concisely my attitude toward the war." She also explained that attitude very concisely in her diary. She and Richard were enthusiastic, jingoistic supporters of it. The French behavior in the lead-up to war she called "a tissue of lies, ignorance, insolence and conceit." Her diary reflects vividly the continuing vital interest of herself and Richard in the course of the conflict. Nonetheless, with their French friends they shared much music in the evenings, and walks and carriage rides during the day.

But Richard was just warming to the subject. On the twenty-fourth, we read, "Richard demands of our French friends that they understand how much we hate the French character." He had written much in similar vein about *the Jews*, but it is doubtful that he ever said the equivalent directly to a Jewish friend about the Jewish character. On the twenty-sixth, "There comes from Richard a long speech on the German character and how difficult it is for us at this moment to consort with French people." On the twenty-ninth the Frenchmen spoke of the alignment of other nations, and, with an obvious effort at objectivity, condemned France's enemies and allies alike. Cosima complained in her diary about "That so-called sage objectivity which accords the same treatment to an honest man — Bismarck — as to a rogue Napoleon," referring to Napoleon III, emperor of France.

On July 30, they learned from Richard's lawyer that the wedding could not take place for another four or five weeks. The French group said farewell and departed, but not before a reading by Villiers of one of his writings. What he read is not mentioned, but Cosima referred to his style as hypocritical and bombastic, the theatrical presentation making "us" thoroughly indignant, whoever besides Richard "us" may include. Richard, she says, "draws their attention to the objectionable nature of their rhetorical poetry." She describes Catulle and Judith Mendès as a good, deeply distressed couple who both posses real beauty of soul. Her kindly feeling toward Judith, however, was not destined to last too many more years.

Their departure did not end the one sided diatribe. Friendly letters from Catulle and Judith were met with officious sermons on the faults and failings of their nation, and the sentimentality, the falseness and narrowness of the French spirit. He tells these Frenchmen, as a year ago he told the Jews, that they must find a "real statesman" who will "tell the French nation what the German nation is and what it wants, for it is this nation ... not the 'Prussians' that is knocking at your doors." The reference is to the new unity of the German states as one nation. The French, he says, must look at the situation like "practical philosophers," and see it as a judgment of God on them. In short, both Jews and French must assimilate to the new Germanism.

Catulle responded with the hope that higher things than war or politics, such as love and music, could unite these friends. As usual, Wagner required the last word. The Frenchman's tone was very nice, he said, but it was discouraging that his countrymen were still resolving to exterminate the invaders. He was still waiting for a single Frenchman with the courage to declare the "truth," namely the justice of the German cause.[1]

Wagner lamented the absence of the one Frenchman with courage as he had the one Jew, and as he would some years later lament the absence of any "real men" in Russia to cure that nation's faults, which he meticulously detailed. As with almost all of Wagner's opinions, there was no room for dissent or contrary view. There was only right and wrong; he being right, any dissent being necessarily wrong. His hatred of the French was matched by his euphoria at the prospect of a new united German nation, a long sought replacement of the confederation of independent states that had plagued German life and politics for a thousand years. Such feelings were shared by most other Germans and are understandable. Much less so was the rude and unprovoked expression of them to friends, citizens of the enemy country though they were.

Yet the possibility cannot be ignored that such an arrogant self assurance was an intricate part of the temperament required to complete the life's task he set out for himself. His French friends, like many others, seemed to understand. After enduring hardships and privations during the lengthy German siege of Paris, Catulle could write that he and Judith were consoled that Wagner was at peace in his Swiss retreat.[2] Whether or not this contained a touch or more of sarcasm, no one now can say.

But, regardless of the nuances of that letter, if the insensitivity of Wagner knew no bounds, the understanding and patience of Catulle ultimately did. In November 1870, during the siege of Paris, Wagner penned a rather juvenile farce, ridiculing the suffering of the French, mocking some of the finest of their writers and musicians, including Schuré and Jules Offenbach. He did not publish it until 1873, over a year after the war ended. Catulle continued in his admiration for Wagner's music and in his attendance of performances of his works. But his personal contacts with Wagner ended.

On August 25, 1870, as the war in all its fury still raged, Cosima and Richard were married. She wrote that her highest pride was that she had given up everything in order to live with him. "May I be worthy of bearing Richard's name," she wrote in her diary. Throughout the 12 years of the marriage, she did her very best, and by any standard must be said to have succeeded. She was not only his wife and the mother of his three children, but his secretary, social secretary, confidant, public relations person, hostess and receptionist to their many distinguished visitors. She loved what he loved, admired what he admired, and hated what he hated. Those who were ill disposed to Richard or his music earned only her contempt. Those favorably disposed earned at least her respect, often her love or admiration. She was the epitome of the nineteenth century wife. She had expressed the hope that they would die together. But she outlived him by 47 years, devoted, while her strength remained, to carrying out his wishes, including performances of his works exactly as "the Master" had decreed, down to the smallest detail.

A letter from Judith explained their absence from the wedding. Catulle would be considered a deserter if he left France at that time. A telegram of congratulations was received, signed by Marie Muchanoff, Karl Tausig, and the artist Franz von Lenbach. Cosima, a devout Catholic, did indeed give up everything, including her religion. Wagner had often expressed contempt for the Catholic religion. At his urging she became a Protestant. He expected everyone around him to be what he wanted them to be. On August 27, he wrote the Frenchman Schuré, urging him to become a German.

26

Death of Tausig

WAGNER'S OBSESSION WITH the Jews as enemies continued apace with his friendship with Porges and Tausig. Just two months after the outbreak of war, he pronounced to Cosima that the Jews had no interest in the formation of a German empire, preferring "cosmopolitanism." A month after that, he and Cosima discussed certain "weird" characteristics of Madame Viardot. Richard, said Cosima, attributed it to her Jewishness: "These people do not possess the soul of their gifts." Viardot's "Jewishness" was entirely a figment of the imagination of Cosima and Richard. The day after Christmas, a friend described the Beethoven festivities in Vienna. To Wagner, the friend's detailed description showed "that it was Judea which celebrated the greatest of our heroes. All of it must have been absurd and ridiculous and, for us, an affront."

On January 1, 1871, Porges was appointed musical director in Munich. Wagner saw this as a trick by Perfall. The papers, he pointed out, were quoting him as saying that he, Wagner, was in effect having himself appointed as manager of the theater, as Porges was known only as a supporter of Wagner. His enemy Wüllner was thus to secure the permanent appointment, as Wagner saw it, since it was known that Porges could not really conduct. On the 16 of the month, Wagner complained of the "clumsy" critical comments about him. People continued to comment, he said, about appointments of his supporters, including Porges and Cornelius, not understanding that "such men can be of use only under my direction." On the 29 came news of Porges's failure as director.

On February 22, Hans Richter told Wagner he had a letter from Munich to the effect that Porges had conducted *Lohengrin* so badly that he would not conduct again. Wagner answered:

I can never forget it when someone has behaved well toward me. It was he who arranged the concert in Prague for me, and in the evil days in Vienna he was the only one to whom I could turn. So he can go on sinning quite a while before I strike him off my good books.

Whatever problems he had with *the Jews* did not extend to this particular Jew. Just a few days earlier, he had expressed surprise that a Jew was editing a humor-oriented newspaper, saying, "The Jews have no wit of their own; though they are excellent subjects for witty observations, they themselves ... have no powers of observation."

By 1871 much in Wagner's life had been clarified. The marriage to Cosima had diminished the possibility of exposing himself or her to further humiliation or attack for the betrayal of husband and friend. Nor was there further necessity for secrecy, contrived explanations or apologies. Nonetheless it was also clear that he wanted nothing further to do with Munich, and its cabal of enemies. *Tristan* and *Die Meistersinger* had been brought to life in productions, he was obliged to admit, that were all that could have been expected. The plans for a theater in Munich had been abandoned and the controversy with the architect Semper had been settled, though not without leaving traces of rancor. It was now time to begin anew his work on *Der Ring des Nibelungen*.

It had been over 12 years since he wrote Liszt that he had left his Siegfried under a Linden tree and said farewell to him. He had completed the second act of that opera, except for full scoring, and lying ahead were composition of the third act and of the final opera, *Götterdämmerung* ("The Twilight of the Gods"). He wanted no more productions in Munich, but the king certainly did, and ordered a production of *Siegfried*. Ludwig was the owner of all rights to the operas, and had the will and the power to have them performed with or without Wagner's cooperation. He asked for the full score. But Wagner was not going to undergo another experience with that third opera of the *Ring* as he did with the first two. Both chicanery and some duplicity with his royal benefactor were of course necessary, but in these matters Wagner was already both skilled and experienced. He worked on, but delayed the final completion of *Siegfried* until it suited his purpose to finish it. After it was finished, he simply said that it was not.

It would suit his purpose to acknowledge its completion when he had found and arranged for a suitable place in which to build his theater, specially designed for his *magnum opus*. He had long imagined that place as a small town, free from the multiple distractions of a large city. It was his wish, expressed as early as 1862,[1] that guests would come to the town to see his operas, not for any other of the "usual entertainments." There, a provisionary theater was to be erected, a very simple one, "perhaps only of wood," the interior designed only for the artistic purpose. One of the key provisions was to be an invisible orchestra, hidden by the stage. Members of the audience were not to be involuntary witnesses to the mechanical movements made by musicians and their leader. He found especially odious the puffed up cheeks of the players in the brass section.

The town that he selected was Bayreuth, in the kingdom of Bavaria, about 150 miles north of Munich. It was in 1835, at the age of 22, that he had first laid eyes on this town, nestled in the valley at the foot of the Fichtelgebirge, the Spruce Mountains, to the north. He was traveling to Nuremberg from Carlsbad, in what was then Bohemia; today, the Czech Republic. His route lay through Bayreuth, which he first saw in the light of the setting sun. It made an indelible impression on him. Now on the fifth of March, 1871, having heard Richard's recollection of the town, Cosima suggested they examine an encyclopedia article about it. They were delighted to read of a beautiful old opera house. It had been built in the previous century by the Margravine Wilhelmina, a sister of Frederick the Great, and was one of several buildings that still stood as monuments to her short stay there. She and her husband, the Margrave Frederick, had moved there from Anspach. After his death she moved back to Anspach with the provincial court.[2]

In April Richard and Cosima journeyed to Bayreuth to inspect the theater. They realized at once that the magnificent rococo structure, though housing the largest stage in Germany at the time, and despite its richly carved and gilded interior, was far too small for Richard's grandiose plans. A new one would have to be built. He would need the cooperation of many townspeople. As it happened, he fell ill on this visit and was treated by one of them, Dr. Karl Landgraf. He became the family doctor not only to the Wagners after they moved to Bayreuth in the following year, but later to the artistic personnel.[3] On the twelfth of May Wagner publicly announced his plans to build a theater in Bayreuth for the production of his *Nibelung* operas. It was a bitter blow to Ludwig, but at least it was to be in his kingdom of Bavaria. As Wagner well knew, it had to be there if he was to enjoy the continued patronage of the king.[4]

Wagner explained not only his vision of the new theater, but expounded at length the details by which it was to be achieved. The cornerstones of the project were the "invisible orchestra," to be situated under the stage, and the unrestricted sight lines, both of which would maximize the illusion of reality on the stage. The prevailing system of tiers of boxes was thus to be excluded. The theater was to be provisional in nature, simple and unadorned. Later was to come a more permanent and grandly designed outer shell, unimportant for the actual performances, and unnecessary at that early stage.

The singers and musicians for that first festival were to receive expenses but no salaries. "He who does not come to me from glory and enthusiasm can stay where he is." He had no use for a singer who came only for the sake of a "silly salary." Nor were the performances to be accessible by admission fees, nor for financial profit to anyone. They were to take place only when costs were covered by voluntary subscriptions of patrons. "Never is there to be a question of recompense to the author."[5] Strange, weird perhaps, as it may sound, there is not the slightest reason to suspect the sincerity of the statements.

Ludwig, as owner of the rights to the operas, could have stopped the project cold, a risk of which Wagner was well aware, but which he was willing to take. Under no circumstances was he going to take up residence again in Munich, even should it mean the loss of the pension he was receiving from the Bavarian treasury. But Ludwig could not tolerate the thought of a rift. He congratulated Wagner and wished him well. His show of good will, and the pension, continued. It was increasingly evident that the king needed Wagner and his music, even more than Wagner needed the king. In matters that were vital to his goals, Wagner was unyielding to anyone, the king included.

In addition to Dr. Landgraf, Wagner enlisted the aid of two other important Bayreuth residents, Friedrich Feustel, a banker and civic leader, and Theodor Muncker, the Bürgermeister, the mayor, of the town. Wagner also gained the full cooperation of two other prominent men: Emil Heckel, a book and music seller from Mannheim, who had been the founder of the first Wagner Society; and Karl Brandt, a prominent stage machinist from Darmstadt.

The first and most important task was financing. The estimated cost of the festival was 300,000 thalers, or 900,000 marks. Wagner knew it was necessary to organize a society of friends and patrons. His choices to undertake this task were Heckel, Countess von Wolkenstein, formerly the Baroness Marie von Schleinitz, and Karl Tausig.

It was Tausig who took the leading role. The group planned to accomplish their mission by means of "Wagner clubs" throughout Europe and America, whose purpose was to collect sufficient funds to finance the project. It was primarily Tausig who worked out the details and the idea of establishing a guarantee fund to be subscribed to by patrons. The goal was to sell 1,000 "patron certificates" at 300 thalers apiece, a free seat for all the performances being included as an incentive. Among the guarantors were Tausig himself, Liszt, and, to add international flavor, the sultan of Turkey.[6] In present times, the process does not seem at all unusual. In 1871 it was as new as the notion of an opera festival itself.

Tausig was "the life and soul" of the project.[7] In early May, Wagner was in Berlin to give a concert. It was part of an ill conceived plan to gain the support of Bismarck and to break loose from his ties with Bavaria and King Ludwig. Upon his arrival there was much excitement, and Tausig had arranged a huge dinner in his honor. He had also planned to organize an orchestra to give special concerts, and later to organize the beginning of the festival orchestra itself. But, not long after his appointment as provisional manager of the fund in April, he fell ill. He was later diagnosed with typhus, and journeyed to Leipzig, where he was nursed by two friends, Countess Elisabeth Krockow and Marie Muchanoff,[8] the latter being the lady to whom Wagner had dedicated the new publication of his "Judaism in Music."

Tausig died in a hospital in Leipzig on the seventeenth of July. On the eighteenth, Wagner was playing for Cosima a portion of the third act of *Siegfried,* on which he had resumed work; the scene known as "Brynhilde's Awakening." Cosima was enthralled by it and tried to imagine which people would be able to appreciate the magnificence of the musical passage. Only two, her father (Liszt) and Tausig, came to mind. Then a letter arrived from Countess Krockow. It was written before the young friend's death. She was in the hospital, she wrote, with Tausig who was dying of Typhus. Cosima's unfeeling, almost chilling, reaction, and almost unfathomable thoughts, should be quoted in full for whatever one might be able to make of them:

> A great shock. Even if he recovers, he is in any case lost to our undertaking; what a lesson to us! To us his death seems to have a metaphysical basis; a poor character, worn out early, one with no real faith, who, however close events brought us, was always conscious of an alien element (the Jewish). He threw himself into Bayreuth with a real frenzy, but can this outward activity help him?... He is too gifted not to be weary of life.

Before her union with Wagner, and after his death, she uttered numerous hateful remarks about both *the Jews* and individual Jews, and unlike her husband, solely because they were Jews. In none of them does she do herself less credit, or show more meanness of character, than in this passage in her diary. That she had just mentioned Tausig as the only one, other than her father, who could properly appreciate the sublimely beautiful musical episode her husband had created, merely serves to make the entire outpouring more macabre. Tausig was important only for his usefulness to her husband and his work. Otherwise his life was irrelevant. Even to her private diary, she must make it explicit that he is a Jew. Nor is it any mitigation that her reference to Tausig's having "no real faith" may not be aimed at his religion, but perhaps at the lack of faith of any kind. In this connection it is well to recall the early exchange of letters between Wagner and Liszt, cryptic in some respects, but obviously dealing with a lack of piety on the young man's part, not on his Jewishness.

As she frequently did, she spoke of "we" and "us" with little or no indication that her thoughts were shared by her husband. In this instance the evidence seems to be entirely contrary. His first reaction: "I have no further wish to live in this world. Now I have you, all I want is to care for the children and just look on; for no matter what one puts a hand to, ghosts arise. Die Fliegende Holländer was nothing compared to me." Richard pens an answer to the letter, and they walk into town to take it to the post office. Cosima wrote "Will it find Tausig still alive?" Richard claimed to have hope. Tausig was like a cat, he said, and would perhaps recover.

But on the twentieth came a letter from the countess. Tausig was dead. From Cosima there was more baseness. "When we received the news of his illness he was already dead. Complete stupefaction, then reminiscence — how many friends already gone." She mentioned Schnorr and a few others. "How many! In Tausig we have certainly lost a great pillar of our enterprise, but that leaves us indifferent." But Richard said he "looks upon it as a cloud; the vapors rise — will they be dispersed or will they form themselves into a life-bringing cloud? God knows."

The conversations continued. Cosima confirmed her inability to see this ingratiating young man as anything but an asset to their venture, otherwise of no value. She was obsessed with his Jewishness, and his humanity means little or nothing to her: "Tausig's sad life; so precocious ... conscious of the curse of his Jewishness; no pleasure in his tremendous virtuosity ... the marriage with a Jewess, ended almost at once; completely finished at 29, yet still not a man." Compared to her, Richard was the soul of an empathetic, caring human being: "What must the sleepless nights of such a person be like? What occupied his thoughts?" He shrugged and complained to his wife about the "stupidity of fate, snatching Tausig away at the moment when a great new activity would have brought him inner joy and satisfaction." That night, they talked a lot more about Tausig. The next day Richard told her he dreamed about him. Two days later came another letter from the countess: In his final days Tausig had called Richard and Cosima "two great natural forces."

He did not get over the loss quickly. On July 25 Richard referred to him as an "unfortunate, interesting phenomenon." Cosima quoted Richard's laments: "Melancholy in Nature and myself, since Tausig's death I have no will for anything but business matters and the children's lessons; I just cannot manage to write personal letters." By September 15, almost two months after Tausig's death, Cosima found him extremely worried and agitated due to problems with the laying of the foundations for the theater.

He claimed to be so "churned up inside that even something like Tausig's death goes in one ear and out the other."

A year later, on September 7, 1872, he wrote an epitaph for Tausig's grave in the Halle Gate Cemetery in Berlin, one that Cosima found "very moving." The epitaph, placed on the tombstone at the time it was raised, was in verse:

> To be ready for death
> Life's fruit slowly ripens,
> To earn its ripeness early,
>   In the sudden blush of spring,
> Was your fate, and your daring —
> Now we must grieve both your fate and
>   Your daring.[9]

The foundation stone for the theater in Bayreuth had been laid on Wagner's fifty-ninth birthday, May 22, 1872. It was the occasion of much ceremony and the presence of many friends, including Porges, and dignitaries, including the newly installed emperor of Germany, William I. One of the high points was a performance of Beethoven's Ninth Symphony. Among the four soloists selected by Wagner for the performance were Albert Niemann and Marie Lehmann, the younger sister of Lilli. Both sisters were to perform in the first festival four years later. Typically, no one from the press had been invited.

Almost a year later, Wagner issued his report to the patrons on *The Festival-Theater at Bayreuth*. He acknowledged the help and support of many friends and acquaintances, but only one of them did he mention by name: Karl Tausig. On the first page of this 19-page report, he stated:

> Only to a handful of more intimate friends did I express my views as to the precise mode in which a solid form might be given to the interest I asked for. The youngest of these friends, the exceptionally talented and energetic Karl Tausig, embraced the matter as a task peculiarly falling to himself ... Hardly had he began to set his scheme in motion, than a sudden death removed him from us in his thirtieth year. My last word to him was committed to his gravestone: the present seems a not unworthy place to repeat it.[10]

The short poem was included in the report. The following evening an incident occurred at a banquet held for many of the distinguished guests. There were present also a number of uninvited guests, namely, members of the press. An argument ensued between the journalists and one of the guests, one Coerper, who thought their presence unwarranted and unseemly. On the advice of another guest, the journalists were ordered out. As Cosima recorded the event, "The entire Jewish contingent from Berlin stood up as one man to defend the gentlemen of the press." This compelled Coerper to apologize, which, according to Cosima, made "Richard and me very indignant."

After the dedication of the cornerstone for the theater, Richard was obliged to find singers for his venture and to give concerts almost incessantly to raise funds. Ominously, Cosima's diary of August 9 reports that the previous day Richard had experienced heart palpitations.

On the eleventh, the Wagners received an announcement from Carlsruhe of a proposed visit by Hermann Levi, and Frau Lehmann and her daughter; which daughter Cosima did not specify. Wagner answered Levi: "Most valued friend, I am here, and looking forward to seeing you at any time. You are most heartily welcome." It is signed "Your devoted servant." The guests arrived on the seventeenth. The next day Levi said something mildly supportive of the Jesuits, apparently opposing some law repressive to them, whereupon "Richard became very angry and depicted in lively words all the damage which the Catholic Church had done to Germany."

Part V

Bayreuth I:
The First Festival

27

Rubinstein and Preparations
for *The Ring*

THE FESTIVAL THEATER WAS constructed at the foot of a hill known as the Bürgerreuth, in the very northern part of town. It affords a panoramic view of the gently rolling landscape that marks the entire Bayreuth area. The ground itself had been purchased by the governing council of Bayreuth and donated for the theater. The site for Wagner's home, situated in the town's center, had been paid for by Wagner in 1872 in the amount of 12,000 guilders. He later named the home "Wahnfried," sometimes translated as "peace from madness," other times, "peace from illusion." Its construction, however, was in need of funding, which was made possible by King Ludwig. In 1871 he had taken patrons certificates in the amount of 25,000 thalers, and now designated them for use in the construction of the new home.

It was built to Wagner's precise and luxurious specifications, including a finely sculpted bronze bust of Ludwig. The idea for the bust was Wagner's, but when work on it was delayed due to the cost, Ludwig had the sculpture done at his own expense and gave it to Wagner as a gift. The composer and his family took possession of the home on April 28, 1874. The bust, in all its dignity, still adorns the lawn in front of the structure, which is now a Wagner museum.

His love for Tausig notwithstanding, the barbs against the Jews continue, most of them by Cosima, but sporadically by Wagner himself. In mid–November, he told Cosima that when Germans are well off, "They become Jews, elegant and indifferent!" On February 5 he returned from Berlin and reported that the "Wagneriana" vanished into thin air. "Much

Jewishness to put up with." It seems that at the dinner arranged by Tausig some months before his death, the young pianist had not introduced the members by name, thus, "so to speak, denying them. Jewish sensitivity and Jewish revenge." It appears, in short, that most of the members of the Wagner club in Berlin were Jews, and feeling slighted that their names had not been mentioned at the banquet, they resigned.

On March 7, 1872, Cosima made a significant entry in her diary: "Letters arrive, among others a very remarkable one from Josef Rubinstein, beginning 'I am a Jew' and demanding salvation through participation in the *Nibelungen*. Richard sends a very friendly reply."

Cosima quoted nothing from the letter except that one initial statement. More fully, it stated, "I am a Jew. By telling you that I tell you everything. All those characteristics noticeable in the present day Jews I too possess." Rubinstein then described how he had been completely dispirited until the day he discovered Wagner's music. He immersed himself in it and was able to forget the outside world. That was the happiest day in his life. Now, however, he was again despondent and had made an attempt at suicide. Further, his condition continually worsened. Obviously familiar with "Judaism in Music," he recognized, he says, that the Jews, himself included, must "go under."[1] Without further explanation, however, he said that he cannot go under through baptism. There remained only death, which he had already tried. The letter continued:

> Perhaps you can yet help me. Of course I do not mean help me from sheer pity ... but could I not be of some use to you in the production of the *Nibelung*? I believe I understand the work even if not perfectly yet. I look to you then for help, for the help I urgently need. My parents are rich. I would have the means to go to you at once. I look for an answer as soon as possible. My address is as follows ... Joseph Rubenstein, c/o Isaac Rubinstein, Kharkov.[2]

This 25-year-old Russian Jew was obviously a very troubled, probably neurotic, man. He was also a very talented one, though that could not have been known to Wagner at the time. He had studied in Vienna with one Joseph Dachs, a pupil of the well-known Karl Czerny, a prolific composer and best known for his instructive studies for piano, still used by countless students. Rubinstein's first public concert was given there at age 18. At age 22, one of Wagner's devoted supporters, the Grand Princess Helene of Russia, made him her personal pianist, and it was in that capacity that he came in contact with Wagner's music. Another friend of Wagner, the composer Alexander Serov, introduced him to *Tristan* and *Die Meistersinger*. It was undoubtedly these works that gave the highly strung, depressed artist a reason to live.

From the letter itself, it can hardly be said that he was seeking salvation from his Jewishness, as Wagner, self-defensively, later claimed. The letter seemed to rule that out. He seemed rather to be looking for escape from his emotional turmoil. For a man who never converted, never changed his name, or converted despite incessant, rampant pressures of the societal hostility of 19th Century Germany, salvation in Wagner's sense did not seem to be his goal. What he was begging for was a more immediate and practical solution, Wagner's consent to his participation in the *Nibelung* undertaking.

What the "very friendly reply" was, Cosima does not say, but it must indeed have been friendly. To tell Richard Wagner "your music gave me a reason to live," and "I want to help you," whether the writer was Jew, Christian, or otherwise, was bound to evoke a very friendly response. It was friendly enough that seven weeks later, on April 21, Rubinstein appeared at Triebschen, unannounced, in the company of a Dr. Cohen, a friend, and perhaps a guardian. As it happened, that was the day before Wagner was to leave permanently for Bayreuth.

Rubinstein, having traveled from Kharkov to see the composer, was probably quite upset to learn of Wagner's imminent departure. Doctor Cohen managed to maneuver Wagner into a private conversation in the boathouse, out of the hearing of Rubinstein, and told Wagner that the man needed to be treated with great consideration. Cosima's entry on that day: "Richard is infinitely kind to the young man and advises him to take things easy, offers him access to Bayreuth." That would necessarily come in the future, when the Wagners were settled there. Rubinstein returned to Kharkov to bide his time.

The following day, Wagner, though not Cosima or the children, did go to Bayreuth, where he stayed at the Hotel Fantaisie, just to the west of town. The packing of the household furniture and articles was supervised by Cosima. She and the children said their tearful goodbyes to their home at Triebschen, then joined him at the Fantaisie on April 30, the first day after the work on the theater had begun. The laying of the foundation-stone took place on May 22, as already noted, after which came a round of concerts and banquets. Rubenstein, in mid–June, wrote to the Wagners of his planned appearance the following month. Wagner had been back in Bayreuth some weeks when, on July 13, Rubinstein made his appearance, having come to assist in plans for production of *Der Ring des Nibelungen.*

His first act was, fittingly, a piano concert for Richard and Cosima, the very evening of his arrival. It pleased both of them tremendously, and Cosima noted that his rendering of a fugue by Bach put them into ecstasies. "It is as if music were really being heard for the first time." Wagner soon had him copying the orchestral sketch for the third act of *Götterdämmerung,* last of the *Ring* operas. He also appointed him as one of four copyists, whom he termed his "Nibelung Chancellery." Initially, the four stayed in the shell of the theater, still under construction.

Interestingly, in October 1874, in a letter to King Ludwig, Wagner mentioned that one of his group of four was a "Russian." Apparently, his continued anti–Semitic vituperations considered, he did not care to mention that Rubinstein was also a Jew, though most often it was the religion, not the nationality of Jews that rated precedence with him. He told the king he was teaching them all to conduct his work, and termed them "extremely capable young musicians."

For most of the next 10 years Rubinstein lived close to, or with Wagner as part of the household, doing most often the two things he had done so quickly upon his arrival. He copied scores, and entertained Richard and Cosima, as well as frequent guests, with his wide range of piano repertoire. For the most part, the Wagners found his performances at least satisfactory, often brilliant, at which times neither Richard nor Cosima mentioned his Jewish heritage. On rare occasion they found his performance less that satisfactory, however, and this they privately attributed to his Jewishness.

What is perhaps one of the strangest juxtapositions in Cosima's diaries, one of the most glaring contradictions, comes in notations less than a month apart. On November 8, 1874, Rubinstein had entertained the couple with the Beethoven Sonata opus 111, the great composer's last, and arguably his finest. Cosima saw minor problems with the first movement, but the magnificent second, echoing her husband no doubt, she termed "very beautifully and delicately" played. On December 3, hardly four weeks later, he performed from piano transcription the "Harp Quartet," which did not please them. Said Richard: "The Jews have no folk feeling and in consequence can neither love nor recognize that quality in Beethoven." If Cosima perceived any contradiction in her husband's position on this subject, she, wisely perhaps, kept it to herself.

Rubinstein was unquestionably a very difficult person. For one thing, he refused to heed any request that did not come personally from Wagner. It would not do for another of the many assistants or family members to convey the request; he must hear it personally from the Master. On at least one occasion Wagner was reported to be enraged at him to the extent that Cosima was obliged to calm him. It is not easy to imagine how two such difficult people as he and Wagner could get along well. But despite a number of flare-ups, and racial insults on the part of Wagner, and provocations and sullenness on the part of Rubinstein, through some strange chemistry they did get along and become fast friends. Wagner had a peculiar affection for him, as he was to demonstrate a number of times.

On May 25, just three days after the cornerstone ceremony, Cosima and Richard discuss again the "Jewish question." The "Israelite" participation in the Wagner Society in Berlin has left them with a very bad taste. Richard, said Cosima, hoped the whole thing would disappear like a sickness. Amalgamation was impossible and, she wrote, "we cannot believe that the Germans will be subjugated by the Jews, our military exploits have shown us to be too strong for that." Nor was Rubinstein personally immune from such comments uttered between the couple in private.

On August 3, following vocal exercises with a tenor being auditioned, the diary included "unpleasant revelations of character in Herr Rubinstein." On this occasion no reference to his Judaism was included. But on the fourteenth, while discussing Rubinstein's playing, Richard comments about the "curiosity" that Jews seemed neither to recognize nor to play any themes. His basis for the incredibly sweeping indictment: In Dresden a Jewish musician played through the entire *Fliegende Holländer* without recognizing the Dutchman's theme. Wagner's broad conclusions, applied to the entirety of the Jewish population, resulted quite frequently from the real or imagined deficiencies of a single individual, sometimes exhibited on a single occasion.

Not all of their negative comments about Rubinstein referred to his religion. The day after his arrival, July 14, as he "makes music" with Richard, Cosima observed that everything inside the young man is in a very raw state and must be developed. On the sixteenth she commented that Herr Rubinstein went through the first act of *Siegfried* and showed great powers of understanding. The following day, the Wagners walked with Rubinstein and "Richard questions him about his study of Schopenhauer, which soon leads the conversation to very deep levels." On the twenty-second, Richard was not feeling well, and "the presence of our good Rubinstein," disturbed and put a strain on him. On the twenty-ninth, "he wished to sing us a song of his own," but the childish delivery and text, plus a break in his voice, caused uncontrollable laughter.

There are other mentions of Rubinstein, sometimes showing mild annoyance, but he was obviously becoming a fixture in the Wagner household. On September 29, five days after the Wagners had moved from the Fantaisie to a house in town, Cosima noted that "Our good Rubinstein" came to say farewell, though she does not tell us where he is going. "Richard reproaches me for having dismissed him coldly, which I very much regret."

Remarks about *the Jews*, however, continue. In November Cosima wrote that their friends were having a bad time at present as "the entire Jewish clique has mobilized against them." In December they were in Bremen and visited the stock exchange. Richard found the atmosphere very dignified, unlike the exchanges in which Jewish traders predominated.

On September 17, Richard had told Cosima that he believed there was something wrong with his heart. Of any serious concern about it there is no mention.

The story of Wagner's efforts throughout 1873 to produce his *Nibelung* tetralogy is one of feverish activity and tireless efforts to raise funds; of the search for suitable singers; of arrangements for construction, postponements of the planned performances, and unending frustrations. Longtime friends commented on the obvious signs of aging, and there were physical pains and illnesses. On May 12, Cosima wrote that Richard "is not well, suddenly spits blood, complains about suddenly being unable to remember words.... He looks worn out and his speech, though still full of feeling, is flat.... I do not wish to admit to myself how worried I am. The doctor says it is nothing."

The furious pace continued. Two architects engaged by Wagner, Karl Brandt and Otto Brückwald, had worked out the details of design of the theater from the original design by Semper. His was intended for Munich, but this building was to be far simpler. In early August 1873 the building was topped out, but there was still much work remaining and construction companies, their bills unpaid, were threatening to walk off the job. The first performance, planned for 1874, had to be postponed for another year. The very idealistic undertaking was being run aground again on mundane matters.

In the fall of that year, Wagner, following his usual custom when desperately short of funds, moved to a comfortable home on one of the finest streets the town had to offer. That his attempts to finance the festival were coming up far short, however, was clear. To Nietzsche and others, he complained of the lack of interest or financial support from the German princes, while steadfastly refusing any compromise on any aspect of his artistic endeavor.

He did receive 500 pounds sterling from the khedive of Egypt. This same Egyptian leader had very recently commissioned an opera from Giuseppe Verdi based on a story set in Egypt. When the great Italian composer hesitated to accept, the khedive had threatened to give the commission to Wagner or to Charles Gounod. Verdi finally accepted, and the result was *Aida*. When threatening him with Wagner, the khedive was either bluffing, or knew not whereof he spoke. Wagner's plate was already full, and nothing was going to divert him from his goal.

In mounting desperation he turned once again to the man he had so sorely disappointed, but who could not live without the dream they both had nourished. The Bavarian king had more or less washed his hands of the project, having been burned too often with it, and did not at once respond.

So in early 1874 Wagner met with the not unkindly disposed Councilor Düfflipp. The councilor agreed to take the matter up with the king, but after doing so, he claimed that the king was somewhat unsettled, and his behavior erratic, behavior that was later to give grounds, or excuse, to his opponents to have him declared insane and deposed.

Thoroughly frustrated and dejected, Wagner spoke of abandoning the project entirely until, some uncertain future time when different circumstances might prevail. Throughout Germany, it seemed, including the seat of the empire in Berlin, doors were being slammed in his face. But if he thought failure was certain, the king did not. Only Wagner could create the art; but the king could bring it to life. Whatever disappointments he had suffered in the past, whatever ingratitude and betrayals, whatever dishonesty, Ludwig could not let the work fail. On January 25 he wrote to Wagner, apologizing for the delay in responding to his request. The response was indeed heartening. "No, no, and again no! It shall not end in this way! It must be helped. Our plan must not be wrecked.... Do not despair and favor me with a prompt letter."[3]

A plan was soon worked out. If the advance sale of tickets and patron certificates could not repay the royal guarantee, an outright loan to be repaid out of actual receipts over time might well succeed. One hundred thousand thalers was advanced. All receipts from performances and the sale of patron certificates plus half of the receipts from concerts given by Wagner to raise money were to go to the court treasury to repay the debt. It was still anticipated by the king and his councilors that the first performance would take place in 1875. Wagner had assured them previously that with sufficient advances that date could be kept.

But to his top financial lieutenants, Feustel and Muncker, he said something different. He announced to them that the festival would definitely now take place in the summer of 1876. Wagner wrote an effusive letter of thanks to the king, but mentioned no postponement of the date of opening. There followed much more intense and often frustrating work, and negotiations, peppered with misunderstandings and disagreements with the king. When Wagner asked that some relief be granted with respect to repayment of previous loans and for use of the patron certificates receipts, all due to unforeseen personal and theater expenses, the king's response was cool. He granted the relief as to the loan repayment, but insisted that no change would be countenanced to the agreement with respect to receipts from the patron certificate sales. Wagner was further told that the king did not want that subject brought up again.

But bring it up again he did. All through 1875 it was broached by Wagner in one form or another. Finally in September, he regretfully advised the king that without use of receipts from the first 600 certificates for certain pressing construction expenses, the scheduled *Ring* performance for 1875 would have to be postponed again. The decision for this postponement had in fact already been made and conveyed to his close associates. The king, though faced with his own difficulties, agreed to permit a substantial portion be given to the theater committee. Once more, the uncanny ability of the composer to pressure the pliable monarch is starkly evident. The last portion of the king's agreement did little to alter that now obvious fact: "I am not disposed to make any more concessions in the matter and consequently must not be importuned about it again."

Nonetheless he was. The final rehearsals were set for the early summer of 1876, the performances in August. By the end of May, however, Wagner, no doubt in all sincerity, found it impossible to continue without more financial assistance. He informed the king that he required a moratorium on repayments for two or three months. The king responded by foregoing repayments until 800 patron certificates had been sold.

Thus there appears no doubt that Wagner's creations were of signal importance to Ludwig, or that there was, to him, something spiritual, noble, and transcendent in them, something to be preserved at all costs. He saw his most important mission as the struggle to bring those works to the life on a stage befitting their extraordinary demands. That goal was to him the most important of his reign. History has vindicated him. It is to his credit, and was a strength rather than a weakness, that he yielded time and time again to Wagner's importunings.

He was not, as shown in other matters, easily manipulated or weak willed. His life's story, most of which is irrelevant to our inquiry here, so proves. But he was a dreamer. Denied his dream of building in Munich the theater to house Wagner's works and of making his capital the center of Wagnerian art, he turned to building projects of his own: castles, Neuschwanstein and Linderhof among them. But, thrusting aside the disappointments and slights from the man whose art he so admired, he persisted in his efforts, as he saw them, in behalf of Bavaria and of German art. He could forgive Wagner his sins; Ludwig, one among few, recognized the goal Wagner pursued as the only important thing about him. Wagner himself would have agreed.

28

The Scapegoats

DESPITE THE OVERWHELMING nature of his task, Wagner still had plenty of time and inclination to comment about his favorite scapegoats. On April 7, 1873, he had a discussion about the Jews with two visiting professors. One suggested that intermarriage was the solution. Richard demurred. German blood was not strong enough to withstand this "alkali." Jewish blood was far more corrosive. Perhaps, he explained, "these fellows" (the quotation marks are Cosima's), would become so arrogant they might even give up speaking German. They should then learn Hebrew in order to keep things running smoothly, but should still remain Germans. With this "joke," added Cosima, the conversation ended. How much was joke, how much was serious, is anyone's guess. If it was serious, it could indicate a reversal of his ideas about the desirability of intermarriage and assimilation. More likely it indicated nothing at all except a desire to make a humorous remark. A more serious comment to the same effect came about five years later in "Know Thyself."

In June there were derogatory remarks about "the Jew Lasker," a politician; Heine, the poet, referred to as a Jew; and a new editor for a Berlin paper, as "probably a Jew." Richard, or Cosima, or both, were upset that a certain nobleman was retiring from government and that a Jew was taking his place. It bears repeating that it is sometimes difficult to distinguish summaries of remarks of Richard from interjections of Cosima. In August, a visitor from Vienna "who turns out to be a Jew, proves tiresome with his self-conscious emotionalism and lack of humor." In mid–January 1874, Cosima said that Richard was not feeling well and was very angry. About a general franchise, giving the ballot to one and all, he remarked that Germany was not suitable for it; that good people abstained from voting and only the "bad," Jews, Catholics and Socialists were active.

On January 28 came a peculiar remark, one that stands out in even in that sea of peculiarity. It concerns a subject that Cosima placed in quotes, "icebergs which have melted in the sea of inferiority." Among them, said Richard, was Karl Ritter. "It was the *Judaism* article which destroyed him as it did poor Tausig, for he had Jewish blood in his veins." There are two mysteries here. From the recorded documents there appears not the slightest evidence to credit Wagner's conclusion about either one of those two friends as having been destroyed by the essay. Further, if Karl Ritter was of any Jewish lineage, only Wagner seems to have known it. And if Tausig had shown any resentment of Wagner, despite the re-publication of the essay in 1869, that too has been a secret kept from everyone else.

Karl Ritter was the son of one of Wagner's friends in his Dresden days. It will be recalled that he was the one to whom Wagner, in 1850 and living in exile, sent his manuscript on *Judaism,* with the request that it be handed to another friend for delivery to the publisher. If Ritter was hurt by that manuscript, that would have been the time to say so. Instead, Ritter maintained a friendship with Wagner, albeit a very up and down one, for a number of years. He gave small sums to Wagner on occasion; his mother, Julie Ritter, much more. And, as we have seen, Karl traveled with him to Venice in 1858. When Wagner left that city in 1859, he told the still friendly Ritter goodbye, and that was the last time the two ever met. Why he should have been suddenly hurt by the re-publication of the essay in 1869 is difficult to imagine, and evidence of it is totally lacking. Nor does it seem as though Wagner could have known of his pique, if any there was. But there is no way to discount it completely.

Tausig, two years after the re-publication of the essay, was recruited by Wagner for a very difficult task, and, by all accounts, including that of Cosima, threw himself into it with tremendous zeal. He might well have known even of its original publication, but during their later friendship could not have failed to be aware of it. On his deathbed he could still refer to Richard and Cosima as "two great natural forces." The only thing that seems to have destroyed Tausig was the typhus from which he died.

Comments such as this may, on one level, be dismissed as unpremeditated and thoughtless. Husband and wife were talking in private, and if Wagner was saying anything that came into his mind, illogical, impossible, ill-considered though it be, we are eavesdropping, and must take it for that. But even as such comments tell us that not everything he says can be taken at face value, or as reflective of any deeply held, fully thought-out opinions, they may still tell us something of significance.

What this particular instance may reflect is possible stirrings of guilt, which no known facts of his life otherwise corroborate. It also raises the possibility that one or both of these friends had told him things that have never been recorded. Obviously we cannot know everything that transpired between them. Perhaps in some quiet moment, he may have regretted causing pain to close friends, even Jewish friends.

Less complex, and less mysterious, is his comment to Cosima on April 2, the day before Good Friday. He was indignant "over the way the Jews are strutting about here in their best clothes, because today is their Easter festival ... walking around in festive garb on our day of mourning! That's what Lessing bequeathed us—the idea that all religions are good, even stupid Mohammedanism." In May he told his wife how good it was to read of ancient relationships and to abandon for a while "our world of Jesuits and Jews, our complete barbarism!" On July 8 he wished to see Bismarck start a war with France just on account of the Jesuits.

On June 1, Rubinstein was again in the Wagner household. He had left over half a year before to spend the winter in Budapest taking lessons from Liszt. It must have benefited him; Cosima remarked that his piano playing had made great strides. Such complimentary remarks are almost always more than balanced by something negative, and only concerning the negative does the religious faith become important. Less than a week later she gave another slant on her father's tutelage of the young pianist. Rubinstein, she said, "in the way of Jews has copied all sorts of things from my father, much to his own advantage." On July 1, Richard was "pleased with Joseph Rubinstein's talent." On the fifteenth, Rubinstein "distinguishes himself by playing from the manuscript of the third act of *Götterdämmerung*." In September he played Strauss waltzes to their "great enjoyment."

In early October, Richard was drinking beer in a beer hall with his dog Rus, when a Jewish piano teacher tripped over the animal. Richard apologized, to which the musician replied that for him Richard's dogs were sacred creatures. Said Richard later to his wife, he was astonished over the propensities of the Jews, who like the Jesuits could "sniff out everything," referring presumably to the piano teacher's knowledge of Wagner's love of dogs. In November he again expressed the dangers he saw in a general franchise, "the Jews, etc." On the fourteenth there was a visit from Rubinstein's father. Not much was said about it, but it became quite clear in time that the father and Richard had quite friendly relations. On the nineteenth, Cosima wrote of Joseph Rubinstein, "Richard agrees with me that this strange man's behavior toward Richard is utterly extraordinary, since he has never in the least been encouraged to settle here." In December Richard expressed pleasure over some of the "strange man's" copying work.

On January 29, 1875, comes another perplexing entry, this one clearly attributable to Cosima. She had been reading to her children *Nathan the*

Wise, a play by Gotthold Lessing, an eighteenth century German drama-
tist, and said she found it "once more" very interesting. It cannot be half
so interesting as the fact that she found it so and that she read it to her children. The play dates from 1779, is set in the Holy Land, and involves Jews,
Christians and Moslems, intermarriage and interfaith adoptions. The central character is the Jew Nathan. The play is very plainly a plea for racial
tolerance. This is the same Lessing whom Wagner blamed, almost seven
months previously, for the notion that all religions are good, "even stupid
Mohammedanism." How much the play influenced Cosima is questionable. Her comment is that "Truth paid out like a coin in the monologue of
Nathan, reminds one of the businesslike attitude of the Jews toward their
God."

The next night, she gives us one more bit to ponder. She had been
reading Friedrich Gfrörer's *Primitive Christianity,* and mentioned a particular saying of the Jews; "One should pray for a good eye, a humble spirit,
and a soul free from desire." It made a "deep imprint" on her mind. A week
before, she noted that Richard, also reading Gfrörer, was much impressed
by the seven-day silence before the seat of judgment, as told by the book
of the Jewish mystics. On February 3, "Rubinstein provides great enjoyment with his piano playing." A few days later they met the wife of Hans
Richter, who would a year later conduct the first *Ring.* They were newly-
weds and Cosima had heard that she is Jewish. She found the bride "strange,
a decidedly Jewish type." In April Richard said of Bismarck that four years
before he had been recommending the Jesuits, but that now he was recommending the Jews. A Jew was now even a minister.

In early September, owing to a dispute with a Paris publisher, Richard
resolved never again to do business with Jews. A week or so later they were
in Prague. Walking the crowded streets at night, Cosima was pleasantly
impressed: "not much Israel." A few days after that she was upset that three
Jews were head of the German Party in Bohemia. Shortly before Christmas,
Richard received a pamphlet on the Jews written by a Herr Beta, badly written and without style, but containing "remarkable insights." The comparison between Antonio's melancholy attitude toward Shylock in Shakespeare's
Merchant of Venice and the behavior of the Germans toward the Jews was
"very apposite." In that same evening, noted Cosima, "a little music making with Herr Rubinstein." On the twenty-seventh of December Richard
had overheard some beerhouse conversation to the effect that villages were
becoming destitute. His comment: "The Jews are buying up the woodlands
and cattle, they raise the prices, everything goes to ruin!"

By the nineteenth of July, the time was fast approaching for the premiere of the *Ring.* Many things were going wrong. During the entire month

there was harsh criticism in the diary, mostly Cosima's comments, echoing, no doubt, Wagner's own judgments about some aspects of the staging and the voices. There was also, during these trying times, outrage about instances of cruelty to animals, which was one of Richard's most keenly felt resentments, and petty complaints about other people's behavior. Only about Rubinstein, however, was a complaint coupled with mention of the religion of the offender. Finally, wrote Cosima, "The piano rehearsals ended with the wholesale dismissal of Herr Rubinstein who here once more displayed all the dismal characteristics of his race."

29

The First Festival

IT WAS TO BE A MUSICAL AND cultural event like none the German nation or perhaps the continent of Europe had ever witnessed. Royalty from all of the German states, the German emperor himself and the first rung of composers from across Europe were expected to attend. The finest musicians and singers to be found had agreed to perform, often at great cost to themselves, remuneration being far smaller than could be expected from other engagements.

It began on August 13, 1876. The final weeks leading up to it, coming as they did following years of agonies and frustrations, would have been enough to completely break the perseverance of a lesser man. Although excuse was lacking for blaming the malice of the press on *the Jews*, justification for his hatred of the press itself was now more than ample. Gleefully the papers around Germany and Austria, led by those of Vienna and Munich, reported and exaggerated each of the always inevitable untoward incidents that plague rehearsals. Where incidents were lacking the press manufactured them. Predictably, subscriptions were drastically reduced.

All problems were compounded manyfold by the press, but the real problems were onerous enough. There were the usual ones with singing, acting and costumes, but difficulties with the scenery and the complex mechanisms for the scenic changes were multiplied many times more than the usual by the increased demands of the gigantic undertaking. It was quite a challenge, from the beginning of the first opera, set under the River Rhine with three swimming Rhinemaidens and a dwarf, and continuing through the end of the last opera, depicting the destruction of the hall of a strange people called the Gibichungs; the immolation of the Valkyrie Brunnhilde;

Valhalla, home of the gods, going up in flames in the distance; and the Rhine overflowing its banks.

There were also problems with casting that went far beyond the usual. Many leading artists were under contract with companies throughout Germany and could be available for performance in Bayreuth only with the concurrence of the respective companies. The directors usually demanded a price: permission to perform one or all of the *Ring* operas, or having Wagner personally conduct a concert or, as in the case of Vienna in late 1875, performances of one or more of his earlier operas. Despite thunderous ovations from the audience there, he reaped more ill will by his refusal, a congenital inability no doubt, to give more praise to performers than he felt they deserved. He did, however, earn much needed cash to be applied toward the huge expenses of the festival.

One of the minor performers at the Vienna opera at the time was Angelo Neumann, the Jewish tenor whom Wagner had seen in Stuttgart performing in *Don Giovanni*. That was, it will be recalled, during those dark days spent fleeing from creditors while Ludwig's emissary searched for him. By 1875, Neumann had already decided that his future was that of an impresario, rather than a singer, and working under Wagner in Vienna at this time, he knew that he wanted to tie his career to the composer of *Lohengrin* and *Tannhäuser*.

Among the singers finally enlisted for the festival of 1876 were Lilli and Marie Lehmann, of whom we have previously heard. Each appeared in *Das Rheingold* and *Götterdämmerung*, the first and last operas of the tetralogy, as one of the three Rhinemaidens, and in *Die Walküre*, as one of the nine Valkyries. Lilli in addition sang the offstage role of the Woodbird in *Siegfried*, the third of the four operas. Albert Niemann was engaged for the role of Siegmund, a major one in the second opera, *Die Walküre*, but not so much of one as the role of Siegfried, appearing so prominently as that character does in each of the last two operas.

This temperamental tenor was not lacking in musical gifts, but was painfully short of self-control. Whether through pique at not being chosen for the role of Siegfried, or some other annoyance, he succeeded in darkening the atmosphere in mid–1875 when appearing for rehearsals. The tone of camaraderie and optimism prevailing during rehearsals for *Rheingold* changed abruptly upon his arrival for *Die Walküre*. It began even before the start of the opera's first rehearsal. Not by any means the only lapse, but one of the more egregious, came during the rehearsal of the first act. Highly agitated, stumbling through his role, he finally vented his frustration by seizing the slender Rubinstein as he accompanied on the piano and began to shake him violently. The stunned participants, including the composer, stared in silence, at a total loss to understand or to make sense of the unprovoked assault. After a few moments, Wagner regained his composure, and somberly said to Niemann, "Please continue." It was not the last episode of unnecessary tension caused by the singer's erratic behavior.[1]

Likewise this was not the only time the unfortunate pianist was the target of sudden and unprovoked assault. One in July 1876, almost a year after the Niemann episode, occurred following one of the final piano rehearsals, shortly before the first performance. This assault was verbal, not physical, but, considering that it came from Wagner, it must have hurt even more. Wagner started off, graciously enough, thanking Rubinstein, in the presence of the assembled artists, for his fine work during rehearsals. But as he continued, he seemed to get more and more agitated, thinking perhaps of the many tense moments resulting from the pianist's presence in the household. Ultimately, as remembered by the conductor Felix Mottl, Wagner snapped, "If we never really grew any closer on a human level, the fault is not mine, but yours. You are a member of a foreign race with which we have no sympathy." Thus what began as an expression of appreciation turned into one of anger. What Rubinstein's reaction was to this gratuitous insult, Mottl leaves to our imaginations.

With regard to Porges there was little cause for anger, nor any such demonstration. In 1872, Porges had written Wagner from Munich promising to assist with the gigantic undertaking then underway. On November 6 of that year, Wagner answered, assuring Porges that he was most grateful, and said "I had already assigned you a particular role in my enterprise which is of the greatest possible importance for the future." He then reminded Porges of his recording of Wagner's instructions to orchestra and artists at the rehearsals for the Ninth Symphony at the laying of the foundation stone for the theater on May 22 of that year. Porges had also written an article on the performance of the symphony, much to Wagner's gratification.

Now he wanted the same done with regard to the rehearsals for the *Ring*, a much larger and more complex project. He wanted Porges to attend all the rehearsals and to write down all of Wagner's remarks, "however intimate," concerning the interpretation and performance of the work and "in that way to establish a fixed tradition." And if Porges desired also to assist in the rehearsals with the individual singers, he would be welcome to do so.[2]

The result of his labors with regard to the rehearsals of these operas was a volume entitled *Wagner Rehearsing the Ring*. It was published in installments between 1880 and 1896, and has proved invaluable as a resource for musicians and stage directors, and later for Cosima Wagner. In 1896, 13 years after Wagner's death, she undertook the production of the Ring in Bayreuth for the first time since the 1876 premiere. She wrote to Nietzsche that Porges had written "some beautiful, profound words of great congeniality."[3] His work has been further described by one Wagner biographer as one of "amazing insight and perception," evidencing his thorough familiarity with the score and an ability to "always locate the endless detail of Wagner's individual instructions."[4]

He seems to have had time for other writing also. A music critic from the *London Times*, attending that first festival, reported that the rehearsals had been much talked about, but that only the most intimate friends of the composer had been admitted to them. Among them, he reported,

> must have been one who, under the signature of Heinrich Porges, has contributed glowing accounts of the rehearsals one after another as they occurred.... They have enlightened not only the inhabitants of Bayreuth in particular and Bavaria in general, but have penetrated through various channels to other more remote corners of the earth. Herr Porges, comparing his demi-god to Aeschylus and Shakespeare, with Beethoven thrown in, leads us to expect much, and if but a fourth part of what he affirms be accepted as gospel, an exhibition without precedent is really in store for us.[5]

Among the intimate friends witnessing the final rehearsal was King Ludwig. The crowd-shy king did not want to make an appearance during the public performance. On that final rehearsal, beginning August 6, Wagner sat with him in the royal box. It was the first time he and Wagner met since that night in June 1868 upon the occasion of the first performance of *Die Meistersinger.*

Mesmerized by the *Ring's* magic, he wrote Wagner with the most effusive of compliments: "You are the human god, the true artist who has brought the holy fire from heaven to earth.... Fortunate Century that saw this spirit arise in its midst!" He beseeched Wagner to "make possible the third series of the performances ... I have a burning desire, like a searing thirst to experience once more that marvelous drama."[6] Despite his antipathy to crowds, he attended the third cycle toward the end of the month.

Emperor William I also attended though, through pressing political exigencies, either real or contrived, he left after the second opera. Upon arriving he had greeted Wagner with the laconic "I never thought you could pull it off." He also congratulated Wagner on this matter of "national" importance. Wagner answered with the full respect due an emperor, but later wondered to others what the "nation" had to do with his work. Except for King Ludwig, they had failed him completely. The emperor of Brazil, who had offered to have Wagner build the theater in his country, also attended. Upon signing the guest book, asked to state his profession, he wrote "Emperor."

If the German royalty had failed him, they were nonetheless out in force to observe the culmination of his efforts. The Princes' Gallery was filled with almost every crowned head of every state in the nation. Also in attendance were musicians and composers from around Europe, including the Russian Peter Ilyich Tchaikovsky, the Norwegian Edvard Grieg, both in their thirties; and the 41-year-old Frenchman Camille Saint-Saëns, who met and took sharp issue with Wagner for his bitterly anti–French pronouncements. All three were present as journalists representing papers in their homelands. In addition there were many other persons of note, including writers and other journalists from Vienna, Paris, Milan, London and Boston. On the special invitation of Wagner, not the first such overture, Liszt was also in attendance. The two, so long estranged, embraced in public and openly shed tears.

The reports on that first festival would fill several volumes. Certainly not all comments were positive, and many viewers were quite hostile. With some, a preexisting bias faded to grudging admiration; with others, eager anticipation was cooled by the complexity of the work. There were undoubtedly not many who had seen *Tristan* or *Die Meistersinger,* which alone among Wagner's operas could have been an adequate preparation, and even those few who had seen them may have been confounded by this tetralogy.

There are in the *Ring* no arias, and, until the last act of *Siegfried* and in *Götterdämmerung,* the final opera, no duets or other ensembles, nor choruses, as was customary in all other operas, including those two earlier Wagnerian works. There were instead monologues and dialogues. Instead of extended melodies there were motifs, that is, short themes, intricately woven together like a fine tapestry, a flood of orchestration from a hidden orchestra that did not merely accompany voices, but, charged with a life of its own, commented on the action like the chorus of a Greek tragedy. Filled throughout with hauntingly penetrating themes, every note existed for no other reason than to heighten the emotional impact of the drama, far beyond what words alone could ever accomplish.

Perhaps the most scathing comments were those from the pen of the Viennese critic Eduard Hanslick. He found almost nothing to admire, save the few most accessible passages, usually of orchestral music. There were other viewers, few though they were, who were enchanted by the entirety.

One of those was Grieg, who seemed quite familiar with the underlying mythology of the Norse gods. Even he, however, was ill prepared for the newness of the musical structure. He first viewed the final dress rehearsal that so impressed the king. After the *Rheingold* performance he wrote that

> In spite of ... the inadequate characterization of the gods, the ceaseless modulations and wearying chromaticism of the harmonies, and the end result of

leaving the listener totally exhausted, this music drama is the creation of a true giant in the history of art, comparable in innovation only to Michelangelo. In music there is nobody to approach Wagner.

But his favorite was the finale, *Götterdämmerung.* Of it he said, "I cannot say that any part of the music is better than any other for it is all divinely composed and to pick out any one passage at random is to pick out a pearl." His overall conclusion: "My impression of the whole work is great, I can hardly express it properly." Whatever the shortcomings of detail, he wrote, one thing was certain: "Wagner has created a great work, full of audacious originality and dramatic merit."

Of those not so favorably impressed, one of the most thoughtful views came from Tchaikovsky. For readers who expected a critical discussion of the merits of Wagner's creativity, he said, he must apologize, as that could come only in the future. He had made himself familiar with the work before coming and believed that he need only hear it once to become completely attuned to it. He was wrong, he admitted; it must be heard often, and only then could the merits or deficiencies become clear. But he allowed himself a few general observations: "Anyone who believes in the civilizing power of art must take away from Bayreuth a very refreshing impression of the great artistic endeavor which will form a milestone in the history of art." He praised Wagner's dedication to his artistic ideals, but would not predict what the future of this new type of music might or might not be. He did agree that "Something has happened at Bayreuth, something which our grandchildren and great-grandchildren will remember."

To his brother, Modest, he was perhaps more open. Writing a few days after the close of the first cycle, he said that *Der Ring des Nibelungen* may "be actually a magnificent work, but it is certain that there never was anything so endlessly and wearisomely spun out."

As with *Tristan* and *Die Meistersinger*, time has sided with the admirers. Among the pithiest comments to come some years later was one by the usually long-winded George Bernard Shaw. In 1898, he wrote that there was in the *Ring,* not a note "that has any other point than the single direct point of giving musical expression to the drama."[7] However much musicologists may quibble, and however much an exact musical-to-literary-phrase relation may be unsustainable, the essence of Shaw's observation stands as entirely valid. By 1921, even such a notorious cynic as the editor and critic H.L. Mencken, in a preface to the Wagner-Nietzsche correspondence, and dwelling mostly on Wagner's personal shortcomings, could grudgingly acknowledge:

> I believe that his music dramas are, by long odds, the most stupendous works of art ever contrived by man — that it took more downright genius to imagine

them and fashion them than it took to build the Parthenon, or to write *Faust*, or *Hamlet*, or to paint the Sistine Frescoes, or even to write the Ninth Symphony.[8]

W.H. Auden, the Anglo-American poet, later in that century was more succinct, even while more all-encompassing: Wagner, he said, for all his notorious difficulties was "perhaps the greatest genius that ever lived." It was undoubtedly this four-opera epic that contributed most to these judgments.

But there was one contemporary observer at that first festival who was at once thoroughly immersed in the beauty of the music, the sweep of the drama, and the remarkable unity of the two. The Jewish impresario-director Angelo Neumann knew now that he not only wanted to promote the operas of Wagner, but that he was determined to bring to opera houses all over Europe and to promote as far and wide as possible his *Ring des Nibelungen*.

There was something of a consensus, if about nothing else, that it was a tremendous undertaking, a milestone in the history of art, and a personal triumph for Richard Wagner. There were, to be certain, numerous predictions or insinuations that it could never happen again, that the cost and effort could not be duplicated, and that the new music would have little or no effect on music in the style in which it had always been known and appreciated. None of these prognostications, all terribly wrong, detracted from the flood of laudatory comments concerning Wagner's perseverance and originality that drowned the petty carping of his enemies in the press.

Was the personal triumph, or even the unstinted praise for the works themselves, gratifying to Wagner? Did it justify in his mind the years of agonizing frustration that brought it about? Anyone who expected that it would, knew little about him. What he saw and heard most vividly were the many faults, perceptible mostly to him alone; problems with the scenic effects, the acting, the singing and the tempo. In his conductor, Hans Richter, who earned much praise from other musicians, he was sorely disappointed.

Two years later, writing his *Retrospect of the Stage Festivals of 1876*,[9] he lamented that although Richter was the best conductor he knew, that he knew of no conductor at all whom he could trust to perform his music in the right way, nor any singer of whom he could expect a proper realization of his characters unless he had taught them everything from the beginning. What had driven him most to despair, what had "horrified" him, was the discovery that "Richter could not maintain the right tempo even when it had been achieved, simply because he was incapable of understanding *why* it should be thus and not otherwise."

As it happened, his next and last opera would be conducted by one whom he indeed could and did trust, one who could maintain the right tempo and did understand why Wagner's music was thus and not otherwise. That would be the Jewish conductor Hermann Levi. His only fault would be his heritage as a Jew. As we will see later, once more, it was Wagner the artist who prevailed over Wagner the racist.

Two of his male singers, one of whom was Niemann, he termed "matadors" and vowed to have nothing more to do with them. That vow was concerned more with their behavior as male prima donnas offstage rather than their performances on stage. By all accounts, Niemann performed masterfully his role as Siegmund, and Wagner apparently agreed. His disgust with the antics of both of his "matadors" did not prevent him from requesting from the king the order of St. Michael for both of them. Brandt, the machinist for the scenic props, was almost as big a disappointment to Wagner as was his conductor.

To a few with whom he was fully satisfied, he wrote glowing letters. One of these was the friend from Prague, the Jewish, half Jewish, or putative Jew, Lilli Lehmann. To her he wrote, "Oh, Lilli, Lilli! You were the most beautiful of all — and you are right, dear child, it will never come again. That was the magic of it all — my Rhinemaidens.... Greetings to Marie, she is so good. Great god, how good both of you were.... Farewell, dear good child! Lilli!"[10]

The outer shell of brick that was to be later added to his theater never materialized. It stands today as it was when first completed, except for certain additions. The reason for the permanence of the original structure these many years is its extraordinary acoustics. The audience is enveloped in the sound, which does not seem to originate in any particular place, and seems at times to float into the theater from outer space. There was, at the time of completion, no place where the sound could be heard better than any other place, and the viewer from any seat in the sloping amphitheater seemed to be a part of the unfolding action. In recent times there have been added a few seats with only a partial view of the stage.

Did Wagner, to whose specifications the theater was built, have some secret knowledge of acoustics, or was the result a lucky accident? Acoustics were very much on his mind from the outset, but even he probably did not anticipate the marvelous results. Acoustical engineers from many countries have tried without success to pinpoint the cause.

30

Neumann

WAGNER WAS NO LONGER LIGHTLY given to euphoria, and the performances at the first Bayreuth festival evoked no such response. It is well they did not, as any such flight of his spirits would have been brought quickly to earth. In addition to the many flaws that he felt must be corrected before the next festival, within a few weeks he learned that the deficit resulting from this one amounted to 150,000 marks. That was more than 12 times that which he had believed at the conclusion of the performances. Before learning the grim truth he had been planning on again giving three cycles of the *Ring* the following year. He was confident enough of it to refuse the requests of other theaters, and their handsome prices, for permission to produce the tetralogy.

Shortly after the conclusion of the festival, he took his entire family through Italy on vacation, including visits to Bologna, Naples, Sorrento and Rome, the expenses being largely covered by a 5,000-dollar fee he earned for a "centennial march." It had been commissioned by the Philadelphia Women's Auxiliary of the United States Centennial Commission. Wagner was never at his best when writing occasional pieces, and he later commented that the best thing about this one was the 5,000 dollars he earned for it.

The Italian vacation was a sojourn he sorely needed. But toward the end of it he learned of the scope of the festival deficit. The impact of these figures left Feustel apprehensive and Wagner thoroughly discouraged about any performances in 1877. In late 1876 he made several attempts with detailed proposals to interest the Reich, that is, the federal government, and the State of Bavaria through King Ludwig, in taking over the project including the debt.

These attempts were all unsuccessful. In early 1877 he tried again with the Bavarian government and negotiated with its representatives, but at this time the king's finances were in no shape to rescue him. Discouraged and depressed, his faith in the German public at an end, he could see in the future only poverty and ruin. A festival in 1877 was now out of the question. As it developed, the *Ring* would not be produced again in Bayreuth until 1896, 13 years after his death, under the leadership of Cosima who had by then taken command of the Bayreuth operation.

But the aging, ailing colossus still had one more mighty music drama left in him, one that he had been turning over in his mind since his Dresden days, over 30 years previous. It was the story of the Grail knight Parsifal, or Parzival as he is known in the legends. In August 1865, having told Ludwig about his plans, the king asked for more details. Wagner at once wrote a complete prose sketch. With minor changes, it became the story of his opera.

With the *Ring* operas completed, his theater constructed, and the operas performed, despite the shortcomings and the insurmountable financial problems, he now turned his attention to bringing Parsifal to life. The major theme of the opera is compassion, Parsifal being depicted as "a pure fool made wise through pity." It is filled with Christian legends and Christian symbols: the Holy Spear, the lance that wounded Christ on the Cross; the Holy Grail, the vessel in which Joseph of Arimathea collected Christ's flowing blood; and the Castle of Montsalvat, the Castle of the Grail. It was completed and first performed in 1882, the performances of that summer preceding his death by only six months.

During these last six years of his life we see in Cosima's diaries some of his most frequently and most vehemently expressed outpourings of anti–Semitism, not to mention comments in letters and essays. They leave little doubt that until the end, he still subscribed to the views expressed in his essay of 1850. It was also a period during which his life most sharply contradicted those expressions of animosity. His great Christian opera was written and produced during his close association with four Jews whom we have already met in these pages.

One, Joseph Rubinstein, returned to Bayreuth where he assisted as a copyist and as pianist in rehearsals, and again entertained the Wagner family and visitors with his virtuosity. Heinrich Porges continued his work with Wagner, now helping to train the chorus of "Flower Maidens" who grace the second act of *Parsifal*. Another, Angelo Neumann, was to be the moving force in having *Der Ring des Nibelungen* performed far and wide across Europe, earning fame for the operas and badly needed funds for the composer. The fourth, Hermann Levi, son of a rabbi, was to serve in a capacity that was arguably the most important of all in any performance, the conductor. It was he who was to lead the first performances of Wagner's last opera, a paean to Christianity.

The immediate need of Wagner was to turn his golden *Ring* into funds, if possible without sacrificing it to second-rate opera houses and treatment of it as "ordinary" opera, a possibility which he viewed with disgust. His salvation lay with Angelo Neumann. In August 1876 Neumann was manager of the Leipzig opera theater, jointly with a Dr. August Förster. The two had agreed that Förster would attend the first cycle of the *Ring* in Bayreuth, Neumann the second. When Förster returned from the first he advised Neumann, "My dear fellow, the thing is not presentable." But upon dining that evening with a friend who had seen the same performances, Neumann was told in no uncertain terms, and with controlled but unmistakable enthusiasm, "It is nothing short of your duty to see this performance no matter what it conflicts with." Neumann arrived in Bayreuth by train with no time to spare. He later wrote that there was tremendous excitement in the town, but that it was probably the adverse opinions that predominated.

At the close of the *Rheingold* performance, Neumann was "incapable of speaking to a soul, so deeply sunk was I in all I had seen and heard." He had for many years been a great admirer of Wagner, but he now realized that the future of the Leipzig opera was to lie along different lines entirely from what had previously been envisioned: "A new field had been opened by the greatest of the world's stage directors." By the time the last notes of the last opera had sounded, he had conceived the idea of "transplanting this whole colossal undertaking to Leipzig and giving it there next year in a complete cycle."

Angelo Neumann, April 1883. From *Personal Recollections of Wagner* by Angelo Neumann.

Among the advantages offered by that centrally located city was the fact that it was the birthplace of the composer.

The idea was conveyed to a friend who presented it to Liszt. Neumann and Liszt appeared in Wahnfried the following morning to discuss the plan with Wagner. Waiting downstairs in the large reception room, the two men conferred on ideas. Then Liszt wrote a hasty note and sent it to Wagner, still in his bedroom upstairs. The note read: "Incomprehensible man. Neumann is here. Come down and talk it over with him." A few minutes later the note came back. On the reverse side Wagner had written: "Still more incomprehensible one. I've nothing on but my shirt — hence can't come down. Have considered Neumann's proposition, but still cling to the hope of repeating the Ring at Bayreuth next season." For the time being Neumann's dream of a *Ring* in Leipzig was in suspension. Both Liszt and Neumann agreed that the hope Wagner still harbored of a repeat performance the next year in Bayreuth was impossible. After months of frustrating negotiations with royalty in Munich and Berlin, Wagner would come to realize this himself.[1]

By February of the following year, the landscape had changed. Neumann's enthusiasm had converted his co-manager Förster, though his dedication to the project never matched Neumann's own. Nonetheless, Förster, in August 1876 and again in February 1877, wrote to Wagner requesting permission to mount a production of the *Ring* in Leipzig. The second letter was prompted by Wagner's recent admission that the festival could not take place that year. This time Wagner was quite encouraging, but not yet committed. He was in a position of strength. Companies all over Germany had been seeking to perform the *Ring* or individual operas of it, most often *Die Walküre*. He was no longer the naive business man, ignorant in matters of finance or unconcerned about remuneration. He was too experienced, and in far too dire straits to remain so innocent.

But Förster too was a hard bargainer, and all the more unyielding owing to his lingering reservations as to the success of the project, reservations that were heightened by strong opposition to it within the opera administration. A lengthy negotiation process conducted through correspondence with Wagner collapsed in mid–May due to several sticking points including the exclusive nature of the contract as it pertained to northern Germany. It ended with both Neumann and Förster, supposedly partners on the same side, questioning each other's good faith.

Neumann was frustrated and upset. Shortly thereafter he attended a breakfast in honor of a soprano with the Leipzig opera. A friend of Förster raised his glass and offered a toast to the "successful" avoidance of the *Ring* undertaking. Neumann declined to join in, and as the assembled group urged him to do so, one of them touched the recalcitrant man's glass as though to hand it to him. Neumann angrily threw it over his shoulder and, as the glass shattered, stormed out of the room.

Neumann did not mean to give it up, and the ball would now pass to his hands. Six months later, he heard rumors to the effect that several cities, including Hamburg and Schwerin, had been given rights to produce the *Ring,* and that rights to *Die Walküre* only were being sold to Berlin. In mid–November he wrote to Wagner that ever since hearing the "gigantic" works in Bayreuth he had one ambition, namely to present them in Leipzig, where the composer was born and better understood than anywhere else. He told Wagner of what he had heard about Berlin and *Walküre* and begged that he be given by Wagner the terms required for the rights to produce the entire *Ring,* which he preferred, or alternatively for any part of it.

Wagner answered at once. He had not given Berlin the rights to *Die Walküre,* as he had no intention of giving up any part of the tetralogy singly. The Hamburg opera had been given the right to produce the *Ring* but with no provision that it be exclusive. He was willing to deal with Leipzig and offered financial arrangements that Förster had originally demanded. Despite Wagner's acquiescence in the previously proffered arrangement, two months later, in January 1878, Förster was still not convinced. He was still working to overcome the opposition of the opera personnel, and to calculate the costs.

It was Neumann's insistence, and persistence, that ultimately forced his hand, using the previous season's deficit as his strongest bargaining point. Förster finally succumbed: "I give you *carte blanche* now; but I fear it's too late. He won't want anything to do with us."[2]

Wagner did indeed have much to do with them. By telegram Neumann requested a meeting at once. In one word Wagner answered: "Gladly." The two men met on January 21. He was met at Wahnfried by Cosima who explained that her husband was still asleep, and hoped that Neumann "would put up with my company for a while." Neumann, in his memoirs, referred to his half hour with her while waiting for Wagner as "a charming talk with this delightful and interesting woman." He described Wagner's manner as most gracious.

The relationship between Wagner and Neumann began on that day and lasted through the remaining four years of Wagner's life. Except for a single incident, the two dealt with each other on a basis of friendship and mutual trust. A bond was formed at once. Wagner's initial comment that day in January: "I can see you're thoroughly in earnest ... you don't look like a man who would take that trip from Leipzig to Bayreuth in the dead of winter simply for amusement." After explaining to Wagner his plan to produce the first two operas in April and the second two in September, and answering all of the composer's pointed questions, Wagner scanned Neumann's face searchingly, then, according to Neumann, turned to his wife: "What would you say about it? Shall I trust this man?" Without reservation Cosima answered in the affirmative. There was some further questioning and finally Wagner, in his own hand, drew up a contract in accordance with their verbal agreement. Neumann claimed that he left and then "flew" rather than walked to his hotel and the train station.

Cosima's diary entry for that day includes the following, somewhat different slant:

> A curious interruption of our sublime life is provided by the visit of the opera director, Angelo Neumann from Leipzig and Israel. He has come for the *Ring* but would also like to have *Parsifal*. Coaxes Richard out of half the royalties for the subscription quota — in short, is just what such gentlemen always are. Richard says he has nothing against his coming, insofar as it shows they still need him — and we need the money, so agreement is reached!

This entry of January 21 is the last that makes any such derogatory comments about Neumann, but it speaks volumes about Cosima, none of it very flattering. We will see later some exceedingly friendly exchanges of letters from both Cosima and Richard to Neumann. She was finally forced to admit, even to her diary, that "Richard does not dislike him." It was a gross understatement.

Förster was delighted with the arrangement, having harbored serious regrets over the failure of his own negotiations, and gave Neumann carte blanche with regards to these productions and authority to make any expenditure he deemed necessary. Problems with casting, scenery and hiring were vexatious, but were overcome. The final rehearsal was held before a full house, the spectators present by invitation only. Friends and foes alike were present. Conducting was a young man, Arthur Nikisch, who with these productions made a name and a reputation. At the conclusion of both rehearsals, there were storms of applause, even from the hostile camps.

Anton Seidl and Hans Richter, who had also attended the rehearsals, met with Neumann after the end of *Die Walküre* for the purpose of offering suggestions for improvement. Both had been skeptical. Seidl began to express certain ideas for change, whereupon Richter broke in to announce that what had been heard and seen was "so superb" that the only thing left was to wire Wagner: "Magnificent! Neumann has done wonders."

The performances of the first two operas were held as scheduled on April 28 and 29 to wildly enthusiastic audiences from all over Germany. On the thirtieth, Wagner wired Neumann an exemplar of the doggerel with which he often amused himself:

All hail the town of Leipzig, beloved native place
All hail its great conductor — the bravest of his race.

"Race" was very important to Wagner. Neumann's "race" was Jewish, that same race that, he had written, was incapable of appreciating true art. This was not the end of their relationship, their business dealings, or their friendship, which would grow closer by the month. Before it ended with Wagner's death he would be obliged to express new ideas about Jewish appreciation of art; never, of course, allowing any possibility of error in his previous writings.

Liszt was so carried away with the performances as to write Wagner, "Neumann has managed the affair in some respects better even than you did in Bayreuth."

We will return later to Neumann and his business and personal dealings with Wagner. In the meantime, both Rubinstein and Porges were still in his service.

We had previously heard of Rubinstein in Cosima's diary a month before the beginning of the festival in Bayreuth, when she referred to his "wholesale dismissal" for his having shown "all the dismal characteristics of his race." The frenetic pace of those days and the intense pressure on everyone can be felt in her short, terse entries. Almost seven months later, on February 2, 1877, she noted that "Herr Rubenstein writes a curious letter, asking forgiveness for his behavior last fall!" What the behavior was we are never told. Neither do we know whether that behavior followed or preceded Wagner's sudden insulting outburst during an intended show of appreciation for the pianist. Both events obviously occurred within, at most, a few weeks of each other

We do not hear of him again until, once more in the diary, he is mentioned as having sent his piano arrangement of the *Siegfried Idyll*. This Idyll was a piece written by Wagner for a small orchestral ensemble and played as a surprise for Cosima on Christmas morning 1870, which was also her thirty-third birthday. It was dedicated to her for having presented Richard with a son on June 6 of the previous year. The couple, it will be recalled, were living at the time in Triebschen. Wagner had apparently asked Rubenstein to prepare an arrangement for piano. Says Cosima: "Richard is pleased with the wonderful, cherished work!"

We hear next on May 16 of the following year, 1878. Rubinstein was having lunch with the Wagners during a visit to Bayreuth and Richard observed, while alone with Cosima, that Jews like him behaved quite differently from Germans as "they know the world belongs to them, we are outcasts of fortune." Not until November did he appear in the diary again, and again only for a visit. He seemed the same as he was years ago, she said, that is, "unmistakably ill." The day was eventful, but, she said, one memory remained: "the *Idyll*, which Herr Rubinstein played in his own very good arrangement." He visited again that evening and discussed with Cosima the relative merits of certain Indian literature. He played the *Centennial March*, "splendidly" but the *Idyll*, "which he did not study with Richard" continued somewhat to elude him.

A month later, December 15, he was back, this time playing Bach fugues. The following day Richard said he got into a discussion with Rubinstein about Catholicism at Angermann's, Richard's favorite local pub. But upon realizing others were listening in, he decided that Angermann's might not be the right place for such a topic. We may be sure he had nothing good to say about Catholicism. Through the end of the month there are mentions of Rubinstein at the piano and discussions of certain erudite matters with Richard.

So by the end of 1878, whatever had transpired in those hectic days before the festival, it appears that Rubinstein was back in Bayreuth as part of the Wagner mélange. We will see more of him in connection with copying parts, and with rehearsals for Parsifal.

Porges, as of February 1878, was once again employed to put to use in behalf of Wagner his skills as a journalist and editor. We last saw him so engaged as assistant editor of the *South German Press,* published under the auspices of the Bavarian government. As an organ of the state, there was necessarily much interference, internal arguing, and limitation on what could be written in Wagner's behalf. Wagner's solution was to start a new journal, one to serve his own purposes without interference. This was the *Bayreuther Blätter*, in English "The Bayreuth Gazette." The editors were Hans von Wolzogen, a financially independent young man thoroughly devoted to Wagner and his cause, and Heinrich Porges. This journal was to be for and in behalf of Wagner and his work exclusively. The beliefs published were to be his, or at least consistent with them. Neither contrary opinions, nor income, advertisements, subscriptions or other financial considerations were to play any role. Porges was obviously one Jewish journalist of whom Wagner did not disapprove.

In one of his first articles, however, Porges tripped. He displeased Wagner somewhat, probably in taking slight issue with Schopenhauer, a philosopher whom Wagner greatly admired; but mainly he roused the ire of Cosima. The offense was apparently minor in Wagner's eyes but of sinister import in Cosima's. We are favored with little of the content but can see that Wagner found the beginning of it, religion as a link between art and the people, "not bad," but decided to ask Porges to shorten the piece. Cosima also read it and decided that "these people" have "no separate inner life ... no real experience of good and evil ... everything they say is shallow and indefinite." Then: "people who lead an inner life and are aware of it *must* affirm Schopenhauer's philosophy."

"These people" could mean anything, but probably means *the Jews.* Whoever they are, Porges was obviously one of them. About this specimen of "these people," she had written Nietzsche in the previous year that Porges was "an exceptionally good man" and was unquestionably the "most noble Jew I have ever known."[3] How much of a compliment that was cannot be precisely quantified.

Porges continued to rate mention in the diaries, but there was none of the controversy we have seen and will continue to see regarding Rubinstein. He remained a loyal, trusted member of the entourage through the remainder of Wagner's life and beyond. In addition to his work on the *Gazette*, he was later asked to assist to train and coach the chorus of Flower Maidens in preparation for the *Parsifal* performance. Lilli Lehmann was also asked repeatedly, begged at times, to recruit and lead in training the 24 women for the chorus. She was prepared to do so, but declined upon learning that Fritz Brandt, the son of Karl Brandt, was now to make the stage arrangements. At the 1876 festival she and Fritz had fallen in love at first sight, but the affair had gone badly. The reason according to Lilli was the uncontrollable jealousy of Fritz, though even from her own account, she appeared more devoted to her mother than to him. Nonetheless, her friendship with Wagner continued.

Part VI

Bayreuth II:
Levi and Neumann

31

The Young Hermann Levi

ASSISTING, COACHING, COPYING PARTS, and accompanying with the piano in rehearsals, all activities executed behind the scenes, were one thing. The role of conductor was quite another. But in addition to Porges and Rubinstein, we will see at those first *Parsifal* performances a Jew wielding the baton. How is it that Wagner, in this most Christian of his works, would have a Jew take what is arguably the most visible and most important role in the opera? As complex as was the life of Richard Wagner, the episode involving Hermann Levi was among the most complex of all.

Even in a place and a period of so many highly talented conductors as nineteenth century Germany, the name of Hermann Levi ranks near the top of anyone's list of the greatest. In his interpretation of the operas of Richard Wagner, he is at the pinnacle. In a critical history of the golden age of the Munich Court Theater, said by the author to begin with King Ludwig's reign in 1864, we can see a vivid picture of Levi's orchestral style:

> He was throughout no show-off conductor or "podium virtuoso." His directing was not for sensation; but when this small man swung his baton, his understated movements brought the orchestra, choir and

Hermann Levi, about 50 years of age. From *Zwischen Brahms und Wagner* by Frithjof Haas.

213

soloists more strongly on track and with greater enthusiasm than the far-reaching, fluttering arm movements of many of our directors of today.[1]

His conducting was often observed by Eugenie Schumann, daughter of Clara and Robert. As she described him:

> The head sat on a small expressively moving body. He had total mastery of his mission, which, as he well understood, was expressed in this quiet bodily bearing. It enabled him to transmit to his fellow artists a large part of that fire of enthusiasm that was the true essence of his character as a musician.[2]

Another contemporary, Ernst von Possart, was actor and stage director and ultimately theater director of the Munich Court Theater from 1864. In 1916 he published an account of his experiences, mentioning and describing many of the artists with whom he worked. Only to Levi did he devote a full chapter, most of it unstinted praise. He spoke of Levi's artistic skills and of his personal qualities, describing his subject as a person of good heart and delightful amiability. He said that when Levi laughed, it was not only with his eyes and mouth, but with his whole body.

> Rich experiences, sharp powers of observation, and a penetrating understanding had developed in him a philosophy of life which, fortunately, kept in check his fiery temperament. It also helped him brush aside the unavoidable disagreements in theater management. Always he kept the ultimate goal in sight, and bore petty annoyances with smiling patience. He had the ability, spiritual resiliency and native cheerfulness to prevent even serious events from disturbing him unduly.[3]

He conducted, according to Possart, more with his eyes than with his baton. Among those closest to him, according to one friend, Levi was "good-natured, affable and benevolent," and it was "his greatest pleasure to do good turns for others."[4] Perhaps it took such a man to work so closely with Wagner in preparation for the composer's last opera, then to conduct it almost a dozen times in the festival theater. He did so during the last summer before the composer's death, and to his entire satisfaction, a rarity in the life of this demanding taskmaster.

Levi was born in 1839 in the small town of Giessen, in central Germany. The milieu of his upbringing and education are not at all irrelevant to our subject. They are important considerations, first, to an understanding of his relationship with Wagner, and second, to a proper perspective on his treatment at the hands of certain modern day authors, both of which matters will be dealt with later.

He often spoke with pride of the 14 rabbis in the last ten generations of his ancestry. His father, Benedict Levi, born in Worms in 1806, was but 23 when he took charge of the pulpit in the synagogue in Giessen. Benedict's father, Hermann's grandfather, was Samuel Wolf Levi, whose synagogue was in the town of Worms. He earned enough respect for his linguistic skills, among other attributes, that after Worms was occupied by Napoleon's troops in 1797 he played an important role in the transition of government. The mayors and district representatives met regularly in his home to receive his translations of the orders of occupation from French to German.

Napoleon took a keen interest in the presence of the Jewish population in Germany, and their role as outsiders, to him a strange and perplexing situation. He granted the Jews full civil

Hermann Levi, right, with his father, Rabbi Benedict Levi. From *Zwischen Brahms und Wagner* by Frithjof Haas.

rights, removing at once all legal disabilities, and created a "Sanhedrin" patterned after the oldest Jewish council from Jerusalem in Roman times. This new one first met in 1807 in Paris, its decrees limited to the occupied areas only, and sat in judgment as to all disputes within the Jewish community. Upon his return from Paris, Rabbi Samuel Levi was granted the title of "Grand Rabbi of the Consistory of the Department of Donnersberg." Shortly before his death Napoleon granted him the honor of a private audience.[5]

So it happened that Samuel Levi settled in Mainz, the capital city of Donnersberg, and that Hermann's father, Benedict, grew up and was educated in that city in both religious and secular subjects. The occasion for his removal to Giessen, then a town of about 8,000 with only a few hundred Jews, was the departure of its officiating rabbi to Copenhagen. Shortly after his assumption of office, the grand duke of the province of Upper Hesse was impressed enough with Benedict to name him rabbi of its entire Jewish population. Three years later Benedict married Henriette Mayer, a talented, 26-year-old pianist from Mannheim.

The Levi home soon resounded with her music, which together with her lively and gregarious nature earned the admiration of many townspeople. After the first year of marriage, a son, Wilhelm, was born. He later studied music and for a time performed as a singer. Three years later came a daughter, Emma, and still another three years thereafter came Hermann. Henriette died in 1842, when Hermann was barely three years old. Two years later, Benedict married the daughter of a businessman, Gitel Worms, from Giessen. She died the following year, a few weeks after giving birth to a daughter, Auguste. For the remaining 54 years of his life, Benedict remained a widower. The wife of a family member took over many of the duties of raising the four children, but Benedict remained faithful to his responsibilities as their father.[6]

Many of Benedict's letters attest to his favoritism toward Hermann, often mentioning that the youngster's artistic gifts most resembled those of Benedict's first wife. Hermann's extraordinary musical talents became apparent early on. In Giessen he was hailed as a Wunderkind, a child prodigy. He was six when he gave a public concert, accompanied by his brother Wilhelm at a second piano. The proud father steered both boys toward careers as professional artists. At ten, Hermann was accompanying the community choral group on the organ.

Biographical material hardly mentions any religious training. The boy's unusual musical talents were always uppermost in the minds of his elders, and throughout his life his spiritual needs seemed to have been met by music. He never showed a serious interest in religion. Music, indeed, as he more than once implied, was his religion. In later years, Benedict joined with a group of other rabbis in attempting to further propagate certain French reforms by subordinating the Mosaic laws to the duties of German citizenship. It was an early Jewish reform movement, and may point to further circumstances resulting in so little pressure on the youngster to temper his love of music with religious studies.

The father decided to send him at age 12 for further education to Mannheim, where he lived with an aunt. It was then an industrial city with a solid musical tradition, though its best days had long passed. The court orchestra conductor in Mannheim, a man of decidedly conservative musical taste, was Vincenz Lachner, youngest of three brothers, all musicians. Through the good connections of the family of Hermann's aunt, they were able to introduce him to Lachner, to have him enrolled in the Lyceum, and to begin musical studies with him. For two years, the boy visited Lachner in the afternoons after school. At the age of 14, in his ninth year of formal education, he left school to devote himself exclusively to music.

He had thus little formal education, but nonetheless harbored an innate thirst for knowledge. He had a particular proclivity for language and ultimately mastered both Italian and French. He later used these skills in developing a profound knowledge of European literature, and was to publish a number of translations of both literary works and opera libretti. Through his studies with Lachner he also enjoyed an ever widening practical musical experience. The repertory of works that he studied is reflected in that of his mentor, who, in his 25 years with the Mannheim Opera, conducted 159 different operas from the German, Italian and French genres.

Without doubt, Lachner realized that the boy would one day eclipse him. Without doubt, also, he quickly developed a paternal interest and affection for him. In 1854, he wrote a letter of recommendation for his pupil, asking that he be permitted to attend a renowned conservatory in Leipzig, the *Cäcilienverein*. The beginning of the letter tells us much about the prevailing anti–Semitism of the age, and gives us some inkling of the hurdles to be overcome by a gifted young Jew, even in the arts. The letter begins:

"Although a Jew from birth, Hermann Levi has not a single one of the unpleasant peculiarities that we prejudge as being inseparably bound with his heritage, and which in truth often do abound in many of those of his heritage and in his co-religionists." After this bit of apologia, Lachner dealt first with the pupil's positive personality traits, deemed necessary in this instance before getting to the small matter of his musical talent. Contrary to those unpleasant traits, he assured the Verein, this young man, then 15, was of "an open, upright, honorable nature in all matters, such as is not often seen." One does not need to know him long before seeing his "likeable, winning personality." That said, he now felt safe in getting to the point:

> Levi came here as a boy of not quite thirteen to study composition with me. He was already an accomplished pianist and fluent sight reader, accompanied by a deep, most decidedly sensitive feel for music. After three industrious, intensive years of study, I advised him to attend the Conservatorium in Leipzig, to continue with his studies ... and importantly, through contact with other young people to be stimulated, and to become acquainted with the new preferred trends as represented in Leipzig.[7]

So, in the summer of 1855, three months shy of his sixteenth birthday, Hermann Levi said farewell to his mentor Lachner and, his very caring relatives, and set out alone for Leipzig to enroll in the renowned conservatory. It had been founded 12 years earlier by Felix Mendelssohn, composer and then conductor of the Gewandhaus orchestra. Mendelssohn died four years after the opening of the conservatorium, at age 37, and was succeeded as orchestra director by one Julius Rietz. Included among Hermann's teachers were Robert and Clara Schumann, Hans von Bülow, violinist Joseph Joachim, and the director Ferdinand Hiller. Joachim and Hiller were former friends of Wagner, both of whom broke personal relations with him after publication of his Jewish essay, though both had already converted to Christianity.

Toward the end of his second year, Hermann expressed doubts to his father as to whether he should continue another year at the conservatorium, whereupon Benedict wrote to Rietz, inquiring as to how things stood with his son's musical education. Rietz's reply showed some exasperation with the 17-year-old as wild and unruly, but added that the wildness of the environment itself was a contributing factor, and he correctly wondered if the question was not prompted by a desire to know whether the lad should transfer to another institution. Decidedly not, was Rietz's answer. "Let him remain here and we will enjoy the most satisfying success. About his piano playing, I hear only good things. He is one of the most skilled of all the students in our local institution."

He stayed another year, and undoubtedly did not regret it. He was trying his hand at composition, with all intentions of devoting his life to creation rather than interpretation. In March 1858 several of his songs were sung in concert, and a few days later he gave a solo piano concert including the delicately beautiful Beethoven Sonata opus 111. The critic for the *New Journal of Music*, the same journal that had printed Wagner's "Judaism in Music," described Levi as "one of the most talented, many sided, and perhaps the most mature students of the institution." This happened to be only a few months before another talented Jewish musician, Karl Tausig, first laid eyes on Richard Wagner in Zurich. In the fall of 1858 Levi left the conservatory to spend the winter in Paris.

It was a fruitful few months. He saw many works of the reigning master of grand opera, Giacomo Meyerbeer, the general enthusiasm for which he did not share. He saw also the new anxiously awaited opera, Charles Gounod's *Faust*, in the general enthusiasm for which he fully participated. He sharpened his knowledge of French and developed a keen interest in French culture, which culminated in his later translations of opera texts of Berlioz and Chabrier. He left Paris shortly before Wagner arrived to test the waters for his *Tristan*. He thus saw some of the massive renovation of the city that was, a few months later, to cause Wagner much grief.

Upon returning to Germany, with the assistance of Lachner he obtained the post of orchestra conductor in Saarbrücken in September 1859. By November, following several concerts, a local newspaper praised his combination of versatility and circumspection, and wished him well for continued success. He stayed his usual two seasons, during which he performed some of his own compositions to apparently less than enthusiastic receptions. He also appeared several times as guest conductor in nearby

Mannheim. With encouragement from Lachner, still reigning in that city as lead conductor, he again introduced compositions of his own, which, from his audience of friends and relatives there, was more warmly received. He never returned to Saarbrücken, but remained in Mannheim. The Saarbrücken critic wrote that a small city like his could not realistically hope to retain such a highly gifted conductor, but that Levi had accomplished much for good music during his tenure there.

By invitation from the Leipzig Gewandhaus he appeared there on November 7, his twenty-second birthday as it happened, in a solo piano concert. Again he played some of his own compositions. The review of the *New Journal for Music* had little good to report about them. It willingly acknowledged the accomplished and elegant performance on the piano, and the skill, study and talent in the handling of the orchestra, but declared that to be the end of its praise. It referred to Levi's composition as a potpourri, thrown together, devoid of any organization or unity. Levi had recently heard of the *Tannhäuser* debacle suffered by Wagner in Paris, but derived little comfort from it. Wagner was one of the best known living composers, he told friends, while he had to first make a name. For the time being, however, the setback only strengthened his resolve to compose.

We next see the young Levi as conductor of the German Opera in Rotterdam, a position secured once again with the help of the faithful Lachner. He spent the now customary two years in the Dutch city, conducted a varied repertory, and earned praise from the local press. Most significant to his future there was his performance of Wagner's *Lohengrin*. He had planned to have Wagner appear as guest conductor for the occasion, and contacted Wendelin Weissheimer to serve as intermediary, but nothing came of it.

The performance, under Levi's direction, was a brilliant success, a matter that was bound to have reached the ears of Wagner. In the second season, as he prepared for a premiere performance of an opera by Ferdinand Hiller, he recommended his older brother Wilhelm for one of the singing roles, only to find that Wilhelm himself was no longer interested in a career in music. He had married a Catholic woman and changed his surname to Lindeck, a matter that disturbed their father very much. Later, in 1868, Wilhelm pursued a banking career in Frankfurt with his wife's family.

Levi was convinced after his second year that there was no advantage to remaining outside of Germany. At the end of April 1864, his contract in Rotterdam having expired, he considered an offer to conduct in Carlsruhe. He was no doubt encouraged by a communication from Lachner listing the advantages of that position, among which was the fact that in such a small city, few would be concerned about religious denomination. He accepted the offer.

He was 25; his years as a student were over. He was experienced and talented and felt he could match the best that his colleagues had to offer. His first performance in Carlsruhe was Wagner's *Lohengrin*. The artistic director, Wilhelm Kalliwoda, and the theater director, Eduard Devrient, sat in the loge together, and both expressed extreme pleasure in Levi's conducting. An unknown spectator expressed his own enchantment with the performance by sending Devrient a bejeweled ring.

32

The Brahms-Levi Friendship

LEVI HAD BY NOW CONDUCTED a wide variety of music, including that of his contemporary Johannes Brahms. He had met Brahms in the summer of 1862 in Hamm, a rural suburb of Hamburg on the Alster Lake, where Brahms was living at the time.[1] Levi was returning to Rotterdam after a short vacation and said he wanted to have a look at the creator of the music he so admired. Two years later he was conducting in Carlsruhe. Brahms, spending the summer in Lichtenthal near Baden-Baden in the Black Forest, was staying in the home of Clara Schumann. He went to nearby Carlsruhe to participate in a performance of the German Musical Arts Society, which he found "ugly, feeble and boring," with one exception. "The whole affair was quite bearable in the company of Hermann Levi, the local music director," he wrote to Joseph Joachim. "That young man, in spite of all the theater-conductor routine, is so fresh and gazes so brightly onto the loveliest heights that it's truly a pleasure."

In the summer of 1865, Brahms returned again to Carlsruhe for the festival and stayed in the same rooming house where Levi resided. Bülow was one of the festival directors. Among the audience was Franz Liszt, accompanied by his daughter, Bülow's wife Cosima, two months pregnant at the time with Isolde, the first child of Richard Wagner. As we have already seen, Bülow either was ignorant of the child's true paternity or skillfully hid his awareness.

Judging by a letter from Brahms to Joseph Joachim, both he and Levi enjoyed exchanging humorous criticisms of the performers. It was during this visit that Levi and Brahms became fast friends. They admired each other's artistry and Brahms seemed taken with the gregarious nature, the mischievousness and the wit of his conductor friend. Eugenie Schumann was witness to much of it and wrote of Levi's infectious laughter and his practical jokes. Brahms had a sharp wit of his own, and it fed at times on Levi's obvious Jewish physical characteristics. Brahms was never accused of anti–Semitism, nor should he have been. He clearly harbored no such prejudice. Yet it is evidence of the nature of the times, and of the place, that he could engage, along with others, in joking about such matters, undoubtedly considering it harmless fun. Levi's reaction was often a wan and halfhearted smile.[2]

At the end of October of that year Brahms came to Carlsruhe to participate with Levi in a performance of his First Piano Concerto. Brahms had been helped considerably by Levi in the scoring of the concerto, as he was in many other compositions. He relied repeatedly, and heavily, on Levi's skill and mastery of the orchestra. Levi placed himself unstintingly in the service of his composer friend, sank himself deeply into his works, and interpreted them with intensity and understanding. "Whether he was listening to Brahms's work, playing them on the piano, studying or directing them, he identified himself completely with them."[3] Such was Levi's dedication to his art, and such was his complete devotion to what he instinctively recognized as greatness in music.

In the summer of 1867 they met again in the home of Clara Schumann near Baden-Baden. The moody Brahms was not in one of his better humors. Levi had been advising Brahms on various compositions, including his *German Requiem,* and felt sufficiently close to show Brahms some of his own compositions. Brahms was apparently quite abrupt. Tact was not one of his better attributes, though by some accounts, Levi's talents as a composer were by no means negligible. Levi felt offended to the extent that he wrote Clara that Brahms was now at a crossroads:

> If he should not succeed in snatching his better self from the demon of abruptness, of coldness, and of heartlessness, then he is lost to us and to his music, for only all-engendering love can create works of art.[4]

Whatever Brahms had said, Levi obviously was wounded. The rift at this time was temporary. But the germ of what would ultimately break the friendship asunder was already clear, at least in retrospect, in the different approach to artistic endeavor to which each subscribed. Levi must have poured out his injured feelings to Brahms by letter, and we can assume that its content resembled that of the letter to Clara Schumann. Brahms answered briefly, assuring Levi that they would meet soon and he would address the matter at more length in person. But his short written reply tells us much. Until they meet, said Brahms,

> Forgive me if I wait until I can ask you in person not to react bitterly to what I said with such sincere good intentions.... What seems so problematic to you, "to dedicate oneself totally" is not at all so to me.[5]

"To dedicate oneself totally." The use of quotation marks in the letter indicates that Brahms was quoting Levi's own words. It was more than merely "problematic" to Levi, it was essential; but not at all so to Brahms. This was the crux of the problem that was to arise a few years hence, when we will see Levi totally succumb to the siren song of Wagner, and devote his entire being to that pied piper and to the overwhelming power of his art. He would do so with a singular intensity almost equaling Wagner's own, an intensity that has been within the capacity of very few, whether composers, conductors, or performers. The fire, in Levi and Wagner both, burned with a white heat. Both were totally consumed by their respective arts, something that could not and need not be understood by a composer of cooler, more classical forms such as Johannes Brahms, a very great, but different, kind of genius.

Brahms ended his letter with still more salt to the wound: "Be of good cheer, be reasonable, allow your wings to grow back, there are seven heavens (the Composers' Heaven you won't get into)." Ultimately Levi did decide that he would rather be, as he then put it, a first-rate conductor than a second-rate composer, but it was a painful decision, and Levi's ambition at the time was given short shift by Brahms.

Not with Brahms nor later with Wagner could Levi separate the man from the artist. As a contemporary of both, and as interpreter of both living composers, he did not have the luxury of dedicating himself completely to the music of either without complete dedication to the composer. He expected no less from them. Brahms was of a different temperament. It seems a justifiable inference from their correspondence that the closer Levi drew, the more restrained became Brahms. Nonetheless, Levi continued to exert himself tirelessly in the service of Brahms, even as he immersed himself in the widest symphonic and operatic repertory as director of the Carlsruhe theater.

One of the operas in which he immersed himself was Wagner's *Meistersinger,* which had premiered in Munich, as we have seen, in 1868. We have seen also Wagner's comment to him, in his correspondence in 1870, about the reports of Levi's excellent performance of the opera earlier that year, an unusual experience indeed for Wagner. The excellence that so pleased the Master did not come easily. Levi had begun preparations for the performance in late 1869 even as he was dedicating himself simultaneously to a performance of Brahms's *German Requiem,* which had been heard in incomplete form in Vienna and Bremen in previous months. The Wagner opera was particularly difficult and presented numerous problems, including the insufficient complement of the Carlsruhe orchestra and chorus, the resistance of the opera administration and their subsequent insistence that the opera be shortened for performance.

But Levi had attended the premiere in Munich, and had there become hopelessly enamored of the work. He persisted and, overcoming all obstacles, presented the work uncut on February 5. The final curtain was followed by a storm of applause and repeated calls by the audience for Levi and the soloists. Later that evening at a social function for many of the dignitaries, Levi stoutly defended Wagner and his work against sharp criticism from an art historian, Wilhelm Lübke. It was during the preparations for this performance that Levi's admiration for the Wagnerian work became one of reverence. He wrote to Brahms that the opera had left him breathless.[6]

The *German Requiem* was performed five weeks later, on the ninth of March. Levi continued to exert himself tirelessly in behalf of Brahms. In 1871, experiencing difficulties with the composition of the *Shicksallied*, "The Song of Destiny," Brahms turned to Levi, who unstintingly worked with him, advising and assisting. Brahms was also seeking a suitable opera libretto, determined to try his hand at that genre, and Levi tried repeatedly though unsuccessfully to secure one to his satisfaction.

By the end of 1872, as we have seen, Levi was engaged as conductor of the Royal Opera in Munich, where he served temporarily in a position subordinate to Wüllner. But Wüllner soon had reason to fear for his authority. Levi's first production was of Mozart's *Die Zauberflöte* (*The Magic Flute*). In the final rehearsal, the singers had the opportunity to judge the now famed artistry of the new conductor. Following the rehearsal, the lead tenor, his face glowing, lay his hand on the shoulder of one of the theater's top administrators and declared: "I don't need to hear anything more. He is a second Lachner." The Lachner referred to was the brother of Vincenz, namely Franz, who had previously conducted in Munich.

Levi's first public performance of *Die Zauberflöte* brought praise from the artists, the public and the press. He was soon in the position of lead conductor for the Munich Opera. Wagner telegraphed his congratulations. Thinking of his own troubles in that cauldron, he told Levi that since he, Levi, believed in a personal God, he should now call on Him for help. None of Levi's successes stood in the way of his closeness and assistance to Brahms.

In the summer of 1873 he assisted Brahms again, this time in the scoring of two quartets he had recently completed and a two-piano arrangement for certain Haydn Variations. In mid–September Brahms read them with Levi at the latter's home in Munich. These were his last compositions before returning to work on his towering First Symphony, which he had previously, temporarily, put aside. One of Brahms's biographers has expressed the opinion that without Levi, Brahms might never have achieved the orchestral virtuosity he finally developed.[7]

In December Levi wrote to Brahms and, possibly sensing the cooling of Brahms's attitude toward him, said, "I have a terrible yearning to see you again." But shortly thereafter he sent the composer another letter, filled with rhapsodic praise for Wagner's *Götterdämmerung*, which probably triggered the resentment that would end the Brahms-Levi relationship. As Wagner had not actually completed the scoring of that opera in 1873, Levi probably had read only the first two acts. A year later, in late December of 1874, Brahms was awarded a high honor by King Ludwig of Bavaria. Many formalities accompany such an event, details with which Brahms was unfamiliar, and probably uninterested. Levi patiently guided him through the thicket, including the necessarily stiff and formal letter of thanks to His Majesty.

The ultimate rupture in the Brahms-Levi relationship was preordained by an event culminating on May 10, 1874. On that date, Levi for the first time conducted *Tristan und Isolde.* He had heard performances of it in Munich under the baton of Bülow during June and August, just a few months before Levi's assumption of the office there as music director. To conduct this masterpiece was for Levi an overwhelming challenge, which he accepted only after much hesitation and painstaking preparations. What the mastery of that opera would mean for him became clear during the performance by Bülow. He later wrote to Wagner that *Tristan* was the work that he loved above all others, and that the turning point in his life he dated from his closer acquaintance with it.[8]

Not everyone who heard that opera was so favorably impressed. In September 1875 Clara Schumann traveled to Munich with her children to attend another opera, but stayed to hear a performance of *Tristan*. They were joined by Joseph Joachim. Clara was but little short of outraged. "The most offensive that I have ever seen and heard," she wrote, "to have to see and hear all evening long such love madness." But the objections and arguments of neither Clara, nor Joachim, nor those of Paul Heyse, poet and playwright and friend of both Brahms and Levi, nor all of their warnings about Wagner the man, or Wagnerian music, were of any avail against the determination of Levi to cast his lot with the creator of *Die Meistersinger* and *Tristan*.

Four years later, in 1879, Levi wrote to Joachim: "You ask me whether I am still a Wagnerian?" After years of study and reflection, he answered, he felt he might really call himself that. "I bless the day on which my eyes were opened (dimly at first through *Meistersinger*, and completely through *Tristan*)." He is entranced by all of Wagner's mature works. "*Tristan, Meistersinger* and the *Nibelung*, although absolutely different in style, are all equally emanations of the same great genius." He urged his friend to overcome his aversion to Wagner, just by listening. One cannot argue about Wagner, continues Levi, "any more than one can argue about religion."

33

The Breach with Brahms

THE BREAK WITH BRAHMS came in the summer of 1875. Brahms was visiting Levi at his home in Munich, having stopped en route to his summer quarters near Heidelberg. In the course of the visit Levi expressed the opinion that the operas of Wagner exceeded in quality those of the eighteenth century composer Christoph Gluck, a statement with which hardly anyone today would quarrel. There must have been a tremendous resentment building in the temperamental composer against Levi, Wagner, or both. He interrupted Levi, saying, "One doesn't pronounce those two names like that, one after the other."[1] What else was said has not been reported, but may be gleaned from Levi's letter to the composer written shortly thereafter. Brahms stalked angrily out of the house, and much to Levi's resentment and sorrow, left Munich without saying farewell, or anything else, to him.

Levi's letter tells us much about the cause for this break. It renders superfluous attempts by some Brahms apologists to put a better face on this tantrum. Brahms had obviously been deeply wounded, not by any slight or injury done him by Levi, but by his own juvenile sensitivities. His reaction was that if Levi was to be a close associate of Wagner, then he could not be a friend of Brahms. This must have been difficult indeed for Levi to understand. As an artist and conductor he saw no reason why something done for one composer should interfere with his personal relations with others. His artistic calling involved service in behalf of many composers, living and dead. He had translated into German the texts of several operas of Mozart and Berlioz, and performed their works together with those of countless other composers. He is in fact credited with beginning a "Mozart renaissance," that composer's masterpieces having been sadly neglected for many decades.[2]

The exact date of his letter to Brahms is unknown, but followed shortly after the abruptly terminated meeting in Munich. Portions of it are quite revealing. Levi left no memoirs, and this may be as close as we come to seeing inside this complex and extraordinarily talented artist.

He was not prepared for the sudden departure, says Levi, and he had set aside the following morning for certain discussions with Brahms, but,

> Your comments of the first day had also pained me deeply. I don't wish to hark back to it again, but there is one thing I would like you to reflect on: that I have in fact dedicated my life to a specific goal, which I must cherish. I take pains to discharge my profession fully and completely. But that can come about only on condition that I enter into it with a fullness of heart. I would consider it a misfortune if I confronted as stranger and foe the material which, as an opera director, I am expected to replicate and represent.

He had, in short, been captivated by Wagner's music, and he realized full well that, whatever his faults, it was the man who wrote the music, and that he must work with him. Others, Brahms included, could separate the two, the man from the music. He could not:

> One who is staunchly self-reliant, like you, or who, like Allgeyer [a celebrated photographer and close friend of both Brahms and Levi], need not deal with the external world and can avoid everything which is disagreeable to his nature, is free to go his way, untouched by his own time — and to rise above it. For me there was ... the genuine interest of the theater person, and finally the need to give an accounting of this interest to myself, and to defend it against those who differ. To my mind this has nothing at all to do with "transformations."

The quotation marks around "transformations" tells us that it was a term, accusatory in nature, no doubt, that Brahms pinned on Levi during their conversation in Munich.

> It is instead a natural progression, and anyone who, for instance, saw me after the *Schicksallied*, would consider it unthinkable that anything that I ever truly loved could pale for me as a result of more recent impressions. The fact that I shy away from any conceivable association with the future gang, and am thoroughly hated by it, might also give you pause to ponder whether I had actually deserved your cruel words.

The "future gang" refers to the committed acolytes who gathered around Wagner and adopted as gospel the empty phrase which had come to be associated with his music: "music of the future." His acknowledgment of their "hatred" at this early date should be noted with interest. He was fully aware of the anti–Semitism surrounding Wagner, much of which far exceeded Wagner's own. The letter continues:

I have not often plagued you with my own affairs since we have known each other, and would also like to leave it at that today, after this brief *oratio pro domo* [a speech for use within the household]. Should you need someone to jump into a great deep in your behalf, turn to me. And besides, it's absolutely no business of yours that I hold you dear.

In unalterable loyalty and devotion

Your Hermann Levi

Brahms never answered. Four years later, in a letter to his friend Paul Heyse, Levi revealed the depth of his anguish caused by this affair: "A friend whom I always thanked for what I am and what I have, deserted me because he cannot have anything in common with a Wagnerian. That was the most painful experience of my entire life."[3] By this time, however, Heyse had also distanced himself from Levi, and for the same reason.

Brahms could, and did, tolerate other directors who conducted Wagner's music. Brahms himself admired much of it. But he could not abide the close personal relationship that was developing between his friend Levi and Wagner. The breach with Brahms was the most egregious, but was not the only strain on Levi's relationships with friends that was to result from his growing absorption with Wagner. In early 1875 Julius Allgeyer had answered a concern expressed by Clara Schumann about Levi. He wrote that he no longer was of the same mind as Levi in all things, but hoped that a coming concert Levi was to conduct of Brahms's music would perhaps show him the difference between "musical poison and truly noble art."

Levi saw it differently. He acknowledged to Clara that strictly as a musician Brahms was superior to Wagner, but that "When Wagner puts music in the service of drama, he does it with a force like no one before him." Therefore, he says, he sees no reason why a genuine admiration for his creations cannot exist together with an equally honest admiration for Bach, Beethoven and Brahms. His opinion of Brahms's work is not lessened by his belief in *Tristan* as a great work of art.[4]

It was all without effect. The breach was never healed, though circumstances often brought them in close contact. In vain, friends tried to bring them together. From a distance, through others, Brahms expressed concern over his former friend, particularly for his health, which was soon to see a rapid decline. But the tension was exacerbated in 1877 over a remark by Brahms that under better circumstances would have been brushed aside.

In November 1876, the same year as the first *Ring* performance in Bayreuth, Brahms had conducted his monumental First Symphony in Carlsruhe. He completed the Second Symphony the following summer. In late fall, Levi requested that Brahms permit its performance in Munich, preferably with the composer conducting. Brahms replied that the symphony would first be performed in Vienna with Wüllner conducting. At the time, Levi was preparing to conduct the first Munich performance of the *Ring.*

It happens that in the first *Ring* opera there are two giants, Fasolt and Fafner, who fight over possession of the magic ring until one kills the other. Brahms remarked on the rivalry of Wüllner and Levi, referring to them as Fasolt and Fafner, implying a struggle between them for money or fame. Levi was outraged, and the breach, if not previously so, was now irrevocable.

In June 1899, less than a year before his death, Levi answered a question from Countess Anna von Hesse about this breach of his friendship. From the perspective of 22 years, the ailing 62-year-old Levi could speak with detachment, with a bird's-eye view as he termed it. He now saw his intimate relationship with Brahms as a mere point of passage. "As this change in my direction was completed, under the colossal impression of *Tristan* and *Meistersinger* my personal relationship with Brahms had to cease; we parted in the year 1877, without really saying so, without argument, only in the feeling that we had nothing more to say, and from then on I have not seen him again."[5]

Aside from Clara Schumann and Allgeyer, who were sharply critical of the path Levi chose, others besides Brahms openly broke with him. His friendship with Paul Heyse, though not broken, was severely strained. Next to Brahms, the most painful breach must have been that with his friend and mentor, Vincenz Lachner. In 1880, he wrote to Levi in words that must have cut him to the quick: "I see you as one of the most professional priests of art, forever fettered to something that to me is a sickness, yes, that I must see as a national misfortune. You appear to me as a victim of a spiritual, brilliant, but inwardly false, destructive cause."[6]

None of them reckoned with the inner steel or the unswervable purpose of this quiet, seemingly pliable, self-effacing musician. It was obviously unsettling for his contemporaries to see such stubbornness in this man who so craved and valued friendships, who sought always to avoid tension and controversy. To Heyse he wrote, "Many years ago I thought it impossible to lose someone other than through death; since then I have had to learn to cry over the living dead."[7] But Levi knew who he was, what he was, and the meaning of his life. It was music. Music permeated his being as it did that of few others, and the new music of Wagner beckoned him as though from a spirit world. Nothing was going to stand in his way.

The "false destructive cause" of Wagner and "Wagnerism" that so disturbed Lachner was troubling to many, including more than a few who were immersed in the world of music. What it threatened was the traditional, the tried and true forms of the classical structure. In its place was the melodic line that never seemed to come to rest, the continually shifting keys and abruptly changing moods of the orchestra, the orchestra itself as a character in the drama, commenting, evoking memories of prior scenes and foretelling what was to come. It seemed so formless. His was not the cultured, cultivated garden, the geometrically correct structures that were the bedrock of great music for several centuries. But it was not formless at all. The form around which this penetratingly evocative music wrapped itself was the drama. Never, in the history of opera, was there such cohesion between drama and music. This remarkable magician seemed able to squeeze music out of the drama itself.

These ragged cliffs, mountain ranges with jutting peaks of no immediate discernable order, unsymmetrical coastlines, wild, untamed nature, things that seemed the stuff of Wagner's music were found by many to be threatening to their comfortable cultivated musical domain. To others it was an exciting new world. Where other composers so beautifully expressed the well traveled paths of emotions and feeling of a civilized humanity, Wagner reached deep into the human psyche and explored the depths of feelings and emotions long buried. Where many were content to leave these darkly troubling ghosts from the unconscious undisturbed, others, such as Hermann Levi, were fascinated, hypnotized, by the newness, the novelty, and the power of this world of dark spirits. It was not at all for frivolous reasons that so many invested in him so much of their fortunes, and that others devoted to him a lifetime of energy and industry.

About 12 years after Levi's performance of *Tristan* in Munich, another Jew, an adolescent named Bruno Schlesinger, later known to the world as Bruno Walter, attended a performance of the same opera in Berlin. In his home and as a pupil in the Stern Conservatory in that city, he had heard many denigrating comments about Wagner's later works, as opposed to his early ones, such as "dangerous sensuality." Brahms on the other hand was heralded as the pinnacle of the classical tradition. He had heard and loved Brahms, but had never heard Wagner's later operas, so the youngster decided to see for himself. He bought a ticket for *Tristan*. The only seat he could afford was one in the topmost balcony.

His expectations and excitement were high, but left him totally unprepared for the experience. In his own words written almost 60 years later: "From the first sound of the cellos my heart contracted spasmodically. The magic, like the terrible potion ... 'burst raging forth from heart to brain,'" a quote of a line from the third act. All he had been taught of the sanctity of the classical forms was swept away on that evening in the Berlin opera house:

Never before had my soul been so deluged with floods of sound and passion, never had my heart been consumed by such yearning and sublime blissfulness, never had I been transported from reality by such heavenly glory. I was no longer in this world. After the performance, I roamed the streets aimlessly. When I got home I didn't say anything and begged not to be questioned. My ecstasy kept singing within me through half the night, and when I awoke on the following morning I knew that my life was changed. A new epoch had begun: Wagner was my god, and I wanted to become his prophet.[8]

It could well have been said a dozen years earlier by Levi. At the cost of valuable friendships and of the respect and esteem of still others, Levi turned to Wagner. In place of his comfortable musical circle, he knowingly put himself in another, one he well knew to be permeated with virulent anti–Semitism. He was as prepared to tolerate the stings and psychic wounds of the new milieu as he was to give up the adulation and comfort of the old. It was for neither fame nor money; it was the pursuit of an ideal in music, one that had penetrated his entire being. This is the essence of character, and of abounding self-confidence, of knowledge of oneself and one's purpose in life. It is necessary to say this, as for his dedication he has been vilified in recent times as lacking in character, and as a case of "self-hatred."

34

A Study in Malice

LEVI CHOSE TO ENLIST IN the cause of those who in matters of music were his soul mates. In matters of heritage and "race" he was in hostile territory, something he knew in advance. Like many other Jews of the time to whom religion meant little, he found himself adapting to the views of his countrymen. Even before his complete seduction by the music of Wagner, he talked and behaved like most of his fellow Germans, even in sporadic expressions of disdain for the "foreign" traits of his fellow religionists, converted and unconverted. Many Jews did convert. Some few became vociferous anti–Semites. Karl Marx, born a Jew, and converted by his father at the age of 6, was one of the most rabid of that particular brand.

Levi never converted or changed his name, but to a much lesser degree, some of the same syndrome may have affected him. It has been mentioned by author Peter Gay, whose disdain for Levi we will examine shortly, that on one occasion Levi denigrated members of his family as showing "typically Jewish" traits for their interests in monetary matters such as banking,[1] for which he, like Wagner, had little concern. Gay has also mentioned that Levi once rejected a Jewish soprano as not suitable for a role that required a Germanic characterization. This, however, was hardly novel in the casting practices of the time. He, like many others, was convinced that certain roles should not be portrayed by artists whose appearances were not fitting for them. Levi had also found distasteful the works of many contemporary Italian and French composers that he felt were written in styles not suited to their talents. In short, he was ripe for what was to follow his awestruck dedication following introductions to *Tristan und Isolde* and *Die Meistersinger*.

Levi was not a perfect human being, but being no less than human, he

232

began to adapt, increasingly often, to some of the attitudes of the anti–Semitic coterie surrounding Wagner, as well as the hurtful remarks of the Wagners themselves. Those of Richard, and later of Cosima, often made in Levi's presence and sometimes directly to him, were often wounding, sometimes unintentionally so, and other times perhaps even well meant. They truly believed that Jewishness was a curse, and seemed to have more sympathy for the conductor than animosity.

But rarely were Wagner or Cosima, unlike some others of their friends, motivated by malice, nor were they ones to engage in ridicule. They had too much respect for Levi's talent for that, though not enough to keep them from anger. Wagner displayed his temper at times to everyone, and neither Levi nor Cosima herself were exempt.

As a result of the path he chose, Levi was cut off from two of his most enduring and valuable friendships, met with frequent hostility in his new surroundings, and was there looked upon as flawed from birth by his Jewishness. He made the choice willingly, and never looked back. He endured much for his decision. So, in different ways, did Liszt, Wesendonck, Bülow, King Ludwig, and a host of others. What they experienced was, for them, the supreme satisfaction of contributing in some way to the creation of great art that had so moved them emotionally. Not surprisingly, Levi used whatever defensive mechanisms he could muster to endure what inevitably came with his choice.

What he endured can be well exemplified by a passage from a young conductor, Felix Weingartner. He wrote that on one occasion in Wahnfried, seeing Levi addressed insolently by one of the children, he took Levi aside and asked why a man of such renown should tolerate this type of treatment. Sadly, said Weingartner, Levi looked at him and answered, "You certainly have an easy life in this house — you an Aryan."[2]

How his defenses came to his rescue, and how little it affected his own self-esteem as an individual, even as he turned at times against his own culture, is shown in a now-controversial letter to Cosima, more than 10 years after Richard's death:

> It has become dogma in Wahnfried that a Jew has certain characteristics, that he thinks and acts in a certain way and that, above all, he is incapable of unselfish dedication. Everything I do and say is judged by this precept, everything is considered offensive or strange at least. I will not censure anybody for this judgment. I know quite well the content of "Judaism in Music" and share the view of that glorious book. But to demand that I ascribe all the characteristics of the Jews to myself, that I protest against. I know that my own nature is very different.[3]

Many modern writers on this subject have treated Levi rather harshly for this seemingly unnecessarily compliant attitude toward the scurrilous essay. We must understand, however, that this letter was not a public document. It was not intended for the eyes of anyone other than Cosima, that unquestioning, rigidly dedicated, devout worshipper of her deceased husband. To question anything he wrote, or anything he said or did, was enough to mark the author of such impertinence as an enemy worthy only of excommunication.

But the words Levi used were probably not so much through fear of her anger, as through sympathy, and perhaps a touch of pity for this single-minded widow. Arrogant and officious as she often appeared, she bristled with outrage, and no doubt a good deal of pain, to hear her deceased husband's operas or writings challenged. Such words were like darts and struck at the very core of her being. Her entire existence was one-dimensional. As a close friend, Levi well knew this. He was, in this letter, protesting some prevailing skepticism regarding his own presence, and obviously felt it politic, perhaps, humane, to disclaim any intent to, the good Lord forbid, take issue with the Master's pronouncements in his essay.

But some modern writers have become more than merely critical; they have become enraged, not only for this letter, but for the entire direction of Levi's career. For his decision to dedicate his talents to Wagner and his work Levi has been vilified and slandered as few others in the history of music. These fulminating scholars have pinned on him a libelous, calumnious epithet, painting him as a study in self-hatred. The first application of this term to Levi seems to have been authored by Peter Gay in 1978.[4] The phrase is pungent enough, and the political climate receptive enough, that the term has been picked up in the general Wagner literature. In the manner sometimes peculiar to scholars, it has been accepted as an enduring truth.

The truth, however, is that Gay's chapter about Levi is not a study in self-hatred. It is a study in anger, namely his own, and he divides it impartially between Wagner and Levi. Wagner struggled in an environment equally as hostile as that in which Levi had found himself, namely in the classical and artistic world that was nineteenth century Europe. He persevered against tremendous societal inertia, hostility and ridicule, and bequeathed to humanity some of the most profound and evocative art in history. But he is painted by Gay as a grotesque caricature of personified evil.

We are to understand from Gay's writing not that Gay hated Levi, but rather that Levi hated himself. Gay's own writing belies that conclusion; his contempt for Levi oozes from his pages, despite a superficial veneer of objectivity.

To presume to analyze these human relationships without an appreciation of the music that emanated from the difficult genius that was Richard

Wagner is a task doomed to failure. But Gay is apparently deaf to the music. One can read his tract from beginning to end and find no trace of any understanding of the artwork that captivated so many so deeply, Christians and Jews alike.

As Gay sees it, Wagner cost Levi the friendship of Lachner and of Brahms. In short, the breach was Wagner's fault, or it was Levi's; or both. In no respect was it the fault of Brahms or Lachner. It was a failing on the part of Levi in that he did not give up what was most important to him, and behave as Gay would have preferred. And it was part of the evil nature of Wagner to tear Levi from his friends, as though Levi were a child in Wagner's care.

Except as some scholars and others have made it a term of art with their own peculiar definition, it was not self-hatred at all. Traditional religion never meant very much to Levi; his religion was music. In saying that Levi became anti–Semitic himself, Gay attempts to place him in a group of the converted who notoriously did couple their change in religion with a show of anti–Semitism, as if to trumpet the completeness of the renunciation. Karl Marx is only one example.

But if Levi, who did not convert, was a Jewish anti–Semite, it was in a very strange form. His love and honor for his father is alone sufficient to nullify such an appellation. Alfred von Mensi-Klarbach, in his *Altmünchener Theater Erinnerungen* ("Recollections of the old Munich Theater"), writes that "Levi was dedicated with a touching show of love to his elderly father, which, as well known, is nowhere more strongly nor so well defined as with the Jews."[5] He contributed his musical talents as composer to synagogues in Mannheim and Giessen, and as late as 1881, he was sponsor and benefactor of the cantor in Munich.[6]

In referring to his behavior as evidence of self-hatred there is no validity at all, except by twisting the words hideously out of their common meaning. Levi's behavior has been described by many authors on this subject, but never, until Gay and his followers, as self-hatred. Gay also calls it an addiction, and cannot forgive Levi for not giving it up, as though love of great art were in a class with alcoholism, or drug addiction.

The plethora of Jewish conductors and artists who have continued to find pleasure and fascination in Wagner's work would undoubtedly see things differently from Gay. They would probably agree with a modern Jewish conductor, Georg Solti. In his 1997 autobiography he wrote that he was not interested in Wagner's political or philosophical ideas, and said, "To me, anybody who can create such beauty, whether he be half–Jewish, anti–Semite ... or royalist, is first and foremost a musical genius and will remain so as long as civilization lasts."[7]

35

Declining Health,
Worsening Temperament

IN THE SUMMER OF 1875 rehearsals for the *Ring* were to begin in earnest. Levi wrote to Wagner asking to be allowed to take part in these preparations, in whatever capacity he might deem helpful. Wagner readily accepted, responding at once to his "most worthy friend." In early August Levi spent five days in Bayreuth listening to rehearsals of *Siegfried* and *Götterdäm-merung.* He was fascinated by, among other things, the unique acoustics of the festival theater. Every morning he would rehearse one act with the orchestra alone, and in afternoons add the soloists. In the evenings he was a guest in Wagner's home in Wahnfried. It was an overwhelming experience.

To his father, after describing the exciting impressions, he wrote: "I am too old to kid myself — and I tell you that what will happen in the coming year in Bayreuth is a radical change in our artistic life." The marvels of the theater he described in detail, the unrestricted sight lines and the clarity of the acoustics throughout the building, all brought to fruition by this "simple German musician." As for Wagner himself, "He was charming to me, and welcomed me most sincerely." The relationship of Wagner to Perfall, however, he said could never be healed. Wagner exploded in anger, said Levi, when one spoke his name. He mentioned also his having renewed many old acquaintances and made a number of new ones.[1]

Though he mentioned no names, among old acquaintances were Porges and the conductor Hans Richter, who would conduct the first *Ring*. During a rehearsal of *Siegfried*, Levi was treated to a firsthand look at a specimen of Wagner's well known temperamental outbursts. Displeased with something, he raged and shouted, shook his fist and stamped his feet. Then, suddenly, he played the clown, put a horn on his head (an instrument blown on stage by the lead tenor), and ran with it toward the stomach of a prominent invited guest.

The following year, from mid–June until mid–August, Levi was again in Bayreuth assisting in the final preparations and partaking in festivities involved with the festival itself. Among the new acquaintances he met during these two months was the conductor Felix Mottl, then only 19, but destined to play a significant role in Bayreuth after Wagner's death. He was also introduced to an art philosopher from Munich, Conrad Fiedler, and his 22-year-old wife, Mary. Levi, years later after Fiedler's death, was to be her second husband.

The visit was beneficial to Wagner as well as to Levi, as the composer now had a friend in the Munich opera. Owing to Levi's position, he was able to assist in Wagner's goals in a number of respects, notwithstanding the animosity between Perfall and Wagner.

So in the beginning, all seemed sunny and bright, with not a cloud in the sky. It would continue so for several years. Levi's friendship with the Master, for all his help and assistance, was still not very visible to the public. As long as it was not, it caused no problem to Wagner. Problems would come later with his selection of Levi for one of the highest honors that could befall a conductor: to conduct the premiere of an opera by a world renowned composer. This was especially true of what would be the composer's final opera, and even more especially one as eagerly anticipated, and as certain to enter the permanent repertory as was the hypnotically beautiful *Parsifal.*

There would be problems, but Levi's fine sense of irony, his tact, and his touch of cynicism laced with wry humor would see him through. One vignette may tell us much. Baron Perfall, as administrative director of the Munich opera, gave a soirée for all of the opera's high ranking personnel. Levi sought to excuse himself for the reason that his brother Wilhelm would be in Munich that day, and Levi wanted to spend the time with him. Perfall graciously assured the conductor that his brother would be welcome also. It will be recalled that Wilhelm had changed his name from Levi, a patently Jewish name, to Lindeck, which hinted at no trace of Jewish heritage.

When the two brothers entered, Levi introduced his brother, Wilhelm Lindeck, to Perfall. Later, apparently in all innocence, Perfall privately inquired of Levi as to why, if they were brothers, he should be Levi and the brother Lindeck. Replied the quick witted conductor, with perhaps a bit of exasperation: "Well, you see, Your Excellency, my name also used to be Lindeck, but that sounded too Jewish, so I changed it to Levi."[2]

On January 20, 1877, Levi, having just concluded a performance in Munich of *Die Meistersinger,* was sufficiently exhilarated that he could not resist an immediate visit to Wahnfried. He went to Bayreuth and announced his presence with a letter explaining that after such a successful perform-ance he could no longer bear not visiting Wagner. Five days later, Cosima noted in her diary that Richard began work on *Parsifal.* He was to spend the next five and one-half years on this work, and for the last year and a half of that period, it would throw him and Levi into close and sometimes continual contact. Never would he work so closely with so many Jewish artists as then, in the last years of his life, and never would his anti–Semi-tism be more frequently and more bitterly expressed, mostly in private to his wife, but on occasion in letters and in his prose writings.

Raw numbers tell something of the story. Of the approximately 400 days in which anti–Semitic comments appear in Cosima's diaries, 177 appear in the first nine years, from 1869 through 1877. During the next five years and 43 days of his life, there are 223 days with such comments. It must be noted nonetheless that the volume of entries for the later period equals that for the longer, earlier one. Perhaps the more advanced age of the children and their lessening requirement of supervision may account for the more detailed account by Cosima of those last five years.

But numbers do not tell the whole story. More of the later remarks than those in the earlier years seem to be those of Richard, rather than Cosima's own thoughts. They are also more mean spirited, more contemp-tuous, and at times show less evidence of any lightheartedness or attempts at humor, though those qualities are not always lacking. His bitterness is pervasive, directed at many, not only at the Jews. Groups, such as the Jesuits; nationalities, such as the French, and many individuals are targets of his stinging remarks. But primarily his prey was *the Jews.*

Even he must have realized the deadening effect of the repetitive nature of his attacks. On November 28, 1878, on a walk with Cosima he explained, "I find it embarrassing to keep coming back to the subject of the Jews, but one can't avoid it when one is thinking of the future." Any reasons deduced now for this growing obsession can be speculative only.

In partial mitigation it should be borne in mind that his health, dur-ing these later years was in decline; he endured a number of "chest spasms," some of which may have been heart attacks, and he suffered pain and dis-comfort from others of his many ailments. Two such spasms were men-tioned in 1879; by 1881 there were five. For two weeks in December 1879, on the eve of a trip to Italy, there was a bout of erysipelas, the 'roses' as he called it, and a recurrence of it for a week in February while vacationing with the family in Naples. The chest spasms must have been frequent enough that not all were mentioned. In February 1882, Cosima reports that a sponge bath staved off another episode. But a month later, during a visit to Italy with his family, he suffered a severe one.

There were also reports from time to time of abdominal catarrh, coughs and sore throats as well as dental surgery, performed, as was the custom then, in the home. On July 26, 1882, the day of the first *Parsifal* performance and just seven months before his death, she described her husband's restless night, and his calling out, "Children, I am going, suffering." At lunch the next day it was obvious he had forgotten some events of the previous evening.

His growing cynicism, bitterness, and contempt for the world in general was exacerbated also by his constant struggle with that world for the recognition and help to which he felt entitled, and which he so desperately needed. These traits had hardened during his last years, though they often showed themselves in a crudely delivered wrapping of irony and humor. In September 1881 he startled his wife by proclaiming that "everything, everything is a lie," a statement he supported with a number of trivial examples.

The following day, during a walk together, she discussed with him his "curious and demoniac habit of his hurting people without the slightest evil intent." She gently took her husband to task for wounding, with an acid comment humorously intended, a Russian stage designer who had come to help in the *Parsifal* venture. She had felt obliged to explain to the Russian that when agitated her husband would "stick out his claws" with a talent for "hitting unerringly on one's weak point."

She was eminently qualified to make such an explanation. On December 8 of that year she noted that Richard was somewhat irritable (probably a gross understatement), and, she continued, "I frequently call upon the God within me to give me strength against evil spirits." She knew that he wrote that day in his Brown Book that he could not get along with others because of "foolish questions he is asked, which drive him to despair." On February 27, 1882, he was driving in town with Cosima when he suddenly called out to no one in particular, "Very well, you gentlemen overflowing with ideas, try to write a melody like the Prelude to the second act of *Tristan und Isolde*."

The Russian Cosima had mentioned was Paul von Joukowsky, a wealthy young painter with a home in Naples. The son of a Russian father and a German mother, he had attended the festival of 1876 at Bayreuth and was fascinated by the possibility of meeting and working with the Master. He first met Richard and Cosima in their temporary home at the Villa d'Angri in Naples on January 18, 1880, and enjoyed a pleasant evening. After Joukowsky left, Richard expounded to Cosima his views about Russia:

I know how Russia can be helped but no one asked me for my opinion. The Tsar should set fire to St. Petersburg with his own hand, transfer his residence first of all to Odessa, and then go to Constantinople. That is the only way to show what there is in the Slav race. But to do that would need a stout fellow, and that sort isn't made anymore.

Years later, this artist, who was to serve as scenic designer for the first performances of *Parsifal*, wrote:

No one who has not known Wagner in the intimacy of his home can have any idea of the goodness of his nature, his childlike lovableness. Frau Wagner was right when she compared him to the child with the orb whom St Christopher carries across the stream; he was a child in spirit, with a whole world within him.[3]

Considering the private comments to his wife and some continuing public invective against the Jews in his writings, it would be tempting to dismiss these words as naïve impressions of an all too trusting and inexperienced young artist, comments made only in ignorance. So they may be. Yet his judgment is also supported by testimony in memoirs and letters of other contemporaries, including those of some of his Jewish friends. None of them unfortunately kept diaries or daily accounts of his comments, nor did Joukowsky. The only such record comes from Cosima, the human being closest to him, and one perhaps harboring vitriolic animosity against the Jews equal at least to that of any of her husband's most rabid acquaintances. From the others we have only conclusions and opinions.

Still, whatever his compulsion for the continuing invective while speaking to Cosima, it apparently did not motivate him to any such outpouring to most others. Nor is any of it to be found either in his autobiography intended for public consumption, nor in his private diary, the "Brown Book," intended only for himself and ultimately for Cosima.

36

The Strangest Synagogue

IT IS ALSO DIFFICULT TO correlate the insensitive and outwardly mean, callous remarks in Cosima's diary with the spiritual, delicate sensitivity of the music that he was composing and preparing for performance. *Parsifal* is comparable to *Tristan* in the depth of inspiration that underlies its conception, in inventiveness and resourcefulness, and in the marvel of variations in thematic content. In the nature, the tone, and the pace of the music, however, the dramatic difference renders it sometimes difficult to realize that both creations were the product of the same mind.

Where *Tristan* breaks over us with the fury of the storm, *Parsifal* is a cooling breeze bearing exotic scents. *Tristan* is a flood tide of emotion that plays on the nerves like an extended primal cry, a source of tension that ends, as it must, with the death of one and the transfixion of the other of the lovers. *Parsifal* is a reflecting pool of clear water, silken in its texture, transparent and translucent, mirroring changing shapes and colors of the surrounding landscape. Thus where the life's blood of the earlier opera is tension, that of the final opera is reflection. The excitement in the yearning that burns in the young lovers of *Tristan* has given way in *Parsifal* to soul searching, meditative calm.

In April he finished the poetic rendering of the story, which had existed previously only in prose sketches. In September he began the composition sketch and then the orchestral sketch of the first act. He worked slowly, taking infinite pains. The opera was not completed until January 1882. It was performed 16 times in July and August of that year.

And the vitriol against *the Jews* continued. In July 1877, the Wagners drove to Triebschen in the rain, just to see it again. They found, among other unpleasantries, that it was neglected and overgrown, and that some

French Jews now lived there, all of which is "too much for one time" for Richard. When viewing a book on the Sistine Chapel, Wagner saw too much of fanaticism, mourning and hate, melancholy of sensuousness, and sorrowful benevolence, all of which he ascribes to a predominant Jewish element.

In May 1878, as already noted, Josef Rubinstein returned and had lunch with the Wagners. A few days later, Cosima favors us with her opinion: The "gifted musician from Israel ... plays with such tingling fluency, his eyes darting everywhere, as if engaged in a business deal!" Later that month, responding to a text relating "solely to those Jews who have remained Jewish," Wagner stated, contrary to his earlier pronouncements, that Jews could never really become anything else. In June, speaking of the rich men who would not promote the festival performances, he observed that they were all Jews, or if not, they are frightened off by the press. He was told that Bismarck has forbidden the election of Eduard Lasker, leader of the National Liberals in the Reichstag. It may or may not have been for opposing Bismarck's liberal attitude toward the Jews. Wagner laughed and said that Lasker would find out what it costs to attack a Jew.

On July 2 we get a view of a different side of this chameleon. Levi came for a visit. According to Cosima, he "touches Richard by saying that, as a Jew, he is a walking anachronism. Richard tells him that if the Catholics consider themselves superior to the Protestants, the Jews are the most superior of all, being the eldest." But a few days later, in conversation with Carl Glasenapp, later to be one of Wagner's most prolific, and uncritical, biographers, Wagner said that "Either the Jews possess a past, in which case they are connected with the Talmud, or they are finished.... But whatever the Jews may be, the main blame lies with the Germans.... They play with us as if we were sparrows." Unhappy with certain actions of the Congress, he complained that the Jews were pulling its strings. In August, a visitor at lunch refused to fold his hands for grace. He got a lecture on religion from Wagner who complained that the people now saw nothing more than "just a Jewish God."

It should be noted that Wagner's views on God were no less contradictory than any other aspects of his personality. He wrote and spoke repeatedly about God, giving every indication of being a believer. But in two of his clearest statement on the subject he said otherwise. On September 20, 1879, in discussing with Cosima the introduction to *Philo of Alexandria,* he stated, "I do not believe in God, but in godliness, which is revealed in a Jesus without sin." In October, in a letter to Ernst von Weber, an activist in the crusade of the antivivesectionists, he wrote: "I do not believe in God, but in the divine as revealed to us by the person of a sinless Jesus."[1] Whether this was a lifelong belief, or lack of belief, or a passing notion, we cannot know for certain. Friedrich Nietzsche, close friend of Wagner for over a decade beginning with the Triebschen days, referred to him as "an avowed atheist," and the philosopher's sister, Elizabeth, termed him also "a pronounced atheist."[2]

Philo of Alexandria, referred to by Wagner, is a history of the origins of Christianity. The author, August Friedrich Gfrörer, a contemporary of Wagner, ascribes its origins to Judaism, in stark contrast to depicting Christianity as its bitter enemy. He also authored the *History of Christian Mythology.* On September 3 of the following year, Wagner, surprisingly, expressed his approval of Gfrörer as "the most sensitive of writers in the handling of religious matters," as opposed to Ernest Renan. Renan, also a contemporary, was a notorious anti–Semite.

In October he spoke of Indian mythology, which he admired, and described the whole Jewish mythology in comparison as just hack work. About "Elizabeth's Prayer" in *Tannhäuser,* Wagner said that a modern audience, "the Jews," would be bored by it. Speaking of how melancholy and dreary Vienna had become during his previous visits, he said that there was nobody there but a "few Jews with good for nothing women," and all so dull. Christianity, during the Roman Empire, has torn down the national barriers, and now the Jews were completing the work. He anticipated a return to "a kind of state of nature," for the Jews would also meet their doom. Not always should we blame Wagner for the nonsequiturs and disjointedness of the thoughts; the summaries are those of Cosima.

One November day he declared that a thousand days would be needed to cleanse the Revelation of the Old Testament. Soon he was singing a folk song, but interrupted himself to ask, "What can a Jew make of something like that?"

He read of a financial calamity in England, which he ascribed to the "Israelites." People so separated from them by religion, he exclaimed, should have no right to make their laws. "But why blame the Jews? It is we who lack all feeling for our own identity."

Still later in November he railed that he could not write anything for the Bayreuth Gazette. He could not say what he thinks of the Catholic Church out of consideration for Cosima's father and the king; nor about the Jews because of Levi. Cosima noted parenthetically that a contributor to the paper had asked whether he might attack Levi, "which is hardly possible." Further, Wagner complained, he could say nothing about musicians like Schumann whom he considered insignificant. So he could say nothing at all, as the only value of his words was the "unsparing truth."

In the midst of these paroxysms of anger came a series of uncharacteristic flirtations with the realm of reason. Between November 22, 1878 and mid–January 1879 his view of *the Jews* seemed to sporadically mellow. On November 21 Rubinstein had visited, provoking the observation of Cosima that he seemed exactly the same as he did years ago, "unmistakably ill." Wagner, whether motivated by Rubinstein's presence or otherwise, said, "If ever I were to write again about the Jews, I should say I have nothing against them, it is just that they descended on us Germans too soon, we were not yet ready enough to absorb them." Ten days later, he stressed the fact that "the Jews have been amalgamated with us at least 50 years too soon.... We must first be something ourselves. The damage now is frightful."

Two weeks after that he lamented that he was vexed at feeling shy now about mentioning the Jews, "just out of consideration for three or four of them." In late December, after a discussion, in the words of Cosima, of "the evils the Jews have brought on us Germans," Richard, according to Cosima, said that

> Personally he has had some very good friends among the Jews, but their emancipation and equality, granted before we Germans had come to anything had been ruinous. He considers Germany to be finished. And that worries him, for there were signs to suggest this might happen. The Germans have been exploited and ridiculed by the Jews, and abroad they are hated. So they have become indolent, besotted, wanting to do everything as the Jews do; their faith and loyalty have been undermined. Certainly much of the blame lay with the governments. But it was all ordained by fate. He, Richard, has no hope left.

In mid–January there was a "very pleasant" visit from Levi and other guests. Cosima described at length the serious discussions between Levi and her husband about *Parsifal,* the characters and the orchestration. Then, according to Cosima,

> Friend Levi stays behind after our other friends have gone, and when he tells us that his father is a rabbi, our conversation comes back to the Israelites— the feeling that they intervened too early in our cultural condition, that the human qualities the German character might have developed from within itself and then passed on to the Jewish character have been stunted by their premature interference in our affairs, before we have become fully aware of ourselves.

Other material in this same diary entry may give us an instructive glimpse into Levi's mind and his inner turmoil.

> The conductor speaks of a great movement against the Jews in all spheres of life; in Munich there are attempts to remove them from the town council. He hopes that in twenty years they will be extirpated root and branch, and the audience for the *Ring* will be another kind of public — we "know differently"!

The quotes indicate the last remark to be that of her husband. There is often much in Cosima's entries that cry out, in vain of course, for further explanation. But the absence of explanation invites speculation, and the evidence at hand furnishes much fuel for it.

Cosima was never averse to using quotation marks when she felt it appropriate. There are none for Levi here. How many of the words are his, and how many are those of Cosima is questionable. The language, "extirpate root and branch," does not have the tone of that used by the soft spoken conductor in anything he has written or in his speech that has been quoted. It has the ring of both Cosima and Wagner, especially when speaking about the Jews.

"Another kind of public" for the *Ring* may well be something that Levi, musician that he was, would have wished for. We have seen something of the antipathy of Jewish audiences toward Wagner's operas, beginning with the re-publication of "Judaism in Music," ten years before this diary entry. That animosity, justified though it was, manifested itself in many incidents of hissing and vocal interruptions of performances. In March 1872, for one instance, there is the diary entry to the effect that Jews were spreading the story that a song in *Die Meistersinger* was an old Jewish song that Wagner was trying to ridicule. There was the hissing at the same opera in Mannheim, and there was the forced postponement of a Berlin *Lohengrin* performance. That such animosity existed should, of course, be singularly unsurprising. But Levi, as did many other Jews, looked past the malice to the artwork, and he may well have been unable to forgive his fellow Jews for not following suit. In any event, following Levi's departure that evening, Richard, obviously pleased, termed the session "indescribable."

Later that same evening, Cosima, thinking no doubt not only of him, but of Tausig, Porges, Rubinstein, Neumann, and others, spoke of "the curious attachment individual Jews have for him." Wagner agreed, and added that "Wahnfried will soon turn into a Synagogue." What Cosima did not mention was the curious attachment Wagner had for so many individual Jews.

But Wagner soon reverted to form, and in fact had never turned from it. Even during the brief two months of such relatively reasonable comments, there was still a flow of malicious, often gratuitous ones. And there was more to come.

37

Distance from Porges,
Closeness to Rubinstein

THROUGH IT ALL, PORGES WENT quietly about his work. In these years of preparation for *Parsifal*, that work involved his literary contributions to the *Bayreuther Blätter* and his new assignment as coach and instructor to the chorus of Flower Maidens that adorns the second act of the opera. This new assignment was in blatant contradiction of everything Wagner had written in his essay and elsewhere about the inability of the Jew to understand acting, singing or art in general.

The subject of race or religion was seldom mentioned concerning Porges, even in the private conversations between Richard and Cosima. Her last recorded mention of that nature was her description of him to Nietzsche as the most noble Jew she had ever known. Even when Richard saw fit, as he did from time to time, to ridicule or denigrate Porges's literary contributions or talents, there is no reference to his Judaism. About his work with the Flower Maidens there appear no adverse comments. Even Cosima seemed remarkably able to mention him without voicing the usual haughty disdain for any allegedly Jewish traits. The relationship of Porges with Wahnfried was relatively problem free. That is not by any means to say that demeaning references are not to be found, only that his religion escaped mention with them.

Hardly a year after the first printing of the *Bayreuther Blätter*, Richard told his wife that after reading one of Porges's articles, he could not remember a word of it, and that Porges wrote things that others had said ten times better. In late 1880, Cosima mentioned both Porges and Rubinstein as two of the friends with whom they took an evening stroll. One of the subjects of conversation was Friedrich Wilhelm von Schelling, a German philosopher of whom Wagner was highly critical. Months later, at lunch, Wagner showed his irritation with Porges for his assumed support of Schelling, though actually Porges had said little. After a tirade about Schelling's shortcomings, Wagner left for a short while to calm down.

A few months prior to this episode, during an evening's discussion, Richard had exclaimed to Porges and two other friends, "My God, what bores you are!" Porges, one day at lunch, read to the Wagners and their children his article on *Tristan*, which elicited no adverse comments. But a few days thereafter his rendering, together with composer Engelbert Humperdinck, of an excerpt from *Parsifal* was not to Wagner's liking. It produced some tension in the atmosphere, and Richard later told his wife that he felt as though he was living among "rotten lettuces."

One day in September 1881, as the work on *Parsifal* was nearing completion, there was an explosion against Porges for some remark about a mutual friend of whom Wagner apparently disapproved in some respect or other; we are not told. Two months later came private amusement over an article Porges wrote about Liszt, which Richard judged as lacking in clarity. He was soon further amusing his wife by commenting that he found it strange, since Porges was now writing for the newspaper so rarely, that the circulation was not increasing.

This was the man whom Wagner invited and begged to cast his life with him so that he might have an intelligent friend about him. Porges had not changed, but Wagner indeed had. The continual tension, the animosities he had incurred, and the struggles he had endured had taken their toll. His character, temperament and joy in life had been largely sacrificed to his artistic goals. Bitterness and cynicism permeated these last years, even as the fame and admiration of his friends and the public grew apace with the contempt of his enemies.

Porges was contributing less to the journal because his time was taken up more and more with his work with the Flower Maidens. Humperdinck, later the composer of *Hänsel und Gretel,* but now only 28, was also an inveterate admirer of Wagner. He assisted in the final preparations for *Parsifal* and observed firsthand the work of Porges, whom Wagner termed the *Blumenvater,* the "flower father," and spoke admiringly of him.

Wagner's more genial side showed itself during his first meeting with the 19-year-old Felix Weingartner, later to become a renowned conductor. After one of the first *Parsifal* performances, Weingartner had insisted that Porges introduce him to Wagner. Porges did so during a social gathering at Wahnfried. Apparently the meeting was rather jovial, and the conductor-to-be came away with a thoroughly pleasant impression.[1]

At those first *Parsifal* performances Wagner was nothing less than thrilled with the Flower Maidens, a rare reaction for this severely demanding composer-producer. His unadulterated joy at the artistry of this group of 24 first-rate female singers resounded in a letter to King Ludwig on September 8, ten days after the last performance. Nor did he begrudge full and unstinted credit to his two Jewish participants: The scene, he says, was "utterly unsurpassable, and probably the most masterly piece of direction in terms of music and staging that has ever come my way.... Thanks to the zeal of our admirable conductor, Levi, whose enthusiasm I cannot praise highly enough, this was a total success.... The admirable Porges had played a significant part in rehearsing them also."[2]

If Wagner ever, during this period, praised Porges directly, there is no record of it. Ample as is the record of his life, however, we do not know everything that transpired. Though evidence of any close or warm friendship between them in the later years seems lacking, most of the record is that contained in Cosima's diaries. And much in that was filtered, consciously or otherwise, through the sieve of her mindless contempt of Jews and Judaism.

It was different with Rubinstein. His relationship with the Wagners, both Richard and Cosima, was both closer and more problematic. His Jewishness is something we are never allowed to forget, except, that is, when he performed, to their liking, at the piano, which was quite often indeed. He was often jokingly introduced and referred to by Wagner as his "house pianist," or, as in a letter to the king, as his "grand house pianist." Nonetheless, his faults, real or as uniquely perceived by Wagner, were laid at the door of his "race," a very important matter in the Wagner household.

Without doubt there were long periods when he resided in that household, and there were other times when he stayed elsewhere but visited often, and at various times of the day or night. It is difficult to tell exactly when he was staying and when residing elsewhere. Wagner's life, including his comings and goings, are an open book; Rubinstein's much less so. Many of Cosima's entries tell us that Rubinstein arrived with Wolzogen, a reference to Hans von Wolzogen, editor and writer for the *Bayreuth Gazette*, Or, he arrived with Stein, a reference to Heinrich von Stein, also a contributor to the newspaper, but best known for being entrusted with the education of young Siegfried. We can assume that Rubinstein was on a friendly basis with both.

Rubinstein was often a difficult man, sullen, insensitive to the feelings of others, insulting at times, and at times offensive. But his musical gifts, for Wagner, overrode all of it. He was a piano virtuoso of concert quality, something Wagner was not. And beyond question, grating on Wagner many times though he did, there was an obvious warmth between them. Rubinstein also contributed articles to the *Gazette,* most, apparently, to Wagner's satisfaction, much more so than the writings of Porges. Concerning an article about Schumann in July 1879, Richard said that "His ideas are good and his style concise." If his style was truly concise, Wagner could well have learned something from him.

He also frequently joined the Wagners and their guests in whist, a card game popular at the time. For this nervous, neurotic and disruptive houseguest, Wagner, despite himself, developed a genuine empathy. Often Cosima took walks with Rubinstein and seems to have enjoyed his company, though without ever having said so, at least in her diaries.

And, her overt racist worldview notwithstanding, she was at times so carried away in rapturous delight by his piano virtuosity that she seemed to forget the musician's heritage. In March 1879 she took "great delight" in his playing of a piece by Bach. He played a passage from *Parsifal* that "echoes inside me like an eternal blessing." In September, "Herr Rubinstein played parts of the second act of *Tristan*. These sounds echo inside me like an irresistible call from my homeland: 'Know'st thou where my homeland is?'... I feel as if I were following some secret power without knowing whither it is leading me." In June 1881 she made what was for her a rather remarkable statement. When Richard commented that something he read concerned race, she replied that "*Tristan* is the music which removes all barriers, and that means all racial ones, as well."

On another evening Richard asked Rubinstein to play a Bach fugue. "Rubinstein chooses the B Minor, to our supreme joy." Successive pieces on the same evening by request of each of the Wagners bring similar praise.

The concerts continued, usually with comments by Richard only about the composition or the composer, a sure sign that the piece was well or satisfactorily played. On occasion, there were remarks also about the pianist, some quite complimentary: In December 1880, "Friend Rubinstein plays Beethoven's E-flat Major Quartet to us, and very well, to Richard's very great delight." And in the same month, "Friend Rubinstein plays the American March very nicely and to the delight of us all, including Richard." The following month, Richard himself was having trouble with the slow movement of a Mozart symphony, but then came Rubinstein, who played the first part of a Beethoven sonata; Cosima wrote, "Our delight is boundless!" Two months later he played a portion of the music from *Tannhäuser* and she saw Richard "for the first time, taking great pleasure in it." A few days thereafter Richard asked him to repeat it. A Beethoven quartet was played "very nicely."

Such comments, though rare, are sprinkled throughout her diaries.

To our enjoyment, said Cosima, Rubinstein played some mazurkas and also a Chopin waltz. Richard "gets Rubinstein to play" various things from the *Ring* and was pleased with the impression made, particularly on the ladies. On another evening, Rubinstein played excerpts from Wagner's operas "to our great satisfaction." Richard "gets Rubinstein to play the first movement of 106 [Beethoven Sonata] and he takes tremendous delight in it, kissing me as it was being played, then telling me he was pleased by the way I was listening."

No less than 65 times during Wagner's last five years, Cosima explicitly stated that Rubinstein played for them. Her usual introduction is that "Richard asked Rubinstein ..." or "Richard gets Rubinstein to play ..." Often it was Bach, or Beethoven, even more often excerpts from his own operas, excerpts that Rubinstein himself had transcribed for the piano, and which Cosima often referred to as "pictures." Other requests included selections by Mozart, Chopin, Mendelssohn, Brahms, Weber and Gluck.

Otherwise the relationship is, like most relationships in Wagner's life, a mass of contradictions. On May 5, 1879, Cosima noted "a slight argument with friend Rubinstein revealing once more the unbridgeable gulf between people of his kind and ourselves...." She added a further observation indicating that her husband may at least have been trying to establish a bridge with this one person of "that kind": "Richard uniquely kind and friendly, so touching in all the ways he tries to inspire trust in this poor distrustful man." On November 8 Cosima referred to a conversation involving herself, Richard and two friends, part of which concerns Rubinstein, "always a painful topic." On December 26, 1879 Richard told her that an article of Rubinstein's was not "all bad" and that he was a "civilized man."

On New Year's Eve the Wagner family set out from Bayreuth, arriving in Naples on January 4, 1880. They stayed in a large country house known as the Villa d'Angri. It was there that they met the Russian stage designer Joukowsky.

On April 6 Wagner, still in Naples, wrote to Rubinstein, then in Berlin, where he was presumably giving concerts. It was Wagner at his concerned and caring best. He had just received a letter from the pianist, the contents of which we do not know. It evoked words of comfort and encouragement: "I see you are still protected by the magic enchantment of hope.... That is because of your faith, and, since you are young, there is still a good deal you can live to see." His "faith" of course was still Jewish. As for himself, wrote Wagner, he hoped to be able yet to produce something that would enable him to forget the misery of the world. He asked Rubinstein about his plans. Was he planning to go to his home in Kharkov, or to Naples? He complimented his friend on his last article for the Gazette and offered him "every good wish for your continuing prosperity."[3]

It seems quite possible that Wagner, scarred and bloodied from his lifelong war with the "philistines" and *the Jews* saw in Rubinstein a fellow sufferer; one, like himself, of extraordinary sensitivity in a hostile world. Rubinstein joined them in Naples later that month, and Richard and Cosima were both pleased, at least with the music that again was heard in their home. They did not return to Bayreuth until November 17.

In January 1881, back now in Bayreuth, during a conversation with Levi, Richard spoke of Rubinstein, describing "how he is always preoccupied with himself, and in spite of his good qualities can never throw this off." In August he told his wife of some peculiar behavior of their house pianist, and complained, "If he knew how difficult we find him, he would make things easier for us."

The 1880 sojourn was not the last time the Wagners spent extended time in Italy, nor the last time that Rubinstein spent time with them in that country. Most of the cost of these Italian vacations in the last years of Wagner's life was paid by Ludwig. Between the first and fifth of November 1881 the family traveled to Palermo. They were motivated, partially at least, by the glowing, picturesque accounts of that town and of Sicily itself given by Rubinstein, who had been living there for some time. They traveled via Munich, Verona, and Naples, and upon arrival in Palermo were greeted by him. They stayed at the Hôtel des Palmes in rooms with a terrace overlooking a garden. On February 7, 1882, despite adverse circumstances, including Richard's confinement to bed, they celebrated Rubinstein's birthday. It was in Palermo that Wagner completed the full orchestral scoring of *Parsifal*. They did not return to Bayreuth until May 1, 1882, a scant three months before the first performance.

After the *Parsifal* performances during that summer, the Wagners, accompanied by Rubenstein, again left for Italy, this time for Venice, staying at the Palazzo Vendramin on the Grand Canal. Rubinstein, after lunching with the Wagners, left on October 22, possibly for a concert tour. In November, Cosima read to Richard a letter from him, precipitating a remark from her husband on "how extraordinarily cultured" he is.

It is clear that not all of Richard's or Cosima's complaints about their pianist's temperament were unfounded. He was indeed a difficult person. As a member of the "Nibelung Chancellery," as we have seen, he would take instructions or requests from Wagner only, and required personal delivery; they could not be communicated through any other person. He was often rude to Cosima. If such conduct was partially provoked by his sensing of her unspoken disdain, his own conduct may well have exacerbated that disdain. For his perplexing show of animosity toward his mild-mannered countryman Joukowsky, however, there does not readily appear any rational explanation.

Cosima, in her letters to Daniela, a daughter by her marriage to Bülow, mentioned Rubinstein's difficult nature and would also describe his behavior on his better days as being "very human," an indirect but scathing indictment of his behavior on other occasions. In one letter she referred to him humorously as "Malvolio" Rubinstein,[4] a good but morose character in Shakespeare's *Twelfth Night*.

In 1923, at the age of 54, Wagner's son Siegfried, in his published memoirs, *Erinnerungen* ("Recollections"), wrote of a sojourn to Italy with the family accompanied by Rubinstein. As to which of their several trips to Italy it was, his recollection may be faulty. He ascribes it to the year 1876, following the first festival, at which time he would have been but seven years old, probably too young for the impressions he describes, and at a time when it is most unlikely that Rubinstein would have been present. And the pianist would almost certainly not have been preparing a vocal score for *Parsifal*, which at that time Siegfried's father had not yet begun. It was probably the journey of 1880. His description of Rubinstein is enlightening:

> The unhappy Joseph Rubinstein, busy preparing the vocal score of *Parsifal*, was not one of the more attractive characters among our circle of friends. He made it clear to my mother and to us children that he was there only because of our father and that the family was really an unnecessary and tiresome adjunct. My mother bore this calmly, since she recognized his good points, but for us children he became so unsympathetic that our mother had to remind us not to show our disapproval quite so openly.[5]

Could Siegfried's memoirs or his recollection of Rubinstein have been colored by his own anti–Semitism? It appears that that can be discounted. There was indeed evidence of such bias on Siegfried's part early in adulthood, but he seems to have outgrown it entirely. In 1921, two years before the publication of his *Recollections*, as director of the Bayreuth theater, he wrote a letter to one Herr Pürringer, who had complained about the large number of Jewish patrons and artists in the festivals. Siegfried's answer should put to rest any doubt about his own feelings on this matter:

> I must tell you that I cannot share your views at all. We have a great number of loyal, honest and unselfish Jewish friends. They have frequently given us proof of their devotion. You demand that we should turn all these people from our doors for no other reason than that they are Jews? Is that human? Is that Christian? Is that German?... If the Jews are willing to support us, they deserve our particular appreciation, for my father attacked them in his writings. They are entitled to hate Bayreuth, and yet many of them revere my father's works

with genuine enthusiasm.... If among a hundred thousand Jews there should be no more than a single one who loved my father's works with his whole heart and whole soul, I would feel ashamed to turn my back on him, just because he is a Jew. It is a matter of complete indifference to us whether a human being is a Chinese, a Negro, an American, a Red Indian or a Jew. But we could well take a lesson from the Jews in solidarity and in helping one another.... Bayreuth must be a true abode of peace.[6]

That the letter was written in 1921 makes it all the more remarkable. After the advent of Hitler and discovery of the full extent of his hideous crimes, such sentiments could be easily, and were frequently, expressed. In 1921, the rampant anti–Semitism in Germany following the first World War rendered such sentiments as expressed by Siegfried both unusual and courageous. Considering the atmosphere in which he was raised it may be all the more remarkable.

Or perhaps it instead tells us something of the true atmosphere predominating between his parents and the many Jews in and out of their home. In 1924, with the rise of the Nazis, Siegfried placed a banner over the entrance to the festival theater: "Our Aim Is Art." It was a continuation of his determination to employ Jewish singers and musicians. Perhaps the surest proof of his tolerance was Adolph Hitler's later observation that Siegfried had been "somewhat in the hands of the Jews."[7]

His father wrote and often spoke in an entirely different vein from Siegfried. But the way his father lived was not really so different. Never did he refuse the help or the friendship of anyone because he or she was a Jew, or on any other racial or religious ground. Twice he was asked, in the summer of 1880, to sign a petition to the Reichstag protesting the recent grant of full rights of citizenship to Jews. Twice he refused, explaining that such actions were not really his style, that he preferred to just write, and to leave such mundane things to others. Further, he explained, he had signed a petition protesting the vivisection of animals for scientific or other purposes, and it accomplished nothing. Neither was a very good reason not to sign this one.

Biographer Ernest Newman, a harsh critic of the man as opposed to the artist, suggested with much logic that even Wagner may have found it too much to sign such a petition when Levi was then attracting audiences from all over Germany with his Wagner performances in Munich; when Rubinstein was living in his home; and when Neumann was making plans to produce Wagner's *Ring* the length and breadth of Europe, to Wagner's great financial benefit.[8] Not to mention, of course, his devoted helper Porges and assistance from Lilli Lehmann. Bülow, who did sign the petition, complained that Wagner had poked the ashes, but let others get their fingers burned.

On December 22, 1881, Rubinstein let it be known that his father, Isaac, who had been sending him small sums as spending money, was putting pressure on him to further pursue his own career, fearful about his spending so much time in the service of another. Implicitly or overtly, he seemed to be threatening to cease all financial support. The anguished pianist asked Wagner for help. Richard started to write the elder Rubinstein, then hesitated; but finally, a month later, did so. It was obviously not the first time that he and Isaac had corresponded:

> Honored Sir,
> Pray permit me to write to you briefly once more about your son Joseph, in the hope of persuading you to adopt an attitude toward the young man that I believe would be beneficial.... Joseph's honorable efforts to comply with your wishes concerning the exercise of his talent to establish a position in life have been as honorable in intent as they have been rendered useless in effect by his own temperament. Without doubt one reason for this lies in certain morbid dispositions, which, I believe I am right in saying might lead to the most regrettable excess if he was obliged obstinately to persist in those efforts. In him the recognition of the essence and the value of true art has grown to a truly religious belief, rooted in his soul where it has engendered a sensitivity that amounts to a passion. If you will assure him, without opposition, of the modest needs for his exceptionally sober and temperate mode of life, you will support him contentedly in the service of a noble cause.[9]

"Morbid dispositions ... the most regrettable excesses"! It seems certain that Wagner feared this depressed young man, who had spoken from the beginning about committing suicide, might do just that were he forced to abandon his life with Wagner, the only thing he had found that gave meaning to his existence. If that is in fact what Wagner meant, his instincts were sound. Wagner died in February 1883. Shortly thereafter, Rubinstein returned to Lucerne where he first met the composer. Eighteen months after Wagner's demise, he shot himself to death.

Concerning his letter of reply, Cosima noted that it put something of a strain on her husband. Richard complained about having such things demanded of him, but spoke very warmly of "our friend." In mid–February, Richard received an answer from Rubinstein's father who wrote "in a very decent manner." Richard sent the letter on to Rubinstein advising him to do "as his father wishes," whatever that might have been.

On August 20, 1882, the day of the twelfth of the 16 *Parsifal* performances that summer, Isaac Rubinstein was at breakfast with his son and the Wagners. Richard's impression is interesting indeed. Just as those who make a bad impression on him are often assumed to be Jewish even if they are not, those making a good impression are sometimes assumed not to be Jewish even if they are. Isaac looks "un–Semitic," reads Cosima's diary, causing

Richard to suspect that his family, like "so many heathen ones in Russia, assumed Judaism, and that the men then married Jewesses." To this gratuitous bit of free association, there appears no good reason to attach the slightest significance except for whatever it may show us of the mysterious workings of Wagner's mind.

Felix Weingartner, as we have noted, was present in Bayreuth in that August of 1882 for the *Parsifal* performances. He saw three of them. It was after his third, which was the last of the 16, that Porges introduced him to Wagner. After the second, as he recounts in his memoirs, he and a friend, upon seeing a carriage outside of Wahnfried, had waited to catch a glimpse of the great composer. Presently he heard Wagner's well-known Saxon accent and saw Cosima emerge from the home, accompanied by Josef Rubinstein, and enter the carriage. Weingartner described Rubinstein as an "intimate friend of the Master," and the man who had arranged *Parsifal* for the piano. Then Wagner came out and entered the carriage. But before doing so, he turned to Rubinstein and was heard to say, "Well, goodbye, my dear Rubinstein, hope we meet again soon, remember me to your father." As we have seen, Rubinstein did join the Wagners again in Venice in November.

About 20 years later Weingartner described his thoughts as the carriage drove away in the darkness, his mind still whirling from the mystical, enchanting sounds of *Parsifal*: "I gazed after it almost bereft of my senses. What a tremendous life, what gigantic power was being carried away in that insignificant vehicle. How negligible and almost unreal the physical presence seemed in comparison with the magnitude of the spirit it encased."[10]

38

Neumann and the Berlin *Ring*

THERE WAS OF COURSE A dark side of this gigantic power. Perhaps that dark side was merely its outer shell, but it cannot be ignored. From 1879, as already observed, the bitterness increased. In that year, reading a nature magazine about predators and prey, he learned how in nature even the most heroic must perish, men as well as animals, "and what remains are the rats and mice — the Jews." He described to the children the consequences of the emancipation of the Jews: middle classes pushed to the wall and lower classes led into corruption. He read a pamphlet someone has sent to him that described the Jews as "calculating beasts of prey," and was "greatly pleased" by it. At one point, in contradiction to so many of his statements before and after, he said he was in favor of expelling the Jews entirely.

Discussing the Russian communes he said that they should have hanged a few Rothschilds. About a pamphlet he had been reading to the effect that the Jews had given up their own language, he said, "Fine fellows," commenting that a language is what a people preserves the longest. "It shows they are there mainly to live like parasites in the body of others." After reading a book about the Talmudic Jews and their "peculiar laws," he wished all Jews would drop off him "like warts," for which there was no known remedy; "one should not try to check them, just ignore them."

In the following year there was no letup. When Joukowsky spoke of the French who disrupted *Tannhäuser*, Richard went into a rage: It was not the French, but the German Jews. Picking up again on a favorite theme, he continued: "And never mind the Jews— It is we ourselves, we weaklings who can only sigh over the terrible things going on." When Cosima asked how it is that falseness has gained the upper hand in Germany, Richard had a ready answer: "You can depend on it, the Jews are to blame." When they talked about the attachment to Richard of so many Jews, his rejoinder was "Yes, they are like flies—the more one drives them away, the more they come." As the year draws to a close, we hear that a Jew can only be "demanding, greedy and cunning"; otherwise he would have to look very touching and worthy of pity.

In January 1881 he scoffed at the statement that Jesus was a Jew, and equated it to saying Mozart was a credit to the people of Salzburg. But this was progress. In November 1878 he had denied Jesus's Jewishness altogether. He said, jokingly according to Cosima, that if civilization came to an end it didn't matter, but if it came about through the Jews, that would be a disgrace. He shuddered at the present day public. At a performance of *Tristan*, for instance, "nothing but hooked noses, and on top of that, those accents!" Reports of Jew baiting in Russia he saw as an expression of the people's strength. He got angry at a guest for advocating nondenominational schools. Caught between the Jesuits and the Jews, he exclaimed, German Protestantism would perish. He amused the children with his description of the present day world: Fine horses, good hard-working coachmen, and "inside the carriage, master of all these creatures, a bloated Jewish banker!"

On December 17 Cosima mentioned reports of a fire at a theater in a Jewish neighborhood in Vienna. "The fact that 416 Israelites died in the fire does not increase Richard's concern over the disaster." The next day Richard complained that "One adds fuel to these fellows' arrogance by having anything to do with them, and we, for example, do not talk of our feeling about those Jews in the theater in front of Rubinstein, 400 unbaptized and probably 500 baptized ones." According to Cosima, "He makes a drastic joke to the effect that all Jews should be burned at a performance of *Nathan the Wise*."

This was just a month before his letter to Rubinstein's father asking for his continued support for his son, and warning of possible "regrettable excesses" should he be pushed too hard to end his association with Wagner. We may assume that this was one Jew whom Wagner would not have liked to see burned in the theater. We may assume further that this was also one Jew with whom he did not feel that he should have nothing more to do. Had Wagner wished to swat this one away "like a fly," he missed an excellent opportunity to do so, with the help of the miscreant's own father.

Rubinstein was not the only Jew playing a large role in Wagner's life at this time. There was, for one, the impresario-director Angelo Neumann. We last saw him conducting *Das Rheingold* and *Die Walküre*, the first two *Ring* operas, in Leipzig, Wagner's birthplace, in April 1878. Liszt personally congratulated Neumann on the excellence of the performances and wrote Wagner that "Neumann has managed the affair in some respects even better than you did in Bayreuth!" Wagner himself, wrote Neumann "hastily, — and with a carbuncle on my leg," expressing his delight "at your whole interpretation of the dramas."

The following month, the director wrote asking Wagner's concurrence for presenting the entire *Ring* in Berlin. The letter was answered by Cosima, in Richard's behalf, conveying his consent, making a few suggestions for changes in artists, and concluding with heartiest congratulations to "my dear Neumann, on the success of your plucky venture and the friendliest greetings from my husband." From herself she offers only "yours with deepest respect."[1] No one was going to accuse her of hypocrisy.

In September came the performances of the last two *Ring* operas in Leipzig, *Siegfried* and *Götterdämmerung*. Telegrams from Neumann and the young conductor Anton Seidl described the enthusiastic reception of both operas. Wagner wrote to Neumann in response and the letter was published in newspapers. In it he thanked Neumann and the other participants, but continued, "The great assiduity of our artists surprises me less than the efficiency of the director: this latter quality is something I have encountered very seldom among our theater directors."[2] The following month, in a letter to August Förster, co-director, with Neumann, of the Leipzig theater, he referred to "Our inimitable colleague Angelo Neumann."

A flow of correspondence between the composer and Neumann continued throughout the year and into 1879. Wagner wrote to Neumann, "Dear Friend and Ally," urging him in great detail as he continually did to all: "You must keep your performances always on the same level of perfection, yes, even improve on them.... If I could find even one conductor in all Germany on whose tempo I could depend with absolute security, I should be willing to go quietly down to my grave."[3] It is impossible to read any part of Wagner's voluminous correspondence without recognizing his single mindedness in striving for perfection in the performances of his works, his desperate need for money notwithstanding. Perhaps the best summation of his criteria for excellence was contained in a letter to August Förster on June 11, 1879: "Dramatic unity is the greatest factor of any performance."[4]

Neumann wished to give *Tristan* in Leipzig, and began correspondence with Wagner, then in Naples, concerning his permission to do so. Through misunderstandings, a lost letter of Wagner's, and other letters crossing in the mail, Wagner became very perturbed and wrote a rather scathing note to the conductor: "So you want me to spit out my venom again ... these misunderstandings are driving me mad." He set out forcefully that *Tristan* could only be given if he, Wagner, were present to personally drill the performers in their parts. "I hope you will understand my feeling of bitterness." If however, he continued, the misunderstandings were due to his own mistake, and "in case I have no right to be irritated, I beg you on my part to forgive me. Above all, I hope this will cause no further breach in our usual pleasant relations."[5] *Tristan* was not produced in Leipzig until two years later.

Neumann then turned his full attention to Berlin. There were many obstacles to production of the entire *Ring* planned there: casting, arguments over which theater was to stage it, and other matters, above all animosity between Wagner and Botho von Hülsen, director of the Royal Opera Company of Prussia. Until convinced otherwise by Neumann, Hülsen insisted that *Die Walküre* was the only one of the four fit for the stage. When that hurdle was overcome, the consent of Berlin was later withdrawn because of objections to the "conduct of the composer." Wagner for his part had been determined that Hülsen would never get his hands on his *Ring*. He wanted a different Berlin house, the Victoria Theater. Through some rather exhausting work and diplomacy, plans were finalized for the *Ring* at the Victoria Theater.

Much of the correspondence was between Neumann and Cosima, as secretary for her husband, as well as with Wagner directly. Cosima was, as always, courteous and respectful, with perhaps of touch of genuine warmth that may have been developing between them. In February an anti–Semitic party in Berlin publicly, and falsely, proclaimed that Wagner was a member. Neumann, recognizing the controversy and possible disruption that might ensue were this true, wrote Cosima to enquire and received an answer directly from Wagner. Nothing was further from his thoughts, he declared. He advised Neumann to see a forthcoming article in the *Bayreuth Gazette* that would prove conclusively that people of sense would find it impossible to connect him with the cause.

Neumann suggested ways to counter the rumor. The reply from Cosima to "My dear and valued Herr Director" thanked him for his trust in her judgment and assured him that Richard had no hand in the agitation, and hoped that his task would not be made more trying. "I repeat my thanks for your kind thoughts ... and add once more the assurance of my highest regards." The forthcoming article Wagner referred to was "Know Thyself," about which we will see more later.

On occasion, Cosima's calming diplomatic skills resulted in compromises between steps taken by Neumann and angry objections by Wagner. The most serious of these involved a dispute over the merits of a lead baritone for whom Wagner had little regard and whose peremptory dismissal he demanded. It was settled by Cosima's intervention on the side of Neumann and his suggestion for Wagner's attendance at a rehearsal. The rehearsal ended with Wagner rushing backstage and hugging and kissing the baritone, and shouting "That was glorious! Man alive, where did you get that voice!"

On the thirtieth of December he wrote to King Ludwig, reporting on various current matters, and spoke most enthusiastically about his opera director from Leipzig, "Angelo Neumann, of Jewish heritage, singularly energetic, and very devoted to me, something which, oddly enough, I find now only among the Jews."[6]

In May 1881 the entire *Ring* was performed four times in Berlin, conducted by Anton Seidl, to wildly enthusiastic audiences. Wagner was not present for the entire time, owing most probably to indisposition. With his family he did attend the final cycle. After each opera's performance, the audience refused to be satisfied until Wagner came to the edge of his box to take a bow. After the *Siegfried* performance, the third of the cycle, the audience, according to Neumann, "raved and shrieked for Wagner. It was five minutes before he appeared to be greeted by "a hurricane of applause and thundering hurrahs."

But after *Götterdämmerung*, the final opera, an incident occurred that was to temporarily poison the relationship between the two men, and could well have resulted in a permanent rupture.

A celebratory arrangement for acknowledgments at the conclusion had been arranged in detail, including the assembled nobility and many distinguished participants, beginning with the kaiser. Neumann began by saying, "First let me thank the august members of our reigning house..." whereupon Wagner turned, quickly left the stage, and returned to his box. Neumann continued as planned, thanking all royalty, artists and other participants, then fairly shouted to Wagner's box the most lavish praise. This was followed by cheers and applause that forced Wagner to come to the front of his box.

But over the participants on stage, "thunderstruck and disappointed," a hush had settled. According to Neumann, they ascribed this action of the composer to an unaccountable tantrum, caused by acknowledgment of the Prussian royalty of whom he was known to disapprove, and believed that it was intended it as an insult to the monarch.

The indignant Neumann wrote to Wagner the next day declaring that in view of these events he thought it best that all further personal intercourse between them should cease. Wagner sent Seidl and a member of the cast to convince Neumann that it had been a heart attack that forced him to withdraw. Neumann did not believe him. Wagner wrote to Neumann insisting that a violent spasm had been the cause of his withdrawal. The "insult," said Wagner, would disappear as soon as Neumann understood that which he had tried in every way to explain. "I have given every possible evidence, both in word and in deed, of my sentiments toward you," continued Wagner, "and no momentary spectacular action could call this now in question.... I for my part, see no reason for breaking off our personal relations."[7]

Neumann still did not believe him. Wagner now wrote to Förster. After praising Neumann's skill and devotion, he asked the co-director to tell Neumann that he would like him to continue with his stagings of his *Nibelung* cycles. Förster's reply, a masterpiece of tact and wisdom, set the stage for a rapprochement, and he urged Neumann to write directly to Wagner.

This Neumann did, suggesting a personal meeting in Bayreuth for July 1. In his answer, Wagner agreed, and assented also to several concessions for which Neumann had asked, including rights to produce performances in various cities in Europe. "Nothing was ever intended in the matter that came between us," continued Wagner. "What happened shall never be repeated, and so—let's drop it!"[8]

The planned meeting took place on the twenty-first of July at Wahnfried. A number of serious matters were discussed. But not until Neumann, accompanied by Wagner, walked down the front path from the home was the Berlin affair mentioned. Wagner assured his friend that his action resulted only from his feeling that he would faint had he stayed a moment longer on the stage. He took Neumann's hand and placed it on his heart: "If you only knew how it beats in here, how I suffer with it! Will you believe me now?" Neumann wrote that Wagner looked at him "with his deep, earnest eyes." But even then he could not tell Wagner that he could. Wagner abruptly flung Neumann's hand away, placed his own hand on his forehead as if in despair, and bitterly exclaimed, "Ah, why should it be so impossible to find a trusting soul?"

As they reached the gate, the two men stood for a moment in silence, whereupon, without speaking, Wagner kissed and embraced Neumann, and the two men parted. In 1909, Neumann wrote in his memoirs, "It was fully two years later, when the sad news came up from Venice of the Master's sudden death from heart failure, that I was finally convinced of the tragic sincerity of his words." He had not of course read Cosima's still unpublished diaries. Had he been able to do so, as we shall soon see, even Wagner's death from heart failure may not have been able to change his initial impression, one shared by the artists on stage.

39

Neumann and the Traveling Wagner Opera Company

AFTER THEIR RECONCILIATION he and Wagner entered into contracts. They bargained as two experienced businessmen would be expected to bargain, and their relationship was not again put to any serious strain. Neumann had already been making plans for Wagnerian performances in other cities throughout Europe, including the *Ring* in Paris and London. The planned performance fell through in Paris for political reasons, but the *Ring* was heard, as were other of Wagner's operas, in London. Before Wagner's death, Neumann had taken his traveling Wagner Opera Company, with exclusive rights to the *Ring* and certain other operas, to many cities in Germany. The *Ring* was performed in Amsterdam and Brussels, and concerts were given in Ghent and Antwerp. After Wagner's death, there were *Ring* performances in Prague, Moscow and St. Petersburg. Plans for America, however, came to nothing.

Communications between Neumann and both Wagners had been most cordial and friendly. There were repeated expressions of admiration and trust by both Richard and Cosima. Surprisingly, the trust was reflected even in discourse between husband and wife in the privacy of Wahnfried. A look at the diary entries for the corresponding period is interesting indeed.

On November 28, 1880, during the early stages of negotiations between Neumann and Hülsen, Cosima wrote: "We compare Neumann's energy and resourcefulness with Hülsen's narrow-mindedness and vindictiveness and have to laugh over Israel's predominance." Two days later: letters to Cosima and Richard from Herr Neumann, "very friendly in tone. Richard is insisting on the Victoria Theater."

Beginning with entries on May 29 we hear of the Berlin affair, Wagner's retreat from the stage, from the Wagners' viewpoint. It appears, unfortunately, that Neumann's mistrust of Wagner's explanation may have been well founded, and his sorrowful acceptance of it upon the composer's death unwarranted. It seems that Richard was already upset by "various things," and that "When Herr Neumann starts an ovation for him according to his own taste," Wagner "rushes away." Cosima prevailed on him to acknowledge the audience from his box and they "managed to laugh merrily" about it on the way home, for "Truly there is something disconcerting about this Israelite affair." The diary entry of course falsifies any claim of a heart attack or any other physical spasm.

The next day, Richard received Neumann's letter, which, as we know, was intended as a break in the relationship. Later a guest mentioned something about the crown prince, causing Richard to "very forcibly" state his opinion of the prince's behavior toward him over the years. A week later there was a discussion between husband and wife over the fact that "Herr Neumann is quite incapable of understanding Richard's indignation," since he, Neumann, meant the acknowledgment as an act of homage, which apparently Richard could not stomach. The diary entries on June 12 take up the subject again. Richard answered on that day the firm but tactful letter received from Förster trying to reconcile the two men. Richard was unimpressed by the letter, however, and complained about being obliged to respond to "untruthful, narrow-minded, phrase-making people [Förster] who are nevertheless devotees."

On July 20, a day before the scene at the garden gate at Wahnfried, Wagner was quite mellow. He remarked that it had been a very nice day yesterday. "His opinion of Herr Neumann is also a favorable one; he says he has personality; and he adds that he no longer knows any Germans at all, everything has become so blurred." Then came this summary by Cosima of the Master's next observation: "He recalls having maintained in the year '52 that no Jew would ever become an actor — and now!" Whether this statement constitutes a statement of regret or a seldom seen admission of error is not clear. In August came another bit of proof of the true motive for the Berlin matter. Joukowsky lamented that he had not achieved much in that year, 1881. In response, Richard joked that had he not "run away from Neumann" he would have accomplished nothing at all.

In June the following year, he complained loudly about a singer, but "In contrast, Richard praises Herr Neumann" who, before giving up his directorship in Leipzig, was staging all of Richard's works there. Recently Richard wrote to him, "I admire you." In October 1882, he deplored the "foolishness of the public, which cares only for *Die Walküre*," but praised Herr

Neumann, who was disseminating the entire *Ring* abroad. His comment on that anomaly: "How curious that it should have to be a Jew!" In January 1883, less than a month before Wagner's death, there was a telegram from Neumann that resulted in the observation that Richard felt sympathy for him, going through all his difficulties "with Semitic earnestness."

A most interesting aspect of the relationship between the two men involves the matter of *Parsifal*. Wagner had always referred to it as a "stage consecration festival play." During the *Ring* performances of 1876, he had first become fully aware of the unique acoustic qualities and the purity of sound in the festival theater. *Parsifal* was the first, and only, opera written with those qualities in mind. This music, he told Cosima, was to have the softness and shimmer of silk. He never wanted *Parsifal* to be performed anywhere but in Bayreuth, something he made clear in conversations with Cosima.

Wagner had started on the opera within six months after the close of the 1876 festival. In September 1878 he told her how he hated the thought of abandoning *Parsifal* to the theaters with "all those costumes and grease paint," and "those dreadful artists' balls." Having created the invisible orchestra, he would, he joked, now like to invent the invisible theater. He dreaded the thought of having this opera performed on the usual operatic stage. By the twenty-sixth of April he had completed the orchestral sketch of the third, the last, act. By the seventh of August he began preparations for writing the score.

On the thirteenth, Neumann, his mind never at rest, wrote Wagner about a fascinating and daring idea. He proposed giving *Parsifal* first in Leipzig. Wagner answered that by agreement with the Munich opera, that company, through the king, had placed its orchestra at his disposal. As part of the agreement, if Wagner for any reason, could not give the performance in Bayreuth, it must be given in Munich. The contract did so provide, and stated further that the work thereafter, in any event, was to belong to Munich. Certain royalties were to be paid to Wagner in retirement of his debt to the company. Later, however, Wagner wrote the king expressing horror at the thought of this opera being performed on any stage in Germany under prevailing conditions, except in Bayreuth. He urged that the provisions concerning performances in Munich be cancelled. The king thereupon cancelled the contract and assured Wagner that the opera would be performed nowhere but in Bayreuth.

In October 1881 this determination was emphasized again by Wagner. He and Neumann, at Neumann's request, had been communicating about a Wagner Opera Company that would perform all of the Wagnerian repertory throughout Europe and America. After laying down his standards for such a theater, Wagner told his impresario friend in no uncertain terms that

> *Parsifal* is to be given nowhere else but in Bayreuth; and this from private and personal motives that my gracious benefactor the King of Bavaria so thoroughly understood, that even he waived his privilege of having it given at the Munich Theater.... I cannot and will not ever allow it to be given in any other theater; unless it were that I fitted out a real Wagner theater.

That said, he assured Neumann that if he remained steadfast in his ideas the time might come when he would indeed trust his *Parsifal*, not to any "court theater," but to the great "Wandering Wagner Opera Company." On the thirteenth of June, Wagner wrote to Neumann, "If anything on earth could astonish me, it would be you! Heavens, what energy, what faith, what courage!"

The first performance of the opera took place in Bayreuth on the July 29, 1882. Neumann wrote, "A lofty ecstasy came over me and I felt I had taken part in a sacred service." That evening at dinner at the Fantasie, the critic Hanslick sat next to Neumann, and according to Neumann, joined in the general enthusiasm, and seemed still to be under the spell of the music. If so, it must have been a time of much self-examination for the Viennese critic.

Following a dinner at Wahnfried a few days later, during business discussions with Wagner, Neumann tried again to touch upon the subject so important to him, the rights to *Parsifal*. To Neumann's amazement, Wagner's reaction this time was encouraging. He invited Neumann to bring along a proposed contract for *Parsifal* together with that for the *Ring*, which had been the main topic under discussion. On August 5, Wagner sent a note to his "Dear friend," asking him to stay over until the seventh so he could speak with him about their business. It is likely that the softening of Wagner's position resulted from the crushing burden of debt that still hovered over the Bayreuth enterprise and himself.

On the appointed day Neumann appeared with both contracts. Wagner, no doubt, was looking to this artist-businessman to save him. "Neumann, help me out of Bayreuth," he pleaded. There was some discussion of details. Then, without hesitation, Wagner signed the contract for the *Ring*. Neumann then handed him the contract affording himself exclusive rights to production of *Parsifal*. What happened next, Neumann recounted in his memoirs:

> He was just about to sign the contract, when suddenly he paused. With his pen poised over the paper he sat there lost in reflection; then suddenly turning slowly to me, he said in a low, gentle voice: "Neumann, I did promise you — and if you insist, I'll sign the contract. But you would be doing me a great

favor if you should not insist at this time. I've pledged you my word — no one shall ever have *Parsifal* but you.

I answered: "Master, if you say I should be doing you a great favor, then naturally that is quite enough for me!" Wagner wrung my hand and kissed me eagerly, saying with touching emphasis, "Thank you, Neumann, thank you!" and so closed one of the most important incidents of my life.[1]

Neumann told his seven-year-old son later that day that when he relinquished *Parsifal* he relinquished many millions.

Whatever problems may have existed between them, there can be little doubt that Wagner and Neumann dealt with each other on a basis of friendship and mutual respect. Even to Cosima, Wagner had nothing to say about Neumann of a derogatory nature; it was almost entirely laudatory, and nothing untoward about his religion or heritage. As with Porges, but unlike with Rubinstein and Levi, the subject never reared its head in the course of personal contacts. It was mentioned by Wagner only in his light-hearted ditty after the Leipzig *Rheingold*, wherein he termed Neumann "the greatest of his race."

Part VII

Bayreuth III:
The Second Festival

40

Levi and *Parsifal*

THINGS WERE PROCEEDING smoothly between Hermann Levi, now the leading conductor of the Munich opera, and the Wagners. He was a frequent guest in their home. Levi did a small favor for Cosima and received a warm note of thanks from Richard. He went to lunch at Wahnfried and stayed the whole afternoon. For some reason, Levi, Wolzogen, whom Wagner admired for his work, and Ferdinand Jäger, a tenor whom he admired much less, are called the "upright men." They often appeared in Wahnfried together. Levi sometimes sent books and pamphlets, which the Wagners enjoyed, even if not so much so as other pamphlets received on the subjects of race and the Jews. Toward the end of 1879 Levi tried to heal the break between Wagner and the director of the Munich opera, Baron von Perfall, but Wagner would have none of it. En route to Naples, the Wagners celebrated New Year's Eve in Munich at the Hotel Marienbad with Levi, the artist Franz von Lenbach, and Ludwig von Bürkel, secretary of the Munich theater.

On October 31, 1880, returning from Italy, the Wagners stayed 17 days in Munich at the home of a friend on the Briennerstrasse. A few days after arriving they spent the evening at Levi's home with Lenbach and two other friends, and continued to see much of Levi throughout their stay. On one occasion after a walk with Joukowsky, Wagner returned in an agitated mood, announcing that he has antipathy toward Lenbach. He said to Levi that as a Jew Levi had only to learn to die, an offensive remark, "but Levi shows understanding," or so said Cosima. The night before leaving for their return to Bayreuth, he spoke openly, before Levi, of the "dismal influence of the Jews on our present conditions, and warns Levi of the implications for him." Levi apparently accepted this "good-humoredly," but with some melancholy. A few days previous he had told Levi that he fussed too much about his soul. In all likelihood, Levi was becoming inured to such blandishments.

There were other, more important matters involving Levi. As conductor of the Munich orchestra, he had prepared an impressive program for the Wagners. It started in early November with Beethoven's *Missa Solemnis*. On November 4, the Wagners attended a performance of *Der Fliegende Holländer,* and Cosima said that "in spite of the shortcomings of the performance," Richard, affected, "bursts into tears." On the seventh they attend a performance of *Tristan*, and "Richard, very affected, tells us that he feels with every character ... he feels he is each of them — the orchestra is very good. The second act the crowning glory." On the eleventh, came Mozart's *Die Zauberflöte* (*The Magic Flute*). Wagner was quite obviously favorably impressed, and he so wrote to Ludwig in September.

According to Levi's biographer, Frithjof Haas, during this visit Wagner had seen clearly that Levi could serve very well as director for *Parsifal*, and that from the point of view of artistry, there was hardly anyone better. Haas further expressed the belief that Wagner's only hesitation was the fact of Levi's Jewishness.[1] The Wagners left Munich on November 17, and Levi was at the station to see them off. He had not yet been told of Wagner's plan to have him conduct that opera.

Seven months earlier, on April 28, 1880, while still in Naples, Wagner, after receiving a letter from Levi, had remarked, "I cannot allow him to conduct *Parsifal* unbaptized, but I shall baptize them both, and we shall take Communion together." This is the first mention in the diaries, letters, or elsewhere, that Levi is to conduct *Parsifal*. The "both" he referred to undoubtedly includes Rubinstein, who has been living in Wahnfried from time to time. Not until January 19 of the following year was the subject mentioned again, this time directly to Levi. He arrived in the early evening and Richard played some ballads, following which he announced to Levi, "to his astonishment," that he is to conduct *Parsifal*.

Cosima quoted her husband: "Beforehand," he said to Levi, "we shall go through a ceremonial act with you. I hope I shall succeed in finding a formula which will make you feel completely one of us." Her diary continues: "The veiled expression on our friend's face induces Richard to change the subject," but after Levi departs, she and Richard discuss it further. As Cosima saw the difficulty, the community into which Levi would be accepted "has itself abandoned Christ, though it still writes about him." When they parted temporarily that evening, Richard "jokes" according to Cosima: "What an accursed subject you have brought up here!"

Later that same evening wrote Cosima, "we agree that this alien race can never be wholly absorbed into our own." She then wrote down something that Richard had repeatedly said to her "with very great earnestness and not a trace of mockery." He said that "when our friend modestly approached him and kissed his hand, Richard embraced him with great inner warmth, and from what emanated between them, he came to feel with extraordinary precision what a difference of race and separateness really mean. And thus the good Jew always suffers a melancholy lot in our midst."

Levi was never baptized, nor was Rubinstein, but Levi did indeed conduct performances of *Parsifal* in the summer of 1882 as lead conductor. How this anomaly came to pass has been the subject of certain questions that have been raised, questions that need to be examined. More than any episode in Wagner's life, this episode may tell us what was really important to him. It has been accepted in the literature that Levi was forced on him by King Ludwig. Under the terms of the contract of 1878, the orchestra and personnel of the Munich Opera were to be used, courtesy of King Ludwig, as Wagner could not assemble a representative orchestra and cast of musicians together otherwise. And, so the story goes, Levi, as chief conductor of the Munich Opera, came with the orchestra.

Weingartner, for instance, wrote in his memoirs that Levi was first rejected by Wagner because he was a Jew, and that if Wagner had not withdrawn the objection, Ludwig would not have permitted the Munich orchestra to cooperate. Humperdinck wrote that it had not been easy for Levi to overcome the original opposition of Wagner as he had his heart set on a conductor of "Aryan extraction, but by his ceaseless devotion and reliability" he won the Master over and became his most intimate friend. In his chronology of events of this period, Stewart Spencer wrote that in 1878, Ludwig allowed his Munich forces to give the first performance in Bayreuth, adding parenthetically, "The conductor Hermann Levi is part of the deal."[2] It is a proposition that has never been examined, but should have been. To do so now we should look more closely at the events leading up to that summer of 1882 and the first *Parsifal* performances.

As originally signed in 1878, a clause of the contract between Wagner and the king provided in part that "the first performance ... shall be given with the orchestra, the singers, and the artistic personnel of the Court Theater." It is not irrelevant to point out that there were two conductors of the theater, Hermann Levi and Franz Fischer. Further, the very next clause provided that "Wagner shall be at liberty to supplement the Munich forces from outside quarters as he may think fit."[3] A few months later, at Wagner's urging, motivated by his unwillingness to have the opera performed outside of Bayreuth, the king invalidated the entire contract. He substituted for it a single paragraph. Nonetheless, that clause just quoted reveals much of what was intended by both parties, involving Wagner's freedom of choice of artists. The new paragraph, in its entirety, read:

> I decree that the orchestra and the chorus of my Court Theater shall be at the disposal of the Bayreuth undertaking for two months in each year from 1882 onwards; my General Director Baron von Perfall and my Court Secretary von Bürkel ... are to come to an agreement with the Patrons' Group in Bayreuth for the choice of these months in conformity with the requirements of the Munich Theater and with regard to the settlement of the costs... I further decree that all previous contracts with regard to the production of ... *Parsifal* are hereby annulled.[4]

Hence, it stipulates that the Munich orchestra and chorus are "at the disposal of Bayreuth," not that Bayreuth is required to use them. And neither Perfall nor Bürkel are endowed with any authority except to agree as to time and settlement of costs. These are matters that will be of import in connection with the one bit of so-called evidence of Wagner's unwillingness to accept Levi and of this conductor having been forced on him.

Nowhere in all the voluminous correspondence between Ludwig and Wagner, or between others in their behalf, is there any controversy over who the conductor shall be. Nowhere in the painfully detailed diaries of Cosima is there any discussion between husband and wife wherein any objection or uncertainty is discussed concerning the suitability of Levi. It seems to have been understood between them that Levi would conduct. We will turn shortly to the one tale, involving events supposedly occurring in 1882, that is too often unquestioningly taken as contrary proof. First, however, it would be well to examine an episode that took place in mid–1881, as it will help in evaluating this story.

On June 26, 1881, Levi arrived at Wahnfried prepared to spend a week in preparation for rehearsal for *Parsifal*. On the twenty-ninth an anonymous letter was received by Wagner taking him to task for having a Jew conduct the holy Christian opera he is writing, and demanding that he discharge Levi and retain a Christian. The letter itself no longer exists. This much would be nothing new. If one of Wagner's subsequent letters to the king is to be believed, he had received many such letters. However, to this one there was more.

It accused Levi of having a clandestine affair with Cosima. As should be clear by this point, there is no possibility of this having occurred and no possibility of Wagner having believed the charge. Cosima's diary is instructive and believable: "Around lunchtime he comes to me in a state of some excitement: 'Here's a nice letter.' I: 'Something bad?' 'Oh, you'll see.' I read it, am at first astonished, but then join in Richard's lively merriment."

When Levi returned for lunch after a walk into town, Wagner, after first upbraiding him for being late, told Levi that he had placed a letter upstairs in his room and asked him to read it before eating. At lunch Levi was asked by Wagner why he was so silent. Levi replied by asking why Wagner had not torn up the letter immediately. Wagner responded that had he done so, something of it would have rankled within him. "But now I can assure you that not the slightest memory will remain with me." Levi said nothing but after lunch packed his bag and traveled to Bamberg.[5]

From Bamberg, he sent a letter asking to be relieved of his post. Wagner answered by telegram: "Friend, you are most earnestly requested to return to us quickly to get the main matter in hand." Levi's response was to repeat his wish to be relieved of his assignment. Wagner then wrote a letter:

Dear best friend,

I have the greatest respect for your feelings, though you are not making things easy for yourself or for us! What could so easily inhibit us in our dealings with you is the fact that you are always so gloomily introspective! We are entirely at one in thinking that the whole world should be told about this shit, but what this means is that you must stop running away from us, thereby allowing such stupid suspicions to arise. For God's sake come back at once, and get to know us properly! Do not lose any of your faith, but have the courage to go on with it. Perhaps this will be a great turning point in your life — but in any case — you are my *Parsifal* conductor. Now, come on! Come on!

Yours, R.W.[6]

On the following day, July 2, at about 1:00 P.M. Levi returned, very relaxed, according to Cosima, and in a very cheerful mood. At lunch, "Richard calls for *Hebrew* wine!" When Levi described the beautiful cathedral in Bamberg, Wagner talked to him about the simplicity and feeling of the Protestant services, presumably in contrast to Catholicism as represented by the cathedral. Despite his letter, he also told Levi that he had been thinking of having him baptized and of both Levi and himself taking Holy Communion together. It never happened.

There do not seem to have been any further controversies or tension between the two men. In October 1881, he wrote to Levi, "For all musical preparation for next year's Parsifal performances, you are my *plenipotentiary*, my *alter ego*."[7] It is extremely doubtful if Wagner, always determined to keep all details within his control, and never completely satisfied with anyone, ever wrote such a letter or gave such authority to anyone else. His complete trust and satisfaction with Levi is evident.

On March 15, 1882, in Palermo, where he had been with his family since the prior November, Wagner wrote to Levi, starting with a cry of agony about his heart, but seeming more in good spirits over the progress in preparations for *Parsifal*: "Oh Hermann — Hermann. Why, Hermann, does my heart hurt so much? Yet! It seems to happen; Good fortune can also come with a bad front," turning on its head a German saying that one should cope with bad luck with a good front. There followed detailed discussions, generally upbeat, about the planned performances.[8]

Levi's father, Benedict, the rabbi in Giessen, was proud of his son, and recognized the honor that was bestowed upon him by his position in the coming festival. Such an honor assured his son of immortality in music history. He wrote to Hermann in April 1882, about four months before the first performance, a letter that Hermann found "very refreshing and stimulating." Apparently though his father also said, "If only I could like Wagner!" Hermann answered:

> You certainly can and you should. He is the best and noblest of men. Of course our contemporaries misunderstand and slander him. It is the duty of the world to darken those who shine. Goethe did not fare any better. But posterity will one day recognize that he was just as great a man as an artist, which those close to him know already. Even his fight against what he calls "Jewishness" in music and in modern literature springs from the noblest motives. That he harbors no petty anti–Semitism like some country squire or Protestant bigot, is shown by his behavior toward me, toward Joseph Rubinstein, and by his former relationship with Tausig, whom he loved dearly. The most beautiful thing I have experienced in my life is that I was permitted to be close to such a man, and I thank God for it every day.[9]

Levi conducted most of the 16 performances of *Parsifal* the following summer. Several days before the first performance, Wagner told his wife that were he a member of the orchestra, he would not like to be conducted by a Jew. It was perhaps the least he could do to make amends to Cosima, and to himself.

This letter has posed difficulties for the Wagnerphobes. It is usually passed over by them as an attempt by Levi to mollify his father and to minimize the "tortures" he was enduring at Wahnfried — like a soldier in a foxhole writing home that he is fine and happy. Wagner's appointment of him as his *plenipotentiary* and *alter ego* is similarly either ignored or passed off as an attempt by Wagner to put a bold face on a bad situation forced upon him. We need now to look at the evidence of Wagner's alleged unsuccessful attempt to ditch Levi for a Christian.

41

Lichtenberg and the Knieses

IN 1931, THERE WAS published in Leipzig a book entitled *Der Kampf zweier Welten um Das Bayrreuther Erbe*[1] ("The Struggle of Two Worlds for the Bayreuth Heritage"). It was published by Julie Kniese, the daughter of Julius Kniese. He was one of many musicians dedicated to helping with the festival of 1882, and worked primarily as a chorus master. The title of this book conceals more than it reveals. The "struggle" is one envisioned by Julius Kniese, as well as his daughter, between the "Jewish element" in Bayreuth and the "Aryan." The burden of their theme is the determination of the Master to keep the festival in Aryan hands, and, to that end, to show the involuntary nature of his employment of Levi. The book also attempts to make the case, through Julius's letters to his wife, Olga, of the ineptitude of Levi and his lack of understanding of this Christian opera.

Of the 133 pages in this book, 49 are taken up by a preface authored by one "Professor Dr. Reinhold Freiherr v. Lichtenberg." Lichtenberg claims to have been told by Alexander Ritter (the husband of a niece of Wagner's, and the brother of Karl Ritter, Wagner's one-time friend), that he, Alexander Ritter, personally witnessed the following:

> In 1882 it was not possible to assemble an orchestra with the best artists from all Germany. So Wagner turned to the Munich directorship with the request that it make available to him the court orchestra. Soon he received the report that the orchestra would on a certain day arrive in Bayreuth with Levi as conductor. Wagner wrote in his answer that he didn't want Levi, but wanted to select the conductor himself. From Munich however came the information that the orchestra was to be with Levi, or would not be available.
>
> Ritter was personally present as Wagner received this letter. Seized with the greatest agitation, the Master stood in silence for a long time, tapping the pane

275

with his fingers, then turned and spat out the words: "So, now I open my beautiful festival theater to the Jews."

No one, of course, can completely eliminate the possibility that this happened. But it has all the earmarks of a contrived story, made to order. All circumstances point to the near certainty that the entire story is bogus.

The identity of this Lichtenberg is rather difficult to determine. He seemed to know something about Wagner, but his name appeared in none of the indices of the major biographies nor in Cosima's diaries, though half of Europe's population seems to be there. As for the supposed witness to this melodramatic scene, Alexander Ritter, except for passing mention of his name in connection with this book of Kniese, he shows up only twice in the last volume of Newman's exhaustively researched four-volume biography. That final volume, dealing with the last 16 years of Wagner's life, refers to him once, namely in 1873, nine years before that supposedly devastating letter, and once after Wagner's death. His name appears twice in Cosima's diaries of the last five years, once in 1873 when Wagner wrote him a letter, and again in May 1881 when the Ritter children arrived for a visit, with no mention of any presence of Ritter himself. There is no mention of him at all in 1882.

Lichtenberg's preface for this book is dated 1927. In the 45 years between the alleged event and the written account of it by Lichtenberg, who else did either Ritter or Lichtenberg tell? Why do we not hear anything about it from anyone else, including Ritter? When did he tell Lichtenberg? It must have been before 1897, as Ritter died in 1896, 31 years before his account to Lichtenberg was put in writing. Wagner told much about the *Parsifal* matters to Cosima, who, in turn, seemed to commit to writing many of his comments. Yet she said nothing about his alleged request or its rejection, supposedly so upsetting to her husband.

More troubling than the lack of other testimony is the question of the date. We are left to guess as to when this incident is supposed to have taken place. 1882 seems out of the question. We know that Wagner did not first turn to the "Munich Directorship" in 1882; he turned to King Ludwig in 1878. Further, the year 1882 would be after the episode with the anonymous letter and Wagner's persistence in having Levi return. It would also be after authority was bestowed on Levi to handle all matters involving the musical aspect of the *Parsifal* performances, specifically giving to him the authority to confirm all engagements with musicians. It would further be after Wagner's letter to the king on September 19, 1881 praising Levi and expressing his satisfaction with what he heard of Levi's conducting the previous November in Munich. This letter will be examined shortly in more detail.

But most troubling of all about a date of 1882 is the fact that from November 1, 1881, until May 1, 1882, the Wagners were in Palermo, Sicily. On the very day of their return, Levi, who had by then been studying the score for almost a year, arrived in Bayreuth to begin preparations for the production. This was a scant three months before the first performance. There is no mention anywhere of the Ritters being in Palermo with the Wagners at any time, and no reason to suspect that they were. Was Wagner truly toying with the idea of changing conductors in May? After everything that had happened that pointed to his complete acceptance of Levi?

Could Lichtenberg have been wrong about the date? Anyone familiar with Wagner's life and work during this period, as Lichtenberg seems to have been, would know the date of 1882 as the premiere of *Parsifal* as surely as a literate American would know the year 1492. And any musician would know the impossibility of a sane person thinking of changing conductors three months prior to the performances of this new and difficult opera. Let us assume the unlikely, namely that he meant 1881 or '80. Assuming that a mistake in date was made, there are still serious problems with this yarn.

He quotes Ritter as speaking of letters between Wagner and the directorship. Where are the letters? Letters to the Court Theater have been preserved, as have copies of letters from the theater to Wagner. Anything can be lost, but it is passing strange that this should be two of a very few, if not the only ones so unavailable. And the directorship meant Perfall, the man with final authority in that quarter, and the man whom Wagner despised. We know from voluminous correspondence, already mentioned, that the agreement was negotiated with the king, not Perfall. Wagner wanted nothing to do with Perfall, and said so to the king himself. There was bad blood between them. Why would Wagner ask permission from Perfall, who would be difficult if not impossible to deal with?

By the terms of the agreement as redrawn by the king in 1878, four years before the alleged episode, Perfall, as well as other personnel of the opera, had been stripped of all authority in this matter other than agreeing upon the time of the production and rehearsals, and matters of finances. Even had he any authority, would we not expect Wagner to look to the king to overrule any unfavorable response from him? Most of the correspondence between Wagner and Munich is in fact directly between him and the king. In all matters of any import, Wagner dealt with the king directly, certainly not Perfall or lesser personnel.

The last time the king had refused Wagner anything, except some exorbitant requests for money, was in connection with the Munich performances of *Das Rheingold* and *Die Walküre*. When the king, in possession of the scores, persisted in having them performed over Wagner's objections, Wagner wrote to Wüllner, the king's chosen conductor, "Hands off my score, Sir, or the devil take you." That was to a Christian conductor he did not want. To a Jewish conductor he did want, he wrote, "For God's sake man, come back ... in any event, you are my conductor for *Parsifal*." It was not religion that mattered to him. It was artistry. Had Wagner truly not wanted Levi, for whatever reason, neither the king nor anyone else would have been able to force him down Wagner's throat.

If, in the summer of 1881, a year before the festival, Wagner truly did not want Levi, if Levi was being forced on him, why would he have made such a determined effort to have Levi return after the episode with the anonymous letter? Why would he, in any event, not have accepted Levi's refusal to return after that first telegram? Why would he not have written the king to the effect that "I asked him to come back, but he won't. It isn't my fault. We'll have to get someone else."?

There is another theory advanced by a few writers, some of whom are Wagnerphobes, some of whom are simply trying to make sense of it all. This theory is that Wagner accepted Levi precisely because of the anonymous letter. Had he not done so, the argument goes, it would have appeared that there was some truth to the sordid letter. A nice try, but it rings false. The one thing that mattered to Wagner at this point in his life was a performance of *Parsifal* that comported with his exacting standards. He proved time and again that he would prefer not to have his works performed at all if not properly presented. No one with the slightest understanding of the man was going to suspect that he could be swerved from that single-minded purpose by a slanderous anonymous lie.

Kniese himself advanced that supposed motivation in a letter to his wife dated July 17, 1883, five months after Wagner's death. He had just learned of the anonymous letter of June 1881 and told his wife that the reason that Wagner accepted Levi was that he had to in order to avoid causing a scandal. That was Kniese's contrivance and is at odds with Lichtenberg's later story.

And who would have been Wagner's alternative to Levi? Wüllner? The man he called a mere "time beater"; the man he accused of knowing nothing at all? Or Hans Richter, with whom he was so disappointed for his conducting of the *Ring*? Mottl was still too young and untried, as was Seidl. Franz Fischer, who was the other Munich music director, was Levi's understudy, respected by Wagner but still unripe enough that he asked Levi to take him in hand. For obvious reasons Bülow was out of the question, and Liszt was busily engaged in his own projects and activities. Nor is there a shred of evidence that Wagner asked Liszt, or anyone else; or that he ever thought about asking anyone else to conduct.

Peter Gay, a dedicated Wagnerphobe, hit on the valid observation that

"To have mastered the Wagnerian repertory was to have become indispensable, almost irreplaceable. This mastery gave Levi whatever internal stability and external authority he commanded."[2] That mastery was observed by Wagner firsthand during his 16 days in Munich in November 1880, upon his return from Italy. According to his own utterances, he was deeply impressed.

Was there a motive to deliberately falsify a story such as this? Both Kniese and Lichtenberg, the relater of the tale, were enlisted in a cause that was driven wholly or in part through hatred of the Jews. Within months following Wagner's death on February 13, 1883, Kniese began to organize a conspiracy against Levi. He may have used Levi's Jewishness merely as a weapon against him in a conspiracy motivated by genuine, if misplaced, concern about Levi's competence. If so, he used it like an expert. Or, more likely, the motive may have been the fact of his Jewishness.

Whatever the case, the effort of Kniese to undermine Levi was determined, aggressive and foul. The rehearsals for the 1883 *Parsifal* performances, the summer following Wagner's death, with Levi conducting, began July 1, just a month before the scheduled performances. According to Haas, Levi's biographer, it was there that Kniese began to lay the germ of a "dangerous controversy" by suggesting how the future festivals should be organized. Bülow was to be chief director and Liszt would be president. Levi's role would be minimized. Haas referred to Kniese's effort as driven by "feelings of hate."[3]

George R. Marek, one of Cosima's biographers, termed Kniese "as rotten a character as he was excellent as a chorus director."[4] Marek had good reason for doing so. In a letter of July 26 of that year, to cite only one instance, Kniese wrote to his wife, referring to Levi as the "cunning Jew." Wagner, though using perhaps the equivalents of such a term in referring to that amorphous faceless entity, *the Jews,* never made use of such invective about any individual Jew. Kniese's letters are filled with personal hatred for Levi.

Artistic control of the performances that summer of 1883 were under the control of two of the male lead singers. Thereafter, Cosima came out of her self-imposed seclusion following Richard's death and took complete charge of the festivals. One reason for doing so was information she received that the stagings had deteriorated from those of her husband during the previous summer. The other reason, as described by Geoffrey Skelton in the postscript to Cosima's diaries, was the attempt by Wagner's "more nationalistically minded supporters" to persuade Liszt and Bülow to "rescue the festivals from the Jewish influence of Levi." Although there was no likelihood of that occurring, "Cosima realized that the time had come for her to assert her authority." Despite Kniese's attempts to appeal to Cosima's own racism, she persisted. Levi would conduct *Parsifal*, and, as it turned out, would be the leading conductor at Bayreuth for another decade. As for administration of the festivals, she alone was now in charge. She would brook no interference from Kniese. "With the ice-hard politeness Cosima could summon, she asked Kniese to leave."[5]

It was with Julie Kniese, the daughter of Julius, that Lichtenberg was allied in the publication of Julius's letters. In her narratives she wrote that the idea that "the Aryan mysticism of Bayreuth would be led by the completely spiritually foreign Judaism is an absurdity and impossible." She saw her father as motivated by "piety and veneration," and the struggle as one of "intrigue and baseness" against "pure idealism." She also wrote of the "holy Aryan inheritance of Bayreuth" as endangered: "Hardly anyone had struggled more to free the German art from the pressure and spirit of Judaism in word and writing than Richard Wagner."[6]

Lichtenberg outdid them both. He spoke of Levi's "unreliability in artistic and human relationships." Kniese, on the other hand, according to him, was motivated by "piety and veneration" and was "strong in his goodness and genuineness of belief." Further, he was a "true guardian of the grail."

Julius, his daughter Julie, and Lichtenberg all at one time or another wrote of Levi, with a good deal of frustration, as "the mightiest representative of the Bayreuth matters," and of his "authoritative position." From where did the authority come? It came from Cosima. As with her deceased husband, when her own, even more deep seated, contempt for all Jewry came into conflict with her all consuming determination to produce his operas precisely as the Master had dictated, it was the devotion to the Master that prevailed.

Every note of music, every nuance and gesture, every bit of staging, had to be as the Master had wanted. Had she ever suspected that Levi had been forced upon her husband, we may be certain she would not have permitted him to set foot in the theater. But after her husband's death, and *after the death of Ludwig in 1886,* the man who would have to have had the final say in supposedly foisting Levi on him, on four different occasions between 1889 and 1894 she invited Levi to return and conduct *Parsifal.* Levi had also conducted in 1886, after Ludwig was forcibly removed from the throne. Further, there was no longer the dire need for the Munich orchestra in those years.

There can hardly be any greater evidence than Cosima's actions with respect to Levi to rebut the notion that Ludwig, or anyone else, had forced Levi upon Richard Wagner. There were three conductors upon whom she relied repeatedly: Levi, Mottl and Richter. She had pet names for each. Levi was called Major, and he was considered the head conductor, because he was not only the finest conductor but, as she put it, "the most spiritual." From that position he was indeed able to make things uncomfortable for Kniese after reports of his scheming were revealed to him by Daniela, one of Cosima's daughters by Bülow, and by Fritz Brandt, the machinist.

Why, then, if Ludwig, or his surrogate, Perfall, did not foist Levi on him, did so many, such as Humperdinck, Weingartner and others say that he did? The author who most probably best perceived the truth was Alan Aberbach in his *The Ideas of Richard Wagner.*[7] Addressing just this issue, he wrote:

> Contrary to popular belief, Wagner was not forced by the king to accept Levi or lose the Munich orchestra. His decision in favor of Levi was made almost three years before the performance. However as a ploy and a way out of an embarrassing predicament, Wagner would have enjoyed the popular rumor that it was Levi or no Munich orchestra.

If Wagner truly did ask Perfall to remove Levi, the only credible hypothesis would be that he knew the request would be summarily rejected, but would give him cover for the anomaly of engaging a Jew for this Christian opera. But such a scheme was unlikely and unnecessary. More probable is Aberbach's theory that Wagner simply, falsely, spread it around that Levi had been forced on him.

We should consider also Levi's surprise when told by Wagner that he would conduct. The contract with the king for use of the orchestra dated from 1878, two and one half years previously. Were Levi destined from the beginning to conduct, could he possibly have been so surprised to receive that news in 1881?

Such an obviously spurious, concocted story is normally not worth such lengthy treatment. It is presented here only because it has been so widely, and uncritically accepted among Wagner scholars, including such usually skeptical ones as Ernest Newman.

Relevant to this controversy is an interesting exchange of correspondence between Wagner and the king in September 1881, just two and one-half months after the episode with the anonymous letter. There are aspects of the letters by Wagner that have been seized upon by many writers to explain his engagement of a Jew for this Christian opera. Taken in the context of Wagner's behavior and past history with the king, however, this is clearly just one more case of Wagner offering lame and rather absurd excuses for his association and friendship with Jews.

In the course of reporting on the progress with the *Parsifal* preparations, Wagner mentions difficulties with locating sufficient worthy flower maidens for his chorus. The burden, he says, was taken over by director Levi:

> His superior zeal and his almost passionate devotion I believe can be fully trusted and I seek on that account to reassure him about his Judaism. Despite the fact that many surprising complaints about this come to me that *Parsifal*, this entirely Christian work, should be conducted by a Jewish conductor, and that Levi himself, moreover, finds himself confused and perplexed, I hold firmly to one thing, that my gracious King has generously and magnanimously put at my disposal his orchestra and chorus as the only means of attaining an exceptional performance of this unusual work. Consequently, I accept the heads of these musical bodies, just as they make themselves available in your service, equally thankful without asking if this one may be a Jew, the other a Christian.... Furthermore, I must freely confess that during my last visit to Munich I was more satisfied with the musical direction of my operas than anywhere else. And if I can judge from the tradition maintained in Munich as just witnessed, it is to be anticipated with great pleasure that these standards will be continued.[8]

In short, he was using Levi, though he was a Jew, because he was the finest conductor to be found and also because he was, after all, part of His Majesty's orchestra. That he would have felt the need to explain something that was already a *fait accompli,* and had never been an issue, is quite an anomaly.

On October 11 the king, in the course of his answer to the many items in Wagner's letter, addressed that subject: "That you, dear friend, make no distinction between Christians and Jews for the performance of your great, holy work is very good; nothing is more offensive, more unpleasant, than such controversies. Men at bottom are all brothers despite the confessional differences."

So said Ludwig II, the "mad king Ludwig." How well the world could use more such madmen. There obviously was not a prejudiced bone in the king's body. In December 1866 he had visited, at the synagogue in Fürth, a Dr. Löwy, the rabbi of the Israelite Cultural Community. The king announced to the rabbi that he was authorizing the declaration that he intended to follow in the footsteps of his father, who had promoted the emancipation of the Jews, and to finish what his father had begun.[9]

He had endured, without answer or comment, repeated derogatory references in Wagner's letters to *the Jews* and to the imagined Jewish takeover of all things German, but thought he might now have seen signs of a change of heart. He did not reckon with the fact that such change would have involved an admission of error in a position Wagner had staked out early on, nor that it was not in the Master's makeup to acknowledge error. His stubborn anti–Semitism more and more often clashed head-on with his determination to have the right artists perform his works, train his singers, or copy his compositions. That determination won out every time.

Wagner answered the letter from Palermo on the twenty-second of November, where he and his family had been residing since the fifth. It was both tactful and respectful. But the anger raged from around the edges. His three-page letter dealt mostly with his progress on preparations for the *Parsifal* performances. About halfway through he mentioned that by "sheer coincidence" there had arrived in Palermo the author of the piano transcription of the opera. In need of a change in climate, says Wagner, the pianist was spending the winter in the south. This led to a lengthy response to the king's unpardonable show of tolerance and the contradiction of Wagner's anti–Semitic pronouncements, both of which must have been rankling him to distraction.

The man in question is the "curious figure" of Joseph Rubinstein, said Wagner, and he repeated the oft told version of Rubinstein's beseeching Wagner to save him from his Jewishness. "I allowed him to have personal dealings with me — he is in any case, an outstanding musician — although it must be said that he — no less than the good Levi — has caused me a good deal of trouble." Then this:

> What both these unhappy men lack is the basis of a Christian education which instinctively enables the rest of us to appear similar in kind — however different we may in fact be — and the result, for them, is the most painful mental anguish. Faced with these circumstances ... I have had to exercise the most extreme patience, and if it is a question of being humane toward the Jews, I for one can confidently lay claim to praise.

For Neumann he reserves a special mention: "But I simply cannot get rid of them; the director, Angelo Neumann sees it as his calling in life to ensure that I am recognized throughout the world." Therefore, he tells the king, he can only put up with this "energetic Jewish patronage," no matter how curious it makes him feel. He then adds a footnote to his letter:

> Because of their dealings in paintings, jewelry and furniture, the Jews have an instinct for what is genuine and what can be turned to lasting value, an instinct which the Germans have lost so completely as to give the Jews what is genuine in exchange for all that is not.

This, as will be readily observed, is in flat contradiction to his "Judaism in Music," republished just 12 years before, wherein he explained at great length that Jews had no appreciation of the genuine. But with so many Jews admiring his own work, some modification of that view could not be avoided.

We have also seen just how hard he tried "to get rid of" Neumann, witness for one thing the scene at the garden gate at Wahnfried just a few months earlier. He never tried to get rid of any of these Jewish friends, because he needed and wanted them. Had he truly wanted to do so, there was, of course, nothing stopping him.

He then gave his answer to the king's expression of tolerance, something that he had to explain however so gingerly: The Jews never impinged upon His Majesty's royal circle: for him they were simply a concept, whereas for the population in general they were an empirical fact.

Then followed the most curious explanation for his own friendships with Jews:

> If I have friendly and sympathetic dealings with many of these people, it is only because I consider the Jewish race the born enemy of pure humanity and all that is noble in man.

Truly, a non-sequitur for the ages. He continued:

> There is no doubt but that we Germans especially will be destroyed by them, and I may well be the last remaining German who, as an artist, has known how to hold his ground in the face of a Judaism which is now all powerful.[10]

This lecture on the finer points of racial prejudice, the king never answered. But none of it lessened in any way his regard for the composer of the operas that held him perpetually spellbound. His very warm and friendly correspondence with Wagner continued, usually concluding with "Your glowing admirer — Ludwig," or something similar. Is there any question as to whether the king would have insisted on Levi over Wagner's objection? There never was any objection expressed to Ludwig about Levi, and very little evidence of any special relationship between the king and Levi. What was special to the king was the opportunity of hearing *Parsifal*. As Ernest Newman phrased it, in another context, Wagner was "the man to whom, as his [the king's] letters show, his lonely heart was more than ever given in these last years."

Levi conducted most of the performances that summer of 1882, Fischer conducting the other few. Wagner was thrilled with Levi's work. After the first performance he went to the front of the theater to congratulate his conductor, who was standing there with his father, then 76. After speaking to Hermann, Wagner turned to Benedict. He shook the rabbi's hand and exclaimed, "Your Hermann, as my *alter ego*, really ought to bear my name, Wagner."[11]

Halfway through the last act of the last performance, Wagner unobtrusively descended into the orchestra pit, an area invisible to the audience, silently took the baton from Levi, and conducted the balance of the act himself. This was not through any displeasure with Levi. In all probability, the seriously ailing and debilitated composer realized that this would be his last chance to conduct, and could not resist the opportunity to do so. As Levi later wrote to his father, he remained standing beside Wagner, concerned lest he make some mistake. He needn't have worried. Wagner conducted, wrote Levi, as though he had been doing nothing but conducting all his life. His concern amused Wagner, who later said that when he added an extra beat to help a singer at one point into a difficult entry, Levi rewarded him with a whispered "Bravo."

At a different pace, in a different way, *Parsifal* is as great an accomplishment as *Tristan*, and its impact on the listener can be just as profound. In 1882 and later there were many renowned composers, musicians and writers who attended performances of *Parsifal* in Bayreuth. Hugo Wolf, the Austrian composer, best known for his many songs, attended in both 1882 and '83, and later wrote that this was "by far the most beautiful and sublime work in the whole field of art." In '83 he was accompanied by Gustav Mahler, the Austrian-Jewish composer, who also described his experience: "Emerging speechless from the Festival Theater, I realized that I had undergone the greatest and most soul-wrenching experience in my life, and that I would carry this experience with me for the rest of my days."[12]

Virginia Woolf, the English author and critic, attended in 1909: "Puzzled we may be," she wrote, "because the music has reached a place not yet visited by sound ... the music is intimate in a sense that none other is; one is filled with emotion and yet possessed with tranquility at the same time."[13]

Chabrier, so overcome by *Tristan* in Munich, first saw *Parsifal* in Bayreuth in 1889, and said of it, "I have never in all my life had an artistic experience at all comparable to this; it is overwhelming; one comes out after each act ... absolutely overcome with admiration, bewildered, distraught, with tears running down one's cheeks, ... It is sublime from beginning to end." His counterpart from Finland, Jean Sibelius, had seen the opera at Bayreuth in 1894 and wrote, "Nothing in the world has ever made so overwhelming an impression on me.... I was beginning to think of myself as a dry old stick but it is not the case.... Everything I do seems so feeble by its side."[14]

And there was Puccini, the great Italian composer, who was so overwhelmed by *Tristan*. He studied the score of *Parsifal*, and prepared himself thoroughly. In 1923, he bought tickets to three of the performances, planning to take in one act at a time. Unable to tear himself away, he saw all three performances in their entirety.[15]

42

Wagnerphobia

Wagner's operas, based as they are on mythology, leave themselves open to all manner of interpretation. One of the most curious concerning Parsifal is that of Robert Gutman.[1] According to his rather ingenious, if somewhat strained, juxtaposition of Wagner's prose writings and his poetic texts, he has determined that Parsifal is one long anti–Semitic diatribe. What he lacks for support in extrinsic evidence, he makes up in creative imagination.

In Wagner's operatic text, knights of the Castle of Montsalvat guard the Holy Spear and the Holy Grail. The outcast, Klingsor, who wanted to join their brotherhood, was refused admission, according to the text, because he chose to ensure his ability to follow the requirement of chastity by emasculating himself. About this deed, the knights were appalled.

According to Gutman, Wagner means for the knights to represent the Aryan race. Further, says Gutman, Wagner intended Klingsor as a symbol of the Jews. After being banished from the brotherhood, to return now to Wagner's text, Klingsor stole the Holy Spear from their castle and, endowed by his mutilation with supernatural powers, created a magic garden. He then lured the knights to their downfall through seduction by beautiful flower maidens. Parsifal himself, the pure knight, was able to resist them, even the most seductive of the flower maidens, Kundry.

For having laughed at Christ on the Cross, Kundry, perhaps the most fascinating female character in all of Wagner's works, has been condemned to live through the ages, unable to die, in expiation for that offense. She was now used by Klingsor in his evil scheme. Parsifal could resist her because, according to Gutman, in Wagner's mind "she herself had fallen victim to Jewry." The other knights, per Gutman who again tells us what was on Wagner's mind, had sold themselves to "Jewish luxury." The spear, we must also understand, was the symbol of purity, outrageously stolen by "Jewry." Says Gutman: "*Parsifal* is an allegory of the Aryan's fall and redemption."

The inventor of this interpretation claims that it is all quite clear from the text and the prose works; but, remarkably, no one noticed until Gutman came along to explain it. It must be said here also, as with Lichtenberg, that any response to such flights of fancy should be unnecessary, but in the political and social climate prevailing for many decades after World War II, there were few to dispute it. Most said: "How true. What an ugly suit of clothes the emperor does have!"

It is sometimes advanced as a brilliant piece of detective work. But it is not as though Wagner's intentions are a closed book. He wrote in detail about this, as about all his operas, and discussed them with Cosima in the privacy of their home. Evidence abounds as to Wagner's thoughts on this drama, but it is ignored by Gutman since it falsifies this specious interpretation.

During the last four days of August 1865, in response to the king's request to learn something of Wagner's proposed opera about the Grail, Wagner made a detailed prose sketch of the story and the characters. About the allegedly Jewish Klingsor, he gives his own description, as he does of all the other characters. Having heard Gutman's interpretation, it is nothing less than fair that we should hear Wagner's:

> Concerning this sorcerer dark things are said. No one has seen him; he is only known by his power. The power is magic. The castle is his work.... Who is Klingsor? Vague, incomprehensible rumors. Nothing else is known of him.... It is supposed that Klingsor is the same man who once so piously inhabited the place now so changed: he is said to have mutilated himself in order to destroy that sensual longing which he never completely succeeded in overcoming through prayer and penance. Titurel refused to allow him to join the knights of the grail, and for the reason that renunciation and chastity, flowing from the innermost soul do not require to be forced by mutilation.... concealed in that castle are the most beautiful women in the world and of all times. They are held there under Klingsor's spell for the destruction of men and of the knights of the Grail.[2]

And that is all. Except to compare Kundry, quite reasonably, to the wandering Jew of the legend, there is not a mention of Jews or Jewishness in the entire 14-page sketch. Wagner, dense as he was, apparently did not realize what his story was all about. He spoke also to Cosima, in March 1878, about his ideas of Klingsor: "In Klingsor the peculiar quality which Christianity brought into the world; just like the Jesuits, he does not believe in goodness, and this is his strength but at the same time his downfall, for through the ages one good man does occasionally emerge!"

Wagner always showed the highest reverence for Jesus, but seemed to hold Christianity, at least as practiced, in contempt. Not a word does he say here about the Jews. Perhaps that omission was in deference to Cosima's sensibilities. Perhaps he felt it would have offended her to hear a derogatory remark about the Jews. Strangely, however, he did not seem to mind speaking against Christianity, of which Cosima was such a devout practitioner, nor, as he so often did, against the Jesuits, of whom one was her father.

Gutman's book is *Richard Wagner: The Man, His Mind, and His Music.* In his analysis of Wagner's music, Gutman grudgingly finds much to say that is favorable; of the man or his mind, nothing at all. The composer's every utterance is twisted to fit into the author's conception of the demoniac character of Wagner the monster. His operatic texts and prose works alike are contorted by Gutman beyond recognition, and mixed in with that author's opinions in such a fine mesh that it is difficult, and for the uninitiated hardly possible, to tell where one ends and the other begins. He sometimes seems oblivious to the fact that most of the operas are based on age-old legends despite his passing mention of the legends. Every word uttered by Wagner, according to Gutman, seems to have been steeped in anti-Semitism.

One example suffices. In a statement teetering on the border of intellectual dishonesty he says, in his analysis of *Parsifal,* "Klingsor represented not only the Jew, Wagner told Cosima, but the Jesuit too."[3] The clear implication is that Wagner told Cosima that Klingsor represented the Jew. He, in fact, told her nothing even implying such a thing. Nonetheless, Gutman can tell us, without embarrassment, that "This painful interpretation of *Parsifal* has been traced largely with the creator's own words."

Gutman is also determined to find great influence upon Wagner and on *Parsifal* by one Count Joseph de Gobineau, French diplomat and author of short stories, accounts of his travels and racist tracts, among other works. In 1855 he wrote his *Essay on Inequality of the Human Races.* What he wrote does not square very well with the writings of Wagner, but fits much better with Gutman's distortions of them. Gutman writes that in October 1880, while in Venice, Wagner "pursued his friendship with Count Gobineau" and "pored over" his essay. Gutman calls Gobineau one of the "validating spirits hovering over the completion of *Parsifal.* In fact, claims Gutman, Gobineau's writings "influenced Wagner in much the same way Goethe's and Schopenhauer's had." It was "the ambitious duty of *Parsifal,*" he adds, "to provide a framework in which the catchword of 'racial decline' could be expounded and reconciled with two other catchwords of Wagner's earlier years, 'redemption' and 'renunciation.'"[4]

Gutman's strained interpretation aside, it would be difficult to support any influence by Gobineau on Wagner. With regard to *Parsifal* the dates themselves tell the tale: The first prose sketch of the opera was in 1857 while the Wagners were living in the Asyl. In August 1865, at the request of Ludwig, he did a first complete prose draft of the story, and in 1877 completed the second prose draft, with relatively minor changes from the first. The same year he did the poetic text.

The meeting with Gobineau on October 22, 1880, in Venice, mentioned by Gutman, was a visit the count paid to the Wagners at their home there, the first time they had met since November 30, 1876. That earlier meeting was a casual introduction, of one person among many, at a soirée in Rome. During the 1880 visit in Venice, according to Cosima, Richard found it hard either to speak or to understand the guest's French. Despite his extended residence in France on several occasions, Wagner never mastered the French language.

Between those two meetings neither man pursued a friendship. There is no doubt that they became friends later, but that does not fill Gutman's requirements. He needs the friendship to begin before the opera text was completed.

Not until December 1880 did Wagner read anything at all by Gobineau, and that was *Amadis,* which has nothing to do with race. He first heard of *The Inequality of Races* on February 14 of the following year, four years after completing the *Parsifal* text, and 16 years after completion of the prose draft. At that time, namely in February 1881, Wagner saw a discussion and criticism of the Gobineau tract but had not read it. He began reading it on March 19, and according to Cosima he was not very pleased by it. His main concern then was the upcoming production of *Parsifal* and the voluminous correspondence about it. He finished Gobineau's book of about 215 pages two months and ten days later. This is what Gutman presumably meant by poring over it. They did become friends, but Wagner disagreed with as much in the essay as he agreed with, and it is difficult to find, even in Wagner's late essays, any influence of Gobineau. The French writer would never have approved of "Know Thyself," published by Wagner in 1881.

Nonetheless, manufacturing interpretations of this sort seemed like such a good idea that other scholars quickly followed suit. It became a cottage industry. It was a gold mine of material for books and articles, and they began to find one operatic villain after another to be a Jew in disguise. The most frequently mentioned, and accepted by a pliant, impressionable throng of authors and directors, was Mime, one of two dwarfs in *Der Ring des Nibelungen*. Because he seeks after gold, he is considered to be Wagner's caricature of the Jew; never mind that the gold is sought by almost everyone else in the operas.

Mime's brother dwarf is Alberich, hence presumably also a Jew. In the same conversation wherein Wagner told Cosima his thoughts on Klingsor, he also spoke about Alberich: "Richard tells me he once felt every sympathy for Alberich, who represents the ugly person's longing for beauty. In Alberich, the naiveté of the non Christian world." Naiveté, it must be understood, to Wagner was not a negative trait. His hero Siegfried was naive; *the Jews* were anything but. Further, in Wagner's mind Jews were the exploiters. The hapless Mime was as much the exploited as exploiter.

We have even more direct testimony from the diaries concerning Mime. In November 1882, in Venice, vacationing after *Parsifal*, she wrote: "This morning we went through all the characters of *Der Ring des Nibelungen* from the point of view of race: the gods white; the dwarfs yellow (Mongols); the blacks the Ethiopians; Loge the half caste." Wagner said many things about the Jews. Never did he call them part of the "yellow race." On May 3, 1881, after attending a Berlin rehearsal of *Siegfried* in connection with the upcoming *Ring* performance there, Wagner gave his wife his impressions: "Mime, a Jewish dwarf, but excellent." The performer was Julius Lieban, son of a Jewish cantor. The "but" tells us plenty about Wagner's views, or lack of them, on this subject.

Beckmesser in *Die Meistersinger* has also been frequently mentioned, the only instance of its kind with some grain of justification. It was not *the Jews* that were being stereotyped however, but narrow-minded, pedagogic critics, in this case one, namely Hanslick, whom Wagner considered to be Jewish because of his Jewish mother.

Wagner has also been saddled with some responsibility for the ghastly crimes of Hitler. To read some of these scholars and pseudo-scholars, one might gain the impression that except for Wagner, the Holocaust would never have occurred; that Hitler might have been a pro–Jewish activist, a Zionist perhaps. Hitler set out, in the 1930s, a detailed statement of his hatred for the Jewish people in his *Mein Kampf*. In that entire thousand-page hate-filled book there is but one mention of Wagner. Hitler makes passing note of him in the same sentence with Martin Luther, pointing to both of them as men who got it right in their contempt for the Jews. Otherwise he is not mentioned, nor is there a single line in that book from Wagner's writings. Nonetheless Gutman seems to derive some perverse satisfaction from comparisons of Wagner with Hitler, one of the most creative minds in history with the most destructive.

Both counts of these indictments, his use of Jewish stereotypes and his influence on Hitler, have been thoughtfully and adequately answered by one of the few objectively presented books on the subject: *The Darker Side of Genius,* by Jacob Katz, professor emeritus of Jewish educational and social history at the Hebrew University of Jerusalem.

The critics of the post–Nazi period, concludes Katz, followed the example of the Nazis themselves, "seeing at times in Wagner's anti–Semitism the key to interpreting his art and in turn establishing his anti–Semitism on the basis of this interpretation. In fact, without forced speculation, very little in the artistic work of Wagner can be related to his attitude toward Jews and Judaism."[5] With regard to the accusations relating to Hitler, Katz succinctly states that the known facts dating from Wagner's lifetime prove incriminating enough without burdening him in addition with the horrible deeds of Hitler.

His admonition to historians who deal with this complex and emotion-laden subject is also worth noting. They must not assume, he writes, that Wagner's attitude was fixed once and for all. "Wagner was far from being bound to a system of thought or from aiming at one. His creative power was devoted to the realization of artistic plans, while his ideas ... original as they might seem, lack disciplined composure and consistency." They were, says Katz, hardly more than "inspirations of the moment, often expressions of the transient phases of his intellectual development, and sometimes emotional reaction to events and experiences."[6]

It is precisely this prescient analysis of the man's mind that so escaped the understanding of Gutman and his fellow Wagnerphobes. They see his every word and thought as part of a monolith, unchanging and uncomplicated, every nuance of his behavior reflective of his evil nature. The only virtue the man possessed, they would have us believe, was his fortuitous ability to compose music. From his relationship with women to his financial affairs, to his relationships with Jews, they find only cynicism and egoism. In the focus of their lens, every relationship with a Jew was manipulative, something always more insulting, it must be noted, to the ones manipulated than to the manipulator. Any possibility of genuine warmth or friendship is discounted.

43

Glimpses of the Other Side

WAGNER'S VIRULENT ANTI–SEMITIC comments and outlook lasted till the end of his days. But throughout his life, his writings and remarks to his wife are laced with perplexing, perhaps grudging expressions of admiration for Jews in general, or at least a softening of his animosity. About individual Jews, as we have seen, there were many complimentary comments. Some of the ones about *the Jews* we have also seen, but there were others. On June 3, 1881, Richard "exploded in favor of Christian theories in contrast to racial ones." On April 5, 1882, "Support for his works comes only from Jews and young people." In September he turned to "that curious book about Judaism he once read and says that such clairvoyant, pessimistic people achieve some kind of progress, the present-day historians and scientists none at all."

On June 27 he commented on one of the few consistencies in his life. He never lost his early feelings of friendship or admiration for the Jewish composer Halévy. Cosima's diary for that day reads: "At lunch he remarks on the beauties of *La Juive,* the Passover celebrations, the final choruses, also the final first act, and says it contains the best expression of the Jewish character."

This last phrase is not such an isolated phenomenon as it may seem. Many students and scholars of Wagner have found much in his works that shows evidence of his interest in Jewish mysticism and legends.

Dieter Borchmeyer, a scholar from Heidelberg, has recently recounted his recollection of an episode told him by Joseph Tal, the Israeli composer. In the presence of his father, a rabbi, Tal played the prelude to *Parsifal.* The surprised rabbi exclaimed: "That is musical *Kabbalah.*" That term means literally "The Received." It arose in the thirteenth century as a reaction to the religious laws of the Talmud, the most sacred of Jewish books. Composed of knowledge handed down for many generations, it contains much mysticism. It was studied by late medieval Jewish scholars and was the subject of considerable writing. It was also studied in the Renaissance by many Christian humanists together with the rabbis. Like much in modern culture, it has become something of a cult.

Another scholar present expressed astonishment over the apparent use by Wagner of what he saw as Jewish influence in the story and ceremonies of *Parsifal,* in view of his persistent anti–Jewish views in his prose writings. He theorized that Wagner, in the romantic tradition, reconstructed the original Judaism as a pure "art religion," to which the secularized Judaism of the present was opposed.[1]

In short, according to this view, what Wagner admired in the earlier aspects of Jewish religion was its aesthetic quality. It was a mirror image of what Levi admired in the Christian, namely the magnificence of the cathedrals such as he saw in Bamberg. Levi commented once that, under the influence of *Parsifal,* he unconsciously walked faster past the open door of a church, so compelled did he feel to enter. It was not the religion that drew him in; it was the grandeur and the aesthetics that were working their spell.

Wagner's remarks on Mendelssohn, however, are mixed. In September 1878 he said he had often sung to himself themes from Mendelssohn. In November he praised his *Calm Sea and Prosperous Voyage* overture, and mentioned Mendelssohn's "good sense of the orchestra," though in the following June he found in it certain "weak sentimentalities." In December Wagner referred to him as a fine musician. Reflecting on his personality the following January, he says he was gifted when young, but became stupid as his strength increased. Aspects of his *Antigone* were also termed stupid. In June, he found Mendelssohn's *Hebrides* overture "truly masterly," and a few days later he claimed it to be his masterpiece. *A Midsummer Night's Dream* got conflicting reviews, but he continued to play it. The *Songs without Words* "astonishes us," wrote Cosima, "with their poverty of invention and their Italianisms."

The pessimism over the "triumph" of the Jews over the Germans continued apace in his last years, as did his frustration with the degrading effects of the Jews on the German culture. More and more he saw the Jews as a result, not a cause, of the German decline. But there were some unusual and interesting wisps of change. In his *Heroism and Christianity,* an essay published in September 1881, he wrote, "The blood of the Savior, the issue from his head, his wounds upon the cross, — who would impiously ask its race, whether white or other?"[2]

Then there is the other essay of that year, "Know Thyself," mentioned by Wagner to Neumann as proof of his lack of animosity toward the Jews. Martin Gregor-Dellin, writer and Wagner biographer, summarizes this essay as a prediction by Wagner that "it would be possible someday to coexist with the Jews because they were fundamentally 'the noblest of all.'"[3] Gregor-Dellin is no starry-eyed Wagner idolator; he deals rather harshly with his subject's human failings. Nonetheless, his conclusion here concerning the meaning of this obtusely worded essay is not readily discernible from the essay itself. The noblest of all phrase was Wagner's statement made, as previously noted, on July 2, 1878, to his friend Levi in an attempt to cheer him up during morose reflections on his status as a Jew in Germany. There is nothing of that nature in this essay. There is nonetheless reason to agree that there is evidence in it of a more broadly humanistic outlook, and perhaps even a touch of optimism.

In "Know Thyself" Wagner describes his own 1850 essay on the Jews as rousing the bitterest ill will though dealing only with "ethical aesthetics." Now, he says, the same subject, when applied to civic intercourse and party politics, we hear about in "vulgar brutal tones." He suggests a reawakening of the German instinct: "As however, we have been obliged to discard all idea of its being a purely racial instinct, we might perhaps search for something higher: a bent ... of far nobler origin and loftier aim ... the spirit of the purely-human."

He suggests that answers to German uncertainty can be found "not in ourselves, but in the truly human." Germans, he says, should look with pride on their ancestry, but with "unclouded eye," and should be "able to rightly estimate those foreigners, and value them according to the spirit of true humanity indwelling in their work. For the sterling German instinct asks and seeks for nothing but this purely human." As always, "foreigners" was a euphemism for Jews. He thus seemed to accept, at least temporarily, a commonality of humanity in lieu of racial tensions.

This is not always the way Wagner wrote, or spoke, or would again write and speak. But that is the way he lived. He judged all individuals by one criterion only: not by their ethics, morals, strength of character, or religion, but by their artistic talent or their willingness to help in a great cause, namely his own. There is not an instance in his well documented life wherein he refused the help or the friendship of anyone because he or she was a Jew, or anything else. He cared only about their talent, helpfulness, or understanding of himself and his aims.

Hans Keller, a Jewish refugee and musicologists from Austria, living in England, wrote less than 30 years ago:

> We desperately cling to Wagner's weaknesses, such as his anti–Semitism ... or his anti–French posture, both of which turn out to be so silly and boring, such

thoughtless generalizations of unpleasant personal experiences, that they don't cause the present writer, a pretty conscious Jew, more than a yawn. They are, in fact, out of character — Wagner's otherwise extremely well-integrated character, and obtrude, like lifeless desert islands from the boiling sea of his ever restless imagination."[4]

Levi paid dearly for his unswervable friendship with Wagner and his dedication to his music, a matter set forth earlier in these pages in connection with the unwarranted charges against him of self-hatred. Wagner, too, paid a price. He had been born in 1813 in the section of Leipzig known as the Brühl, but known also as the Jewish section. His father, Carl Friedrich Wagner, died six months after Richard's birth. Nine months later his mother, Johanne, married Ludwig Geyer, an artist and actor, who had long frequented the Wagner home.

There have been suspicions and speculations, both about Geyer's possible paternity of Richard and the possibility that he was a Jew. The question of paternity still lingers, though barely; the question of Geyer's Jewishness does not. Neither Johanne, Ludwig Geyer, nor Carl Friedrich were Jewish, nor did any of them have any traceable Jewish ancestry. Modern genealogy has run those questions down through many generations. There are those who would have loved nothing better than to prove that Richard, the arch anti–Semite, had Jewish ancestry.

None of that of course disposes of the possibility that Wagner may have thought that he did. It is one proposition that has been advanced in support of his antipathy to Jews and Judaism. The belief, or supposed belief, that he was of Jewish ancestry first seems to have surfaced in the late 1870s, though as early as 1869, one Albert Hahn asserted that "Wagner's nose was not German." Just as Levi had been seen as a traitor to his people, as well as to the accepted forms of music, Wagner was now seen as not only a dangerous influence on music and German culture, but also, by some, as possibly a Jew, and thus outside of the pure Germanism he was supposed to espouse. Newspapers in Vienna and Munich led the way.

In 1876, the year of the first festival and performance of the *Ring*, an article appeared in the Vienna *Fremdenblatt* by Ludwig Speidel, a critic hostile to Wagner since at least 1872. He claimed unequivocally that Wagner, born in "the Jewish Quarter" of Leipzig, was of Jewish descent. This was only a precursor of what was to come in articles and cartoons. He was derided in many journals as "the rabbi of Bayreuth." Four years after the first festival, the Vienna *Floh* published a cartoon showing Wagner seated at a piano on which rested a bust of Jules Offenbach, a Jewish composer, and surrounded by children of obvious and exaggerated Jewish features. Wagner's own nose is likewise markedly of the Jewish stereotype. A drawing in 1882 in another Vienna newspaper, the *Kikerkiki,* shows an audience of all Jews applauding *Parsifal.* In 1880 Daniel Spitzer, a Viennese critic, unsatisfied with newspaper attacks, published a supposedly humorous novel, *Enamored Wagnerians,* in which the composer, Goldschein, is obviously Jewish and obviously also a caricature of Wagner.[5]

It all must have been very rankling to him, and the talk must have been common. Even Cosima seemed to believe that Geyer was his father, even if not a Jew. The day after Christmas 1878, following Richard's observation that young Siegfried resembled his own "father Geyer," meaning his step-father, Cosima replied that "Geyer surely must have been your father." To Richard's reply of disbelief, Cosima persisted: "Then why the resemblance?" Answered Richard: "My mother loved him at the time — elective affinities," a reference to a similar situation in the Goethe novel of that name.

He presumably could have avoided much if not all of the malicious gossip and ridicule by sending his Jewish friends and supporters away. But that occurred to him as little as it occurred to Levi to avoid the animosity of his former friends, the sometimes hurtful comments of Wagner, and the taunts of other anti–Semites, by abandoning Wagner. Their joint dedication to their respective arts and their friendship for each other survived all of it, just as did the relationship between Levi and Cosima after Richard's death.

44

The Final Days

FOLLOWING THE END OF THE *Parsifal* performances, on September 14, accompanied by von Stein, Siegfried's tutor, and Rubinstein, Wagner and his family left for Venice, where they stayed at the Palazzo Vendramin. He was ill, cranky, quarrelsome and full of acid comments laced often with humorous cynicism. It seems to have been known or sensed by many, including Cosima, that he must soon succumb to the strain of his lifelong battles. Between his arrival in Venice and his death there on February 13, there visited many friends and acquaintances from both his distant and not so distant past. They included Liszt, Gross, Joukowsky and Humperdinck among others. Levi visited twice.

On October 3, shortly after the Wagners' arrival in Venice, Cosima noted, "Friend Levi visits us, by no means unwelcome to Richard, who, sitting in the smoking niche, is content looking back on the Parsifal days." Levi left five days later, but returned on February 4. Wrote Cosima: "We are expecting Levi, he arrives toward 4 o'clock, most welcome to all of us." About the arrival of no one else do we read such expressions of pleasure.

He left on the twelfth. On Tuesday the thirteenth, Wagner skipped lunch with the family to work on an essay, "On the Womanly in the Human." He clearly was not well, but refused to see even Cosima. The maid heard him sigh and moan, obviously in great distress. Finally, in desperation he rang the bell. Moments later the family was told by the frantic maid that he wanted the doctor and his wife. It was too late. He suffered a massive heart attack and died in Cosima's arms. The shattered woman remained with him over 24 hours, then cut off her hair and placed it in the coffin in which he was carried away. For days she refused all offers of food, and for months remained in seclusion.

Wagner was found to have suffered from an enlarged heart, fairly extensive enlargement of the stomach, and an internal hernia that had been aggravated by maltreatment. It was enough to exacerbate anyone's negative disposition, let alone Wagner's sour moods.

Two days later Levi, in Munich, wrote to his father: "In my terrible, indescribable pain, I think about you with love. Later generations will measure what the world possessed in him, and what it has lost." He reported that Wagner had been ill the previous week, but by Thursday had recovered. However, Levi himself was not entirely well then and was confined to bed. The doctor could confirm only a "general nervous disorder." Until Monday noon he spent most of the day in bed but was visited often by Wagner and joined the others during the evenings. Monday at noon he felt well enough to travel and, he wrote, "Wagner accompanied me to the stairs, kissed me repeatedly — I was very moved — and twenty-four hours later!!"[1]

When first given the news, Ludwig could only manage a "Frightful! Terrible! Let me be alone." A few days later, learning of the tremendous outpouring of grief and of praise for the great composer, he exclaimed: "This artist whom the world now mourns, it was I who was the first to understand him; it was I who rescued him for the world."

Richard Wagner, probably about age 57. From *Wagner at Home* by Judith Gauthier (1909).

Word came to Brahms in Meiningen as he conducted a rehearsal for his *Gesang der Parzen,* "Song of the Fates." He lay down his baton and announced to the assembled musicians, "Today we sing no more. A master has died." Clara Schumann's condolences went to Levi: "Though we may be unfortunate enough to disagree with you about Wagner, yet I know what he meant to you, and I feel for you warmly in the sorrow that has come upon you."[2] Giuseppe Verdi, genuine, direct and uncomplicated as always, said nothing publicly, but wrote his publisher, Tito Ricordi, the following day: "Sad, sad, sad.... I was crushed. A great individuality has gone, a name that will leave a most powerful impress on the history of art."

Neumann received the news from Förster in Aix where they were to begin producing the following day a performance of the *Ring*. He reeled into the next room and clutched the bed. After consultation with the director, Seidl, and with the cast, they decided to go ahead with *Das Rheingold*. He appealed to every theater in Germany to give a benefit performance for young Siegfried, then 13 years old. Lilli Lehmann attended a *Parsifal* performance in Bayreuth that summer despite her pain from the unhappy love affair with Fritz Brandt: "What cried for salvation in him wailed loudly in me also, and finally found relief in tears. I wept for the genius who was no longer there and could never return to us."[3] We have no memoirs from Rubinstein, nor information as to when or how he heard. We know only that a year and a half later, in Lucerne, he died by his own hand and was buried in the Jewish cemetery in Bayreuth.

Wagner's funeral train moved slowly from Venice to Bayreuth where, at Wahnfried, he had long before prepared graves for himself and Cosima. The train was greeted everywhere by huge and silent crowds, and at Innsbruck was boarded by Levi and Porges. The burial ceremony was on February 18. The public was excluded, but the ceremony was attended by hundreds of friends, acquaintances and dignitaries. When Wagner was lowered to his grave, among the 12 pall bearers were Levi and Porges, two of his closest Jewish friends.

There were of course the usual paeans of praise, speeches and accolades, that habitually accompany the passing of the great, the type of ritual that never meant a thing to Wagner. But there was little put into words that had not been often said before, by many others. Much of it was similar to an often quoted tribute some years earlier by a French literary historian and acquaintance of Wagner, Gabriel Monod. He wrote,

> You find yourself unable to be too hard on him for lapses of taste, of tact, of delicacy; if you are a Jew, you are inclined to forgive him his pamphlet "Judaism in Music," if a Frenchman, his farce on the capitulation of Paris, if you are a German, all of the insults he has heaped on Germany.... You take him as he is, full of faults— no doubt because he is full of genius.[4]

It was the type of thing that would have thrown Wagner into a rage. There was, he was thoroughly convinced, nothing to forgive him for; it was the world that should seek forgiveness for its shabby treatment of him.

It had been Wagner's custom to note that it should be a privilege to serve or to give to "a man like me." This was, understandably, often seen as egomania or arrogance. In truth he was much too modest. Before his time, some believe, there had been only one man like him, and there have certainly been none since. Twenty years after first seeing *Parsifal*, Gustav Mahler, the Austrian-Jewish composer, for one, would write in a letter to his wife that in music there was Beethoven and Wagner, and "after them, nobody."[5] To a dead certainty, in such an assessment he was not alone.

Appendix:
"Judaism in Music"*

Wagner published his "Judaism in Music" in 1850 and again in 1869. To foster the impression that the second publication was simply a reprint, he retained the 1850 date, but actually he made minor changes to the original. The version printed here, despite the date, is the 1869 version. Translator William Ashton Ellis points out, in footnotes, the discrepancies between this version and the 1850 publication in *Neue Zeitschrift für Musik*. The footnotes (signed Tr. for translator) are original to the Ellis translation, published in 1897 as part of *Richard Wagner's Prose Works*.

(1850)

IN THE 'NEUE ZEITSCHRIFT FÜR MUSIK' not long ago, mention was made of an "Hebraic art-taste": an attack and a defence of that expression neither did, nor could, stay lacking. Now it seems to myself not unimportant, to clear up the matter lying at bottom of all this—a matter either glossed over by our critics hitherto, or touched with a certain outburst of excitement.† It will not be a question, however, of saying something new, but of explaining that unconscious feeling which proclaims itself among the people as a rooted dislike of the Jewish nature; thus, of speaking out a something really existent, and by no means of attempting to artfully breathe life into an unreality through the force of any sort of fancy. Criticism goes against its very essence, if, in attack or defence, it tries for anything else.

*To the opening of this article the editor of the Neue Zeitschrift appended the following footnote: "However faulty her outward conformation, we have always considered it a pre-eminence of Germany's, a result of her great learning, that at least in the scientific sphere she possesses intellectual freedom. This freedom we now lay claim to and rely on, in printing the above essay, desirous that our readers may accept it in this sense. Whether one shares the views expressed therein, or not, the author's breadth of grasp (Genialität der Anschauung) will be disputed by no one."—Tr.

†"Erregtheit"—in the N.Z. this stood as "Leidenschaftlichkeit," i.e. "passion."—Tr.

Since it here is merely in respect of Art, and specially of Music, that we want to explain to ourselves the popular dislike of the Jewish nature, even at the present day, we may completely pass over any dealing with this same phenomenon in the field of Religion and Politics. In Religion the Jews have long ceased to be our hatred foes, — thanks to all those who within the Christian religion itself have drawn upon themselves the people's hatred.* In pure Politics we have never come to actual conflict with the Jews; we have even granted them the erection of a Jerusalemitic realm, and in this respect we have rather had to regret that Herr v. Rothschild was too keen-witted to make himself King of the Jews, preferring, as is well known, to remain "the Jew of the Kings." It is another matter, where politics become a question of Society: here the isolation of the Jews has been held by us a challenge to the exercise of human justice, for just so long as in ourselves the thrust toward social liberation has woken into plainer consciousness. When we strove for emancipation of the Jews, however, we virtually were more the champions of an abstract principle, than of a concrete case: just as all our Liberalism was not very lucid mental sport†— since we went for freedom of the Folk without knowledge of that Folk itself, any, with a dislike of any genuine contact with it — so our eagerness to level up the rights of Jews was far rather stimulated by a general idea, than by any real sympathy; for, with all our speaking and writing in favour of the Jews' emancipation, we always felt instinctively repelled by any actual, operative contact with them.

Here, then, we touch the point that brings us closer to our main inquiry: we have to explain to ourselves the *involuntary repellence* possessed for us by the nature and personality of the Jews, so as to vindicate that instinctive dislike which we plainly recognize as stronger and more overpowering than our conscious zeal to rid ourselves thereof. Even to-day we only purposely belie ourselves, in this regard, when we think necessary to hold immoral and taboo all open proclamation of our natural repugnance against the Jewish nature. Only in quite the latest ties do we seem to have reached an insight, that it is more rational (*vernünftiger*) to rid ourselves of that strenuous self-deception,‡ so as quite soberly instead to view the object of our violent sympathy and bring ourselves to understand a repugnance still abiding with us in spite of all our Liberal bedazzlements.§ To

---

*In the N.Z. this clause ran: "thanks to our pietists and Jesuits, who have led the Folk's entire religious hatred toward themselves, so that with their eventual downfall Religion, in its present meaning (which has been rather that of Hate, than Love), will presumably have also come to naught!"— Tr.

†"Nicht sehr hellsehendes (in the N.Z. "luxuriöses") Geistesspeil."— Tr.

‡"Selbsttäuschung'" in the N.Z. "Lüge," i.e. "lie."— Tr.

§"Vorspiegelungen"; in the N.Z. "Utopien."— Tr.

our astonishment, we perceive that in our Liberal battles* we have been floating in the air and fighting clouds, whereas the whole fair soil of material reality has found an appropriator whom our aërial flights have very much amused, no doubt, yet who holds us far too foolish to reward us by relaxing one iota of his usurpation of that material soil. Quite imperceptibly the "Creditor of Kings" has become the King of Creeds, and we really cannot take this monarch's pleading for emancipation as otherwise than uncommonly naïve, seeing that it is much rather *we* who are shifted into the necessity of fighting for emancipation from the Hews. According to the present constitution of this world, the Jew in truth is already more than emancipate: he rules, and will rule, so long as Money remains the power before which all our doings and our dealings lose their force. That the historical adversity† of the Jews and the rapacious rawness of Christian-German potentates have brought this power within the hands of Israel's sons— this needs no argument of ours to prove. That the impossibility of carrying farther any natural, any 'necessary' and truly beauteous thing, upon the basis of that stage whereat the evolution of our arts has now arrived, and without a total alteration of that basis— that this has also brought the public Art-taste of our time between the busy fingers of the Jew, however, is the matter whose grounds we here have to consider somewhat closer. What their thralls had toiled and moiled to pay the liege-lords of the Roman and the Medieval world, to-day is turned to money by the Jew: who thinks of noticing that the guileless-looking scrap of paper is slimy with the blood of countless generations? What the heroes of the arts, with untold strain consuming life and life, have wrested from the art-fiend to two millennia of misery, to-day the Jew converts into an art-bazaar (*Kunstwaarenwechsel*): who sees it in the mannered bricabrac, that it is glued together by the hallowed brow-seat of the Genius of two thousand years?—

We have no need to first substantiate the be–Jewing of modern art; it springs to the eye, and thrusts upon the senses, of itself. Much too far afield, again, should we have to fare, did we undertake to explain this phenomenon by a demonstration of the character of our art-history itself. But if emancipation from the yoke of Judaism appears to us the greatest of necessities, we must hold it weighty above all to prove our forces for this war of liberation. Now we shall never win these forces from an abstract definition of that phenomenon *per se*, but only from an accurate acquaintance with the nature of that involuntary feeling of ours which utters itself as an

---

*In the N.Z. "auf gut christlich," i.e. "like good Christians."— TR.

†"Elend" may also mean "exile." In this sentence the N.Z. had "Romo-Christian Germans," in place of "Christian-Germanic potentates."— TR.

instinctive repugnance against the Jew's prime essence. Through it, through this unconquerable feeling — if we avow it quiet without ado — must there become plain to us *what* we hate in that essence; what we then know definitely, we can make head against; nay, through his very laying bare, may we even hope to rout the demon from the field, whereon he has only been able to maintain his stand beneath the shelter of a twilight darkness — a darkness we good-natured Humanists ourselves have cast upon him, to make his look less loathly.

—————

The Jew — who, as everyone knows, has a God all to himself — in ordinary life strikes us primarily by his outward appearance, which, no matter to what European nationality we belong, has something disagreeably* foreign to that nationality: instinctively we wish to have nothing in common with a man who looks like that. This must heretofore have passed as a misfortune for the Jew: in more recent times, however, we perceive that in the midst of this misfortune he feels entirely well; after all his successes, he needs must deem his difference from us a pure distinction. Passing over the moral side, in the effect of this in itself unpleasant freak of Nature, and coming to its bearings upon Art, we here will merely observe that to us this exterior can never be thinkable as a subject for the art of re-presentment: if plastic art wants to present us with a Jew, it mostly takes its model from sheer phantasy, with a prudent ennobling, or entire omission, of just everything that characterizes for us in common life the Jews appearance. But the Jew never wanders on to the theatric boards: the exceptions are so rare and special, that they only confirm the general rule. We can conceive no representation of an antique or modern stage-character by a Jew, be it as hero or lover, without feeling instinctively the incongruity of such a notion.† This is of great weight; a man whose appearance we must hold unfitted for artistic treatment — not merely in this or that personality, but according to his kind in general — neither can we hold him capable of any sort of artistic utterance of his‡ [inner] essence.

—————

*This adverb (unangenehm) was preceded in the N.Z. by another, "unüberwindlich," i.e. "unconquerably"; whereas "instinctively" (unwilkürlich) was absent from the next clause. — Tr.

†Note to the 1869, and later editions:— "To be sure, our later experiences of the work done by Jewish actors would afford food for many a dissertation, as to which I here can only give a passing hint. Since the above was written not only have the Jews succeeded in capturing the Stage itself, but even in kidnapping the poet's dramatic progeny; a famous Jewish "character-player" not merely has done away with any representment of the poetic figures bred by Shakespeare, Schiller, and so forth, but substitutes the offspring of his own effect-full and not quiet un-tendentiose fancy — a thing which gives one the impression as though the Saviour had been cut out from a painting of the crucifixion, and a demagogic Jew stuck-in instead. On the stage the falsification of our Art has thriven to complete deception; for which reason, also, Shakespeare & Co. are now spoken of merely in the light of their qualified adaptability for the stage. — The Editor" (i.e. Richard Wagner).

‡In the N.Z. "purely human" stood in the place of "his." — Tr.

By far more weighty, nay, of quite decisive weight for our inquiry, is the effect the Jew produces on us through his *speech*; and this is the essential point at which to sound the Jewish influence upon Music.*— The Jew speaks the language of the nation in whose midst he dwells from generation to generation, but he speaks it always as an alien. As it lies beyond our present scope to occupy ourselves with the cause of this phenomenon, too, we may equally abstain from an arraignment of Christian Civilisation for having kept the Jew in violent severance from it, as on the other hand, in touching the sequelæ of that severance we can scarcely propose to make the Jews the answerable party.† Our only object, here, is to throw light on the æsthetic character of the said results.— In the first place, then, the general circumstance that the Jew talks the modern European languages merely as learnt, and not as mother tongues, must necessarily debar him from all capability of therein expressing himself idiomatically, independently of therein expressing himself idiomatically, independently, and conformably to his nature.‡ A language, with its expression and its evolution, is not the work of scattered units, but of an historical community: only he who has unconsciously grown up within the bond of this community, takes also any share in its creations. But the Jew has stood outside the pale of any such community, stood solitarily with his Jehova in a splintered, soilless stock, to which all self-sprung evolution must stay denied, just as even the peculiar (Hebraïc) language of that stock has been preserved for him merely as a thing defunct. Now, to make poetry in a foreign tongue has hitherto been impossible, even to geniuses of highest rank. Our whole European art and civilization, however, have remained to the Jew a foreign tongue; for, just as he has taken no part in the evolution of the one, so has he taken none in that of the other; but at most the homeless wight has been a cold, nay more, a hostile looker-on. In this Speech, this Art, the Jew can only after-speak and after-patch — not truly make a poem of his words, an artwork of his doings.

In a particular does the purely physical aspect of the Jewish mode of speech repel us. Throughout an intercourse of two millennia with European nations, Culture has not succeeded in breaking the remarkable stubbornness of the Jewish *naturel* as regards the peculiarities of Semitic pronunciation. The first thing that strikes our ear as quite outlandish and unpleasant, in the Jew's production of the voice-sounds, is a creaking, squeaking, buzzing snuffle§: add thereto an employment of words in a

---

*The clause after the semicolon did not exist in the N.Z.

†This sentence occurred as a footnote in the N.Z., and the next sentence was absent.— TR.

‡In the N.Z., "in any higher sense."— TR.

§"Ein zischender, schrillender, summsender und murksender / autausdruck."

sense quite foreign to our nation's tongue, and an arbitrary twisting of the structure of our phrases—and this mode of speaking acquires at once the character of an intolerably jumbled blabber (*eines unerträglich verwirrten Geplappers*); so that when we hear this Jewish talk, our attention dwells involuntarily on its repulsive *how*, rather than on any meaning of its intrinsic *what*. How exceptionally weighty is this circumstance, particularly for explaining the impression made on us by the music-works of modern Jews, must be recognized and borne in mind before all else. If we hear a Jew speak, we are unconsciously offended by the entire want of purely-human expression in his discourse: the cold indifference of its peculiar "blubber" ("*Gelabber*") never by any chance rises to the ardour of a higher, heartfelt passion. If, on the other hand, we find *ourselves* driven to this more heated expression, in converse with a Jew, he will always shuffle off, since he is incapable of replying in kind. Never does the Jew excite himself in mutual interchange of feelings with us, but — so far as we are concerned — only in the altogether special egoistic interest of his vanity or profit; a thing which, coupled with the wry expression of his daily mode of speech, always gives to such excitement a tinge of ridiculous, and may rouse anything you please in us, only not sympathy with the interests of the speaker. Though we well may deem it thinkable that in intercourse with one another, and particularly where domestic life brings purely-human feelings to an outburst, even the Jews may be able to give expression to their emotions in a manner effective enough among themselves: yet this cannot come within our present purview, since we have are listening to the Jew who, in the intercourse of life and art, expressly speaks *to us*.

Now, if the aforesaid qualities of his dialect make the Jew almost* incapable of giving artistic enunciation to his feelings and beholdings through *talk*, for such an enunciation through *song* his aptitude must needs be infinitely smaller. Song is just Talk aroused to highest passion: Music is the speech of Passion. All that worked repellently upon us in his outward appearance and his speech, makes us take to our heels at last in his Song, providing we are not held prisoners by the very ridicule of this phenomenon. Very naturally, in Song — the vividest and most indisputable expression of the personal emotional-being — the peculiarity of the Jewish nature attains for us its climax of distastefulness; and on any natural hypothesis, we might hold the Jew adapted for every sphere of art, excepting that whose basis lies in Song.

The Jews' sense of Beholding has never been of such a kind as to let *plastic* artists arise among them: from ever have their eyes been busied with far

---

*In the N.Z. "durchaus," i.e. "altogether."— TR.

more practical affairs, than beauty and the spiritual substance of the world of forms. We know nothing of a Jewish architect or sculptor in our times,* so far as I am aware: whether recent painters of Jewish descent have really created (*wirklich geschaffen haben*) in their art, I must leave to connoisseurs to judge; presumably, however, these artists occupy no other standing toward their art, than that of modern Jewish composers toward Music — to whose plainer investigation we now will turn.

The Jew, who is innately incapable of enouncing himself to us artistically through either his outward appearance or his speech, and least of all through his singing, has nevertheless been able in the widest-spread of modern art-varieties, to wit in Music, to reach the rulership of public taste — To explain to ourselves this phenomenon, let us first consider *how* it grew possible to the Jew to become a musician. —

From that turning point in our social evolution where Money, with less and less disguise, was raised to the virtual patent of nobility, the Jews — to whom money-making without actual labour, i.e. Usury, had been left as their only trade — the Jews not merely could no longer be denied the diploma of a new society that needed naught but gold, but they brought it with them in their pockets. Wherefore our modern culture, accessible to no one but the well-to-do, remained the less a closed book to them, as it had sunk into a venal article of Luxury. Henceforward, then, the *cultured Jew* appears in our Society; his distinction from the uncultured, the common Jew, we now have closely to observe. The cultured Jew has taken the most indicible pains to strip off all the obvious tokens of his lower coreligionists: in many a case he has even held it wise to make a Christian baptism wash away the traces of his origin. The zeal, however, has never got so far as to let him reap the hoped-for fruits: it has conducted only to his utter isolation, and to making him the most heartless of all human beings; to such a pitch, that we have been bound to lose even our earlier sympathy for the tragic history of his stock. His connexion with the former comrades in his suffering, which he arrogantly tore asunder, it has stayed impossible for him to replace by a new connexion with that society whereto he has soared up. He stands in correlation with none but those who need his money: and never yet has money thriven to the point of knitting a goodly bond 'twixt man and man. Alien and apathetic stands the educated Jew in midst of a society he does not understand, with whose tastes and aspirations he does not sympathise, whose history and evolution have always been indifferent to him. In such a situation have we seen the Jews give birth to Thinkers: the Thinker is the backward-looking poet; but the true Poet is the foretelling Prophet. For

"In our times" did not appear in the N.Z. article. — TR.

such a prophet-charge can naught equip, save the deepest, the most heart-felt sympathy with a great, a like-endeavouring Community — to whose unconscious thoughts the Poet gives exponent voice. Completely shut from this community, by the very nature of his situation; entirely torn from all connexion with his native stock — to the genteeler Jew his learnt and payed-for culture could only seem a luxury, since at bottom he knew not what to be about with it.

Now our modern arts had likewise become a portion of this culture, and among them more particularly that art which is just the very easiest to learn — the art of *music*, and indeed *that* Music which, severed from her sister arts, had been lifted by the force and stress of grandest geniuses to a stage in her universal faculty of Expression where either, in new conjunction with the other arts, she might speak aloud the most sublime, or, in persistent separation from them, she could also speak at will the deepest bathos of the trivial. Naturally, *what* the cultured Jew had to speak, in his aforesaid situation, could be nothing but the trivial and indifferent, because his whole artistic bent was in sooth a mere luxurious, needless thing. Exactly as his whim inspired, or some interest lying outside Art, could he utter himself now thus, and now otherwise; for never was he driven to speak out a definite, a real and necessary thing, but he just merely wanted to speak, no matter what*; so that, naturally, the *how* was the only 'moment' left for him to care for. At present no art affords such plenteous possibility of talking in it without saying any real thing, as that of Music, since the greatest geniuses have already said whatever there was to say in it as an absolute separate-art.† When this had once been spoken out, there was nothing left but to babble after; and indeed with quite distressing accuracy and deceptive likeness, just as parrots reel off human words and phrases, but also with just as little real feeling and expression as these foolish birds. Only, in the case of our Jewish music-makers this mimicked speech presents one marked peculiarity — that of the Jewish style of talk in general, which we have more minutely characterized above.

Although the peculiarities of the Jewish mode of speaking and signing come out the most glaringly in the commoner class of Jew, who has

---

*In the N.Z. "but he just merely wanted to speak" appears to have been skipped by the printer, leaving a hiatus in the sense; moreover, after "no matter what," there occurred; "sheerly to make his existence noticeable."— Tr.

†In the N.Z. this sentence was continued by:— "and this was just the proclamation of its perfect faculty for the most manifold Expression, but not an object of expression in itself (nicht aber ein Ausdruckswerthes selbst). When this had happened, and if one did not propose to express thereby a definite thing, there was nothing left but to senselessly repeat the talk; and indeed" &c.— Perhaps I may be forgiven for again recalling Wagner's own parrot, from the Letters to Uhlig (see Preface to Vol. ii. of the present series).— Tr.

remained faithful to his fathers' stock, and though the cultured son of Jewry takes untold pains to strip them off, nevertheless they shew an impertinent obstinacy in cleaving to him. Explain this mishap by physiology as we may, yet it also was its reason in the aforesaid social situation of the educated Jew. However much our Luxury-art may float in wellnigh nothing but the æther of our self-willed Phantasy, still it keeps below one fibre of connexion with its natural soil, with the genuine spirit of the Folk. The true poet, no matter in what branch of art, still gains his stimulus from nothing but a faithful, loving contemplation of instinctive Life, of that life which only greets his sight amid the Folk. Now, where is the cultured Jew to find this Folk? Not, surely, on the soil of that Society in which he plays his artist-rôle? If he has any connexion at all with this Society, it is merely with that offshoot of it, entirely loosened form the real, the healthy stem; but this connexion is an entirely loveless, and this lovelessness must ever become more obvious to him, if for sake of food-stuff for his art he clambers down to that Society's foundations: not only does he here find everything more strange and unintelligible, but the instinctive ill-will of the Folk confronts him here in all its wounding nakedness, since — unlike its fellow in the richer classes— it here is neither weakened down nor broken by reckonings of advantage and regard for certain mutual interests. Thrust back with contumely from any contact with this Folk, and in any case completely powerless to seize its spirit, the cultured Jew sees himself driven to the taproot of his native stem, where at least an understanding would come by all means easier to him. Willy-nilly he must draw his water from this well; yet only a *How*, and not a *What*, rewards his pains. The Jew has never had an Art of his own, hence never a Life of art-enabling import (*ein Leben von kunstfähigem Gehalte*): an import, a universally applicable, a human import, not even to-day does it offer to the searcher, but merely a peculiar method of expression — and that, the method we have characterized above. Now the only musical expression offered to the Jew tone-setter by his native Folk, is the ceremonial music of their Jehova-rites: the Synagogue is the solitary fountain whence the Jew can draw art-motives at once popular and *intelligible to himself*. However sublime and noble we may be minded to picture to ourselves this musical Service of God in its pristine purity, all the more plainly must we perceive that that purity has been most terribly sullied before it came down to us: here for thousands of years has nothing unfolded itself through an inner life-fill, but, just as with Judaism at large, everything has kept its fixity of form and substance. But a form which is never quickened through renewal of its substance, must fall to pieces in the end; an expression whose content has long-since ceased to be the breath of Feeling, grows senseless and distorted. Who has not had occasion to convince himself of the travesty of a divine service of song, presented in a real Folk-synagogue? Who has not been seized with a feeling of the greatest revulsion, of horror mingled with the absurd, at hearing that sense-and-sound-confounding gurgle, jodel and cackle, which no intentional caricature can make more repugnant than as offered here in full, in naïve seriousness? In latter days, indeed, the spirit of reform has shewn its stir within this singing, too, by an attempted restoration of the older purity: but, of its very nature, what here has happened on the part of the higher, the reflective Jewish intellect, is just a fruitless effort from Above, which can never strike Below to such a point that fount itself. He seeks for the Instinctive, and not the Reflected, since the latter is *his* product; and all the Instinctive he can light on, is just that out-of-joint expression.

If this going back to the Folk-source is as unpurposed with the cultured Jew, as unconsciously enjoyed upon him by Necessity and the nature of the thing, as with every artist: with just as little conscious aim, and therefore with an insuperable domination of his whole field of view, does the hence-derived impression carry itself across into his art-productions. Those* rhythms and melismi of the Synagogue-song usurp his musical fancy in exactly the same way as the instinctive possession of the strains and rhythms of our Folksong and Folkdance made out the virtual† shaping-force of the creators of our art-music, both vocal and instrumental. To the musical perceptive-faculty‡ of the cultured Jew there is therefore nothing seizable in all the ample circle of our music, either popular or artistic, but that which flatters his general sense of the intelligible: intelligible, however, and so intelligible that he may use it for his art, is merely That which in any degree approaches a resemblance to the said peculiarity of Jewish music. In listening to either our naïve or our consciously artistic musical doings, however, were the Jew to try to probe their heart and living sinews, he would find here really not one whit of likeness to *his* musical nature: and the utter strangeness of this phenomenon must scare him back so far, that he could never pluck up nerve again to mingle in our art-creating. Yet his whole position in our midst never tempts the Jew to so intimate a glimpse into our essence: wherefore, either intentionally (provided he recognises this position of his toward us) or instinctively (if he is incapable of understanding us at all), he merely listens to the barest surface of our art, but not to its life-bestowing inner organism; and through this apathetic listening alone, can he trace external similarities with the only thing intelligible to his power of view,

---

* *In the N.Z. "wondrous";*

†*"unconsciously";*

‡*"capacity," as also in the preceding sentence where now stands "fancy."—* TR.

peculiar to his special nature. To him, therefore, the most external accidents on our domain of musical life and art must pass for its very essence; and therefore, when as artist he reflects them back upon us, his adaptations needs must seem to us outlandish, odd, indifferent, cold, unnatural and awry; so that Judaic works of music often produce on us the impression as though a poem of Goethe's, for instance, were being rendered in the Jewish jargon.

Just as words and constructions are hurled together in this jargon with wondrous inexpressiveness, so does the Jew musician hurl together the diverse forms and styles of every age and every master. Packed side by side, we find the formal idiosyncrasies of all the schools, in motleyest chaos. As in these productions the sole concern is Talking at all hazards, and not the Object which might make that talk worth doing, so this clatter can only be made at all inciting to the ear by its offering at each instant a new summons to attention, through a change of outer expressional means. Inner agitation, genuine passion, each finds its own peculiar language at the instant when, struggling for an understanding, it girds itself for utterance: the Jew, already characterised by us in this regard, has no true passion (*Leidenschaft*), and least of all a passion that might thrust him on to art-creation. But where this passion is not forthcoming, *there* neither is any calm (*Ruhe*): true, noble Calm is nothing else than Passion mollified through Resignation.* Where the calm has not been ushered in by passion, we perceive naught but sluggishness (*Trägheit*): the opposite of sluggishness, however, is nothing but that prickling unrest which we observe in Jewish music-works from one end to the other, saving where it makes place for that soulless, feelingless inertia. What issues from the Jews' attempts at making Art, must necessarily therefore bear the attributes of coldness and indifference, even to triviality and absurdity; and in the history of Modern Music we can but class the Judaic period as that of final unproductivity, of stability gone to ruin.

By what example with this all grow clearer to us— ay, wellnigh what other single case could make us so alive to it, as the works of a musician of Jewish birth whom Nature had endowed with specific musical gifts as very few before him? All that offered itself to our gaze, in the inquiry into our antipathy against the Jewish nature; all the contradictoriness of this nature, both in itself and as touching us; all its inability, while outside our footing, to have intercourse with us upon that footing, nay, even to form a wish to further develop the things which had sprung from out our soil: all these are intensified to a positively tragic conflict in the nature, life, and art-career of the early-taken FELIX MENDELSSOHN BARTHOLDY. He has shewn

*"*Die durch Resignation beschwichtigte Leidenshaft.*" In the N.Z. this ran: "*der Genuss de Sättigung wahrer und edler Leidenshaft,*" i.e. "*the after-taste of true and noble passion satisfied.*" The change, or rather advance, of view-point is highly significant.— Tr.*

us that a Jew may have the amplest store of specific talents, may own the finest and most varied culture, the highest and the tenderest sense of honour — yet without all these pre-eminences helping him, were it but one single time, to call forth in us that deep, that heart-searching effect which we await from Art* because we know her capable thereof, because we have felt it many a time and oft, so soon as once a hero of our art has, so to say, but opened his mouth to speak to us. To professional critics, who haply have reached a like consciousness with ourselves hereon, it may be left to prove by specimens of Mendelssohn's art-products our statement of this indubitably certain thing; by way of illustrating our general impression, let us here be content with the fact that, in hearing a tone-piece of this composer's, we have only been able to feel engrossed where nothing beyond our more or less amusement-craving Phantasy was roused through the presentment, stringing-together and entanglement of the most elegant, the smoothest and most polished figures— as in the kaleidoscope's changeful play of form and colour†— but never where those figures were meant to take the shape of deep and stalwart feelings of the human heart.‡ In this latter event Mendelssohn lost even all *formal* productive-faculty; wherefore in particular, where he made for Drama, as in the Oratorio, he was obliged quite openly to snatch at every formal detail that had served as characteristic token of the individuality of this or that forerunner whom he chose out for his model. It is further significant of this procedure, that he gave the preference to our old master BACH, as special pattern for his inexpressive modern tongue to copy. Bach's musical speech was formed at a period of our history when Music's universal tongue was still striving for the faculty of more individual, more unequivocal Expression: pure formalism and pedantry still clung so strongly to her, that it was first through the gigantic force of Bach's own genius that her purely human accents (*Ausdruck*) broke themselves a vent. The speech of Bach stands toward that of Mozart, and finally of Beethoven, in the relation of the Egyptian Sphinx to the Greek statue of a Man: as the human visage of the Sphinx is in the act of striving outward from the animal body, so strives Bach's noble human head from out the periwig. It is only another evidence of the inconceivably witless confusion of our luxurious music-taste of nowadays, that we can let Bach's lan-

---

*In the N.Z. "from Music." — TR.

†A slight change has been made by our author in the construction of this sentence, since the time of the Neue Zeitschrift article; but, while improving the general 'run,' it has given rise to almost the sole instance of a "false relation" in all his prose. — TR.

‡Note to the 1869, and subsequent editions: "Of the Neo-Judaic system, which has been erected on this attribute of Mendelssohnian music as though in vindication of such artistic falling-off, we shall speak later."

guage be spoken to us at the selfsame time as that of Beethoven, and flatter ourselves that there is merely an individual difference of form between them, but nowise a real historic distinction, marking off a period in our culture. The reason, however, is not so far to seek: the speech of Beethoven can be spoken only by a whole, entire, warm-breathed human being; since it was just the speech of a music-man so perfect, that with the force of Necessity he thrust beyond Absolute Music — whose dominion he had measured and fulfilled unto its utmost frontiers— and shewed to us the pathway to the fecundation of every art through Music, as her only salutary broadening.* On the other hand, Bach's language can be mimicked, at a pinch, by any musician who thoroughly understands his business, though scarcely in the sense of Bach; because the Formal has still therein the upper hand, and the purely human Expression is not as yet a factor so definitely preponderant that its *What* either can, or must be uttered without conditions, for it still is fully occupied with shaping out the *How*. The washiness and whimsicality of our present musical style has been, if not exactly brought about, yet pushed to its utmost pitch by Mendelssohn's endeavour to speak out a vague, an almost nugatory Content as interestingly and spiritedly as possible. Whereas Beethoven, the last in the chain of our true music-heroes, stove with highest longing, and wonder-working faculty,† for the clearest, certainest Expression of an unsayable Content through a sharp-cut, plastic shaping of his tone-pictures: Mendelssohn, on the contrary, reduces these achievements to vague, fantastic shadow-forms, midst whose indefinite shimmer our freakish fancy is indeed aroused, but our inner, purely-human yearning for distinct artistic sight is hardly touched with even the merest hope of a fulfilment. Only where an oppressive feeling of this incapacity seems to master the composer's mood, and drive him to express a soft and mournful resignation, has Mendelssohn the power to shew himself characteristic —characteristic in the subjective sense of a gentle‡ individuality that confesses an impossibility in view of its own powerlessness. This, as we have said, is the tragic trait in Mendelssohn's life-history; and if in the domain of Art we are to give our sympathy to the sheer personality, we can scarcely deny a large measure thereof the Mendelssohn, even though the force of that sympathy be weakened by the reflection that the Tragic, in Mendelssohn's situation, hung rather over him than came to actual, sore and cleansing consciousness.

---

*In the N.Z. this stood: "he yearned to pass beyond Absolute Music and mount up to a union with her human sister arts, just as the full and finished Man desires to mount to wide Humanity."— Tʀ.

†"Wunderwirkenden Vermögen" and "eines unsäglichen Inhaltes" did not occur in the N.Z.— Tʀ.

‡"Zartsinnigen"— in the N.Z. "edlen," i.e. "noble."— Tʀ.

A like sympathy, however, can no other Jew composer rouse in us. A far-famed Jewish tone-setter of our day has addressed himself and products to a section of our public whose total confusion of musical taste was less to be first caused by him, than worked out to his profit. The public of our Opera-theatre of nowadays has for long been gradually led aside from those claims which rightly should be addressed, not only to the Dramatic Art-work, but in general to every work of healthy taste.* The places in our halls of entertainment are mostly filled by nothing but that section of our citizen society whose only ground for change of occupation is utter 'boredom' (*Langeweile*): the disease of boredom, however, is not remediable by sips of Art; for it can never be distracted of set purpose, but merely duped into another form of boredom. Now, the catering for this deception that famous opera-composer has made the task of his artistic life.† There is no object in more closely designating the artistic means he has expended on the reaching of this life's-aim: enough that, as we may see by the result, he knew completely how to dupe; and more particularly by taking that jargon which we have already characterised, and palming it upon his ennuyed audience as the modern-piquant utterance of all the trivialities which so often had been set before them in all their natural foolishness. That this composer took also thought for thrilling situations (*Erschütterungen*) and the effective weaving of emotional catastrophes (*Gefühlskatastrophen*), need astonish none who know how necessarily this sort of thing is wished by those whose time hangs heavily upon their hands; nor need any wonder that in *this* his aim succeeded too, if they but will ponder well the reasons why, in such conditions,‡ the whole was bound to prosper with him. In fact, this composer pushes his deception so far, that he ends by deceiving himself, and perchance as purposely as he deceives his bored admirers. We believe, indeed, that he honestly would like to turn out artworks, and yet is well aware he cannot: to extricate himself from this painful conflict between Will and Can, he writes operas for Paris, and sends them touring round the world — the surest means, to-day, of earning oneself an art-renown albeit not an artist. Under the burden of this self-deception, which may not be so toilless as one might think,§ he, too, appears to us wellnigh in a tragic light: yet the purely personal ele-

---

*The last clause, "but in general" &c., was absent from the N.Z. article.— Tr.

†Whoever has observed the shameful indifference and absent-mindedness of a Jewish congregation, throughout the musical performance of Divine Service in the Synagogue, may understand why a Jewish opera-composer feels not at all offended by encountering the same thing in a theatre-audience, and how he cheerfully can go on labouring for it; for this behaviour, here, must really seem to him less unbecoming than in the house of God.— R. WAGNER.

‡To the N.Z. article there here was added a foot-note: "'Man so thun!' sagt der Berliner," i.e. "'It's to be done!;' as they say in Berlin."— Tr.

§This subsidiary clause did not exist in the N.Z.— Tr.

ment of wounded vanity turns the thing into a tragi-comedy, just as in general the un-inspiring, the truly laughable, is the characteristic mark whereby this famed composer shews his Jewhood in his music.—

From a closer survey of the instances adduced above — which we have learnt to grasp by getting to the bottom of our indomitable objection to the Jewish nature — there more especially results for us a proof of the *ineptitude of the present musical epoch*. Had the two aforesaid Jew composers* in truth helped Music into riper bloom, then we should merely have had to admit that our tarrying behind them rested on some organic debility that had taken sudden hold of us: but not so is the case; on the contrary, as compared with bygone epochs, the specific musical powers of nowadays have rather increased than diminished. The incapacity lies in the spirit of our Art itself, which is longing for another life than the artificial one now toilsomely upheld for it. The incapacity of the musical art-*variety*, itself, is exposed for us in the art-doings of Mendelssohn, the uncommonly-gifted specific musician; but the nullity of our whole public system, its utterly un-artistic claims and nature, in the successes of that famous Jewish opera-composer grow clear for any one to see. These are the weighty points that have now to draw towards themselves the whole attention of everyone who means honestly by Art: here is what we have to ask ourselves, to scrutinise, to bring to plainest understanding. Whoever shirks this toil, whoever turns his back upon this scrutiny — either since no Need impels him to it, or because he waives a lesson that possibly might drive him from the lazy groove of mindless, feelingless routine — even him we now include in that same category, of "Judaism in Music."† The Jews could never take possession of this art, until that was to be exposed in it which they now demonstrably have brought to light — its inner incapacity for life. So long as the separate art of Music had a real organic life-need in it, down to the epochs of Mozart and Beethoven, there was nowhere to be found a Jew composer: it was impossible for an element

---

*Characteristic enough is the attitude adopted by the remaining Jew musicians, nay, by the whole of cultured Jewry, toward their two most renowned composers. To the adherents of Mendelssohn, that famous opera-composer is an atrocity: with a keen sense of honour, they feel how much he compromises Jewdom in the eyes of better-trained musicians, and therefore shew no mercy in their judgment. By far more cautiously do that composer's retainers express themselves concerning Mendelssohn, regarding more with envy, than with manifest ill-will, the success he has made in the "more solid" music-world. To a third faction, that of the composition-at-any-price Jews, it is their visible object to avoid all internecine scandal, all self-exposure in general, so that their music-producing may take its even course without occasioning any painful fuss: the by all means undeniable successes of the great opera-composer they let pass as worth some slight attention, allowing there is something in them albeit one can't approve of much or dub it "solid." In sooth, the Jews are far too clever, not to know how their own goods are lined!— R. WAGNER.— In the Neue Zeitschrift this note formed part of the body of the text.— TR.

†In the N.Z. this ran: "of Judaism in Art, whereto the actual Jews have merely given its most obvious physiognomy, but in nowise its intrinsic meaning. The Jews could never take possession of our art" &c.— TR.

entirely foreign to that living organism to take part in the formative stages of that life. Only when a body's inner death is manifest, do outside elements win the power of lodgment in it — yet merely to destroy it. Then indeed that body's flesh dissolves into a swarming colony of insect-life: but who, in looking on that body's self, would hold it still for living? The spirit, that is: the *life*, has fled from out that body, has sped to kindred other bodies; and this is all that makes out Life. In genuine Life alone can we, too, find again the ghost of Art, and not within its worm-befretted carcase.—

I said above, the Jews had brought forth no true poet. We here must give a moment's mention, then, to HEINRICH HEINE. At the time when Goethe and Schiller sang among us, we certainly know nothing of a poet-ising Jew: at the time, however, when our poetry became a lie, when every possible thing might flourish from the wholly unpoetic element of our life, but no true poet — then was it the office of a highly-gifted poet–Jew to bare with fascinating taunts that lie, that bottomless aridity and Jesuitical hypocrisy of our Versifying which still would give itself the airs of true poe-sis. His famous musical congeners, too, he mercilessly lashed for their pre-tence to pass as artists; no make-believe could hold its ground before him: by the remorseless demon of denial of all that seemed worth denying was he driven on without a rest,* through all the mirage of our modern self-deception, till he reached the point where in turn he duped himself into a poet, and was rewarded by his versified lies being set to music by our own composers.— He was the conscience of Judaism, just as Judaism is the evil conscience of our modern Civilisation.

Yet another Jew have we to name, who appeared among us as a writer. From out his isolation as a Jew, he came among us seeking for redemption: he found it not, and had to learn that only *with our redemption, too, into genuine Manhood*, would he ever find it. To become Man at once with us, however, means firstly for the Jew as much as ceasing to be Jew. And this had BÖRNE done. Yet Börne, of all others, teaches us that this redemption can not be reached in ease and cold, indifferent complacence, but costs— as cost it must for us— sweat, anguish, want and all the dregs of suffering and sorrow. Without once looking back, take ye your part in this regener-ative work of deliverance through self-annulment†; then are we one and un-dissevered! But bethink ye, that one only thing can redeem you from the burden of your curse: the redemption of Ahasuerus—*Going under*!

---

* In the N.Z. there appeared: "in cold, contemptuous complacency," and the sentence ended at the "self-deception"— a footnote being added, as follows: "What he lied himself, our Jews laid bare again by setting it to music." Moreover in place of "seemed" there stood "is," and in the next sentence the predicate "evil" did not occur.— TR.

†In the N.Z.: "an diesem selbstvernichtenden, blutigen Kampfe."— TR.

Chapter Notes

1. The Asyl

1. J. Wille and W.G. Zimmermann, *Richard Wagner in Zürich*.
2. S. Spencer, *Wagner Remembered*, 76.
3. S. Spencer, *Wagner Remembered*, 94–97, quoting R. von Hornstein, *Memorien*.
4. R. Wagner, *Correspondence of Wagner and Liszt*, vol. II, letter 244.

2. The Fugitive

1. W. Lippert, *Wagner in Exile*, 84.

3. Minna

1. E. Newman, *The Life of Richard Wagner*, vol. I, 353.
2. R. Wagner, *My Life*, 274.
3. R. Wagner, *Letters of Richard Wagner: The Burrell Collection*, 251–253.
4. R. Wagner, *Letters of Richard Wagner: The Burrell Collection*, 256.
5. E. Newman, *The Life of Richard Wagner*, Vol. II, 147.
6. S. Spencer, *Wagner Remembered*, 105.
7. R. Wagner, *Letters of Richard Wagne: The Burrell Collection*, 369

4. The Paris Jews

1. R. Wagner, *Letters of Richard Wagner: The Burrell Collection*, 291.
2. R. Wagner, *My Life*, 250, 251.
3. R. Wagner, *My Life*, 614, 615.

4. R. Wagner, *My Life*, 313.
5. R. Wagner, *Letters of Richard Wagner: The Burrell Collection*, 167–178.
6. R. Wagner, *Richard Wagner, sämtliche Briefe,vol 2*, letter 55.
7. R. Wagner, *Richard Wagner, sämtliche Briefe, vol 2*, letter 86.
8. R. Wagner, *Richard Wagner, sämtliche Briefe, Zweiter Band*, letter 96.
9. R. Wagner, *My Life*, 210.
10. R. Wagner, *Selected Letters of Richard Wagner*, letter 23.
11. R. Wagner, *My Life*, 255.
12. R. Wagner, *Richard Wagner's Prose Works*, vol. VII, 175–200, at 179, 181, 190.

5. The Essay

1. W.A. Ellis, *Life of Wagner*, vol. III, 93.
2. R. Wagner, *Correspondence of Wagner and Liszt*, letter 59.
3. R. Wagner, *Richard Wagner's Prose Works*, vol. III, 75–122.
4. R. Wagner, *Correspondence of Wagner and Liszt*, letter 96.
5. R. Wagner, *Correspondence of Wagner and Liszt*, letter 143.
6. R. Wagner, *Correspondence of Wagner and Liszt*, letter 165.
7. R. Wagner, *Correspondence of Wagner and Liszt*, letter 183.
8. R. Wagner, *Selected Letters of Richard Wagner*, 322.
9. R. Wagner, *Correspondence of Wagner and Liszt*, letter 190.
10. R. Wagner, *Selected Letters of Richard Wagner*, 374.

11. R. Wagner, *Selected Letters of Richard Wagner*, 335.
12. R. Wagner, *Richard Wagner on Mathilde und an Otto Wesendonck*, 28–29.
13. N. Demuth, *An Anthology of Musical Criticism*, 226–253.
14. R. Wagner, *Correspondence of Wagner and Liszt*, letter 259.
15. R. Wagner, *Correspondence of Wagner and Liszt*, letter 220.

6. Tausig

1. E. Newman, *The Life of Richard Wagner*, vol. III, 300,
2. R. Wagner, *Richard Wagner's Prose Works*, vol. VI, 264–274 at 271.
3. M. Gregor-Dellin, *Richard Wagner: His Life, His Work, His Century*, 464.

7. The Break with Minna

1. W. Lippert, *Wagner in Exile*, 96–97.
2. R. Wagner, *Richard Wagner, Letters to Mathilde Wesendonck*, letter 66.

8. *Tristan und Isolde*

1. R. Hartford, *Bayreuth, the Early Years*, 182.
2. F. Nietzsche, *The Nietzsche-Wagner Correspondence*, 138
3. W. Brockway and H. Weinstock, *Men of Music*, 426.

9. Tannhäuser in Paris

1. E. Newman, *The Life of Richard Wagner*, vol. II, 593–594.
2. R. Wagner, *Selected Letters of Richard Wagner*, 411.
3. S. Spencer, *Wagner Remembered*, 119–120.

10. Vienna

1. R. Wagner, *Letters to Mathilde Wesendonck*, letter 117.
2. R. Wagner, *Richard Wagner: Letters to Minna Wagner*, letter 213.

11. Penury

1. R. Wagner, *Richard Wagner's Prose Works*, vol. I, 269–270.

2. R. Wagner, *Richard Wagner's Letters to August Roeckel*, 4.
3. E. Newman, *The Life of Richard Wagner*, vol. III, 169.
4. P.B. Beeson, *Textbook of Medicine*, 177–179.
5. F. Praeger, *Wagner As I Knew Him*, 251–252.
6. R. Wagner, *Correspondence of Wagner and Liszt*, letter 200.
7. R. Sabor, *The Real Wagner*, 160–161.

12. Biebrich on the Rhine

1. R. Wagner, *The Diary of Richard Wagner: The Brown Book*, 135.

13. The Vienna Jews

1. R. Münster, "Heinrich Porges (1837–1900), Dirigent und Chorleiter."
2. A.D. Low, *Jews in the Eyes of the Germans*, 327.
3. K. Hermann, "Wagner and Levi: Cooperation or Resentment?" 183.
4. L. Lehmann, *My Path Through Life*, 50.
5. L. Lehmann, *My Path Through Life*, 54.
6. C. Wagner, *Cosima Wagner's Diaries*, vol. I, 214.
7. L. Lehmann, *My Path Through Life*, 93.
8. J. Swafford, *Johannes Brahms*, 276.
9. E. Hanslick, *The Beautiful in Music*, viii.
10. R. Wagner, *My Life*, 845.
11. S. Spencer, *Wagner Remembered*, 137.
12. M. Cross and D. Ewen, *Milton Cross' Encyclopedia of the Great Composers and Their Music*, 869.
13. E. Hanslick, *Vienna's Golden Years of Music*, 116–131.
14. E. Hanslick, *Vienna's Golden Years of Music*, xxii–xxiii, quoting *Deutsche Rundschau* (January 1894), 56.

14. Flight from Creditors

1. R. Wagner, *Richard Wagner's Prose Works*, vol. III, 282.
2. R. Wagner, *My Life*, 876.
3. E. Newman, *The Life of Richard Wagner*, vol. III, 303n.
4. S. Spencer, *Wagner Remembered*, 154–158, quoting E. Wille, *Richard Wagner an Eliza Wille*.
5. A. Neumann, *Personal Recollections of Wagner*, 5–6.

6. S. Spencer, *Wagner Remembered*, 158–162, quoting W. Weissheimer, *Erlebnisse mit Richard Wagner ua* (Stuttgart: Deutsche Verlags-Anstalt, 1898).

15. King Ludwig

1. E. Newman, *The Life of Richard Wagner*, vol. III, 215.

16. Cosima

1. E. Newman, *The Life of Richard Wagner*, vol. III, 242.
2. R. Wagner, *The Diary of Richard Wagner: The Brown Book*, 194.
3. R. Wagner, *Richard Wagner: Letters to Minna Wagner*, letter 160.
4. C. Wagner, *Cosima Wagner's Diaries*, vol. II, 1126.
5. R. Wagner, *Letters to Minna Wagner*, letter 234.
6. R. Wagner, *Selected Letters of Richard Wagner*, 605–606.
7. R. Wagner, *Selected Letters of Richard Wagner*, 607–608.
8. R. Wagner, *Selected Letters of Richard Wagner*, 613–617.
9. G. Marek, *Cosima Wagner*, 236–237.
10. R. Wagner, *The Diary of Richard Wagner: The Brown Book*, 64–65.

17. The First *Tristan*

1. R. Wagner, *Selected Letters of Richard Wagner*, 621–622.
2. S. Spencer, *Wagner Remembered*, 178.
3. K. Ludwig, R. Wagner, *König Ludwig II und, Richard Wagner, Briefwechsel*, vol. I, LXXI.
4. K. Ludwig, R. Wagner, *König Ludwig II und, Richard Wagner, Briefwechsel*, letters 83 and 84.
5. R. Wagner, *The Diary of Richard Wagner: The Brown Book*, 144.

19. Triebschen

1. K. Ludwig, R. Wagner, *König Ludwig II und, Richard Wagner, Briefwechsel*, letter 216.
2. R. Münster, "Heinrich Porges."
3. K. Ludwig, R. Wagner, *König Ludwig II und Richard Wagner, Briefwechsel*, letter 414.
4. E. Newman, *The Life of Richard Wagner*, vol. IV, 158.

5. E. Newman, *The Life of Richard Wagner*, vol. III, 546.
6. K. Ludwig, R. Wagner, *König Ludwig II und, Richard Wagner, Briefwechsel*, letter 272a.
7. E. Newman, *The Life of Richard Wagner*, vol. IV, 133–134.

20. *Die Meistersinger*

1. R. Mander and J. Mitchenson, *The Wagner Companion*, 181.
2. W. Brockway and H. Weinstock, *Men of Music*, 433–434.
3. N. Cardus, *Composers Eleven*, 43–45.
4. G. Pourtales, *Richard Wagner*, 304–306.
5. G. Pourtales, *Richard Wagner*, 306.
6. B. Magee, *The Tristan Chord*, 357.

21. Cosima's Diaries

1. D. Aberbach, *The Ideas of Richard Wagner*, 228.
2. E. Brody, "The Jewish Wagnerites."

22. "Judaism in Music": The Second Publication

1. A. Low, *Jews in the Eyes of the Germans*, 331.
2. E. Newman, *The Life of Richard Wagner*, vol. IV, 179–180.
3. R. Wagner, *Selected Letters of Richard Wagner*, letter 378; *Richard Wagners Briefe*, letter 2121.
4. H. von Bülow, *Letters of Hans von Bülow*, 50, 64, 66, 71, 79, 108.
5. J. Joachim, *Letters from and to Joseph Joachim*, 337.
6. H. von Bülow, *Letters of Hans von Bülow*, 33.

23. *Das Rheingold* Brouhaha

1. E. Newman, *The Life of Richard Wagner*, vol. IV, 214.
2. M. Gregor-Dellin, *Richard Wagner: His Life, His Work, His Century*, 390.
3. K. Ludwig, R. Wagner, *König Ludwig II und, Richard Wagner, Briefwechsel*, letter 173.
4. E. Newman, *The Life of Richard Wagner*, vol. IV, 238.

24. The Turn of *Die Walküre*

1. R. Gutman, *Richard Wagner: The Man, His Mind and His Music*, 339.

25. Wagner and the French

1. E. Newman, *The Life of Richard Wagner,* vol. IV, 270–272.
2. E. Newman, *The Life of Richard Wagner,* vol. IV, 272.

26. Death of Tausig

1. R. Wagner, *The Bayreuth Letters of Richard Wagner,* 7–9.
2. R. Hartford, ed. *Bayreuth, the Early Years,* 23.
3. R. Wagner, *The Bayreuth Letters of Richard Wagner,* 17–19.
4. R. Hartford, ed. *Bayreuth, the Early Years,* 24.
5. R. Wagner, *Richard Wagner's Prose Works,* vol. V, 321–340.
6. W. Wallace, *Richard Wagner, As He Lived,* 220–221.
7. R. Wagner, *The Bayreuth Letters of Richard Wagner,* 23–24.
8. M. Gregor-Dellin, *Richard Wagner: His Life, His Work, His Century,* 401.
9. R. Wagner, *The Diary of Richard Wagner: The Brown Book,* 192–193.
10. R. Wagner, *Richard Wagner's Prose Works,* vol. V, 321.

27. Rubinstein and Preparations for *The Ring*

1. J. Katz, *The Darker Side of Genius,* 95.
2. C. von Westernhagen, *Wagner,* 443; K. Ludwig, R. Wagner, *König Ludwig II und, Richard Wagner, Briefwechsel,* note, 229. Partially quoted in both; location of original is not identified.
3. K. Ludwig, R. Wagner, *König Ludwig II und, Richard Wagner, Briefwechsel,* letter 478.

29. The First Festival

1. G. Skelton, *Richard and Cosima Wagner,* 208.
2. R. Wagner, *Selected Letters of Richard Wagner,* letter 415.
3. R. Jacobs, "Translator's Preface," in H. Porges, *Wagner Rehearsing the Ring,* x.
4. R. Jacobs, "Translator's Preface," in H. Porges, *Wagner Rehearsing the Ring,* vii, quoting C. Westernhagen, *Wagner: A Biography.*
5. R. Hartford, *Bayreuth, the Early Years,* 97.
6. K. Ludwig, R. Wagner, *König Ludwig II und, Richard Wagner, Briefwechsel,* letter 502.

7. G.B. Shaw, *The Perfect Wagnerite,* ix.
8. H. Mencken, introduction to *The Nietzsche—Wagner Correspondence,* xii.
9. E. Newman, *The Life of Richard Wagner,* vol. IV, 486–487.
10. L. Lehmann, *My Path Through Life,* 238–239.

30. Neumann

1. A. Neumann, *Personal Recollections of Wagner,* 15–23.
2. A. Neumann, *Personal Recollections of Wagner,* 53–57.
3. F. Haas, *Zwischen Brahms und Wagner,* 194.

31. The Young Hermann Levi

1. A. Mensi-Klarbach, *Alt=münchner Theater Erinnerungen,* 95.
2. E. Schumann, *Erinnerungen,* 184. Cited in H. Frithjof, *Zwischen Brahms und Wagner,* 162.
3. E. Possart, *Erstrebtes und Erlebtes,* 309, 311.
4. A. Mensi-Klarbach, *Alt=münchener Theater Erinnerungen,* 94.
5. F. Haas, *Zwischen Brahms und Wagner,* 10–14.
6. F. Haas, *Zwischen Brahms und Wagner,* 15–16.
7. F. Haas, *Zwischen Brahms und Wagner,* 20–22.

32. The Brahms-Levi Friendship

1. F. Haas, *Zwischen Brahms und Wagner,* 93.
2. J. Swafford, *Johannes Brahms,* 287.
3. F. Haas, *Zwischen Brahms und Wagner,* 93
4. J. Swafford, *Johannes Brahms,* 312.
5. J. Brahms: *Johannes Brahms, Life and Letters,* letter 211.
6. F. Haas, *Zwischen Brahms und Wagner,* 122–127.
7. J. Swafford, *Johannes Brahms,* 380.
8. F. Haas, *Zwischen Brahms und Wagner,* 188.

33. The Breach with Brahms

1. J. Swafford, *Johannes Brahms,* 398.
2. W.P. Jacob, *Zeitklänge,* 80–84.

3. F. Haas, *Zwischen Brahms und Wagner,* 199.

4. F. Haas, *Zwischen Brahms und Wagner,* 196.

5. F. Haas, *Zwischen Brahms und Wagner,* 362.

6. F. Haas, *Zwischen Brahms und Wagner,* 251.

7. F. Haas, *Zwischen Brahms und Wagner,* 196.

8. B. Walter, *Theme and Variations,* 40.

34. A Study in Malice

1. P. Gay, *Freud, Jews and Other Germans,* 189–230.

2. E. Werner, "The Wagners' Jewish Friends," 170.

3. K. Hermann, "Wagner and Levi: Cooperation or Resentment?" 190–191.

4. P. Gay, *Freud, Jews and Other Germans,* 189–230.

5. A. Mensi-Klarbach, *Alt=münchener Theater Erinnerungen,* 94.

6. K. Herrmann, "Wagner and Levi: Cooperation or Resentment?" 179.

7. G. Solti, *Solti on Solti,* 116–117.

35. Declining Health, Worsening Temperament

1. H. Levi, "Hermann Levi an Seinenvater," 6–7.

2. A. Mensi-Klarbach, *Alt=münchener Theater Erinnerungen,* 93–94.

3. E. Newman, *The Life of Richard Wagner,* vol. IV, 623.

36. The Strangest Synagogue

1. G. De Pourtales, *Richard Wagner,* 365, quoting H. von Wolzogen, *Erinnerungen an Richard Wagner.*

2. F. Nietzsche, *The Nietzsche-Wagner Correspondence,* 294.

37. Distance from Porges, Closeness to Rubinstein

1. R. Hartford, *Bayreuth, the Early Years,* 134.

2. R. Wagner, *Selected Letters of Richard Wagner,* 926.

3. R. Wagner, *Selected Letters of Richard Wagner,* 900.

4. E. Newman, *The Life of Richard Wagner,* vol. IV, 640–641.

5. S. Spencer, *Wagner Remembered,* 272–273.

6. R. Sabor, *The Real Wagner,* 181.

7. D. Large, "The Bayreuth Legacy," in *The Wagner Compendium,* 391.

8. E. Newman, *The Life of Richard Wagner,* vol. IV, 626.

9. D. Aberbach, *The Ideas of Richard Wagner,* 226.

10. R. Hartford, *Bayreuth, the Early Years,* 132.

38. Neumann and the Berlin *Ring*

1. A. Neumann, *Personal Recollections of Wagner,* 72–73.

2. A. Neumann, *Personal Recollections of Wagner,* 83.

3. A. Neumann, *Personal Recollections of Wagner,* 95.

4. A. Neumann, *Personal Recollections of Wagner,* 97.

5. A. Neumann, *Personal Recollections of Wagner,* 103–104.

6. K. Ludwig and R. Wagner, *König Ludwig, Richard Wagner Briefwechsel,* letter 567.

7. A. Neumann, *Personal Recollections of Wagner,* 169–171.

8. A. Neumann, *Personal Recollections of Wagner,* 180.

39. Neumann and the Traveling Wagner Opera Company

1. A. Neumann, *Personal Recollections of Wagner,* 235.

40. Levi and *Parsifal*

1. F. Haas, *Zwischen Brahms und Wagner,* 250.

2. S. Spencer, *Wagner Remembered,* 214.

3. E. Newman, *The Life of Richard Wagner,* vol. IV, 578.

4. E. Newman, *The Life of Richard Wagner,* vol. IV, 613.

5. P. Gay, *Freud, Jews and Other Germans,* 220.

6. R. Wagner, *Richard Wagners Briefe an Hermann Levi,* letter 28.

7. R. Wagner, *Richard Wagners Briefe an Hermann Levi*, letter 30.
8. R. Wagner, *Richard Wagners Briefe an Hermann Levi*, letter 32.
9. H. Levi, "Hermann Levi an Seinen Vater."

41. Lichtenberg and the Knieses

1. J. Kniese, *Der kampf zweier Welten um das Bayreuther Erbe.*
2. P. Gay, *Freud, Jews and Other Germans*, 230.
3. F. Haas, *Zwischen Brahms und Wagner*, 282.
4. G. Marek, *Cosima Wagner*, 210.
5. G. Marek, *Cosima Wagner*, 210.
6. J. Kniese, *Der kampf zweier Welten um das Bayreuther Erbe*, 128–129.
7. D. Aberbach, *The Ideas of Richard Wagner*, 236.
8. K. Ludwig and R. Wagner, *König Ludwig II und, Richard Wagner Briefwechsel*, letter 579.
9. K. Ludwig and R. Wagner, *König Ludwig II und, Richard Wagner Briefwechsel*, letter 580.
10. R. Wagner, *Selected Letters of Richard Wagner*, 918.
11. K. Herrmann, "Wagner and Levi: Cooperation or Resentment?" 186.
12. D. Large, "The Bayreuth Legacy," in *The Wagner Compendium*, 381.
13. R. Hartford, *Bayreuth, the Early Years*, 248.
14. R. Hartford, *Bayreuth, the Early Years*, 182, 193.
15. P. Hodson, *Who's Who in Wagner*, 110.

42. Wagnerphobia

1. R. Gutman, *Richard Wagner: The Man, His Mind, and His Music*, 463–469.
2. R. Wagner, *The Diary of Richard Wagner: The Brown Book*, 46–51.
3. R. Gutman, *Richard Wagner: The Man, His Mind, and His Music*, 465.
4. R. Gutman, *Richard Wagner: The Man, His Mind, and His Music*, 457–458.
5. J. Katz, *The Darker Side of Genius*, ix.
6. J. Katz, *The Darker Side of Genius*, 130–131.

43. Glimpses of the Other Side

1. W. Hartwich, "Jüdische Theosophie in Richard Wagners 'Parsifal,'" 122.
2. R. Wagner, *Prose Works*, vol. VI, 280.
3. M. Gregor-Dellin, *Richard Wagner: His Life, His Work, His Century*, 467.
4. R. Taylor, *Richard Wagner: His Life, Art and Thought*, 235.
5. E. Newman, *The Life of Richard Wagner*, vol. II, 612–613.

44. The Final Days

1. H. Levi, "Hermann Levi an Seinen Vater," 12–13.
2. J. Swafford, *Johannes Brahms*, 482.
3. L. Lehmann, *My Path Through Life*, 305.
4. E. Newman, *The Life of Richard Wagner*, vol. IV, 700.
5. A. Mahler, *Gustav Mahler: Memories and Letters*, 205–206.

References

Aberbach, David. *The Ideas of Richard Wagner*. Rev. ed. Lanham, Md.: University Press of America, 1988.

Altmann, Wilhelm. *Richard Wagners Briefe*. Wiesbaden: Martin Sändig oHG, 1971. First published, Leipzig: Breitkopf und Härtel, 1905.

Bassett, Peter. *Wagner's Parsifal: The Journey of a Soul*. Kent Town, South Australia: Wakefield Press, 2000.

Beeson, Paul B., and Walsh McDermott. *Textbook of Medicine*. Eleventh edition. Philadelphia: W.B. Saunders, 1963.

Boyden, Matthew. *Richard Strauss*. Boston: Northeastern University Press, 1999.

Brahms, Johannes. *Johannes Brahms, Life and Letters*. Selected and annotated by Styra Avins. Trans. Josef Eisinger and Styra Avins. Oxford, England: Oxford University Press, 1997.

Brockway, Wallace, and Herbert Weinstock. *Men of Music*. Rev. and enlarged ed. New York: Simon and Schuster, 1958.

Brody, Elaine. "The Jewish Wagnerites." *The Opera Quarterly* 1, no. 3 (autumn 1983): 66–80.

Bülow, Hans von. *Letters of Hans von Bülow*. New York: Vienna House, 1972.

Burbidge, Peter, and Richard Sutton, eds. *The Wagner Companion*. New York: Cambridge University Press, 1979.

Cardus, Neville. *Composers Eleven*. New York: George Braziller, 1959.

Carner, Mosco. *Puccini: A Critical Biography*. Third ed. New York: Holmes and Meier, 1992.

Cross, Milton, and David Ewen. *Milton Cross' Encyclopedia of the Great Composers and Their Music*. Vol. II. New rev. ed. Garden City, New York: Doubleday, 1962.

Danuser, Hermann. "Universalität oder Particularität," in *Richard Wagner und die Juden*, edited by Dieter Borchmeyer, Ami Maayani and Susanne Vill. Stuttgart: Verlag J.B. Metzler, 2000. 79–102.

Demuth, Norman, compilation. *An Anthology of Musical Criticism*. London: Eyre and Spottiswoode, 1947.

Fehl, Phillip P. "Wagner's Anti-Semitism and the Dignity of Art," in *Wagner in Retrospect*, edited by Shaw, Leroy R. et al. Amsterdam: Rodopi, 1987. 197–202.

Finck, Henry T. *Richard Strauss: The Man and His Works*. Boston: Little Brown, 1917.

Gay, Peter. *Freud, Jews and Other Germans.* New York: Oxford University Press, 1978.
Giesberg, Robert I. "Wagner and France," in *Wagner in Retrospect,* edited by Shaw, Leroy R. et al. Amsterdam: Rodopi, 1987. 106–116.
Goehr, Lydia. *The Quest for Voice.* Berkeley: University of California Press, 1997.
Gregor-Dellin, Martin. *Richard Wagner: His Life, His Work, His Century.* Trans. Maxwell Brownjohn. San Diego: Harcourt Brace Jovanovich, 1980.
Gutman, Robert W. *Richard Wagner: The Man, His Mind, and His Music.* New York: Time Incorporated, 1968.
Haas, Frithjof. *Zwischen Brahms und Wagner: Der Dirigent Hermann Levi.* Zurich: Atlantis Musikbuch-Verlag, 1995.
Hanslick, Eduard. *Aus Meinem Leben.* 2 vols. Berlin: Allgemeiner Verein für Deutsche Litteratur, 1894.
_____. *The Beautiful in Music.* Gustav Cohen, trans. Indianapolis: Liberal Arts Press, 1957; originally published 1854.
_____. *Vienna's Golden Years of Music.* Trans. and ed. by H. Pleasants III. New York: Simon & Schuster, 1950.
Hartford, Robert, ed. *Bayreuth, the Early Years.* Cambridge University Press, 1980.
Hartwich, Wolf-Daniel. "Jüdische Theosopie in Richard Wagners 'Parsifal,'" in *Richard Wagner und die Juden,* edited by Dieter Borchmeyer, Ami Maayani and Susanne Vill. Stuttgart: Verlag J.B. Metzler, 2000. 103–122.
Hermann, Klaus J. "Wagner and Levi: Cooperation or Resentment?" in *Wagner in Retrospect,* edited by Shaw, Leroy R. et al. Amsterdam: Rodopi, 1987. 172–196.
Hodson, Phillip. *Who's Who in Wagner.* New York: Macmillan, 1984.
Hornstein, Robert von. *Memoiren.* Munich: Süddeutsche Monatshefte, 1908.
Horowitz, Joseph. "Wagner und der americanische Jude — eine persönliche Betrachung," in *Richard Wagner und die Juden,* edited by Dieter Borchmeyer, Ami Maayani and Susanne Vill. Stuttgart: Verlag J.B. Metzler, 2000. 238–250.
Jacob, Walter P. *Zeitklänge.* Buenos Aires: Editorial Cosmopolita, 1945.
Jacobs, Robert L. "Preface." In Heinrich Porges, *Wagner Rehearsing the Ring.* Trans. by R. Jacobs. London: Cambridge University Press, 1983.
Joachim, Joseph. *Letters from and to Joseph Joachim.* Selected and translated by Nora Bickley. New York: Vienna House, 1972.
Kapp, Julius. *Richard Wagner, sein Werk, sein Leben, seine Welt.* Berlin: Max Hesses Verlag, 1933.
Katz, Jacob. *The Darker Side of Genius: Richard Wagner's Anti-Semitism.* Hanover and London: University Press of New England, 1986.
Kesting, Hanjo, ed. *Richard Wagner Briefe.* Selected, introduced and annotated by Hanjo Kesting. Munich: R. Piper, 1983.
Kienzl, Wilhelm. *Weltgeschichte in Karakterbildern.* Munich: Kirchheim'sche Verlagsbuchhandlung, 1904.
Kniese, Julie. *Der Kampf zweier Welten um das Bayreuther Erbe.* Leipzig: Verlag Theodor Weicher, 1931.
Knust, Herbert. *Wagner, the King and "The Waste Land."* University Park, Pennsylvania: Pennsylvania State University, 1967.
Köhler, Joachim. *Nietzsche and Wagner: A Lesson in Subjugation.* New Haven: Yale University Press, 1998.
Lehmann, Lilli. *My Path Through Life.* Trans. Alice Benedict Seligman. New York: Arno Press, 1977. Reprint of 1914 edition, G.P. Putnam's Sons, London.
Lessing, Gotthold Ephraim. "Nathan the Wise." Trans. W.A. Steel, in *Lacoön, Nathan the Wise, Minna von Barnhelm.* London: J.M. Dent and Sons, 1967.
Levi, Hermann. "Hermann Levi an Seinen Vater," in *Bayreuther Festspiele Programm, 1959, Parsifal,* 6–22.

Lippert, Woldemar. *Wagner in Exile*. Trans. Paul England. London: George G. Harrap, 1930.

Low, Alfred D. *Jews in the Eyes of the Germans*. Philadelphia: Institute for the Study of Human Issues, 1979.

Ludwig II (King) and Richard Wagner. *König Ludwig II und Richard Wagner. Briefwechsel*. 5 vols. Bearbeitet von Otto Strobel. Carlsruhe: G. Braun, 1936.

Magee, Bryan. *The Tristan Chord*. New York: Metropolitan Books, 2000.

Mahler, Alma. *Gustav Mahler: Memories and Letters*. Trans. by B. Creightor. New York: Viking, 1946.

Mander, Raymond, and Joe Mitchenson. *The Wagner Companion*. New York: Hawthorn Books, 1977.

Marek, George R. *Cosima Wagner*. New York: Harper and Row, 1981.

Mensi-Klarbach, Alfred von. *Alt–Münchener Theater Erinnerungen*. Munich: Verlag Von Knorr and Hirth, 1924. 91–98.

Millington, Barry, ed. *The Wagner Compendium*. New York: Schirmer, 1992.

Münster, Robert. "Heinrich Porges (1837–1900), Dirigent und Chorleiter" in *Geschichte und Kultur der Juden in Bayern*. Munich: Haus der Bayerischen Geschichte, 1988. 157–162.

Neumann, Angelo. *Personal Recollections of Wagner*. Translated for the fourth German edition by Edith Livermore. London: Archibald Constable, 1909.

Newman, Ernest. *The Life of Richard Wagner*. 4 vols. Cambridge: Alfred A. Knopf, 1946.

Nietzsche, Friedrich, and Richard Wagner. *The Nietzsche-Wagner Correspondence*. Edited by Elizabeth Foerster-Nietzsche. Trans. Caroline V. Kerr. New York: Liveright, 1949.

Philippi, Felix. "A Meeting with Verdi," in *Encounters with Verdi,* edited by Marcello Conati. Trans. Richard Stokes. Ithaca: Cornell University Press, 1984. 326–322.

Possart, Ernst von. *Erstrebtes und Erlebtes*. Berlin: Königliche Hofbuchhandlung, 1916. Copyright 1916 by E.S. Mittler and Sohn, Berlin.

Pourtales, Guy de. *Richard Wagner: The Story of an Artist*. Lewis May, trans. from the French. New York: Harper and Brothers, 1932.

Praeger, Ferdinand. *Wagner As I Knew Him*. London: Longmans, Green, 1892.

Prawy, Marcel. *Nun sei bedankt*. Munich: Wilhelm Goldmann Verlag, 1983.

Rose, Paul Lawrence. *Wagner: Race and Revolution*. New Haven: Yale University Press, 1992.

Sabor, Rudolph. *The Real Wagner*. London: André Deutsch, 1987.

Schumann, Eugenie. *Erinnerungen*. Stuttgart, 1927.

Shaw, George Bernard. *The Perfect Wagnerite*. 1898. Reprint, New York: Time Inc., 1972.

Shaw, Leroy R. et al., eds. *Wagner in Retrospect*. Amsterdam: Rodopi, 1987.

Skelton, Geoffrey. *Richard and Cosima Wagner: Biography of a Marriage*. London: Victor Golancz, 1982.

Sokoloff, Alice Hunt. *Cosima Wagner: Extraordinary Daughter of Franz Liszt*. New York: Dodd, Meade and Company, 1969.

Solti, Georg. *Solti on Solti*. London: Chatto and Windus, 1997.

Spencer, Stewart. *Wagner Remembered*. London: Faber and Faber, 2000.

Stein, Leon. *The Racial Thinking of Richard Wagner*. New York: Philosophical Library, 1950.

Swafford, Jan. *Johannes Brahms*. New York: Knopf, 1997.

Taylor, Ronald. *Richard Wagner: His Life, Art and Thought*. New York: Taplinger, 1979.

Treml, Manfred, and Wolf Weigand. *Geschichte und Kultur der Juden in Bayern*. Unter Mitarbeit von Evamaria Brockhoff. Munich: Haus d. Bayerischen Geschichte, 1988.

Wagner, Cosima. *Cosima Wagner's Diaries*. Edited and annotated by Martin Gregor-Dellin and Dietrich Mack. Trans. and with an introduction by Geoffrey Skelton. 2 vols. New York: Harcourt Brace Jovanovich, 1977.

_____. *Das Zweite Leben, Briefe und Aufzeichnungen 1883–1930.* Edited by Dietrich Mack. München: R. Piper, 1980.

_____, and Houston C. Chamberlain. *Cosima Wagner und Houston C. Chamberlain im Briefwechsel.* Edited by Paul Prezsch. 2nd ed. Leipzig: Phillipp Reclam, 1934.

Wagner, Richard. *The Bayreuth Letters of Richard Wagner.* Trans. and ed. by Caroline V. Kerr. New York: Vienna House, 1972.

_____. *Diary of Richard Wagner: The Brown Book 1865–1882.* Presented and annotated by Joachim Bergfeld, trans. George Bird. London: Victor Gollancz, 1980.

_____. *Letters of Richard Wagner: The Burrell Collection.* Edited with notes by John R. Burk. New York: Vienna House, 1972.

_____. *Letters to Anton Pusinelli.* Trans. and ed. with critical notes by Elbert Lenrow. New York: Vienna House, 1972.

_____. *Letters to Mathilde Wesendonck.* Trans. by W.A. Ellis. New York: Scribner, 1905; reprint, New York: Vienna House, 1972.

_____. *My Life.* 2 vols. Authorized translation from the German. St. Clair Shores, Michigan: Scholarly Press, 1977; original English publication, New York: Dodd, Mead, 1911.

_____. *Richard Wagner an Mathilde und an Otto Wesendonck.* Berlin: Schreitersche Verlagsbuchhandlung, n.d.

_____. *Richard Wagner: Letters to Minna Wagner.* 2 vols. Trans. William Ashton Ellis. New York: Vienna House, 1972.

_____. *Richard Wagner, sämtliche Briefe.* 1st 4 vols. Leipzig: Veb Deutscher Verlag für Musik, 1979.

_____. "Richard Wagners Briefe an Hermann Levi." *Bayreuther Blätter* xxiv (1901): 13–42.

_____. *Richard Wagner's Letters to August Roeckel.* Trans. Eleanor C. Sellar, with an introductory essay by Houston Stewart Chamberlain. Bristol: J.W. Arrowsmith, 1914.

_____. *Richard Wagner's Letters to His Dresden Friends.* Trans. and with a preface by J.S. Shedlock. New York: Vienna House, 1980.

_____. *Richard Wagner's Prose Works.* Trans. William Ashton Ellis. 8 vols. New York: Broude Brothers, 1966; reprinted from the 1897 London edition by arrangement with Routledge and Kegan Paul.

_____. *Selected Letters of Richard Wagner.* Trans. and ed. by Stewart Spencer and Barry Millington. London: J.M. Dent and Sons, 1987.

_____. *Wagner Writes from Paris.* Ed. and trans. by Robert Jacobs and Geoffrey Skelton. New York: John Day, 1973.

_____, and Franz Liszt. *Correspondence of Wagner and Liszt.* 2 vols. Trans. by F. Hueffer. 2nd ed., rev. by W.A. Ellis. New York: Scribner, 1897; reprint New York: Vienna House, 1973.

Wallace, William. *Richard Wagner, As He Lived.* New York: Harper and Brothers, 1925.

Walter, Bruno. *Theme and Variations.* Trans. by James A. Galston. New York: Knopf, 1946.

Weiner, Marc A. *Richard Wagner and the Anti-Semitic Imagination.* Lincoln: University of Nebraska Press, 1995.

Werner, Eric. "Juden um Richard und Cosima Wagner: Eine Konfrontation nach einem Jahrhundert," in *Anzeiger der Österreichischen Akademie der Wissenschaften* 121, no.1–9 (1984): 131–169.

_____. "The Wagners' Jewish Friends," in *Wagner in Retrospect,* edited by Shaw, Leroy R. et al. Amsterdam: Rodopi, 1987. 165–171.

Westernhagen, Curt von. *Wagner.* 2 vols. Cambridge: Cambridge University Press, 1978.

Wille, Eliza. *Richard Wagner an Eliza Wille.* Berlin: Schuster and Loeffler, 1908.

Wille, Jürg, and Werner G. Zimmermann. *Richard Wagner in Zürich.* Zürich: Präsidialabteilung der Stadt Zürich, 1987.

Index